EUROPE AND AMERICA:
THE END OF THE TRANSATLANTIC RELATIONSHIP?

EUROPE AND AMERICA

The End of the Transatlantic Relationship?

FEDERIGA BINDI

EDITOR

BROOKINGS INSTITUTION PRESS
Washington, D.C.

The Brookings Institution is a private nonprofit organization devoted to research, education, and publication on important issues of domestic and foreign policy. Its principal purpose is to bring the highest quality independent research and analysis to bear on current and emerging policy problems. Interpretations or conclusions in Brookings publications should be understood to be solely those of the authors.

Library of Congress Cataloging-in-Publication Data
Names: Bindi, Federiga M., editor.
Title: Europe and America : the end of the transatlantic relationship? / Federiga Bindi, editor.
Description: Washington, D.C. : Brookings Institution Press, 2019. | Includes bibliographical references and index.
Identifiers: LCCN 2019011294 (print) | LCCN 2019011514 (ebook) | ISBN 9780815732815 (ebook) | ISBN 9780815732808 (pbk. : alk. paper)
Subjects: LCSH: United States—Foreign relations—European Union countries. | European Union countries—Foreign relations—United States. | United States—Foreign relations—Europe. | Europe—Foreign relations—United States. | United States—Foreign relations—21st century. | European Union countries—Foreign relations—21st century. | Europe—Foreign relations—21st century.
Classification: LCC JZ1480.A54 (ebook) | LCC JZ1480.A54 E87 2019 (print) | DDC 327.4073—dc23
LC record available at https://lccn.loc.gov/2019011294

9 8 7 6 5 4 3 2 1

Typeset in Janson Text

Composition by Westchester Publishing Services

Contents

Foreword   vii

1 Introduction   1
FEDERIGA BINDI

PART I

The Foreign Policy of the EU and of Its Member States

2 EU Foreign and Defense Policies and
Transatlantic Relations: Friends and Foes   11
FEDERIGA BINDI

3 The Foreign Policy of France: Continuity and Change   31
ALEKSANDER LUST

4 The Foreign Policy of Germany: Economic Giant,
Foreign Policy Dwarf?   67
JAN TECHAU

5 Italy: The Middle Country   91
FEDERIGA BINDI

6 Great Britain's Foreign Policy Dilemmas 109
KLAUS LARRES

7 Spain: Foreign Relations and Foreign Policy 137
JOAQUÍN ROY

8 From Soviet Satellite to Regional Power: Poland after 1989 161
MICHELA CECCORULLI AND SERENA GIUSTI

9 Danish Foreign Policy: From Pastry to Bloody Denmark? 179
JONAS PARELLO-PLESNER

10 The Foreign Policy of the Czech Republic:
Domestic Politics Back with a Vengeance 199
DAVID CADIER

PART II

The Cold War Superpowers in a Hot World

11 Russia's Staunch Foreign Policy in a Wavering Landscape 219
SERENA GIUSTI

12 The Foreign Policy of the United States:
Indispensable No More? 239
JUSSI M. HANHIMÄKI

13 Conclusion: The Unbearable Weight of History and the
End of Transatlantic Relations? 269
FEDERIGA BINDI

Contributors 299

Index 301

Foreword

FEDERIGA BINDI

Books have a life of their own, and this one is no exception. Originally thought of in 2010 as a book comparing the foreign policies of the EU member states with those of the EU itself and the major world powers, it ended up in 2018 as a book on transatlantic relations.

The original coauthors met in Rome, in July 2011, at a conference organized by our EU Center of Excellence at the University of Rome Tor Vergata, in cooperation with the Italian Ministry of Foreign Affairs, the Italian National School of Administration, SAIS Johns Hopkins University, and the European Council on Foreign Relations (ECFR). I am particularly grateful to Foreign Minister Franco Frattini, to the School President—and my Tor Vergata colleague—Giovanni Tria, to ECFR Italy's director, Silvia Francescon, and to Erik Johns for their collaboration and support.

The conference was cofinanced, like most of my academic activities, by the Jean Monnet Action. To Luciano Di Fonzo, then leader of the Jean Monnet Action, thank you for a support that through the years has definitely been more than financial. And how not to mention my (then) grad students Marco Amici, Giulia Bianchi, Irina Angelescu, Valeria Contu, and Ilaria Agozzino?

As we were working on the book, I was named to lead the Italian Cultural Institute in Brussels. The very intense pace of the work there made the book linger until my return to research in 2015.

As the chapters were finally coming in, the world started to dramatically change. In November 2016, an earthquake shook our sensible world. "Was it the end of transatlantic relations?" we questioned with my wonderful editors at Brookings Institution Press, Janet Walker and William Finan.

Why were the Europeans not comprehending what was happening on this side of the Atlantic, and sharply reacting to it? Could they not see how business as usual was dead, possibly forever? What else should the Twitter-in-Chief do, to have the Europeans finally open their eyes? And yet, despite a totally different and upsetting style, how much of the substance of transatlantic relations was actually changing? These questions bugged me.

Then the Europeans finally started to move. A provision in the Lisbon Treaty never used before was enacted, giving birth to PESCO—the Permanent Structured Cooperation. This time it was Washington that surprised me. On past occasions, the various American administrations had moved quickly, determined to directly or indirectly prevent any further EU integration in security and defense. Yet this time, PESCO had gone totally unnoticed in D.C.

And why was the U.S. defense industry not creating mayhem about it, the way business had done at the time of the Single European Act, fearing a "Fortress Europe"? A colleague at *Foreign Policy* shared my views, and we prepared a proposal for American defense industries: we wanted to look into the possible effects of PESCO for them. In our mind, since the EU is using a strategy similar to the one successfully employed for the Single Market, it will prospectively shift defense acquisitions from American producers to European ones. Much to our surprise, they could not see it.

All this did not make sense to me. These questions needed to be investigated further. More evidence was required. I asked my wonderful coauthors to make one more effort. I needed them to better refine their research and answer a few additional questions. My colleague Alex Lust was providential in replacing a coauthor who dropped out due to maternity leave. I put my research assistants to work: Gregg Nelson and Matt Holbrook did a lot of background research to help the authors. The two of them, Kathleen Doherty, Robbie Pope, and I had endless discussions in my office, upsetting—with our loud laughs and our desperate need for chairs—my next-door colleague. Having read, over and over, the different chapters,

Which were the main variables in determining the transatlantic partners' foreign policies? I asked them; Why so much mutual misunderstanding?

Little by little, things started to make sense, like a puzzle that finally starts to reveal a picture. As in good spy stories, I won't reveal the answers or the full picture here—for that you will have to wait for the conclusions. But I do surely hope that you will enjoy our collective work, and will come back for comments!

ONE

Introduction

FEDERIGA BINDI

We live in turbulent times. The unlimited access to information, one of the benefits of modernity, is also its curse. With too much information—not to mention fake news—it is becoming increasingly harder to understand what really matters. This is particularly true in foreign policy, where distance, different languages, and cultural norms further complicate the picture. Transatlantic relations are not exempted. Americans do not fully understand Europeans, and Europeans think they know Americans because of Hollywood movies. However, while Hollywood can legitimately be considered the United States' most relevant soft power tool, the image conveyed is far from accurate in describing the complexities of American society.

The narrative about transatlantic relations is not exempt from this trend. In the time of Trump, *twitterplomacy*, and fake news, our understanding of the state of transatlantic relations seems to reflect more what each of us wish they were, rather than their actual reality. Wishful thinking, however, is extremely dangerous in policymaking, especially in foreign policy. With the end of the Cold War constraints, transatlantic relations have become more complex, rather than simpler. Twenty years of wars—of which we are not seeing the end—have dispersed the moral capital that the United States acquired with the two world wars and the Marshall Plan, in a way that it is not comprehended in the United States. Similarly, Europeans only partially appreciate the effect of Donald Trump's election on Americans—both to his emboldened supporters, and his outraged adversaries.

All these factors combined risk ending whatever little is left of transatlantic relations. The contributors to this book, however, share the belief that vital transatlantic relations are today more important than ever. Refounding transatlantic relations requires a better understanding of each other and, in particular, of the determinants of foreign policy decisions, both in Europe and in the United States.

This book, by comparatively analyzing ten national case studies, aims to better understand which variables determine the foreign policies of the transatlantic partners, a necessary step to try to foresee the future of transatlantic relations. We therefore selected eight representative member states of the European Union: the four "big" EU member states (Germany, France, Italy, and the soon-to-be-ex-member, the United Kingdom), two "midsize" countries (Spain and Poland), and two smaller member states (Czech Republic, Denmark). The countries were also chosen to be geographically representative—with a balance between the south (Italy, Spain, France), the north (United Kingdom, Germany, Denmark), and Eastern Europe (Poland, Czech Republic)—as well as between EU founding countries (Germany, France, Italy), mid-termers (United Kingdom, Denmark, Spain), and newcomers (Poland, Czech Republic).

To these eight cases studies, we added chapters about Russia and the United States. Ever since the end of World War II, however, European countries have in fact been suspended between the West (the United States) and the East (USSR, then Russia). Any decision in foreign policy had to take into consideration—at least to some extent—either or both of these countries' preferences. During the Cold War, the USSR pretty much dictated any foreign (and domestic) policy decision for the Central and Eastern Europeans. For Western Europe the picture was more nuanced. Countries like Germany or Italy tried to find a difficult balance between Atlantic obligations and Eastern reality. With the end of the Cold War, both Eastern and Western Europe gained a new freedom of action in foreign policy, though the legacies of the past still loom. Europe's foreign policies can therefore be understood only by including in the picture both American and Russian foreign policies, with particular reference to their policies toward Europe.

As for the European Economic Community/European Union, the bloc has been a foreign policy actor only since the 1970s. The EEC/EU foreign policy has at the same time supported the foreign policies agendas of its member states and shaped its own agenda. The role of the EU as a united actor in foreign policy depends on the bloc's institutional advancements, but also appears to be inversely proportional to the health of transatlantic relations. To better understand EU-U.S. relations, we also added a history chapter chronologically reviewing the relation. As the chapter will show, there seems to be a pattern in EU-U.S. relations: historically, the EU has integrated further in foreign and defense policies during periods of crises in the transatlantic relationship. The Permanent Structured Cooperation (PESCO) created in December 2017 is just the latest case in point.

We built the book in a way to make quick referencing and comparability easier. Each chapter gives a historical overview and an introduction to the most important priorities of the national foreign policy. An analysis of the country's most important geographic relations (relations with Russia, the United States, the Balkans, the Middle East, Latin America, Africa, China) and of eventual thematic areas of interest (energy, environmental protection, defense, trade policy, international organizations) follows. Geographic and thematic policy areas were chosen by each author to reflect the main priorities of the country in question.

In his chapter about Germany, Jan Techau argues that the country is a major player in international economic and trade policies but a minor one in the fields of foreign and security policies, and that Germany's foreign policy has not substantially changed since the beginning of the Cold War. It was an approach built on "three plus three" pillars. The first three pillars represent close relationships with Germany's most important bilateral partners: the United States, France, and to a lesser extent and on very different terms, Russia. The other three pillars represent Germany's multilateral engagements with the North Atlantic Treaty Organization (NATO), the European Community (today the EU), and later, the United Nations. Keeping this pillars construction intact remains Germany's unspoken primary foreign policy goal. In what constitutes remarkable continuity, the major turning points in German postwar history—rearmament in the mid-1950s, the 1968 cultural shift, *Ostpolitik*, UN membership in 1973, NATO's dual-track policy in the late 1970s and early 1980s, unification in 1990, and the more assertive period after Helmut Kohl's ousting from office after 1998—had no real game-changing impact on the overall strategic culture established in the 1950s. In essence, Germany is operating its foreign policy in the twenty-first century based on a strategic culture from the 1950s: Germany is an ambitious world player in international economic affairs but shows no sign that it desires to be a significant political player on the world stage. Defense and security policies thus remain a weak spot for Germany, whose strategic culture remains largely unchanged from the one that emerged in the newly established federal republic after the country joined the Western alliance. It is marked by an instinctive rejection of military power as a means of international problem-solving and a strong reluctance even to debate matters of security and defense publicly. Remarkably, historic developments since 1990—the Kosovo War; the attacks of September 11, 2001; Afghanistan; Libya—have not significantly changed Germany's strategic culture.

In a similar way, argues Federiga Bindi, Italy's foreign policy has been influenced by the country's fascist past. This started from the rejection of the "national interest," which was replaced with a vaguer "European interest." Though today there is a shared consensus that national interests should be at the center of Italy's foreign policy, this has proved hard to define and execute because of the other historical legacy of the country: the Cold War. Until 1989, Italy held a privileged geopolitical role because of its unique geographic location in the middle of the Mediterranean Sea, between East and West. After that, like Germany, Italy has struggled to redefine its role in world affairs. If the symbol of the new German foreign policy is the fight for a permanent seat on the UN Security Council (UNSC), the symbol of post–Cold War Italy is the fight *against* a German seat on the Security Council, masked as a need for a global reform of the UNSC (admittedly a good point per se). As with Germany, the key pillars of Italy's foreign policy have thus remained consistent since the 1950s: strong support for European integration and transatlantic relations, counterbalanced by collaboration with Russia and an attention to its neighbors: the Balkans and the Mediterranean area.

France has a different historical legacy. As Aleksander Lust argues, France's foreign policy is mainly defined by its colonial past. Today, France generally accepts that it is a medium-size power with a limited ability to shape world events, but it remains willing to use its position as a UNSC permanent member to challenge U.S. policy in those regions where it has strategic and economic interests. The presence of French territories in numerous parts of the world, military bases in Africa and the Middle East, and a large diplomatic body—France has embassies in 160 countries, more than any other country except the United States—physically root France's claim to a global role.

Similarly, the contradictions of British foreign policy stem from its colonial past, Klaus Larres argues. As Dean Acheson said in 1962, Britain lost an empire and has not yet found a role. British foreign policymakers continue to view the United Kingdom as a major international power. The general perception outside the United Kingdom—be it in Washington, Beijing, or Berlin—is somewhat different, however. For instance, the United States has used the "special relationship" with Britain only when useful to Washington, never really considering London on a level of parity. Even the Brexit decision—like the decision not to join the European Communities at the outset—was influenced by this hypertrophic vision of the country's role in world affairs, and what Larres describes as Britain remaining caught in a Churchillian foreign policy framework.

Denmark, a small country situated at the northern tip of the European continent, does carry out a full-fledged foreign policy, argues Jonas Parello-Plesner. The trends in Danish foreign policy have been shaped by history and geography, as well as by the conditions encountered by any small state with limited room to maneuver in the international system. Nevertheless, Denmark has sought to make a small but clear mark in global politics in several specific policy areas, leading President Barack Obama to remark that Denmark punched well above its weight. This has been particularly true since the end of the Cold War, with an activism that took a stronger military bent, moving Denmark beyond the blue helmets of UN peacekeeping missions and foreign aid—two traditional tenets of Danish policy—and into the wars in Iraq and Afghanistan. Global developments such as terrorism, poverty, climate change, fragile states, piracy, and cyberwarfare are what Denmark perceives today as threats to its freedom and prosperity, although Russia's threatening posturing also raises concerns.

After the demise of the Francisco Franco regime, the Spanish government adopted a frantic agenda of *Apuntarse a todo* ("Sign up for everything"), explains Joaquín Roy. Spain ratified the UN Universal Declaration of Human Rights and became a member of the Council of Europe in 1977; it joined NATO in 1981 and acceded to the European Community (EC) in

1986. Relations with the rest of Europe and the United States have monopolized the attention of Spain's governments since the rebirth of Spanish
democracy. Spain's mediation role was recognized at the Middle East Peace
Conference, convened by the United States in Madrid in 1991, and in the
Mediterranean process, founded by the EU and its southern partners in
1995. The record of Spain's membership in the European Union has proved
to be truly impressive. From being a country that was a net receiver of aid
from the EC, Spain is today a net payer. However, that does not mean that
Spain has forgotten other parts of the world, in particular Latin America,
which Spain successfully managed to elevate to EU policy.

Poland, too, argue Michela Ceccorulli and Serena Giusti, constitutes a
successful model of the EU's transformative power, rapidly becoming a
front-runner and a regional power in Europe. Since 1989, Polish foreign
policy has progressively become more proactive, assertive, and pragmatic.
Warsaw has used the EU tactically to pursue its own interests: It has revived regionalism as a means of advancing the interests of the Central and
Eastern European countries and, in turn, it is using its role to acquire more
leverage both within the EU and Central and Eastern Europe. There has
been a dramatic reassessment of relations with countries that once were
considered hostile, such as Germany and Russia. Yet Poland is looking
carefully at Russian moves on the regional landscape. The Georgia war
and the annexation of Crimea have persuaded Warsaw to review its more
lenient posture toward Russia. Poland also has encouraged regional cooperation with the near abroad through the Eastern Partnership to dilute
potential instabilities in the periphery and create a buffer with Russia.
Hence, Poland has emphasized its role as a bridge between the West and
Eastern Europe and Russia and has made the promotion of democracy a
new part of its external projection. Poland's Atlanticism seems to have
turned out to be quite pragmatic, with Warsaw adopting a more equidistant position between the United States and the EU. Poland's strong
support for strengthening Europe's defenses is a case in point. Poland's
mounting power is due in part to its formidable economic performance. The
Polish leadership has put forward an ambitious strategy for accomplishing
foreign policy goals and has domestic public opinion on its side.

The story of the Czech Republic is different, argues David Cadier. If
the "new Europe" label traditionally refers to congenital Atlanticism, a proactive and teleological (that is, neoconservative-like) approach to democracy promotion and a certain reluctance toward the process of European

integration, then the Czech Republic is probably the one state to which this label can be most accurately applied. The Czech Republic has in fact systematically prioritized NATO over the EU's Common Security and Defense Policy. For instance, the Czech Republic had sought to participate in the Ballistic Missile Defense system envisioned by the George W. Bush administration, it has been the most vocal critic of the Cuban regime and the staunchest supporter of Israel within the EU foreign policy arena, and it has not hesitated to join the United Kingdom's "splendid isolation" on certain European questions such as the fiscal compact. Today, however, the Czech Republic finds itself at a crossroad. Major structural evolutions have affected its international and regional environments, such as the rebalancing of U.S. priorities, the economic rise of China, the reshaping of EU institutional and power structures, and the resurgence of Russia.

For centuries, Russian foreign policy was marked by expansion, militarization, and border defense, writes Serena Giusti. Russia's very identity was forged by the country's capacity to spread out and conquer new territories. Unlike other empires, the Soviet Union did not fall because it was defeated in war, but rather because the political and economic model on which it was based failed. Contemporary Russian foreign policy has been determined by both history (Russia's self-image as a great power) and the sense of frustration that the country felt after the implosion of the Soviet system, which was accompanied by a deep economic slump. When Vladimir Putin became president in 2000, his foremost priority was to restructure the economic foundations of the country in order to bring about economic recovery and to restore Russia's international dignity. Once Russia got back on its feet economically, thanks to its energy revenues, its priority has been to consolidate its international role and expand its influence in strategic areas. Putin explicitly committed his government to regaining Russia's status as a great power. Putin's conception of the process for developing Russia's foreign policy followed a linear sequence: first, strengthen the Russian state politically and economically; second, restore Russia's international status; third, act assertively on the international scene. The Kremlin is strengthening its leverage by widening its network of partners and creating new organizations. Putin is, for instance, willing to consolidate the BRICS (Brazil, Russia, India, China, and South Africa) as both an economic and a political force in order to counterbalance U.S. power, especially after its exclusion from the 2014 Group of Eight (G-8).

On the other side, the United States emerged from the Cold War victorious, prosperous, and confident, argues Jussi Hanhimäki. The collapse of the Soviet Union was interpreted as proof of the superiority of liberal capitalism over totalitarian socialism. The United States was "bound to lead," Joseph Nye wrote. The confident tone remained a trademark in the 1990s. The reaction to September 11, 2001, reflected the United States' status as the self-appointed indispensable nation: the Bush administration acted unilaterally for the most part, alienating most of its allies. The war in Iraq created a multitude of long-term problems that linger on. In January 2009, Barack Obama moved into the White House burdened by unrealistically high expectations. Many expected that the forty-fourth president would reverse course. However, much remained the same. The Obama administration's priorities were, as they had to be, *American* priorities: protecting U.S. national security and reviving the U.S. economy. In fact, one of the striking things about the first years of the Obama administration was the degree of continuity. America's standing with its European allies certainly improved after 2009. There was the signing and ratification of a New START (Strategic Arms Reduction Treaty). Some, albeit lackluster, efforts were made to repair America's difficult relations with the Muslim world, a task made more complicated by the Arab Spring of 2011. All such efforts can, however, be seen as part of a long-term continuum of U.S. foreign policy. Rather than a radical departure with the past, Obama's foreign policy can be regarded as a mixture of President Bill Clinton's emphasis on multilateral engagement and democratic enlargement and the Bush Doctrine's assertions about the American need to reserve for itself the right to take unilateral military action. What is most incredible, however, is that despite the U.S. withdrawal from the Iran nuclear agreement, the possibility of a trade war with China and the EU, Trump's rebuke on NATO, and his unclear relation with Vladimir Putin, the United States' relations with the rest of the world have yet not fundamentally transformed. Incredibly, world leaders are still looking at the United States, convinced that sooner rather than later it will go back to business as usual. Will it, before all is lost? The answer is at the end of this book.

PART I

The Foreign Policy of the EU and of Its Member States

EU Foreign and Defense Policies and Transatlantic Relations

Friends and Foes

FEDERIGA BINDI

Since the end of World War I, Western Europe and the United States have had a long history of working together, though their relationship has oscillated: the high points being the end of World War II and immediately after 9/11, and the lows being the Suez Crisis in 1956, the 1970s, the post–Iraq War years of George W. Bush's presidency, and most recently, following the election of Donald Trump as U.S. president.

Europeans' foreign policy and defense cooperation has in turn seen highs and lows; interestingly, EU integration in foreign and defense policies appears to be inversely proportional to the highs and lows in the transatlantic relationship: As crises appeared in the transatlantic relationship, Europeans generally progressed toward more integration in foreign and defense cooperation, as this chapter shows. This last crisis is no exception, but the difference is that its consequences for transatlantic relations and, especially, U.S. leadership in international relations may be far more important and irreversible than in the past.

The Making of Transatlantic Relations

The developments in Eastern Europe after World War II encouraged the Western European countries to search for a new system of alliances where the USSR, rather than Germany, would be the potential enemy. The first step in this direction was the signing of the Treaty of Brussels on March 17, 1948, by France, England, and the three Benelux countries. It called for military cooperation and mutual defense, though it also included clauses for economic, social, and cultural cooperation.

Slowly, the idea of a defense system bringing Western Europe and the United States together started to develop. With a historic vote, the U.S. Senate voted on the Vandenberg Resolution (June 1948), allowing the U.S. government to join alliances in times of peace outside the American continent. The Pentagon Talks thus began between Britain, the United States, and Canada, later to be joined by France, Holland, Belgium, and Luxembourg. Numerous difficult questions emerged: What would the aim of the treaty be? What kind of responsibilities would members have? Which states should be included?

Before the draft of the treaty could be completed, more European countries expressed their interest in joining: namely, Norway, Denmark, Italy, and Iceland. When Norway requested to participate, at the end of February 1949, France initially opposed the inclusion of Norway in favor of Italy to guarantee the strategic protection of Corsica and Algeria. England strongly opposed Italy's participation due to its fragile economic and political landscape. For the United States, Italy represented a serious problem: From a geographic point of view, it was not an Atlantic country; in addition, the United States thought Italy would contribute very little, in terms of military resources, to Western European security. Politically, however, Italy's exclusion from the North Atlantic Alliance was dangerous. Without ties to Western Europe, Italy could become isolationist or, worse, gravitate toward Eastern Europe, given its strong Communist Party. Despite the reluctance of several U.S. senators, the United States decided to allow Italy to join as one of the founding members of the North Atlantic security system.

The decision concerning Spain's entrance into the alliance was opposite. The Pentagon wanted Spain included, but the United States finally succumbed to the British and Canadian views. Both countries were wary of including a fascist dictatorship in the alliance. Interestingly, however, the (fascist) government of António de Oliveira Salazar in Portugal was seen as less of a problem; given the geopolitical strategic importance of the Azores and Madeira islands, Portugal's membership was never really questioned. Ironically, the hardest part proved to be convincing Salazar—who had signed a nonaggression treaty with Francisco Franco's Spain. The Portuguese ambassador to the United States, Pedro Pereira, played a fundamental role in convincing the two Iberian leaders that the North Atlantic Treaty was compatible with their treaty.

Finally, the North Atlantic Treaty was signed on April 4, 1949, in Washington, D.C.

The EDC: A Failed Opportunity

While the creation of the European Coal and Steel Community (ECSC) in 1951 was strongly supported by the United States—which viewed it as a way to reinforce Western Europe and, most of all, insert Germany in a web of relations that would have prevented a repeat of another post–World War I situation—the ECSC did not solve the problem of German rearmament. German disarmament had created a security vacuum in the heart of Europe, which was felt as particularly problematic after the Korean War. The United States suggested that an integrated, operative structure within the North Atlantic Alliance be created: the North Atlantic Treaty Organization (NATO), where a German army could participate under direct American control. As the French rejected the idea, they had to present an alternative. Once again, the proposal originated from one of Jean Monnet's ideas: French Prime Minister René Pleven announced his plan to the French National Assembly on October 24, 1950.

The Pleven Plan proposed to create a European army, headed by a European defense minister. The soldiers—coming from all participating countries, including Germany—would be integrated into a European army. The proposal was submitted to all the members of the North Atlantic Alliance, but the only countries to meet in Paris to discuss it in February 1951 were France, Germany, Italy, Belgium, and Luxembourg. Holland joined a few months later, in October; the United States, Great Britain, Canada, Norway, and Denmark sent observers. The European Defense Community (EDC) Treaty was signed on May 27, 1952, the day after Germany's sovereignty in the field of defense was restored.

Between 1953 and 1954, the EDC treaty was ratified by Germany and the Benelux countries. However, in Italy and France, changes in governments cooled down the enthusiasm for the ECD. With the public opinion divided between *cedistes* (favorable to ratification) and *anticedistes* (opposed), the vote on the Treaty in France was postponed *sine die* on August 30, 1954, thus effectively killing the ECD.

To solve the problem of German rearmament, the British foreign minister, Anthony Eden, resumed the American proposal: In 1954, Germany joined the North Atlantic Alliance. Italy and Germany also signed the Brussels Pact, now transformed into the Western European Union (WEU). The WEU was effectively a talk shop without military capability, which essentially left European security exclusively in NATO's hands. Consequently, in 1955, Germany was also admitted into NATO.

In 1957, the European Economic Community (EEC) included some provisions dealing with external relations, including external trade (the Common Commercial Policy) and a common external trade tariff (as a key feature of the customs union). Beginning with the 1963 Yaoundé Convention, the EEC took its first steps to form a development policy. In 1964–67, the EEC represented its members in the General Agreement on Tariffs and Trade (GATT) Kennedy Round negotiations.

The First Crises

By the beginning of the 1970s, the EEC began to feel pressure from the international community to engage further in international affairs. The Arab-Israeli wars, the oil crisis, and the Vietnam War were all external events pushing Europeans together as transatlantic relations became strained. Until the end of the John F. Kennedy administration, the United States had been generally supportive of the European integration process. That started to change in the late 1960s. By the 1970s, the United States perceived the EEC as an economic competitor and held it responsible for the deficit that the United States experienced in its balance of payments.

U.S. behavior vis-à-vis the EEC became rather contradictory. The United States insisted that Europe should contribute more to NATO expenses while the U.S. president, Richard Nixon, affirmed the principle of American leadership over the organization. Similarly, Secretary of State Henry Kissinger called 1973 the "Year of Europe." Yet the idea was essentially that the United States had global responsibilities and interests while Europe's interests were and could only be regional.

In response, on December 14, 1973, the EEC foreign ministers adopted in Copenhagen a "Declaration on European Identity." The objective was to better define the EEC's relations and responsibilities to the rest of the world and the place they occupied in world affairs. According to the declaration, the Nine were to play an active role in world affairs. In 1974 it was also decided that the country holding the EEC rotating presidency should consult with the United States on behalf of its partners.

The United States, however, continued to disagree with the Europeans on several foreign policy issues, including the Middle East. The Europeans themselves were divided until the Six-Day War in 1967. October 1973 brought a new war and the subsequent OPEC oil embargo on the United States and the Netherlands. Between October and November of that year, the Nine agreed on a common view and a common declaration regarding the legitimate rights of the Palestinians. The Nine greeted the Camp David peace talks (1977–79) without any noticeable enthusiasm. In the Venice Declaration of June 12–13, 1980, they reaffirmed the Palestinians' right to self-determination and advocated for the Palestinian Liberation Organization (PLO) to be included in peace negotiations. The election of U.S. president Ronald Reagan, who was resolutely against any European initiative outside Camp David, and the Israeli invasion of Lebanon (June 6, 1982) put an end to European activism in the area. Still, the EEC took action in favor of the Palestinians and became gradually more critical of Israel.

A similar story took place in neighboring Iran. When on November 4, 1979, the U.S. embassy in Tehran was seized and sixty-three hostages were taken, the United States immediately responded with a boycott on imports of Iranian oil and froze Iranian assets in the United States. While the EEC called several times for the release of the hostages, it did not support the U.S. call for sanctions. Only on April 22, 1980, did the EEC agree to sanctions, although only if implemented by the individual states.

Relations with Eurasia were also a matter of contention in transatlantic relations. The EEC and the United States clashed over the question of Poland when martial law was declared on December 13, 1981. While the United States imposed sanctions both on the USSR and Poland and pushed the Europeans to do likewise, the Europeans agreed on March 15, 1982, to only a limited number of restrictions on the USSR (on imports). This was the first time they had used article 113, referring to commercial policy, for political purposes. It took three weeks for the Europeans to formulate a response to the Soviet invasion of Afghanistan in December 1979. Moreover, the Europeans disagreed with the U.S. decision to boycott the 1980 Moscow Olympics. The United Kingdom supported the U.S. position, but France and Germany stood opposed, worried that it would undermine deterrence. Because of the slow EEC response to these events, in 1981 it was decided that three member states could call for an emergency meeting of the European Political Cooperation (EPC).

Because the Europeans needed to cooperate more, they set up the EPC, establishing the practice of regular meetings of EEC foreign ministers, heads of state and government, and political directors of the nine EEC member states, as well as systematic consultation on all major questions of foreign policy, including the decision that the ministers of foreign affairs would meet four times a year and whenever necessary.

The End of the Cold War

The Single European Act of 1986 (SEA) gave the EPC a treaty basis without changing its existing intergovernmental nature and methods of operation. In doing so, the SEA defined the role of the European Council (given the lead role), the European Commission (to assist the European Council), and the parliament (minimal right to be informed) within the EPC. The SEA also established that member states were to define common positions within international institutions or conferences, and were to assist and inform each other of foreign policy decisions and actions.

The year 1989 brought dramatic and unexpected changes in Eastern Europe. On December 8–9, the European Council in Strasbourg approved the German reunification. It was, however, to be counterbalanced by a more integrated community, which was realized with the 1992 Maastricht Treaty, or as it is formally known, the Treaty on European Union (TEU), which established the "European Union." The Maastricht Treaty set the path for a European single currency and created the Common Foreign and Security Policy (CFSP).

However, as the Iraqi invasion of Kuwait in August 1990 and the subsequent First Gulf War in 1991 coincided with the Maastricht Treaty negotiations, it became a source of friction among EEC partners, in particular between the United Kingdom and the others. It led to disagreement over issues of security, majority voting, how to integrate foreign policy into the Community, and whether the philosophical distinction made between security and defense could be abandoned. Different views were also expressed over whether the WEU should be merged with the EU. The United States and the more pro-NATO member states were extremely worried about this possibility and what they saw as an impediment to NATO and Western security.

As a result, CSFP was far from the EU foreign and defense policy initially envisaged. It nonetheless established systematic cooperation between member states in adopting "common positions" in foreign policy matters; in coordinating their actions within international organizations and conferences; in engaging in joint actions; and in refraining from any action contrary to EU policies. The WEU was to be closely associated with the CSFP, acting as a bridge to NATO, and the CFSP was finally permitted to address the previously taboo question of "defense," with the possibility held out in the Maastricht Treaty of gradually moving toward a common defense system. The Council Presidency was to represent the EU in CFSP matters. Abroad, member-states' diplomatic missions and European Commission delegations were to cooperate, and the European Parliament (EP) was to be consulted. Soon afterward (1995), the EU swiftly enlarged to include Austria, Sweden, and Finland.

Meanwhile, tensions started to arise between two parallel processes: the integration of the new Central and Eastern European countries (CEECs) into the EU and into NATO. The end of the Cold War had opened the question of incorporating these recently democratized countries into the EU. Trade agreements had already been signed by the EEC in 1988 (Hungary and Czechoslovakia), 1989 (Poland), and 1990 (Bulgaria and Roma-

nia) and then replaced with Association Agreements (the so-called Europa
Agreements) in 1992 (Hungary and Poland), 1993 (Czech Republic, Slovak
Republic, Bulgaria, and Romania), and 1996 (Slovenia). However, the EU
member states—fearing the costs of incorporating the CEECs into the
EU—tried to delay the enlargement process by embarking on more narrow
negotiations over EU institutional reforms, considered as a precondition
to enlargement. This strategy left Central and Eastern Europeans, who had
previously looked at the EU as a source of inspiration against the Soviet
system, frustrated.

The United States was quick in exploiting the political void left by
the EU by speeding up the process of integration of the new European
democracies into NATO. In November 1991, the North Atlantic Cooperation Council (NACC) was created to enable security discussions with
the CEECs. In 1992, a "consultation forum" was created within NATO
that included the CEECs but excluded Russia. In 1994, the WEU offered the CEECs the status of "associate partners," which would permit
the CEECs to participate in Petersberg-like (peacekeeping) operations,
but they were not offered the prize they most coveted—the West's security guarantee.

Meanwhile, the Europeans had begun talking of a European security
and defense identity (ESDI). This idea, however, was not so well received
in the United States. The U.S. administration of Bill Clinton was in fact
eager for the Europeans to bear more of the defense burden, but not if an
EU-led defense pact would rival NATO. As a result, in a June 1996 NATO
ministerial meeting in Berlin, EU defense ministers agreed to build ESDI
within NATO, while simultaneously stressing the supremacy of the principle of transatlantic cooperation within the alliance.[1] Subsequently, the
U.S. administration pushed for speedy NATO enlargement. On July 8,
1997, the North Atlantic Council in Madrid invited the Czech Republic,
Hungary, and Poland to begin accession talks with a view to joining
NATO by its fiftieth anniversary in 1999. The EU had no option but to
follow suit and, in December of the same year, invited the ten CEECs as
well as Cyprus to join EU membership talks.

At a meeting in Saint-Malo in December 1998, British prime minister
Tony Blair and French president Jacques Chirac, the leaders of the EU's
two nuclear powers, agreed to establish European military cooperation
within NATO. However, U.S. approval came with conditions, articulated
by then U.S. secretary of state Madeleine Albright, that the EU avoid the

"three Ds": no decoupling (of European Security and Defense Policy from NATO); no duplication (of capabilities); and no discrimination (against non-NATO members). NATO members formally endorsed European defense cooperation at its fiftieth anniversary summit (April 25, 1999). (In December 2002, NATO and the EU negotiated a set of agreements, called "Berlin Plus," that govern the sharing of assets between the EU and NATO for crisis management and peacekeeping operations.)

Following the historic NATO summit, at the June 1999 Cologne summit the EU heads of government announced their decision to absorb the WEU into a new European Security and Defense Policy (ESDP)—later renamed "Common Security and Defense Policy" (in the Lisbon Treaty). The former NATO general secretary, Javier Solana, was appointed WEU Secretary General and High Representative for the CFSP. At the Helsinki European Council in December 1999, it was then agreed that by 2003 the EU would be able to deploy up to 60,000 troops within sixty days for at least one year.

9/11 and Its Consequences

George W. Bush took office in January 2001. Eight months later, the attacks of September 11 were to have lasting effects on U.S. foreign policy and, consequently, on transatlantic relations. The new administration was quickly at odds with its European allies on issues such as missile defense, climate change, and relations with Russia and the Balkans.[2] September 11, 2001, and the subsequent war on terror further contributed to tensions. The Anglo-American attack on Iraq in 2003 was supported by some EU member states while others strongly opposed it. With the invasion of Iraq, U.S.-EU relations thus reached what was considered then a historic low. When asked by a Dutch reporter why America's European allies were not more supportive of U.S. calls to hold Saddam Hussein accountable, Secretary of Defense Donald Rumsfeld replied: "You're thinking of Europe as Germany and France. I don't. I think that's old Europe."[3] Realizing the negative impact of such tense relations with Western Europe, the Bush 43 administration sought to correct its policy toward Europe—a process also eased by a number of changes in the new administration's national security and foreign policy teams, most notably the replacement of Donald Rumsfeld with Robert Gates.[4]

Meanwhile, in the attempt to repair divisions within Europe over Iraq—in particular those that had emerged between French president Jacques Chirac and British prime minister Tony Blair—the European Council agreed at the Thessaloniki Summit in December 2003 to a European Security Strategy (ESS) entitled "A Secure Europe in a Better World."[5] The text, drafted under Javier Solana's direction, was considered a counterpart to the U.S. security strategy. It identified a list of key threats Europe needed to deal with: terrorism, proliferation of weapons of mass destruction, regional conflict, failed states, and organized crime. Central to the ESS was the promotion of regional stability in Europe and its "neighborhood,"[6] with the EU's strategic priorities identified as Europe (Balkans, Eurasia, Russia), the Mediterranean, and the Middle East.

The European Defense Agency (EDA), established in 2004, was one of the new institutions to be developed from this new strategy. Then, in December 2007, the Lisbon Treaty was signed. The new treaty introduced a substantial upgrade in the field of European foreign policy. It finally entrusted the EU with legal personality and introduced a series of important innovations both in the fields of EU foreign policy and defense, now an integral part of CFSP. Most notably, the Lisbon Treaty created the High Representative for European Union Foreign Affairs and Security Policy, a "double-hatted position" combining the existing portfolios of the CFSP high representative and the EU commissioner for external relations.

Barack Obama and the Lisbon Treaty

In his pre-election tour in the summer of 2008, Obama was greeted rockstar style in Europe. Obama's vision of foreign policy was a message of change, hope, and audacity. Obama sought nothing less than bending "history's arc in the direction of justice, and a more peaceful, stable global order."[7] He argued for the need to pay more attention to the "global commons," which was threatened by terrorism, nuclear proliferation, climate change, and pandemic diseases.[8] In his July 24, 2008, Berlin speech, Obama spoke of a planet that needed to be saved from famine, rising oceans, and carbon emissions; a world without nuclear weapons; and the redemption of those left behind by globalization by extending to them dignity, opportunity, and justice.[9] At the same time, Obama was promising toughness in

Afghanistan and in the handling terrorists and insurgents in Pakistan, as well as an exit strategy from Iraq. All in all, Obama was promising a major break with the past and a historic change for the future, based on essentially three pillars.[10] The first pillar was a *changed relationship with the rising powers*, manifested in Obama's preference for the G-20 over the G-8, support for a permanent seat for India on the UN Security Council, and the Asia pivot. Except for Gordon Brown, the then British prime minister, and Nicolas Sarkozy, then French president—who both used the G-20 for the purpose of their domestic politics—the other G-8 Europeans and the EU showed uneasiness about a larger table for fear of being marginalized. Such fears were confirmed in December 2009 at the Climate Change Summit in Copenhagen, when the United States made a deal with the Indian, Chinese, Brazilian, and South African leaders, leaving the Europeans and the EU literally out of the room.

The second pillar was *nuclear disarmament and proliferation*. In his Prague speech in April 2009, President Obama declared he was seeking "the peace and security of a world without nuclear weapons."[11] In September 2009, at the UN General Assembly, President Obama chaired a special meeting of the UN Security Council (UNSC) and then hosted in Washington the Summit on Nuclear Proliferation (April 2010) while at the same time launching the U.S. Nuclear Posture Review, which spelled out the new U.S. doctrine in the field: a "no first use" nuclear commitment toward those states that would foreswear nuclear weapons. Any achievement in this area was obviously linked to success in the "reset" of the relations with Russia. The main result of the reset was the signing of the New START Treaty and the positive vote of both Russia and China on the UNSC Resolution of June 2010 mandating tougher sanctions against Iran for its violation of the Non-Proliferation Treaty.

The third pillar was turning Bush's combative *relations with the Muslim world* into a positive partnership, as Obama told the world in his Cairo speech in 2009.[12] Originally, Obama did not include the idea of "exporting democracy"—a principle arguably abused by Bush—and used a more abstract notion of "universal human rights": freedom of speech and assembly, equal rights for women, rule of law, and accountable government. Only later, with the Arab Spring, did the promotion of democracy become a foreign policy priority.

Barack Obama was sworn into office in January 2009. In December of the same year, the new Lisbon Treaty also entered into force. The new treaty was seen in Europe and abroad as a substantial upgrade in the field of European foreign policy.

The person who was chosen to serve as the first EU High Representative (EUHR) in November 2009 was Lady Catherine Ashton.[13] While initially relatively unknown, EUHR Ashton quietly gained the trust of her American counterparts and represented the EU in extremely difficult situations, such as in Cairo (during the ouster of President Mohamed Morsi), Serbia, and Kosovo, and with the Iranians over uranium enrichment. The close personal relationship that EUHR Catherine Ashton and U.S. secretary of state Hillary Clinton forged was later followed by a similarly close relationship with Secretary John Kerry. In parallel, Ashton oversaw the setup of the European External Action Service (EEAS), a sui generis service led by EEAS Secretary General and French diplomat Pierre Vimont and comprising personnel recruited among the member states (one-third) and EU institutions (two-thirds).

The new treaty raised expectations in the United States about future EU foreign policy. Early in his tenure, Assistant Secretary for European Affairs of State Phil Gordon embarked on a tour of European capitals to inquire about the Lisbon Treaty and its implications for the United States and to find out if Europe would finally have "one phone number."[14] A number of adjustments were made at the U.S. State Department to streamline its way of dealing with EU affairs.

In the U.S. Department of State, EU affairs fell under the Bureau of European and Eurasian Affairs (EUR). The bureau was structured to address multiple multilateral and bilateral issues: It consisted of a cluster of functional offices, along with traditional, bilateral regional offices. EUR dealt with the EU, NATO, the Organization for Security and Cooperation in Europe (OSCE), the Russian Federation, and non-EU member states in Europe. Yet most of the work with the EU was still based on traditional bilateral channels, despite the fact that the different EU country "desks" are scattered around different "offices" (for example, the Office of Western Europe, Office of Southern European Affairs, Office of Nordic and Baltic Affairs, Office of Central European Affairs), each of which deals with different EU and non-EU member states. The new Office of European Union and Regional Affairs (ERA), responsible for addressing U.S. relations with the EU and its institutions, initially suffered a number of difficulties.[15] In 2010, however, ERA was finally given charge to deal exclusively with EU affairs, and a skilled diplomat, Elizabeth Dibble, was named as its head.

EU-U.S. relations progressed well on a number of relevant issues, including the ongoing conflict in Afghanistan, the nuclear deal with Iran, the 2011 NATO operation in Libya, and the common problem of counterterrorism. The Iran deal and the war in Libya, in particular, are worth recalling, for rather opposite reasons.

Transatlantic cooperation regarding Iran's nuclear program has been close and extensive. Since the discovery of Iran's covert enrichment activities in 2002, the "EU-3" (France, Germany, and the United Kingdom) have played a leading role in international efforts to curtail them. In 2006 the United States joined the EU-3, along with Russia and China, to form the Permanent Five Plus One (P5 + 1) group that has attempted to conduct negotiations with Iran.[16] Between 2006 and 2010, the EU-3 and the United States successfully pushed for UNSC approval of four rounds of sanctions on Iran (Resolutions 1737, 1747, 1803, and 1929).

With sanctions appearing to put considerable pressure on the Iranian economy, tensions between Iran and the West increased during late 2011 and early 2012. Following a November 2011 report by the International Atomic Energy Agency (IAEA) about Iran's activities in pursuit of nuclear weapons, EU member states began discussing the dimensions of enhanced sanctions. On January 23, 2012, the EU adopted a major new round of sanctions on Iran. Among other measures that included targeting the Iranian Central Bank and Iran's petrochemical industry, EU sanctions banned the import of oil from Iran. The EU had imported approximately 600,000 barrels of oil from Iran per day, accounting for about 20 percent of Iran's total oil exports. In the past, Americans had pointed to European economic ties with Iran as a sign of European reluctance to press Tehran too hard, urging Europeans to adopt tighter sanctions. The EU's willingness to go beyond the UNSC authorizations sent a strong signal and brought the U.S. and European sanctions policy on Iran into broad alignment. The European Union stressed that its sanctions were designed to target sources of finance for Iran's nuclear program and not the Iranian people or legitimate trade activities.[17] Negotiations resumed in November 2013, with High Representative Ashton as the chief mediator for the P5 + 1. The Ashton-Kerry tandem—later to be followed by Kerry-Mogherini—was the driving force behind the agreement.[18] After months of negotiations, on July 14, 2015, the P5 + 1 reached a Joint Comprehensive Plan of Action (JCPOA) to ensure a peaceful Iranian Nuclear Program.[19] In return for sanction relief, Iran would reduce its uranium stockpile by 98 percent, maintain an enrichment level of 3.67 percent, reduce centrifuges by two-thirds for ten years, and not build the heavy-water reactor for acquiring plutonium for fifteen years.[20] International inspectors from the IAEA are to recurrently confirm that these requirements are being fulfilled.[21]

The agreement demonstrated the effectiveness of diplomacy while also serving to strengthen U.S.-EU cooperation. Therefore, more than blocking the Transatlantic Trade and Investment Partnership (TTIP) and breaking away from the Paris climate accord, President Trump created a serious breach in transatlantic relations with his threats to unilaterally leave the Iran deal. The Europeans made it repeatedly clear that the United States has no right to terminate the Iran deal and that even if the United States withdraws, the Europeans would go forward by themselves.[22] The volatility of the new U.S. administration made the Europeans realize, though, that the EU could not count on the United States as it did for the previous seventy years.

The case of Libya is controversial, though important and thus worth recalling. Both the European Union and the United States failed to foresee the coming of the Arab Spring. The response was slow, fuzzy, and controversial. The 2011 Libyan uprising occurred in the context of popular protest movements and political change in other countries in North Africa and the Middle East. In mid-February 2011, confrontations between opposition activists and government security forces in the eastern cities of Benghazi and Bayda resulted in the death of some unarmed protestors. Security forces used military force to subdue subsequent funeral gatherings and protests in incidents that reportedly killed or wounded dozens, if not hundreds, of civilians. Opposition groups seized several police and military facilities and took control of some eastern cities. In the weeks that followed, counterattacks on opposition-controlled areas by supporters of Muammar Qaddafi, and opposition advances toward Qaddafi strongholds, pushed Libya to the brink of civil war.

The French airstrike on March 20, 2011, marked the beginning of the allied operations in Libya.[23] In the first week of Libya operations, the United States dropped bombs from B-2 stealth planes flown from Missouri and roughly 200 missiles launched from submarines in the Mediterranean, causing alarm that any extended campaign would quickly cost billions of dollars more. But after the U.S. military ramped up the operation, other NATO countries shouldered most of the air burden. Americans took a supporting role, providing aerial refueling tankers, electronic jamming, and surveillance. Hence, for the first time since the Cold War, the United States decided to neither exercise leadership nor fully share risks in a war in which it was otherwise participating. However, the United States provided intelligence, refueling, and more precision bombing assistance than Paris or London want to acknowledge.[24]

A majority of NATO and EU members, including Germany, Poland, and Turkey, refused to support the war, notwithstanding an explicit UNSC resolution. Even jointly owned assets such as NATO's fleet of AWACS (airborne warning and control system) radar aircraft were deprived of German personnel, although these were not strike aircraft. In addition, the EU played no identifiable part in the war, exposing EU structural insufficiencies and flaws in the defense field.[25] Ironically, the Libya campaign was generally considered in Washington as an example of successful transatlantic cooperation, most especially because of the reduced costs and of (relatively) reduced direct U.S. intervention. However, subsequent years would prove the strategic success of this operation very limited. Libya deteriorated quickly as rival militias all claiming government legitimacy battled each other, escalating into full-scale civil war in February 2014. This political instability would allow Islamic State militants to use Libya as a staging ground for terror attacks.[26] The "leading from behind" strategy, as applied by the Obama administration in Libya, thus showed its limits to both the United States and the European Union.

2014 and Beyond

When Federica Mogherini arrived in office in October 2014, she found the European External Action Service (EEAS) up and running. Deemed a weak candidate by many observers,[27] Mogherini was initially opposed by many European partners.[28] However, at her confirmation hearing, she clearly showed she was far more than the accidental nominee. One of Europe's most keen observers—Jan Techau, then director of Carnegie Europe—tweeted: "Mogherini clearly has what it takes: maximum verbal flexibility without too many edges that might hurt anyone." The European Parliament's Foreign Affairs Committee greeted her with applause at the end of the hearing, a compliment not paid to other commissioner-nominees. She, however, initially moved timidly on the international scene, playing a corollary role to John Kerry in the Iran deal negotiations.

However, Mogherini managed in the very difficult task, especially for women, to appear authoritative but not aggressive. As Marianne Cooper wrote in the *Harvard Business Review*,[29] "The ones who are applauded for delivering results at work [are] then reprimanded for being 'too aggressive,' 'out for herself,' 'difficult,' and 'abrasive.'" By the time the Obama presidency drew to a close, Mogherini was well grounded and well at the helm of EU foreign policy.

As the new administration took office in the United States, Mogherini was among the first to arrive in Washington and to invite Vice President Mike Pence to Brussels. However, as it became clear that the United States would no longer be the trustable partner of the past, the EU decisively pushed on the integration accelerator with a new Global Strategy: "The Global Strategy has served as a springboard to relaunch the process of European integration after the British referendum . . . we have moved fast—and united—on concrete implementation, starting with security and defense. In this field, more has been achieved in the last ten months than in the last ten years."[30]

In the absence of the United Kingdom—embedded in the Brexit negotiations and unable to say anything about the EU's future—in December 2017, twenty-five member states (all but the United Kingdom, Denmark, and Malta) agreed to step up the European Union's work in the defense area by creating a Permanent Structured Cooperation (PESCO) on security and defense.[31] Through PESCO, member states will increase their effectiveness in addressing security challenges, advancing toward further integration and strengthening defense cooperation within the EU framework. By providing enhanced coordination and collaboration in the areas of investment, capability development, and operational readiness, PESCO will be a fundamental driver of integration in the European defense industry. Massive European financial investments and European-wide procurement procedures are likely to significantly affect the military industry, relaunching the European one and challenging the American one.

As PESCO reinforces the EU's strategic autonomy to act alone, for the first time in seventy years the possibility of NATO subordination to the European Union, rather than the contrary, is hypnotizable and may lead to a dramatic change in the transatlantic defense and security landscape.

NOTES

1. North Atlantic Treaty Organization (NATO), "Final Communique," Ministerial Meeting of the North Atlantic Council, Berlin, June 3,1996 (www .nato.int/docu/pr/1996/p96-063e.htm).

2. John Peterson and Mark Pollack, *Europe, America, Bush: Transatlantic Relations in the Twenty-First Century* (Abingdon, U.K.: Routledge, 2003), pp. 85–98.

3. George W. Bush, *Decision Points* (New York: Broadway Books, 2010), p. 88.

4. Ibid., pp. 87–94.

5. Council of the European Union, "A Secure Europe in a Better World: European Security Strategy," Europa.eu, December 12, 2003.

6. Ibid., p. 6.

7. Martin S. Indyk, Kenneth G. Lieberthal, and Michael E. O'Hanlon, *Bending History: Barack Obama's Foreign Policy* (Brookings Institution Press, 2012), p. 2.

8. Ibid., p. 5.

9. "Obama's Speech in Berlin," *New York Times*, July 24, 2008.

10. Indyk, Lieberthal, and O'Hanlon, *Bending History*, pp. 12–14.

11. Barack Obama, "Remarks by President Barack Obama in Prague as Delivered," Obama White House Archives, April 5, 2009 (https://obamawhite house.archives.gov/the-press-office/remarks-president-barack-obama-prague -delivered).

12. "Text: Obama's Speech in Cairo," *New York Times*, June 4, 2009.

13. European Parliament, "Summary of Hearing of Catherine Ashton, EU High Representative-Designate for Foreign Policy," 2010 (https://multimedia .europarl.europa.eu/en/hearing-of-catherine-ashton-high-representative -designate-for-foreign-policy-afet-audition-de-cather_1477_c).

14. This phrase is often attributed to Henry Kissinger; however, he likely never said it. It refers to the idea that if an outside actor wanted to contact

"Europe," they could dial a single number rather than calling each country individually.

15. U.S. Office of Inspector General, "Inspection of the Bureau of European and Eurasian Affairs," Report ISP-I-11-22, March 2011 (https://oig.state .gov/system/files/161095.pdf).

16. Derek E. Mix, "The United States and Europe: Current Issues," Congressional Research Service (CRS) Report RS22163, March 20, 2013, p. 6 (www .ipmall.info/sites/default/files/hosted_resources/crs/RS22163_130320.pdf).

17. Ibid.

18. Saeed K. Dehghan, "U.S. Hails 'Unprecedented Opportunity' as Iran Halts Enriching High-Level Uranium," *The Guardian*, January 20, 2014; Rick Gladstone, "U.S. Warns against Business with Iran," *New York Times*, January 23, 2014; Michael R. Gordon, "Kerry Presses Iranians to Prove Nuclear Work Is for Peaceful Purposes," *New York Times*, January 24, 2014.

19. U.S. Department of State, "Joint Comprehensive Plan of Action" (www.state.gov/e/eb/tfs/spi/iran/jcpoa/).

20. "The Historic Deal That Will Prevent Iran from Acquiring a Nuclear Weapon," Obama White House Archives, (https://obamawhitehouse.archives .gov/node/328996).

21. Ibid.

22. David M. Herszenhorn and Jacopo Barigazzi, "EU:US Has No Right to Terminate Iran Accord," *Politico*, October 13, 2017.

23. Elisabeth Bumiller, Steven Erlanger, and David D. Kirkpatrick, "Allies Open Air Assault on Qaddafi's Forces in Libya," *New York Times*, March 19, 2011.

24. Steven Erlanger, "Libya's Dark Lesson for NATO," *New York Times*, September 3, 2011.

25. Francois Heisbourg, "Libya: A Small War with Big Consequences," *New York Times*, August 29, 2011.

26. Erin Cunningham and Hassan Morajea, "Libyan Gains May Offer ISIS a Base for New Attacks," *Washington Post*, June 6, 2015.

27. See Yassin Sabha, "Global Trade and Competitiveness, Italy, Rieti, Jordan and the Middle East" (https://yassinsabha.wordpress.com/2014/09/04 /the-appointment-of-federica-mogherini-is-a-missed-opportunity-for-renzi -and-for-italy-to-gain-credibility-internationally/). See also Valentina Pop, "EU Leaders Pick Tusk, Mogherini for Top Posts," *EU Observer*, August 30, 2014.

28. "EU Summit Fails to Reach Agreement on Top Jobs," *DW Akademie*, July 17, 2014 (www.dw.de/eu-summit-fails-to-reach-agreement-on-top-jobs /a-17791114).

29. Marianne Cooper, "For Women Leaders, Likability and Success Hardly Go Hand-in-Hand," *Harvard Business Review*, April 30, 2013.

30. "The EU Global Strategy at 1: Personal Message by Federica Mogherini," Europa.eu.

31. PESCO is a form of enhanced cooperation among European member states as foreseen by the Treaty on European Union, in articles 42 (6) and 46, as well as protocol 10.

THREE

The Foreign Policy of France

Continuity and Change

ALEKSANDER LUST

> A long time ago some Greeks asked Solon the Wise: "What
> is the best form of Constitution?" He replied: "First tell
> me, for what people and in which times."
>
> —Speech delivered by General Charles de
> Gaulle at Bayeux, June 16, 1946

Drawing on political history and historically minded political science, this chapter explores the changes and continuities in French foreign policy in the Fifth Republic. I first discuss the legacy of General Charles de Gaulle, whose idea of France as a nation destined for great deeds, if no longer a great power, and the presidential system of government that he established still shape French foreign policy today. I then show how French presidents since de Gaulle have pursued a policy of military and political independence from the United States, even as they have adapted themselves to American hegemony since the end of the Cold War. I also discuss how France has cooperated with Germany in building the European Union (EU) as a continental economic bloc, although it shares Great Britain's suspicion of supranational government and preference for a more active foreign and defense policy. Finally, I highlight the global reach of French foreign policy, especially its close ties with Africa and growing presence in the Arab world, reflecting its history as a colonial empire and continued search for a leading role on the international stage.

Given the scope of the chapter, I rely mainly on secondary literature on French foreign policy since 1958. As much as possible, however, I also use published primary sources, such as official documents, speeches, and memoirs, to refine the interpretations in the existing scholarship and, above all, to allow the main characters in our story, de Gaulle and his successors, to speak in their own words.

The Founding Father: The Legacy of General Charles de Gaulle

De Gaulle returned to power amid a domestic political crisis that was deepened by the setbacks and humiliations that France had suffered on the international stage. The constitution of the Fourth Republic (1946) was designed to prevent the emergence of an elected dictator, such as the two Napoleons, Philippe Pétain, or de Gaulle himself. The president had a largely ceremonial role, though he could nominate his candidate for the post of prime minister and ratify treaties. Political power was concentrated in the lower house of the parliament, the National Assembly, which passed laws, approved the budget, and appointed the government (Council of Ministers). While in office, the government, especially the prime minister—called the President of the Council to underscore the collegial character of the body—exercised considerable power, supervising the armed forces and the bureaucracy and, if authorized to do so by the Assembly, passing legislation by decree. However, the government could be removed by a vote of censure by the Assembly, at first by a plurality vote. This provision was easily exploited by small parties and ambitious parliamentarians whose ministerial aspirations had been blocked because two large parties—the Communists and the Gaullists—voted against most governments. As a result, France had twenty-six governments from 1946 to 1958, creating the impression that the political class was more interested in dividing the spoils of the office than in solving the country's problems.[1]

Despite the frequent turnover of cabinets, the Fourth Republic took the lead in creating the European Coal and Steel Community (1951) and the European Economic Community (1957) because European integration was supported by senior civil servants and influential business circles. (In 1954, the National Assembly voted down the proposal to create a European Defense Community.) However, it was less successful in halting the decline of French political and military power. France was a founding member of the North Atlantic Treaty Organization (1949), which protected France from a Soviet attack but subordinated French armed forces to American control. France was also fighting a losing battle to maintain its colonial empire. In 1954, the French army suffered a decisive defeat at the hands of the Vietnamese in the Battle of Dien Bien Phu, leading to the withdrawal of France from Indochina. In 1956, France was forced to retreat from the Suez Canal, which it had invaded with Britain and Israel when the Soviet Union threatened to intervene on the side of Egypt and the United States put pressure on the franc. The military situation in Algeria, the oldest French colony in Africa with a large settler population—officially, Algeria was divided into three overseas departments of France—went from bad to worse as desperate French forces used torture to battle the guerrillas of the National Liberation Front (FLN).

In 1958, the conflict in Algeria spun out of control. In retaliation for an FLN raid, the French air force bombed the movement's bases in Tunisia. Facing international protests, the French government accepted the American and British offer to mediate, which angered the military and broad sections of the public sympathetic to the cause of French Algeria. The French troops stationed in Algiers refused to take further orders from the government in Paris, while paratroopers from Algeria seized power on the island of Corsica. The government declared a state of emergency, but was forced to negotiate with the rebels once the navy declined to transport reinforcements to the trouble spots. Sensing that the time for his comeback had come, de Gaulle declared that he was "ready to assume the powers of the republic." He refused to condemn the insubordinate officers, whose actions he saw as part of a broader problem of a "regime of parties" that lacked authority at home and failed to protect national interests abroad.[2] The constitution of the Fourth Republic, he said, was "a bad one, written against me and in spite of me." At the same time, he professed his commitment to democratic principles, asking skeptical journalists: "Why do you think that, at age 67, I would start a career as dictator?"[3] Fearful of a civil war, President Réne Coty appointed and the National Assembly confirmed de Gaulle as prime minister in a coalition government and gave him the task of writing a new constitution.

Approved by a large majority of the electorate—80 percent of eligible voters turned out, and 83 percent of them voted for the draft—the constitution rebalanced political power in favor of the president. In consultation with the government and/or the leaders of the two chambers of the Parliament, the president has the right to submit important issues directly to the consideration of voters in referenda (article 11), dissolve the National Assembly and call new elections (article 12), and take emergency measures when national independence or political order are threatened (article 16), a provision that de Gaulle used to suppress a military coup in Algeria in 1961. In 1962, the constitution was first amended to introduce the direct election of the president (article 6), who can now speak in the name of the people as a whole, while other politicians represent more limited constituencies. The constitution also makes the president the most powerful actor in foreign and defense policy. The president is the commander in chief of the armed forces (article 15) and negotiates international treaties (article 52). Most important, if ambiguously, while the "government shall determine and conduct the policy of the Nation" (article 20), the president "shall be the guarantor of national independence, territorial integrity and due respect for Treaties" (article 5).[4] Interpreting these clauses as broadly as possible, de Gaulle sought to implement his idea of France as an independent actor on the world stage.

As Frédéric Bozo and Maurice Vaisse and, on the other side of the Atlantic, Charles Cogan and William Nester have argued, the first principle of de Gaulle's foreign policy was national sovereignty. In de Gaulle's view, France was an exceptional nation destined for great deeds. However, France had suffered more than its share of misfortunes in recent history, including military occupation by Germany (France's hereditary enemy) during World War II, followed by defeats in ill-conceived colonial wars in Indochina and Algeria and tutelage to a well-meaning but overbearing American superpower during the Cold War. It was the task of the French government to restore France's position as a great power and, along with that, France's national unity and self-respect by pursuing an independent and assertive foreign policy. After he returned to power, de Gaulle built an independent nuclear force, withdrew France from NATO's military organization, and developed ties with communist and developing countries. His successors improved relations with the United States and eventually rejoined NATO's integrated command but continued to pursue an independent foreign policy on issues like nuclear deterrence and relations with the Soviet Union.[5]

As Gérard Bossuat, Georges-Henri Soutou, and Michael Sutton remind us, however, de Gaulle also helped to create the community of nations we know today as the European Union. He twice vetoed the admission of Britain to the European Economic Community (EEC) and fought bitter battles with the European Commission over the distribution of power between the commission and the member states. However, he understood that France was too weak to defend its interests in a world dominated by the United States and the Soviet Union. Therefore, France needed to cooperate with Germany and other countries of continental Europe, with whom France shared a common tradition of a strong, interventionist state, while Britain was too liberal and pro-American to be a reliable partner. Unlike federalist leaders like Jean Monnet, however, de Gaulle believed that this cooperation should take the form of a confederation between independent nations—a "Europe of states"—that would coordinate their foreign and defense policies instead of looking to American leadership on these issues—a "European Europe." As president, he allowed the Treaty of Rome (1957) that created the EEC to come into effect and proposed a plan for a European political and military union (which, however, failed because of opposition from other countries). Today, French leaders are more supportive of supranational institutions but continue to advocate closer European political and military cooperation.[6]

Recent research by Christian Nuenlist, Anna Locher, Garret Martin, and their collaborators emphasizes the global scope of de Gaulle's foreign policy. Though he granted independence to the French colonies in Africa, he remained actively engaged in African affairs, providing economic and technical aid to the newly independent states and intervening militarily to keep friendly governments in power. After he ended the war in Algeria, he developed good relations with several Arab countries that benefited from French arms sales and diplomatic support against Israel. While French involvement in other parts of the developing world was more limited, de Gaulle wanted France to have a symbolic presence across the globe. From Cambodia to Mexico, he traveled widely, advocating the right of national self-determination and criticizing the hegemonic tendencies of the United

States. Today, France generally accepts that it is a medium-size power with limited ability to shape world events, but it remains willing to use its position on the United Nations Security Council to challenge U.S. policy in regions where it has strategic and economic interests (for example, President Jacques Chirac's opposition to the Iraq War).[7]

Transatlantic Relations: Conflict and Cooperation

De Gaulle recognized that there was no fundamental conflict of interest between France and the United States, the only major power with which France had not fought a war. However, he considered the United States an unreliable ally that pursued its self-interest at the expense of France while claiming to uphold the principles of democracy and self-determination. During World War I, "the Anglo-Saxons' cry of 'Halt'"—the armistice of November 1918—brought an end to the fighting at a point when France, which had borne the brunt of the war, was "about to pluck the fruits of victory." "The wishes and promises of the American President" Woodrow Wilson were the dominant factor in shaping the Treaty of Versailles (1919), which returned Alsace and Lorraine to France but "left the enemy's unity, territory, and resources intact" to start a new war.[8] During World War II, "the immobility the United States had observed when the Third Reich attempted to dominate Europe [and] the neutrality she had clung to while France suffered the disaster of 1940" contributed to France's capitulation to Germany. After Germany declared war on the United States and it was finally obliged to enter the war in Europe, the United States continued to treat France "only as a subordinate, as is proved by the fact Washington is furnishing only a limited supply of arms for the French Army." Though France received an occupation zone in Germany, it was not invited to the conference at Yalta that settled the fate of postwar Europe, prompting de Gaulle, who was "offended . . . but not at all surprised," to announce that "France will of course be committed to absolutely nothing that she has not been in a position to discuss and approve."[9]

During the Cold War, de Gaulle supported the United States during the crises over Berlin (1961) and Cuba (1962) in order to stop the spread of the Soviet sphere of influence beyond Eastern Europe. However, he did not hesitate to challenge the United States on issues where French and American interests diverged and where taking an independent position was important for France's international prestige, such as nuclear weapons, NATO, and eventually, relations with communist countries. As he wrote in his *Memoirs of Hope*:

> My aim, then, was to disengage France, not from the Atlantic Alliance, which I intended to maintain by way of ultimate precaution, but from the integration realized by NATO under American command; to establish relations with each of the States of the Eastern bloc, first and foremost Russia, with the object of bringing about a détente followed by understanding and cooperation; to do likewise, when the time was right, with China; and finally, to provide France with nuclear capability such as that no one could attack us without running the risk of frightful injury.[10]

The French nuclear program was launched during the Fourth Republic, but de Gaulle made it his top priority. In his view, an independent nuclear force would allow France to defend itself against a Soviet invasion even if the United States were to withdraw its nuclear protection from Europe or lacked the nerve to launch its intercontinental nuclear missiles against the Soviet homeland after losing a conventional war in Europe. Nuclear weapons would also increase the world's respect for France at a time when the country had been humiliated by the defeat in Vietnam (1954) at the hands of communist guerrillas backed by China and the retreat from the Suez Canal (1956) under diplomatic pressure from the United States. In 1960, France exploded its first nuclear bomb in the Sahara Desert of Algeria. To deliver the bombs, France built a fleet of strategic bombers and a small number of intermediate-range ballistic missiles. Unlike Europe's other nuclear power, Great Britain, France turned down President John F. Kennedy's offer of nuclear missiles in exchange for U.S. control over its arsenal (1962). De Gaulle also declined to join the treaty banning nuclear tests in the atmosphere (1963) because he believed that it would allow the United States and the Soviet Union to maintain their technological superiority over France. He successfully tested France's first hydrogen bomb in 1968.[11]

From his first retirement, de Gaulle supported French membership in NATO as the best way of containing the Soviet Union at a time when Europe was militarily and economically weak. In the 1950s, however, he concluded that NATO's protection came at the price of subordinating

European foreign and defense policy to the United States. After he returned to power, de Gaulle proposed expanding NATO's remit to military operations outside Europe, including French colonies in Africa, and setting up a directory of the United States, Britain, and France to make major decisions for the alliance. When the United States and Britain turned down his proposal, he gradually disengaged France from NATO's military structures. In 1959, he withdrew the French fleet from NATO's Mediterranean command, in part to support military operations in Algeria, and asked the United States to remove its tactical nuclear weapons from France after the United States refused to tell him where they were located. In 1960, he turned down the U.S. request to place France's air defenses under U.S. command and increase American troop strength in France. In 1963, he pulled France out of NATO's Atlantic fleet and declined to participate in NATO's naval exercises. In 1966, he withdrew France from all of NATO's integrated commands (but not the political organization) and asked U.S. troops to leave France (though he concluded a secret agreement with the United States for cooperation in case of Soviet attack). In a letter to President Lyndon Johnson, he explained:

> This is why France is determined to regain on her whole territory the full exercise of her sovereignty, at present diminished by the permanent presence of allied military elements or by the use which is made of her airspace; to cease her participation in the integrated commands; and no longer to place her forces at the disposal of NATO.[12]

As France's relations with the United States deteriorated, its relationship with the Soviet Union improved. While de Gaulle sought to marginalize the powerful French Communist Party at home—the introduction of the majoritarian electoral system in 1958 significantly cut the party's representation in the National Assembly—he believed that the Soviet Union was more interested in protecting Russian national interests than in spreading communist ideology. In 1966, de Gaulle made an official visit to Moscow, the first by a Western head of state, and signed a number of agreements on economic and cultural cooperation as well as a joint declaration calling for normalization of relations between the East and West, disarmament, and an end to the war in Vietnam. A telephone hotline was established between the Kremlin and the Élysée Palace, a symbolic recognition of the equality between the two countries. In a speech on Soviet national television, he argued that through the political upheavals of the twentieth century, "France as it has always been" and "Russia as it has always been"—nations with their unique character but feeling "a special interest and attraction for one another"—continued to exist and would now seek "détente, understanding and cooperation across the whole of Europe so that Europe can provide for her own security after so many combats, such devastation and such torment."[13]

De Gaulle's successors during and after the Cold War adopted a more conciliatory approach toward the United States, but they continued to pursue an independent foreign and defense policy. Georges Pompidou welcomed the continued presence of U.S. troops in Europe and argued that membership in NATO was an "integral part of [French] policy." In turn, Richard Nixon's administration gave France "negative guidance" (that is, saying what would not work) on the development of nuclear missiles and warheads. However, Pompidou expanded economic and cultural ties with the Soviet Union and held annual summits with the Soviet leadership.[14] Valéry Giscard d'Estaing, whose election was welcomed in Washington because he was a liberal, not a Gaullist, increased military spending and made French conventional forces available for "forward defense" of Germany against a possible Soviet attack. However, after the Soviet Union invaded Afghanistan in 1979, he met with Leonid Brezhnev in Warsaw to persuade him (unsuccessfully) to find a face-saving way out of the conflict and refused to impose economic sanctions against the Soviet Union. When strikes against the communist government broke out in Poland in 1980, he said that the leaders of Solidarity needed to take "geographical and strategic realities into account." When critics, including the young Gaullist leader Jacques Chirac, accused him of appeasing the Soviet Union ("that day the spirit of Munich floated above Warsaw"), Giscard responded that France had the right to pursue an independent foreign policy, which corresponded to France's historical tradition and the will of the French people.[15]

Ironically, it was France's first socialist president, François Mitterrand, who significantly improved relations with the United States. He welcomed President Ronald Reagan's decision to place Pershing II and Cruise intermediate-range ballistic missiles (IRBMs) in Germany in response to the Soviet deployment of SS-20s in its western republics. He also started secret negotiations with NATO for reintegrating France into the alliance's military command, while the French general staff drew up plans for joint operations with NATO against the Soviet Union and French troops participated in NATO's military exercises. However, he declined to participate in Reagan's Strategic Defense Initiative ("Star Wars") because he thought that it would provoke rather than deter the Soviet Union, which would fear having its ground-based nuclear forces wiped out in a surprise attack and being powerless to respond. Moreover, unlike Reagan, Mitterrand viewed the Soviet Union not as an "evil empire" but as a great power that pursued its own geopolitical interests. During a visit to Moscow in 1987, he said, "I have never regarded the Soviet Union as an enemy, or even as an adversary. It is simply a large country with its own interests. We have ours, too."[16]

The fall of the Berlin Wall fundamentally altered the security situation in Europe. Mitterrand had mixed feelings about German unification because he worried that it would revive Germany's great power ambitions. As he told Chancellor Helmut Kohl, "You have the right to seek the self-determination of the German people, but I have the duty to take into account the preoccupations of the rest of Europe." However, he overcame his reservations when President George H. W. Bush promised to keep U.S. troops in Europe and Chancellor Helmut Kohl agreed to recognize Germany's eastern borders and remain part of NATO. Mitterrand also used the new arms control agreements between the United States and the Soviet Union, especially the removal of all land-based IRBMs from Europe (1987), to reduce military spending. Thus, he imposed a moratorium on nuclear tests (1993) and canceled the missile development programs that he himself had launched in the 1980s, though he continued the production of France's new generation of nuclear submarines. However, after Iraq invaded Kuwait, he sent a sizable French contingent (12,000 troops) to fight alongside U.S. and British forces in the Gulf War (1991), the first such endeavor since the Franco-British invasion of the Suez Canal in 1956.[17]

Jacques Chirac, the first president elected in the post–Cold War era, sought to adapt the Gaullist tradition to a changing world. While Mitterrand was unwilling to intervene in the post-Yugoslav wars, Chirac worked with President Bill Clinton to impose a peace agreement on Bosnia (1995), concluded in Dayton, Ohio, but signed at the Élysée Palace, which divided the country into a Serb republic and a Croat and Muslim federation. In 1998–99, France participated in NATO's military intervention in Kosovo, forcing the Serbian president, Slobodan Milošević, to withdraw troops from the province, which soon became an independent state. He also continued

the negotiations on rejoining NATO's integrated command, which nonetheless stalled when the United States refused to give France NATO's
southern command. To consolidate Western geopolitical gains after the end
of the Cold War without provoking Russia, Chirac supported the expansion of the EU (2004–07) and NATO (1997–2004) to Eastern Europe.
However, the Chirac presidency also witnessed the biggest quarrel between
France and the United States since the end of the Cold War as France opposed the U.S.-led invasion of Iraq (2003) as a violation of international law
that would destabilize an already fragile region.[18]

Compared with Mitterrand and Chirac, Nicolas Sarkozy and François
Hollande followed a more consistently pro-American foreign policy in the
hope of exerting influence on the United States. As a presidential candidate, Sarkozy visited the United States and all but apologized for Chirac's
behavior, saying that France had an unfortunate tendency to lecture other
countries and take pleasure in their misfortunes. Under his leadership,
France formally rejoined NATO's integrated command (2009), receiving a
senior command post and joining the committees that draw up war plans
for the alliance. While he opposed the admission of Turkey, at that time
America's main strategic ally in the Middle East, to the EU, he took the
lead in NATO's bombing campaign against Libya (2011).[19] Hollande, who
criticized Sarkozy's hyperactive foreign policy as a candidate, launched more
interventions abroad than any other president since the end of the Cold
War. With U.S. technical and logistical support, he sent troops to battle
Islamist insurgencies in Mali (2013), the Central African Republic (2014–16),
and the Sahel region (2014 and ongoing). He also participated in the
U.S.-led air strikes against Islamic State (ISIS) positions in Iraq and Syria
and (unsuccessfully) lobbied the United States for a military intervention
against the government of Bashar al-Assad of Syria.[20]

As Rachel Lee Loan and Pernille Rieker show, the growing convergence
of French and U.S. foreign policy is also on display in Ukraine. Sarkozy
supported the Bucharest declaration of NATO in 2008, which promised
Ukraine that it would become a member of the alliance, and the Association Agreement that the EU initialed with Ukraine in 2012, though he
worked behind the scenes to remove target dates from the documents.
When Russia invaded Ukraine in 2014 to prevent it from slipping out of its
orbit, President Hollande and Chancellor Angela Merkel first tried to mediate in the conflict, sponsoring two cease-fire agreements. When the fighting continued, however, France and Germany blamed Russia, a view that

the United States had taken from the beginning of the conflict. France voted for a U.S.-sponsored resolution (vetoed by Russia) in the UN Security Council that declared the seizure of Crimea an illegal violation of Ukraine's political independence and territorial integrity. With French support, Russia was also excluded from the Group of Eight (G-8) meetings of advanced industrialized countries, a symbolic rebuke to a nation that saw its identity as a Western country vindicated when it joined the forum in 1998. Finally, France has supported the EU's economic sanctions on Russia—less stringent than the ones imposed by the United States but more effective because Russia trades more with Europe than with the United States—which prohibit European companies from selling Russia weapons, dual-use equipment, and oil exploration technology and European banks from extending long-term credit to Russia.[21]

Paradoxically, however, it is recent developments in American politics that have revived the Gaullist impulse in France. Courting white working-class voters angered by stagnating incomes and loss of job security, Donald Trump won the 2016 presidential election by promising to put America first. He argued that NATO was obsolete because it was set up to deal with a threat—the spread of communism—that no longer existed and that European countries were free-riding on the United States, which contributes over 70 percent of the defense spending of NATO countries. While Trump has reversed his stance on NATO and increased the number of U.S. troops in Europe, his election raises the possibility that the United States may eventually withdraw from Europe, as de Gaulle anticipated. In response, and to fend off a challenge from the National Front's Marine Le Pen, the liberal candidate Emmanuel Macron argued during the 2017 French presidential election that European countries needed to strengthen their military cooperation and, if necessary, act independently from the United States:

> To those who have become accustomed for solutions to their problems from the other side of the Atlantic, I believe that current developments in U.S. foreign policy clearly show that we have changed eras. Of course, the alliance with the United States is and remains fundamental, at the strategic, intelligence, and operational levels. . . .
> But for now, the Americans seem to want to focus on themselves. The current unpredictability of U.S. foreign policy is calling into question some of our points of reference, while a wide space has been left

open for the politics of power and fait accompli, in Europe, in the Middle East, and also in Asia. So, it is up to us to act where our interests are at stake and to find partners with whom we will work to substitute stability and peace for chaos and violence.[22]

What role has France played in European integration? Can the EU become a military power? It is to these questions that we now turn.

France in Europe: From a "Europe of States" to the European Union

Preoccupied with the independence and greatness of France, de Gaulle was often a trenchant critic of what we today know as the European Union. From his first retirement, he opposed the first steps toward European integration, such as the European Coal and Steel Community (ECSC, 1951), which exposed French heavy industry to German competition, and the European Defense Community, which would have placed French troops under multinational command (1952, rejected by the French National Assembly in 1954). As president, he sought to modify the terms of the 1957 Treaty of Rome, which founded the more ambitious European Economic Community (EEC). Thus, he threatened to leave the EEC unless it adopted a protective external tariff and permanent financing for the Common Agricultural Policy (CAP) and boycotted the meetings of the EEC Council of Ministers when it was due to adopt majority voting, resulting in a compromise whereby member states kept the power of veto on issues that affected their "vital national interests." He also opposed plans to increase the powers of the European Commission and the European Parliament and to fund the EU from direct taxes levied on European citizens, rather than contributions from the states.[23]

However, de Gaulle opposed not European integration per se, but the federalist version of it. Led by Jean Monnet, the former high commissioner for the ECSC and the chief economic planner in de Gaulle's postwar government, and Walter Hallstein, the president of the European Commission, the federalists sought to create powerful supranational institutions, such as the Commission and the European Parliament, to coordinate the economic policies of European countries, while following the lead of the United States on foreign and defense policy. De Gaulle preferred close cooperation—a "confederation" or a "Europe of states"—among the governments of continental Europe on economic as well as political and military issues (Christian Fouchet's—or, rather, de Gaulle's—plan for a European political and military union, which first mooted the idea of creating a council of EEC heads of state and government), but without a European-level government that would impose its will on individual nations that have different historical experiences and national characters. As he explained at a press conference in 1965:

> Now we know—heaven knows that we know!—that there was a different concept of a European federation in which, according to those who conceived it, the countries would lose their national personalities, and in which, furthermore, for want of a federator—such as in the West, Charlemagne, Otto I, Charles V, Napoleon and Hitler tried to be, each in his fashion, and such as in the East, Stalin tried to be—would be ruled by a technocratic, stateless and irresponsible Aeropagus. We know also that France is opposing this project, which contradicts all reality, a plan for organized co-operation among the States, evolving, doubtlessly, toward a confederation.[24]

De Gaulle's wartime ally, Great Britain, shared his suspicion of supranational governance and technocratic policymaking. However, de Gaulle vetoed—in 1963 and again in 1967—Britain's application to join the EEC. As Piers Ludlow and Andrew Moravcsik have argued, his reasons were partly economic. Britain had a large and competitive industry and service sector but imported most of its foodstuffs from the United States, Latin America, and especially, the countries of the British Commonwealth of Nations, which enjoyed preferential access to the British market. It was also a large recipient of U.S. investment. As a result, Britain could be expected to oppose CAP and support opening the European economy to multinational corporations.[25] However, de Gaulle also thought that Britain followed the United States too closely in foreign and defense policy, as indicated by its purchase of nuclear missiles from the United States and its eagerness to participate in the U.S.-led Multilateral Force, which would have placed European nuclear weapons under U.S. control. (In the end, the plan was abandoned because of French opposition.) Admitting Britain to the EEC would give the United States an additional lever over European affairs. As he told his information minister and confidant Alain Peyrefitte:

[The Americans] now want to construct a "Multilateral Force" to camouflage this hegemony on the nuclear level, just as they created NATO in 1949 to camouflage their hegemony on the conventional level. The English will be their Trojan horse in Europe. For that, it suffices that the European Community open itself to the Anglo-Saxon world, by means of which they will make the law there.[26]

Since Britain was no longer a suitable partner, France had to forge a new relationship with Germany. As prime minister in 1944–46, de Gaulle wanted to prevent Germany from becoming a major economic and military power again by turning it into a loose confederation of states and placing the Ruhr area under permanent international control. With America's domineering policy toward Europe and Britain's failure to support France in its quest for greater independence, however, de Gaulle came to see Germany as a potential ally. Building on the personal rapport he had developed with Chancellor Konrad Adenauer, a Catholic Rheinlander, he concluded a Treaty of Friendship with Germany (1963) in which the two countries promised to consult with each other on "problems relating to the European Communities and European political cooperation" and to "seek to reconcile their [military] doctrines with a view to arriving at common conceptions."[27] The treaty was weakened by the preamble added by the German Bundestag, which stated that Germany would continue to cooperate closely with the United States within NATO and support British accession to the EEC. France and Germany also continued to disagree on issues such as participation in the Multilateral Force, Germany's Eastern borders, and the structure and financing of the EEC. However, the agreement created a "cordial potentiality" for a Franco-German entente, which is a lasting legacy of de Gaulle's presidency.[28]

De Gaulle's prime minister, Georges Pompidou, ran for president by promising "continuity and opening" in French domestic and foreign policy. After Britain agreed to participate in CAP, Pompidou lifted the veto on Britain's membership in the EEC, arguing that European countries needed to cooperate in order to compete with the superpowers economically and politically:

What is the situation of the European nations? A very small territory, with a medium-sized population, an economic capacity which is great but which, in absolute value, remains limited. If, on the contrary,

they are put together, then one obtains a power equal in many areas
to any other [superpower].[29]

A former finance minister in de Gaulle's government, Valéry Giscard
d'Estaing believed that European countries needed to deepen their economic cooperation to deal with international economic shocks, such as
the oil crisis. With Chancellor Helmut Schmidt, he created the European
Monetary System (1978), which fixed the exchange rates of EEC countries
within a narrow band. Giscard also convened the first formal meeting of
the European Council of heads of state and government (1974) to make
major policy decisions, though this was counterbalanced by the direct
election of the supranational European Parliament (1979). As dictatorships
gave way to democracy in southern Europe, Giscard sponsored the admission of Greece to the EEC in 1981 and prepared the ground for the accession of Spain and Portugal.[30]

François Mitterrand, a socialist who had been de Gaulle's main opponent in the 1960s, guided France's response to the dramatic political changes
of the 1980s and 1990s. Despite his frequent criticisms of communist governments, Mitterrand was taken by surprise by the fall of the Berlin Wall
and tried to delay, though not prevent, German unification, arguing that
the people of East Germany should be allowed to express their democratic
choice and that the process should take place under the control of the Allied powers. When events on the ground gained unstoppable momentum,
however, he struck an agreement with Chancellor Helmut Kohl. France
agreed to the creation of a unified and centralized German state while Germany committed itself to closer European integration.[31] The Treaty of
Maastricht (1992), which was narrowly approved by French voters, combined the European Communities into the EU, created an Economic and
Monetary Union, including a common currency issued by the European
Central Bank, and recognized the possibility that Eastern European countries could join the union. In line with a long-standing French preference, the
treaty also said that the EU would "affirm its identity on the international
scene, in particular through the implementation of a common foreign and
security policy," which "might in time lead to a common defense." Anticipating the eventual withdrawal of the United States—and trouble in Eastern Europe as the Soviet Union and Yugoslavia broke up—Mitterrand and
Kohl also proposed creating a European corps that would operate independently from NATO.[32]

Jacques Chirac, who became president when Bosnian Serbs took as prisoners French troops serving as UN peacekeepers, supported U.S. air strikes against Serb positions in Bosnia (1995) and Kosovo (1999). Frustrated by European military weakness but also unhappy with NATO's choice of targets, he met with the British Prime minister, Tony Blair, in the Mediterranean resort town of Saint-Malo in 1998 to design a common European defense policy, with an emphasis on building a "capacity for autonomous action," backed by "credible military forces."[33] The Treaty of Nice (2001) incorporated the ideas that were first broached at Saint-Malo, such as a military staff to advise the EU (but not to conduct military operations). After the French electorate voted down the proposed European constitution, drafted by Giscard d'Estaing, Chirac campaigned for the Treaty of Lisbon (2007), which gives the European Commission more power over foreign policy and includes a mutual defense clause that obligates member states to come each other's aid in case of aggression. Somewhat reluctantly—Chirac said that they "would have done better to remain silent" instead of publicly supporting the U.S. invasion of Iraq in 2003—he also supported the accession of ten Eastern European countries to the EU in 2004–07.[34]

Nicolas Sarkozy's and François Hollande's presidencies were overshadowed by the worst economic and immigration crises in EU history. As the subprime mortgage crisis in the United States shook financial markets, banks in southern Europe, which had lent freely during the boom years following the introduction of the euro, faced insolvency, while governments ran up huge debts in trying to rescue them. Led by Sarkozy and German chancellor Merkel, the EU's response to the crisis reflected an uneasy compromise between the German emphasis on fiscal discipline and structural reform and the French idea of active state intervention. The European Stability Mechanism (2011) extended loans to Greece, Portugal, and Spain while their private creditors were pushed to write off a large part of their debt. In return, the indebted countries agreed to privatize state-owned companies, improve tax collection, and cut public spending.[35] François Hollande ran for office by promising to refocus French—and European—economic policy from austerity to growth, but his attention was soon diverted by the Middle Eastern refugee crisis. While not on the main migration routes or particularly attractive to asylum seekers, France is nonetheless worried because it has a large and restive Muslim population, high unemployment, and an overburdened welfare system. To stem the flow of migrants, the EU launched Operation Sophia (2015) to police the

Mediterranean and agreed to pay Turkey to take back refugees from Greece (2016).[36]

The recession and the refugee crisis have boosted the fortunes of the right-wing populist National Front (FN), which achieved its first electoral successes in the 1980s and whose program combines economic protectionism with exclusionary—that is, non-Gaullist—nationalism. In the decisive second round of the 2017 presidential election, the FN's leader, Marine Le Pen, argued that France needed to leave the euro and the Schengen agreement that allows visa-free travel within Europe, significantly reduce legal immigration, and deport asylum seekers who break the law. The liberal candidate, Emmanuel Macron, who won a difficult but convincing victory, countered that France needed to promote closer European economic and political integration to protect its interests at the global level:

> You see, the kind of independence we are talking about here is not what's meant by those claiming to be primarily concerned with sovereignty, who seek refuge behind borders they hope are hermetically sealed—it is the kind that allows France to make its voice heard, to advocate for its interests on the international stage, the kind that allows it to influence the course of the world rather than being its hostage. The kind that ensures that we are not in thrall to the superpowers, but are their interlocutor. The sovereignty we gain from this independence is open to the world, and it must be collective in nature when the stakes are larger than our national framework.[37]

Macron's economic program involves the kind of liberal reforms that de Gaulle would have abhorred. During his first year in office, Macron's government passed a sweeping overhaul of the French labor law, reducing compensation for unjust dismissals and allowing small firms to opt out of industrywide collective bargaining agreements. Macron's first budget replaced the wealth tax introduced under Mitterrand with a property tax and reduced the capital gains tax, although he imposed a temporary levy on large businesses to bring the French budget deficit under 3 percent of GDP as required by the 1992 Maastricht Treaty. However, Macron's foreign economic policies have a protectionist bent that de Gaulle would find familiar. Thus, he wants to pass a "Buy European Act" for public procurement and impose antidumping duties on Chinese goods in sectors where European companies are uncompetitive, such as textiles and steel. Under the slogan of a "Europe that protects," Macron persuaded a reluctant European Commission to regulate the wages of "posted workers" from Eastern Europe. While he has argued that France needs more foreign investment, he nationalized the largest French shipyard, STX, to prevent it from being sold to an Italian company.[38]

France's defense policy under Macron, too, reflects both a shift away from de Gaulle's focus on national independence and the continued relevance of the Gaullist idea of European military autonomy. In response to the Russian invasion of Ukraine and the rise of Islamist insurgencies in Africa, European countries took a series of steps in 2017 to strengthen the EU as a military power. Using a provision in the 2007 Treaty of Lisbon, twenty-three of the twenty-eight EU countries agreed to cooperate more closely on defense policy (Permanent Structured Cooperation). Supplementing national budgets, a European Defense Fund will finance joint research and development and procurement, especially in intelligence and logistics, where Europe is almost entirely dependent on the United States, but also in conventional weapons such as tanks and helicopters, where EU countries often duplicate each other's efforts. A voluntary annual review of national defenses will allow the EU High Representative for the Common Foreign and Security Policy to identify gaps and areas where countries could productively cooperate. Finally, the EU will establish its own military headquarters in Brussels that can conduct training exercises and, eventually, military operations independently from NATO.[39] De Gaulle, of course, would be horrified by the idea of French troops serving under international command to defeat Muslim rebellions in the deserts of Sahel or to check Russian incursions into the Baltic Sea, but he would recognize his own legacy in an independent European military force, ready to defend France against dangers from all directions.

But how far from the shores of Bayeux should French power reach? And on whose behalf should it be exercised? Here, too, de Gaulle's legacy serves both as a constraint and a resource for French foreign policy.

France and the Developing World: The Search for a Global Role

As prime minister in the provisional government from 1944 to 1946, de Gaulle sought to keep the French colonial empire intact. He dispatched troops to reoccupy Indochina to prevent the United States from taking

advantage of the defeat of Japan, feuded with Britain over who would control Syria and Lebanon, suppressed an Arab uprising in Algeria, and jailed
nationalist demonstrators in Tunisia and Morocco. By the time he returned
to power, however, French global influence was rapidly declining. Indochina
had been irrevocably lost to France in 1954 when the French army, already
heavily dependent on U.S. supplies and logistical support, was defeated by
Vietnamese guerrillas trained and equipped by China. The French man-
dates in North Africa and the Middle East had become independent states,
and Algeria, aided by Egypt and, indirectly, the Soviet Union, was in open
revolt against French rule. The French colonies in sub-Saharan Africa,
nominally part of a French Union as equal members but still administered
by the Ministry for Overseas France, were relatively quiet. However, a new
generation of politicians, many of whom had held elected office or government posts in the Fourth Republic, wanted greater autonomy, especially
after Britain granted independence to Ghana in 1957.

To restore French political and moral standing in the developing countries, de Gaulle first needed to end the war in Algeria. His preferred strategy was to weaken the FLN militarily in order to persuade it to accept
political autonomy within a union with France. In 1958–59, the French army
in Algeria, which now numbered over 500,000 troops, inflicted serious
losses on the FLN. Algeria's border with Tunisia and Morocco was sealed,
which cut the FLN off from its bases and reduced its flow of weapons from
Egypt to a trickle. French forces conducted successful counterinsurgency
operations in the Algerian countryside, killing FLN cadres and tricking
them into executing supposed traitors. Though it only had a few thousand
fighters left in Algeria, however, the FLN declined de Gaulle's offer of a
cease-fire. Impressed by their tenacity and antagonized by an attempted
military coup in Algeria, de Gaulle then started negotiations with the FLN
leadership. In 1962, peace agreements were signed and approved by voters
in both France (91 percent in favor, with a turnout of 75 percent) and Algeria (officially almost 100 percent in favor, with a 92 percent turnout) in
referenda. France granted Algeria political independence and economic
aid in exchange for access to the Sahara desert and security guarantees for
Arabs who had served in the French army and police. The settlers—about
one million people from a population of ten million—were evacuated to
France.[40]

The aftershocks of the war could be felt in both Algeria and France for
years. Officers of the French army in Algeria who felt betrayed by de Gaulle

launched a campaign of terror against Arab civilians and French officials—
an attempt on de Gaulle's life only failed because the bullets missed him in
his car—while the FLN carried out reprisals against Arabs who had collaborated with the French.[41] However, de Gaulle was now free to redefine
France's relationship with Africa and the Arab countries, the two areas of
the world where France could still play a leading, or at least independent,
role.

Africa: The Colonial Legacy

Approved by voters in all the remaining African colonies except Guinea,
the 1958 constitution created a Franco-African Community where the overseas territories were autonomous in their domestic policies but France
controlled the money supply and foreign and defense policy. Within two
years, however, all the territories asked France to recognize them as independent states. De Gaulle reluctantly agreed, explaining to his bewildered
countrymen that France could not keep its colonies without antagonizing
international opinion and sacrificing its own values—even if he, too, felt a
certain nostalgia for the empire:

> To refuse [the right to self-determination] to them would have been
> to contradict our ideal, to start interminable struggles, to draw down
> upon us the censure of the world—and all this for the sake of a re-
> ward that would have crumbled in our hands. It is only natural that
> one should feel nostalgia for everything that went to make up the
> empire, just as one can miss the glow of oil lamps, the splendor of
> sailing ships, the charm of the carriage era. But why? There is no
> policy that it worthwhile apart from realities.[42]

Even as French troops and administrators were leaving Africa, however,
de Gaulle sought to preserve French influence on the continent, which had
rallied to Free France during World War II and was now the only area in
the world where France could still act as a great power. In doing so, he was
supported by moderate African leaders, such as Félix Houghuët-Boigny, the
president of Ivory Coast, who coined the term "Françafrique" to describe
his vision of a partnership between metropolitan France and Francophone
Africa. In 1960–63, France concluded defense treaties with the newly

independent states, promising to train and equip their militaries and protect their territorial integrity and political independence against foreign
aggression. Long criticized as the epitome of European arrogance, France
now courted African votes in the United Nations and other international
organizations. France also maintained a strong economic and cultural presence in Africa. The African franc, the new common currency for western
and central Africa, was pegged to the French franc. France also remained
the main trading partner for its former colonies, which gained preferential
access to the EEC market. Finally, France provided generous economic
and technical aid to Francophone Africa, funding infrastructure development and sending teachers (of which de Gaulle was especially proud), doctors, and engineers to work there.[43]

Underpinned by his personal connections with African leaders, however,
de Gaulle's policy toward Africa also had a coercive and manipulative side—
"Françafrique" in the pejorative sense in which Xavier-François Verschave
uses the term.[44] The defense treaties with the former colonies included secret clauses that allowed France to intervene in their affairs in case of internal conflicts. De Gaulle orchestrated the overthrow of the pro-Soviet
president of Cameroon, Félix-Roland Moumi (1959); sent troops to Congo-
Brazzaville to prevent Congo-Kinsasha and, indirectly, the United States
from spreading their influence there (1963); restored power to President
Léon Mba of Gabon, a longtime associate (1964); intervened several times
in Chad to help President François Tombalbaye fight an insurgency backed
by Libya and Sudan (1968–69); and supported the (ultimately unsuccessful) secession of Biafra from Nigeria, a former British colony (1967–69). The
new states were expected to toe the French line in the UN, where they refrained from criticizing French nuclear tests in the Sahara desert and arms
sales to South Africa and Rhodesia. French development aid came with
strings attached: Senegal, whose president, Léopold Senghor, had written
a poem to de Gaulle during the war and kept in touch with him during his
years in the political wilderness, was rewarded, while Guinea, whose leader
Sékou Touré defied de Gaulle by unilaterally declaring independence, saw
all aid cut off.[45]

Lacking a wartime bond with African leaders, Georges Pompidou was
less interested in Africa than de Gaulle was, but he continued de Gaulle's
policy of active engagement with the continent. Facing growing criticism
over what the opposition parties saw as "France's Vietnam," Pompidou
withdrew the French expeditionary force from Chad in 1971, but he kept

open the military base in N'Djamena (Fort Lamy) and negotiated defense treaties with the former Belgian colonies Burundi, Rwanda, and Zaire. On the initiative of the president of Niger, Hamani Diori, he held the first Franco-African summit in Paris in 1973, a family-like event with no formal agenda. Valéry Giscard d'Estaing was the first in the long line of presidents who promised to "modernize" French policy toward Africa. In 1975, he hosted the Conference on International Economic Cooperation, which resulted in an agreement between the EEC and the countries of sub-Saharan Africa on the price of agricultural products and raw materials such as oil and copper. In the aftermath of the Angolan revolution (1975), however, Giscard sponsored military interventions in Mauritania (1977), Chad (1978, 1980), and Zaire (1978) to keep in power anticommunist governments in the one theater of the Cold War outside Europe where France continued to contest Soviet influence.[46]

François Mitterrand ran for office by promising to end the neocolonial relations between the north and the south. As president, he increased economic aid for Africa but continued his predecessors' policy of supporting anticommunist dictatorships, intervening twice (in 1983 and 1986) in Chad against Libya. After the Soviet threat disappeared, Mitterrand cautiously encouraged African countries on both sides of the Cold War divide to move toward democracy. However, the first democratic election in Algeria in 1991 resulted in the victory of the Islamic Salvation Front, which the government—ironically led by the heirs to the national independence movement—refused to recognize, plunging the country into a civil war. Partial democratization in Rwanda—the Hutu dictatorship legalized the opposition parties and formed a transitional government with the main Tutsi party—encouraged politicians to exploit tribal tensions to gain political support. When President Juvénal Habyarimana, a Hutu, was assassinated in 1994, Hutu militias killed 800,000 Tutsis while French diplomats and military advisers stood by. The genocide only ended with the establishment of a Tutsi dictatorship under President Paul Kagame, who was backed by Uganda and, indirectly, Britain.[47]

As Tony Chafer has argued, the "Françafrique" framework is less applicable to Franco-African relations since the end of the Cold War and the terrorist attacks of 9/11 because geopolitical imperatives and economic interests have replaced personal and cultural ties as the driving force of French foreign policy. In the twilight of his presidency (1994), Mitterrand devalued the African franc by 50 percent, lowering the price France had to pay

for its imports. Jacques Chirac cut French economic aid for Africa and reduced the number of French troops and military advisers in the region. As
an insurance policy, however, both Mitterrand and Chirac maintained good
relations with African leaders who had cooperated with France in the past,
such as Gabon's Omar Bongo, Mauritania's Ould Abdelaziz, and Togo's
Gnassingbé Eyadema. In 1997, France intervened in the civil war in Congo-
Brazzaville on behalf of the deposed president, Denis Sassou Nguesso,
partly out of humanitarian considerations—the war had claimed over a
hundred thousand lives and displaced nearly a million people—but also to
protect the interests of Elf, the Franco-Belgian oil company. In 2003,
France sponsored a power-sharing agreement to end the civil war that had
erupted in Ivory Coast. When the agreement broke down the following
year and armed demonstrators attacked French outposts, French troops
returned fire, killing dozens of people in the country whose first president
had outlined his vision of "Françafrique" half a century before.[48]

Nicolas Sarkozy, who had few personal connections with African leaders before he came into power, promised to put France's relationship with
Africa on a more equal footing. Declaring that France would no longer be
the "gendarme of Africa," he renegotiated the defense treaties with the former colonies and closed the military bases in Senegal and the Ivory Coast.
In a speech in Dakar in 2007, he argued that Africa was poor because Afri-
cans did not believe that they could make choices to improve their lives:

> The tragedy of Africa is that the African has not fully entered into
> history. . . . In this imaginary world where everything starts over and
> over again there is no place for human adventure or for the idea of
> progress. . . . This man (the traditional African) never launched him-
> self towards the future. The idea never came to him to get out of
> this repetition and to invent his own destiny.[49]

Nevertheless, Sarkozy continued to support authoritarian leaders in countries that were strategically or economically important for France, such as
Chad, where French troops put down a rebellion against President Idriss
Déby in 2008, and Gabon, where French officials made it clear that they
favored Ali Bongo, the son of Omar Bongo, in the 2009 presidential
election.[50]

François Hollande argued that France needed to reengage with Africa
in the context of global political changes. In 2013, he was the only Western

head of state who attended a celebration for the sixtieth anniversary of the African Union in Addis Ababa, Ethiopia, while troops from Chad, Mali, and other former French colonies participated in the military parade in Paris on Bastille Day. As Islamist terrorism spread to Central Africa, however, Hollande launched military interventions in Central African Republic (Operation Sangaris in 2014–16 with 2,000 troops), Mali (Operation Serval in 2013–14 with 4,000 troops), and the entire Sahel region (Operation Barkhane since 2014, with 3,500 troops). Authorized by the UN and conducted in conjunction with EU peacekeeping missions, these operations relied heavily on the support of traditional French clients in Africa, such as Idriss Déby of Chad and Blaise Compaoré, the president of Burkina Faso, whom France helped to flee his country after he was overthrown in a popular uprising in 2014.[51]

The Arab World: A Different Policy

De Gaulle also reshaped France's policy toward the Arab world. In the 1950s, France was the main international sponsor of Israel, supplying it with advanced conventional weapons (especially ships and airplanes) and aiding the development of its nuclear weapons program. Israel, in turn, participated in the ill-fated invasion of Egypt (1956), whose president, Gamal Abdel Nasser, was both a sworn enemy of Israel and a strong supporter of the Algerian independence movement. After he granted independence to Algeria in 1962, however, de Gaulle no longer needed Israel as an ally and grew increasingly exasperated by Israeli policies, such as the project to divert the Jordan River to Israel. As tensions between Israel and the Arab countries mounted in 1967, he urged both sides to exercise restraint, telling the Syrian ambassador that Israel's existence was a fact, but warning Israeli prime minister Levi Eshkol not to attack first. When Israel launched the preemptive Six-Day War and occupied strategically important areas—the Sinai Peninsula, the Gaza Strip, the Golan Heights, and the West Bank of the Jordan River—de Gaulle was furious. In what is seen as the beginning of France's "Arab policy," he imposed an arms embargo on the frontline states and supported a Soviet-sponsored resolution in the UN Security Council that would have required Israel to withdraw from the occupied territories as a precondition for peace negotiations.[52]

In the 1970s, France developed close economic ties with many Arab countries, which sold France oil, commissioned French firms to build infrastructure (for example, power plants), and bought French weapons (from small arms to tanks, airplanes, and missiles). As Rémy Leveau has argued, however, outside the economic arena, France's "Arab policy" consisted mostly of symbolic gestures and sporadic interventions that did not significantly change the balance of power in the region. After the 1973 Yom Kippur War, Georges Pompidou called for negotiations between the United States, the Soviet Union, Britain, and France to impose a peace settlement on the Middle East. Valéry Giscard d'Estaing referred to a Palestinian "homeland" and allowed the Palestine Liberation Organization (PLO), which the United States considered a terrorist group, to establish an office in Paris in 1975. François Mitterrand, who became the first French president to visit Israel, gave a speech in the Knesset where he called for Israel to grant Palestinians statehood and for Arab states to recognize Israel's right to exist. While condemning the terrorist attacks carried out by the PLO, he organized the evacuation of Yasser Arafat's fighters from Beirut during the Israeli invasion of Lebanon in 1982.[53]

As David Styan argues, France's dispute with the United States over Iraq needs to be understood in the context of its Arab policy. In the 1970s, Jacques Chirac, then serving as prime minister, developed a good rapport with Iraqi leader Saddam Hussein:

> The man seemed to me intelligent, not devoid of humor, even rather nice. He received me at his home and treated me as a personal friend. . . . [He] appeared not so much a despot as a fierce, determined patriot, possessed of nationalistic pride and enthusiasm that seemed to reflect the great ambitions he nursed for his country.[54]

The Iraqi government, in turn, borrowed money from French banks, allowed French companies to develop Iraqi oil fields, and solicited French help with its nuclear program: France sold Iraq the nuclear reactor at Osirak that Israel destroyed in 1981. After some hesitation, France took part in the 1991 Gulf War to expel the Iraqi forces from Kuwait (Operation Desert Storm) and establish a no-fly zone over northern Iraq (Operation Provide Comfort). After the war, France lobbied the UN for an "Oil for Food" program that allowed Iraq to export oil in exchange for food, medicines, and other essentials. In 1998, France declined to participate in the U.S. and British air strikes against Iraq (Operation Desert Fox), arguing that they would be counterproductive and cause UN weapons inspectors to leave and impose further suffering on Iraqi civilians.[55]

As Frédéric Bozo has argued, however, France also opposed the second Gulf War (2003) for broader geopolitical reasons. Since a seat on the UN Security Council is one of the last remaining vestiges of France's global power, France wants the UN to decide when it is legitimate for countries to use military force. France also believed that Iraq served as a vital counterweight to Iran in the volatile Gulf region and that its destruction would unleash sectarian violence between the Sunnis and Shias. In the run-up to the war, President Chirac and Dominique de Villepin, his minister of foreign affairs, sought to persuade the United States to allow the UN inspectors to determine whether Iraq had dismantled its weapons of mass destruction. When the United States, supported by Britain and Spain, asked the UN Security Council for an authorization to disarm Iraq by force, France, supported by Russia, Germany, and China, threatened to cast a veto. After the United States and Britain, with the support of a motley "coalition of the willing," invaded Iraq and overthrew Saddam Hussein, Chirac criticized the United States for undermining respect for international law and the principle of multilateralism: "In today's world," he said, "no one can act alone in the name of all and no one can accept the anarchy of a society without rules. There is no alternative to the United Nations. . . . It is the [UN Security Council] that must set the bounds for the use of force. No one can appropriate the right to use it unilaterally and preventively."[56]

Outside Iraq, however, France cooperated with the United States in the global "war on terror." After the attacks on the Pentagon and the World Trade Center in 2001, France voted for UN Security Council Resolution 1368 that declared terrorism a threat to international peace and security. Invoking article 5 of the North Atlantic Treaty, France sent 5,000 troops to Afghanistan, including special forces that participated in combat operations against al Qaeda and the Taliban, while French intelligence services shared data on jihadist groups with their U.S. counterparts. France also worked with the United States to weaken Syrian influence in Lebanon. When the pro-Western Lebanese prime minister, Rafik Hariri, was assassinated in 2005, Chirac asked George W. Bush to introduce UN Security Council Resolution 1595, which required Syria to withdraw its troops from northern Lebanon. Under international pressure, Syria withdrew its troops in 2006, although Hezbollah, the Shiite militia backed by Syria, still controls parts of southern Lebanon.[57]

If Chirac selectively supported the U.S.-led "war on terror," Sarkozy and Hollande embraced the idea of regime change in countries that were not allied with the West. At first, Sarkozy responded cautiously to the Arab Spring because he worried that the fall of authoritarian governments would benefit radical Islamist movements. However, after troops loyal to Libya's president Muammar Qaddafi, France's longtime opponent in the region, opened fire on peaceful (and not-so-peaceful) protestors, he changed his mind. In 2011, France and Britain cosponsored the UN Security Council Resolution 1973 that authorized NATO to create a no-fly zone over Libya, persuading skeptical Russia and China to abstain. Interpreting the resolution as widely as possible, Britain, France, and the United States then bombed Libyan airfields and ground forces (Operation Harmattan, which was eventually merged with the U.S. and British efforts into Operation Unified Protector), which gave a decisive military advantage to the rebels, who overthrew and killed Qaddafi but then fell out among themselves. Hollande, in turn, took a more uncompromising line on Syria than any other Western leader, insisting that President Bashar al-Assad's departure was the precondition for political negotiations. France has also been active in the campaign against Assad's main opponent on the ground, ISIS. Since 2014, France has bombed ISIS positions in Iraq and Syria, while French special forces have captured and killed ISIS operatives in Libya (Operation Chammal).[58]

Conclusion

Returning to power at a time of domestic turmoil and international conflict, de Gaulle reshaped French political institutions and foreign policy. He drafted a new constitution that made the president, now directly elected by the people, the most influential actor in French politics, with the power to dissolve the legislature, call referenda, and take emergency measures if the political order is threatened. Crucially, the president is also responsible for protecting the country's territorial integrity and political independence. De Gaulle used these powers to pursue an independent foreign policy. He supported the United States during the major crises of the Cold War but withdrew France from NATO's military organization, developed an independent nuclear deterrent, and cultivated ties with the Soviet Union. After Britain made clear that it identified more closely with the United States than Europe, de Gaulle cooperated with Germany in building up the EEC as an economic and political counterweight to both superpowers. Though he continued to meddle in their affairs, he granted independence to Algeria and the French colonies in sub-Saharan Africa, which allowed him to improve relations with the developing world, especially Arab countries.

Regardless of their ideological convictions and party affiliation, de Gaulle's successors have embraced his legacy to set the political agenda at home and enhance French power and prestige abroad. François Mitterrand (1981–95), a socialist who denounced de Gaulle's institutional reforms as a "permanent coup d'état," took full advantage of presidential authority to divide and weaken the (now Gaullist) opposition and pursued a similar foreign and defense policy, including cooperation with Germany to tie it more closely to Europe and détente with the Soviet Union to end the Cold War. Nicolas Sarkozy (2007–12), a neo-Gaullist who brought France back to NATO's military organization, worked to delay NATO's—and the EU's— expansion to Ukraine and negotiated a cease-fire between Russia and Georgia. More recently, Emmanuel Macron (elected in 2017), a liberal who admires American economic efficiency and cultural diversity, has led the push to make the EU a military power, reviving de Gaulle's idea of European military autonomy from the United States.

At the same time, French foreign policy has also undergone important changes since the end of the Cold War. France's relationship with the United States has improved because France needs to prove its value to the United States in a world where America is the global hegemon, while the main threat to American power comes from China, not Russia. Likewise, de Gaulle and his successors wanted to build a "Europe of states," whereas today's French leaders are more willing to give more power to supranational institutions within the EU to defend French interests in the wider world. Finally, France has shifted its attention and resources from sub-Saharan Africa, a region where France had to compete with the United States, Britain, and Russia for influence and which was personally important for de Gaulle and people of his generation, to North Africa and the Middle East, which are the main battlegrounds of the U.S.-led "war on terror." At once challenging American hegemony but seeking to establish a special relationship with the United States, promoting European political and military cooperation but using the EU to advance its own national interests, and posing as an advocate of Francophone countries but taking advantage of their weakness and dependency—French foreign policy remains a unique blend of continuity and change, power and pretense, and altruism and egoism.

NOTES

Epigraph: Charles de Gaulle, *The War Memoirs of Charles de Gaulle: Salvation, 1944–1946; Documents*, trans. Joyce Murchie and Hamish Erskine (New York: Simon & Schuster, 1960), p. 389.

1. Robert O. Paxton and Julie Hessler, *Europe in the Twentieth Century*, 5th ed. (Boston: Cengage, 2011), p. 537. The figure includes de Gaulle's first cabinet in 1958–59.

2. Quoted from de Gaulle, "Déclaration du 15 mai 1958" (www.charles-de -gaulle.org/wp-content/uploads/2017/03/Déclaration-du-15-mai-1958.pdf). Through intermediaries such as Jacques Soustelle, a veteran of the Resistance and the former governor general of Algeria, de Gaulle may have also encouraged the army to put pressure on the government. Soustelle became minister of state responsible for overseas departments in de Gaulle's government, but soon quit over de Gaulle's policy toward Algeria.

3. Quoted from "Conférence de presse du 19 mai 1958" (www.charles-de -gaulle.org/wp-content/uploads/2017/03/Conférence-du-19-mai-1958.pdf). See also Jonathan Fenby, *The General: Charles de Gaulle and the France He Saved* (New York: Skyhorse, 2012), pp. 373–402, and Jean Lacouture, *De Gaulle: The Ruler, 1945–1970*, trans. Alan Sheridan (New York: Norton, 1993), pp. 164–92.

4. Constitution of the Fifth French Republic (https://en.wikisource.org /wiki/Constitution_of_the_Fifth_French_Republic); "Proclamation," *Journal Officiel de la République Française*, October 5, 1958 (www.legifrance.gouv.fr/jo_pdf .do?numJO=0&dateJO=19581005&numTexte=&pageDebut=09177&pageFin =). Since 2000, the constitution has been amended to limit presidential power. The president is now elected for five, not seven, years and may not serve more than two consecutive terms (article 6), while the parliament may ask the Constitutional Council to review the need for the president's emergency powers within thirty days (article 16).

5. Frédéric Bozo, *French Foreign Policy since 1945: An Introduction*, trans. Jonathan Hensher (New York: Berghahn, 2016); Maurice Vaisse, *La grandeur: Politique étrangère du général de Gaulle* (Paris: Fayard, 1998); Charles Cogan, *Charles de Gaulle: A Brief Biography with Documents* (Boston: St. Martin's Press, 1996); William Nester, *De Gaulle's Legacy: The Art of Power in France's Fifth Republic* (New York: Palgrave Macmillan, 2014).

6. Gérard Bossuat, *Faire l'Europe sans défaire la France. 60 ans de politique d'unité européenne des gouvernements et des présidents de la République française* (Brussels: Peter Lang, 2005); Georges-Henri Soutou, *L'Alliance incertaine. Les rapports politiques et stratégiques franco-allemands, 1954–1996* (Paris: Fayard, 1996); Michael Sutton, *France and the Construction of Europe* (New York: Berghahn, 2007).

7. Christian Nuenlist, Anna Locher, and Garrett Martin, eds., *Globalizing de Gaulle: International Perspectives on French Foreign Policies, 1958–1969* (Lanham, Md.: Lexington, 2010).

8. Charles de Gaulle, *Memoirs of Hope: Renewal and Endeavor*, trans. Terence Kilmartin (New York: Simon & Schuster, 1970), pp. 168–69.

9. Charles de Gaulle, *The War Memoirs of Charles de Gaulle: Salvation, 1944–1946*, trans. Richard Howard (New York: Simon & Schuster, 1960), pp. 94, 96.

10. De Gaulle, *Memoirs of Hope*, p. 202.

11. Vaisse, *La grandeur*, pp. 139–61, 371–80; Bozo, *French Foreign Policy*, pp. 58–61; Nester, *De Gaulle's Legacy*, pp. 51–55.

12. Letter from de Gaulle to Lyndon Johnson, March 7, 1966 (www.cvce.eu /en/obj/letter_from_charles_de_gaulle_to_lyndon_b_johnson_7_march _1966-en-d97bf195-34e1-4862-b5e7-87577a8c1632.html); Frédéric Bozo, *De Gaulle, The United States, and the Atlantic Alliance*, trans. Susan Emanuel (Lanham, Md.: Rowman & Littlefield, 2001), pp. 143–86; Vaisse, *La grandeur*, pp. 113–24, 381–95; Bozo, *French Foreign Policy*, pp. 46–49, 69–71; Cogan, *Charles de Gaulle*, pp. 121–35; Nester, *De Gaulle's Legacy*, pp. 48–50.

13. De Gaulle, "Discours à Moscou, 30 juin 1966" (www.charles-de -gaulle.org/wp-content/uploads/2017/03/Discours-%C3%A0-Moscou.pdf); Vaisse, *La grandeur*, pp. 413–34; Bozo, *French Foreign Policy*, pp. 63–67, 71–73; Cogan, *Charles de Gaulle*, pp. 145–48.

14. Quoted in Nester, *De Gaulle's Legacy*, p. 82; Bozo, *French Foreign Policy*, pp. 86–87, 91–93.

15. Quoted in Bozo, *French Foreign Policy*, p. 109, and Jacques Chirac, *My Life in Politics*, trans. Catherine Spencer (New York: Palgrave Macmillan, 2012), p. 78.

16. Interview in *Izvestiia*, December 3, 1987, quoted in Angela Stent, "Franco-Soviet Relations from de Gaulle to Mitterrand," Report to the National Council for Soviet and East European Research, Harvard University, 1989, p. 12.

17. Quoted in Frédéric Bozo, *Mitterrand, the End of the Cold War, and German Unification*, trans. Susan Emanuel (London: Berghahn, 2009), p. 171, see also pp. 17–18 and 42–43. For broader context, see John Lewis Gaddis, *The Cold War: A New History* (New York: Penguin, 2005), pp. 237–57.

18. Bozo, *French Foreign Policy*, pp. 151–55, 161–65; Nester, *De Gaulle's Legacy*, pp. 156–63.

19. Ben Hall, "The Volte Face," *Financial Times*, March 26, 2009; Alice Pannier, "From One Exceptionalism to Another: France's Strategic Relations with the United States and the United Kingdom in the Post–Cold War Era," *Journal of Strategic Studies* 40, no. 4 (2017), pp. 475–504.

20. *The Economist*, "The Bamako Effect," February 9, 2013; Christopher Chivvis, *The French War on al Qa'ida in Africa* (Cambridge University Press, 2016), pp. 74–111.

21. Rachel Lee Loan, "France," in *National Perspectives on Russia: European Foreign Policy in the Making*, edited by Maxine David and others (Abingdon, U.K.: Routledge, 2013), pp. 30–47; Pernille Rieker, *French Foreign Policy in a Changing World: Practicing Grandeur* (Basingstoke, U.K.: Palgrave Macmillan, 2017), pp. 61–86.

22. Quoted in Natalie Nougayrède, "As America Retreats, Macron Steps Up," *Foreign Affairs*, September/October 2017, p. 7.

23. Bozo, *French Foreign Policy*, pp. 56–58; Nester, *De Gaulle's Legacy*, pp. 56–58.

24. "Press conference held by Charles de Gaulle, September 9, 1965" (www.cvce.eu/en/obj/press_conference_held_by_charles_de_gaulle_9_september_1965-en-169b1692-c7dd-4ad4-b5fb-67e0e28edd02.html); Bossuat, *Faire l'Europe*, pp. 83–118; Sutton, *France*, pp. 127–38.

25. Piers Ludlow, "From Words to Actions: Reinterpreting de Gaulle's European Policy," in *Globalizing de Gaulle*, edited by Nuenlist, Locher, and Martin, pp. 63–82; Andrew Moravcsik, "Charles de Gaulle and Europe: The New Revisionism," *Journal of Cold War Studies* 14, no. 1 (Winter 2012), pp. 53–77.

26. Alain Peyrefitte, *C'était de Gaulle*, vol. 1 (Paris: Fayard, 1994), p. 282, quoted in Jeffrey Vanke, "Reconstructing de Gaulle," *Journal of Cold War Studies* 2, no. 3 (Fall 2000), p. 96; James Ellison, "Britain, de Gaulle's NATO Policies, and Anglo-French Rivalry, 1963–1967," in *Globalizing de Gaulle*, edited by Nuenlist, Locher, and Martin, pp. 135–54; Cogan, *Charles de Gaulle*, pp. 135–41.

27. Quoted in Sutton, *France*, p. 105; Soutou, *L'Alliance*, pp. 149–201, 241–49; Bozo, *French Foreign Policy*, pp. 60–63.

28. Sutton, *France*, pp. 106–08; Carine Germond, "A 'Cordial Potentiality'? De Gaulle and Franco-German Partnership, 1963–1969," in *Globalizing de Gaulle*, edited by Nuenlist, Locher, and Martin, pp. 43–62; Cogan, *Charles de Gaulle*, pp. 141–43.

29. Quoted in Nester, *De Gaulle's Legacy*, p. 86; Bossuat, *Faire l'Europe*, pp. 119–40; Sutton, *France*, pp. 178–92; Bozo, *French Foreign Policy*, pp. 82–85.

30. Bossuat, *Faire l'Europe*, pp. 119–58; Sutton, *France*, pp. 222–29; Bozo, *French Foreign Policy*, pp. 99–101, 109–11.

31. Bozo, *Mitterrand, the End of the Cold War, and German Unification*, pp. 165–88, 233–43, 293–300, 310–31; Bozo, *French Foreign Policy*, pp. 130–34.

32. Quoted in Sutton, *France*, p. 267; Bossuat, *Faire l'Europe*, p. 159–84.

33. Quoted in Sutton, *France*, p. 308; Chirac, *My Life*, pp. 153–64, 216–24; Bozo, *French Foreign Policy*, pp. 152–57, 167–68, 173–76.

34. Quoted in Chirac, *My Life*, p. 275; Bossuat, *Faire L'Europe*, pp. 185–212; Sutton, *France*, pp. 316–24.

35. Gino G. Raymond, "Sarkozy and Europe: Back to the Future," in *The Sarkozy Presidency: Breaking the Mold*, edited by Gino G. Raymond (New York: Palgrave Macmillan, 2013), pp. 79–103.

36. Camille Robcis, "Debt, Refugees, and the Failure of the European Project in 2015," *Modern & Contemporary France* 25, no. 1 (2017), pp. 82–88.

37. "Speech by President Emmanuel Macron—Ambassadors' Week 2017," August 29, 2017, (www.diplomatie.gouv.fr/en/the-ministry-and-its-network /events/ambassadors-week/ambassadors-week-edition-2017/speech-by-president -emmanuel-macron-ambassadors-week-2017/).

38. "President Macron Outlines France's Foreign Policy Goals," August 31, 2017, (https://uk.ambafrance.org/President-Macron-outlines-France -s-foreign-policy-goals); "Transformers?," *The Economist*, December 2, 2017; James McAuley, "Macron Touts Europe's Interests, but Early Actions Put France First," *Washington Post*, August 5, 2017.

39. Nicole Koenig and Marie Walter-Franke, "France and Germany: Spearheading a European Security and Defense Union?," Jacques Delors Institute, Policy Paper 202, July 19, 2017; Oliver Scanlan and Richard Reeve, "European Military Integration: Implications for the U.K.," Oxford Research Group Briefing, November 2017.

40. Fenby, *The General*, pp. 432–53; Lacouture, *De Gaulle*, pp. 262–300.

41. Fenby, *The General*, pp. 463–92; Lacouture, *De Gaulle*, pp. 301–30.

42. Charles de Gaulle, *Major Addresses, Statements, and Press Conferences, May 19, 1958–January 31, 1964* (New York: French Embassy, 1964), p. 82; Bozo, *French Foreign Policy*, pp. 104–05; Nester, *De Gaulle's Legacy*, pp. 46–47.

43. Guy Martin, "Francophone Africa in the Context of Franco-African Relations," in *Africa in World Politics: Post–Cold War Challenges*, edited by John Harbeson and Donald Rotchild (Boulder, Colo.: Westview, 1995), pp. 163–88; Guia Migani, "De Gaulle and Sub-Saharan Africa: From Decolonization to French Development Policy," in *Globalizing de Gaulle*, edited by Nuenlist, Locher, and Martin, pp. 251–70.

44. François-Xavier Verschave, *La Françafrique: Le plus long scandale de la République* (Paris: Stock, 1998). De Gaulle's Africa policy was coordinated by his chief adviser for African affairs, Jacques Foccart, de Gaulle's close colleague in the Resistance and the former secretary general of the Gaullist party, who specialized in covert operations. Foccart also advised Georges Pompidou and, after a long hiatus, Jacques Chirac. Nonetheless, the presidents set the agenda that Foccart implemented.

45. Jean-Pierre Bat, "Jacques Foccart: *Eminence grise* for African affairs," in *Francophone Africa at Fifty*, edited by Tony Chafer and Alexander Keese (Manchester University Press, 2013), pp. 135–53; Alain Rouvez, *Disconsolate Empires: French, British and Belgian Military Involvement in Post-Colonial Sub-Saharan Africa* (Lanham, Md.: University Press of America, 1994), pp. 35–49.

46. Kaye Whiteman, "Pompidou and Africa: Gaullism after de Gaulle," *The World Today* 26, no. 6 (June 1970), pp. 241–49; Pierre Lellouche and Dominique Moisi, "French Policy in Africa: A Lonely Battle against Destabilization," *International Security* 3, no. 4 (Spring 1979), pp. 108–33; Rouvez, *Disconsolate Empires*, pp. 49–56; Bozo, *French Foreign Policy*, pp. 104–05; Nester, *De Gaulle's Legacy*, pp. 106–07.

47. Xavier Renou, "A New French Policy for Africa?," *Journal of Contemporary African Studies* 20, no. 1 (2002), pp. 5–27; Pierre Brana and Bernard Cazenave, *Rapport de la mission d'information parlementaire française sur le Rwanda*, National Assembly, December 15, 2008; Arthur Jay Klinghoffer, *The International Dimension of Genocide in Rwanda* (New York University Press, 1998), pp. 80–90; Rouvez, *Disconsolate Empires*, p. 56; Bozo, *French Foreign Policy*, pp. 136, 144–45.

48. Tony Chafer, "France and 'la Françafrique': No Longer a Family Affair," *Modern & Contemporary France* 13, no. 1 (2005), pp. 7–23; Kathrin Heitz, "Through the Prism of *Cinquantenaire*: Cote d'Ivoire, *Refondation*, and Houghuët's Legacy," in Chafer and Keese, *Francophone Africa at Fifty*, pp. 219–32; Lucy Ash, "Breaking France's Africa Habit," BBC, April 1, 2007 (news.bbc .co.uk/2/hi/europe/6511963.stm).

49. For an English translation of the speech, see www.africaresource.com /essays-a-reviews/essays-a-discussions/437-the-unofficial-english-translation -of-sarkozys-speech.

50. Gordon Cumming, "'A Piecemeal Approach with No Vision': French Policy towards Africa under Sarkozy," in *The Sarkozy Presidency*, edited by Raymond, pp. 104–29; Steven Smith, "How France Maintains Its Grip on Africa," BBC, May 21, 2010 (news.bbc.co.uk/2/hi/africa/8639874.stm); Nester, *De Gaulle's Legacy*, pp. 184–86.

51. Tony Chafer, "Hollande and Africa Policy," *Modern & Contemporary France* 22, no. 4 (2014), pp. 513–31; Chivvis, *The French War*, pp. 112–55; Bozo, *French Foreign Policy*, pp. 189–90.

52. Gadi Heimann, *Franco-Israeli Relations, 1958–1967* (New York: Routledge, 2017), pp. 108–204; Jean-Pierre Filiu, "France and the June 1967 War," in *The 1967 Arab-Israeli War: Origins and Consequences*, edited by Avi Shlaim and William Roger Louis (Cambridge University Press, 2012), pp. 247–63; Bozo, *French Foreign Policy*, pp. 73–74.

53. Rémy Leveau, "France's Arab Policy," in *Diplomacy in the Middle East: The International Relations of Regional and Outside Powers*, edited by L. Carl

Brown (London: I. B. Tauris, 2004), pp. 3–20; Bozo, *French Foreign Policy*, pp. 88–89, 93–95; 105–07; 120–22, 137–38; Nester, *De Gaulle's Legacy*, pp. 86–88, 133–35.

54. Chirac, *My Life*, pp. 55–56.

55. David Styan, *France and Iraq: Oil, Arms, and the Making of French Foreign Policy* (London: I. B. Tauris, 2006); Nester, *De Gaulle's Legacy*, pp. 161–62, 166–68.

56. Chirac, "Speech before the UN General Assembly," September 23, 2003, quoted in Paul Belkin, "France: Factors Shaping Foreign Policy, and Issues in U.S.-French Relations," Congressional Research Service (CRS) Report RL32464, April 14, 2011, p. 8; Chirac, *My Life*, pp. 255–92; Frédéric Bozo, *A History of the Iraq Crisis: France, the United States, and Iraq, 1991–2003*, trans. Susan Emanuel (Columbia University Press, 2016), pp. 247–88; Bozo, *French Foreign Policy*, pp. 166–67, 169–72.

57. Chirac, *My Life*, pp. 181–96, 297–307; Shaun Gregory, "France and the War on Terrorism," *Terrorism and Political Violence* 15, no. 1 (2003), pp. 124–47; Bozo, *A History of the Iraq Crisis*, pp. 289–310; Bozo, *French Foreign Policy*, pp. 172–73; Nester, *De Gaulle's Legacy*, pp. 161, 165–66.

58. Alan J. Kuperman, "Obama's Libya Debacle," *Foreign Affairs*, March /April 2015; Bozo, *French Foreign Policy*, pp. 183–185, 189; Nester, *De Gaulle's Legacy*, pp. 197–98.

FOUR

The Foreign Policy of Germany

Economic Giant, Foreign Policy Dwarf?

JAN TECHAU

Germany has covered a lot of ground since 1945. In roughly seventy years, it has gone from being the isolated, occupied pariah of Europe to the continent's "indispensable nation."[1] It is startling, however, that a similar development has not taken place in Germany's role as a foreign policy player in Europe. Germany's role in the world today is, of course, important, and the country enjoys high rankings in global favorability polls. But Germany's role as a shaper of foreign policy outside Europe still does not match its role as a shaper of Europe internally.

When the Federal Republic of Germany was founded in 1949, Germans were neither territorially united nor citizens of a sovereign nation.[2] West Germany, however, enjoyed political freedom while the German Democratic Republic in the East became a Soviet satellite state under Moscow's firm control. West Germany's primary foreign policy goal after 1949 was to regain sovereignty—a difficult task given the moral bankruptcy of the

I would like to thank Greg Nelson, graduate student at Appalachian State University, for assisting me in the editing and revision process.

nation after World War II and the fact that Germany was occupied and under Allied political and military control. For West Germany, regaining sovereignty was only possible through a carefully balanced approach to the outside world. Its first main element was *Westbindung*, the firm embedding of the new democracy into the Western political sphere, represented by the United States, Britain, and France. Its second main element was restraint and passivity in its dealings with the outside world. This restraint included diplomatic relationships with other countries, the signing of treaties, and of course, all things military.

It was in this first decade of West German democracy that the consensus on German foreign policy, which still exists today, was formed. It was an approach built on "three plus three" pillars. The first three pillars represent close relationships with Germany's most important bilateral partners: the United States, France, and to a lesser extent and on very different terms, Russia. The other three pillars represent Germany's multilateral engagements with NATO, the European Community (today the EU), and later, the United Nations. Keeping this six-pillar construction intact remains Germany's unspoken primary foreign policy goal.

This construction, in combination with extreme foreign policy restraint, reflected the German postwar mantra of "never again, never alone." It allowed for substantial German foreign policy activity only within tight multilateral frameworks. It also led to a culture of military reluctance and passivity, even after rearmament in the mid-1950s, a culture very much intact today.

In what constitutes remarkable continuity, the major turning points in German postwar history—rearmament in the mid-1950s, the 1968 cultural shift, *Ostpolitik*, UN membership in 1973, NATO's dual-track policy in the late 1970s and early 1980s, unification in 1990, and the more assertive period after Helmut Kohl's ousting from office after 1998—had no real game-changing impact on the overall strategic culture established in the 1950s. In essence, Germany is operating its foreign policy in the twenty-first century based on a strategic culture from the 1950s.[3] This stands in odd contrast to Germany's growing importance as a leader and its now decisive power within Europe.

Germany today is a key foreign policy player in Europe almost by default. It holds a nominally strong position among European member states, but it lacks foreign policy ambition. There is neither much appetite for leading the way nor any aspiration to dominate or subjugate the continent under a *diktat* from Berlin. However, the negative side effects of the German elites' unassuming ways define a profound lack of strategic scope and an under-developed sense of Germany's responsibility for Europe's position as a player in the world. Forty years of outsourcing strategic concerns to its Western allies, especially to the United States, have dried up strategic think-ing in Germany. Most crucially, the importance of hard power as a key component of diplomacy and as a much-needed asset in an increasingly dis-orderly and unstable environment is ignored or rejected.

Germany's eminence as a power today comes almost exclusively from its economic strength. This has a long post–World War II tradition. When, after the war, Germany was initially not allowed to conduct its own for-eign policy, the country's only way to build a reputation and influence abroad was through economic relations. The result is an extraordinarily strong influence of German business lobbies over the country's foreign pol-icy. In no other Western country is business influence on the government's foreign policy decisions as profound and direct as in Germany. This is par-ticularly visible in Germany's relations with Russia.

Germany's economic strength allowed it to play a key role in the handling of the European (and international) monetary and economic crisis after 2008. After initial wavering, Germany's course can be described as "condi-tional solidarity." Under this policy, Germany pledged significant mone-tary support for the euro and for ailing economies in the EU's southern periphery in return for structural economic reform and fiscal austerity on their side. Under strong German influence, based on the country's status as the European economic powerhouse, this policy has become the strat-egy of choice for European institutions and many afflicted governments in crisis-hit countries. As the crisis lingers and the economic situation in many countries gets worse instead of better, this policy has come under in-tense criticism. Regardless of whether these policies are deemed the proper response to the crisis, they are the closest thing to leadership Germany is willing to exercise in Europe.[4] The Greek crisis is a direct result of the failure of member states, including Germany itself, to draw the inevitable conclusions from the deep economic integration they voluntarily em-braced. When European leaders failed to create a system of political gov-ernance commensurate with the need to administer an economy united by a single market, a shared trade policy, sophisticated competition laws, and a common currency, they unleashed the powers of political undergovernance. It does not come as a complete surprise that Germany's partial leadership appears in the field of economic affairs, traditionally the area of choice for a strong German role.

Germany's economic leadership is not matched by similar leadership from Berlin in developing a stronger common foreign policy of the EU. Germany is neither showing strong ambition to develop the EU's Common Foreign and Security Policy (CFSP) nor demonstrating any ambition to drive forward the development of the Common Security and Defense Policy (CSDP), the EU's shared approach to security and defense. In these fields, Germany is more of a reactive player. This has not fundamentally changed during the debate about increased EU defense integration that kicked off after Donald Trump assumed office as president of the United States in January 2017. While Germany is supporting increased EU spending on defense research and a few other projects designed to increase the EU's role in CSDP, none of these initiatives has the scope or depth to bring about change of a strategic nature in Europe. The same is true within the NATO context. Germany's support for the alliance's Framework Nation Concept is a welcome infusion of German energy into NATO's modernization, but it is not the kind of hard security currency that a continent thrown into strategic insecurity yearns for. So, Germany is not altogether inactive on these fronts, but its contributions and positions do not match either the stated goals of the Berlin government or the country's growing responsibility as the chief custodian of Europe's future development.

In sum, Germany is an ambitious world player in international economic affairs but shows no sign that it desires to be a significant political player on the world stage.[5] It retains its traditional postwar culture of military passivity and finds it hard to overcome a strategic culture that fails to appreciate a changed environment and the new demands this environment poses to Europe's strongest player. Thus, its foreign policy will continue to show signs of ambiguity and insecurity. Germany will remain a generally reliable but often underperforming partner for its European and transatlantic allies.

The European Union

For much of its history, the Federal Republic of Germany was the quintessential pro-European country. For the young West Germany, Europe was an ersatz-religion that allowed the country to project its hopes, aspirations, and ambitions into something other than the nation—a concept too contaminated after the Nazi era to be of any use for the Germans after 1949. West Germany, culminating in the early Kohl era, equated European interests with its own national interest to a degree that few other nations were willing to accept. Germany was Europe's reserve power, ready to invest more and give up more than others to enable European integration to succeed and progress.

Even today, Germany is still an above-average pro-European country. Binding itself to multilateral arrangements remains the only way, by and large, in which Germans feel comfortable addressing issues beyond their borders. And yet Germany has changed its attitude vis-à-vis the classic EU integration logic. Having once been a surefire supporter of the community method in which member states rely heavily on the EU institutions to conduct affairs, Germany has for the last twenty years been more and more tempted to adhere to the intergovernmental approach to EU decisionmaking. While still supporting the integration project in general (it offers shelter from political isolation and is also dictated by economic necessity), the intergovernmental approach allows the country to better exploit its relative strength as compared with others during negotiations. This tendency became visible under Gerhard Schröder, and it continued under Angela Merkel, who is said to harbor deep-seated mistrust in the Brussels-based institutions, most notably the European Commission.

In recent years, Germany's attitude vis-à-vis the EU has been dominated by the management of the financial crisis that heavily affected the EU's shared currency, the euro. After initial hesitation, Germany stood up to the challenge of stabilizing the euro once it had started to get into dangerous terrain. But the attitude remained ambiguous. While Germany was willing, several times, to pledge enormous amounts of money to stabilize countries that had fallen into fiscal disarray, it did not show unconditional solidarity. Fearful of a euro regime in which issues of stability and proper budgeting were ignored, Germany attached to its aid strong conditions of economic reform and fiscal discipline. This became known as "austerity" politics, and it deeply damaged Germany's image as a good European in the southern parts of Europe. Equally important, it changed German attitudes not so much as compared with the EU itself (even though it did that, too), but with respect to the euro and Germany's role in it. The euro is now often seen as a flawed project, and the economic logic of stabilizing the currency at all cost is increasingly being questioned. A new party, the now staunchly right-wing Alternative für Deutschland, emerged out of the critique of the euro. It has moved away from its roots as an anti-euro party to being a classic extreme right-wing group sporting xenophobic and ultranationalist positions (it wants Germany to leave the EU), but its origins lie in a fairly deep-seated opposition against the EU's shared currency.

The euro will remain the make-or-break issue for the EU. Germany will play a key role in creating a governance system that will make the shared currency sustainable. But the financial crisis has left many scars in the German political landscape, and it will be extremely difficult for the country to embrace the kind of solution that will likely be necessary to put the euro on a stable footing: political union including a massive debt write-off and a euro-wide transfer union in return for very strict shared political oversight over budgeting, spending, and economic policy. The inner logic of the euro dictates such an approach to keep the whole system afloat. But there is very little political capital left in Germany to step into such a revolutionary scheme. Germany will continue to support the euro, as its survival is now a question of economic survival for the eurozone. But it will fall short of going all the way, the way the founders of the euro intended it to be.

Germany's attitude vis-à-vis the EU's Common Foreign and Security Policy can be described as mostly functional. Despite some strong pro-integration rhetoric in this field, Germany has never been eager to break out of the consensus among member states that this domain should remain firmly within the hands of Europe's nations and not be communalized. In that sense, Germany is very much a mainstream European country. Germany has used, on occasion, the EU vehicle to conduct foreign policy that would have otherwise been impossible, such as during the negotiations over the Iran nuclear deal or when imposing sanctions on Russia after the annexation of Crimea. But there is no appetite in Berlin to strengthen the roles of the European External Action Service (EEAS) and the High Representative for EU Foreign and Security Policy.

This is perhaps especially true when it comes to increased defense cooperation at the EU level. Germany has been a reluctant player in this field, just as in all matters of military affairs in general. It is suspicious of French ambitions in this field and generally, without making much noise about it, sees NATO as the primary vessel for hard security in Europe. A small impulse for more defense cooperation was given after the election of Donald Trump as president of the United States, as this led to questions of U.S. and NATO reliability within the European security architecture. But the measures taken in 2017 and 2018 at the EU level, most notably an increase in EU spending on defense research, do not mark a reversal of long-held convictions. Germany, for the foreseeable future, will not put its considerable political weight behind a notably increased security and defense role of the European Union.

Russia

Germany's relationship with Russia is characterized by deep ambiguity. On the one hand, Russia's geographic proximity and Germany's increasing dependence on Russian energy supplies mandate a cooperative and friendly relationship with Moscow.[6] Economic ties with German companies in the energy sector have been very tight since at least the late 1970s and early 1980s, when large gas pipeline projects between Russia and Western Europe were planned and implemented. Also, traditional historical and cultural ties, rooted in hundreds of years of shared history, have given German-Russian relations a basically amicable character even during the coldest of Cold War periods. On the other hand, Germans profoundly dislike the course Russia has taken during the Putin era. Russia's internal development, just as much as its foreign policy, has considerably concerned both the German public and the policymaking elite.

During Chancellor Angela Merkel's Grand Coalition from 2004 to 2009, Germany attempted to bridge the gulf between these two poles in its Russia policy by becoming a forceful proponent of the *Modernisierungspartnerschaft*, a partnership whose goal was to help modernize the Russian economy and society. From the outset, this project suffered from different interpretations of modernization. While the Germans ultimately also sought to bring about democratic reform in Russia, the Russian side was primarily interested in investments and technology transfers aimed at bringing its aging industries up to current standards. While the Germans, apart from cultivating lucrative business relations, wanted to foster political and social change, Russia wanted the opposite. Its sole interest was in strengthening its export-oriented, de facto state-run energy industries, Russia's only relevant sources of revenue. In the absence of a truly participatory political system, the wealth generated by these industries is crucial for Kremlin elites to stay in power in the long run. It enables them to provide generous handouts to key constituencies in Russia, including the military, thereby buying political consent and keeping political disillusionment at bay.

As the asymmetry of the *Modernisierungspartnerschaft* became more and more obvious, German uneasiness grew. After the democratically imperfect Russian parliamentary elections in December 2011, the subsequent protests, and the job-swapping scheme announced by then-president Dmitry Medvedev and then-prime minister Vladimir Putin, Chancellor Merkel became visibly disenchanted with Russia. Her disenchantment grew after the legal procedure against the female members of the Russian rock band Pussy Riot, which was widely perceived in the West as a scandalous political show trial. Merkel, whose personal skepticism of Russian behavior has been known for a long time, publicly distanced herself from Putin on human rights issues in a press conference in November 2012.[7] In addition, shortly afterward, the parliamentary groups of Merkel's ruling center-right coalition introduced a motion in the Bundestag voicing deep concern over the trial and legislation adopted in the Duma and asking for a revamped partnership with Russia, thereby further illustrating the changed views on Russia in Berlin.[8]

A fundamental shift occurred in Germany's Russia policy after Moscow's annexation of Crimea and the subsequent downing of Malaysian Airlines Flight MH17 over Ukrainian territory. Germany, at first reluctantly, and then with much determination, became the front-runner on both the Western sanctions imposed against Russia and the diplomatic efforts to resolve the aggression, supported and steered by Russia, of so-called separatist militias in Eastern Ukraine. Under Merkel's guidance, two agreements were negotiated in Minsk that aimed at sequencing trust-building moves toward a political solution of the conflict in the Donetsk and Luhansk regions. Most important, however, Merkel made a remarkable U-turn on the home front. In a speech in the Bundestag, she announced that yes, sanctions against Russia would be costly for her country, but Germany was willing to shoulder those costs because a bigger issue was at stake—the questions of the post–Cold War peace order agreed in 1990 and 1991. The addressee of this statement was not just Vladimir Putin. It was also Germans back home, especially German business leaders who in the past had lobbied very hard to keep relations with Russia on a soft footing. Their protest was in vain. Merkel stood by the sanctions policy and has defended them ever since. For a country that has often been blamed—and sometimes for good reason—that it deemed its business interests more important than its geopolitical responsibility, this was a remarkable move.

After Crimea and the war in eastern Ukraine, Germans remain deeply ambiguous about Russia. Trust in Vladimir Putin and his regime is low, but Germany's historic reluctance to risk conflict with Russia also still exists. Both on the political left and on the political right, influential Russia-friendly groups exist. Some of them crystallize around the former German chancellor, Gerhard Schröder, whose business ties with state-owned Russian energy giant Rozneft make him a key player in linking German business interests to government policy—at least as long as his Social Democratic Party is part of government. All German parties, with the possible exception of the Greens, have at some point shown that their resolve against an intensified Russian power game against the West is not too steadfast. Much of German Russia policy will depend on how long Merkel can hold on to power and remain the defining force in German-Russian relations. At the same time, because of its key role within the EU, Germany will remain the most important target for Russian diplomacy and propaganda in Europe.

The Middle East

German involvement in the Middle East has traditionally been dominated by its relationship with Israel. History prescribes that it be so. During her chancellorship, Angela Merkel has lived up to this tradition by twice issuing German security guarantees for the state of Israel. She did this once in the U.S. Congress and once in the Knesset, thereby underlining in the most public way possible the historic responsibility Germany has for the existence of the Jewish state.[9] However, Germany has also been a significant contributor of development aid and acted as a diplomatic mediator, an arms exporter to Saudi Arabia, and a financier of the Palestinian Authority after the Oslo agreements. Germany also plays a major role as one of the six powers representing the international community in the diplomatic efforts over the Iranian nuclear program. To be included to serve in this group alongside the five permanent members of the UN Security Council is an acknowledgement of Germany's increased diplomatic weight and its role as a key political player in the international sanctions regime against Tehran.

Germany's engagement in the Middle East is probably the best illustration of what experts have called the country's role as a *Zivilmacht*, a civilian, nonmilitary power.[10] Germany has a strong national interest in stability in the region, which would include reducing Islamist terrorism, limiting the prospect of mass migration from the region to Europe, and securing access to the energy resources of the region. At the same time, it is not a primary geopolitical player in the region's diplomacy. Germany has firmly embedded its diplomatic involvement in the region in the multilateral approaches of the EU and the UN. This has sometimes created conflicts with Arab nations that would have wished for more engagement by Germany in bilateral efforts.[11] In a rare show of military commitment, Germany has been participating in the United Nations Interim Force in Lebanon (UNIFIL) naval mission to prevent weapons smuggling in Lebanese territorial waters since 2006.

In Angela Merkel's second term in office, three topics have dominated German engagement in the Middle East: first, the Arab uprisings, starting in early 2011, and the European reaction to the so-called Arab Spring; second, a string of decisions by the German government to allow the export of German military equipment to Saudi Arabia; and third, the deterioration of support for Israel's position in the Israeli-Palestinian conflict due to Prime Minister Benjamin Netanyahu's policy of expanding settlements on Palestinian territory in the West Bank.

While Germany's reaction to the Arab Spring, in line with established tradition, came for the most part through the EU, Berlin's decision to authorize German arms deals with governments in the region demonstrated a notably higher national profile. In 2011, the Merkel government approved the sale of over 200 German-made battle tanks to Saudi Arabia. In December 2012, Merkel again gave the green light to an arms deal with Saudi Arabia, bringing the total sum of approved exports to the region to US$1.88 billion, with recipient countries including Qatar, Kuwait, Omar, and Bahrain. These decisions were met with harsh criticism in Germany, as these deals had been made with countries with shaky human rights records.[12] Some observers have gone as far as saying that the German government is now operating under the "Merkel Doctrine," a geopolitical strategy that would prohibit German soldiers from being deployed in operations such as the one in Libya, but attempts to pursue German interests by arming countries that promise to provide stability in the region.[13] While this reading of the government's strategy might go too far, the Merkel government's decision to engage on very hotly contested security and defense issues, a behavior not often seen by Berlin, has not been popular. In October 2018, therefore, Merkel halted German arms exports to Riyadh following the killing of journalist Jamal Khashoggi at the Saudi consulate in Istanbul.

The most important development in German Middle East policy, however, concerns its main interest in the region, Israel. Traditionally bound to support Jerusalem on the grounds of a historically rooted raison d'état, the Merkel government has grown visibly cool in its support for the Israeli government under Prime Minister Benjamin Netanyahu. Berlin considers the decision of Netanyahu to press ahead with the building of new settlements in the Palestinian West Bank as detrimental to the proposed two-state solution of the Israeli-Palestinian conflict. In an unprecedented move, Germany abstained in the UN General Assembly vote on Palestinian statehood in November 2012. In the past it had been one of Israel's most reliable allies in UN votes, but its decision to not vote "no" was seemingly unexpected in Jerusalem. Chancellor Merkel is said to "have lost all trust in Netanyahu."[14] While this decision is remarkable, it is by no means certain that it will develop into a new pattern, breaking with long-established German policies in the region. The move is probably more telling about the perceived state of Israeli policies than about Germany's changing interests. Yet it portrays a country that is perhaps more willing to deviate from long-standing positions if it deems that useful.

The United States

The most important factor that needs to be understood in German-U.S. relations is the large extent to which they are multilateralized. In trade relations, Germany is part of the EU's common trade policy and has only limited influence over decisionmaking by the EU Commission. In defense matters, Germany's membership in NATO dictates large parts, but not all, of the relationship between the U.S. und German militaries. In the field of homeland security (the responsibility of the interior ministry in Germany), Europe's policies in the Justice and Home Affairs portfolio of the EU Commission regulate the majority of cooperative schemes. This far-reaching multilateralization is typical for large parts of Germany's relations with its Western partners and allies. The network of institutionalized consultations, summits, working groups, committees, and councils, including the G-7,

G-8, and G-20, is so tightly knit, the established machinery and procedures for dealing with disputed issues so established and generally well oiled, that most issues get relegated to technical status rather quickly. Yet this high level of integration does not make intensive bilateral government contacts irrelevant. Quite the contrary. The newly established foreign policy doctrine of U.S. president Donald Trump puts Germany, for the first time in postwar history, on a direct political collision course with the United States in a structural way, not just with respect to individual policy issues. For Germany, multilateralism is a raison d'état. Despite the occasional unilateral temptation, the country can really only imagine itself as a partner in multilateral political designs, embedding the country firmly in established, rules-based partnerships. The Trump Doctrine, as spelled out by the president in his speeches in Warsaw[15] and before the United Nations General Assembly,[16] stipulates the exact opposite approach: Every country is on its own and has to see after its own interests first.

For Germany, this came as a shock. Like all European nations, its fundamental strategic posture rests on the assumption that the United States sees itself as the guardian of a liberal order based on multilateral institutions such as NATO, the EU, and the United Nations. America itself was the very architect of the multilateral post–World War II global order, underwriting as key capacitator, protector, and enabler institutions like the World Bank, the International Monetary Fund, and the World Trade Organization.

With the rhetoric role reversal that Trump has made concerning multilateralism, a multitude of potential conflicts between the United States and Germany has emerged. And while it needs to be stated that U.S. foreign policy vis-à-vis Europe under Trump has been rather different in deeds than in words (the United States has actually increased its troop presence in Europe and its Europe-related defense spending, and expanded its presence in Germany), trust in U.S. attitudes is shaken in Germany and across Europe. There is less trust in whether the United States is the same reliable ally it has been since the late 1940s. In Germany, this has led to a heated debate over transatlanticism and Germany's role in Europe.

In the past years, three topics have dominated the agenda in relations between Berlin and Washington: first, the European currency and economic crisis, in which Germany's key role is acknowledged by Washington; second, Germany's role as a provider of military security in the NATO framework; and third, the project of a Transatlantic Free Trade Agreement (TAFTA).

Germany's centrality in the euro crisis, like the country's indispensable role in the EU in general, have made Germany America's most important partner in Europe.[17] This role was once reserved for the United Kingdom, which is still Washington's primary European partner in defense, security, and intelligence issues, but has lost its privileged role in the key fields of economic and regulatory policy. During the euro crisis, consultations between Berlin and Washington intensified, with the United States being a key external stakeholder in EU economic stability. The positions of the German and U.S. teams differed significantly on how to best deal with the crisis. While the U.S. president, Barack Obama, favored and repeatedly recommended to Europeans a course similar to the neo-Keynesian economics he applied to the economic crisis in the United States, Chancellor Merkel opted for a course aimed at reforming public finances and ailing economies. Her approach, balancing German willingness to pledge large sums of German taxpayers' money with demands for austerity and structural reform in recipient countries in Europe's south, was greeted with uneasiness by the Americans. As the sense of immediate danger partially subsided in late 2012 and early 2013, tensions over this rift eased. Yet, with a number of uncertainties looming in Europe's economy— namely, an ongoing recession that is particularly severe on the continent's southern periphery, a dismal economic situation in France, and the downgrading (for the first time in history) of the United Kingdom's AAA credit rating to AA1 by the ratings agency Moody's—Germany's perceived strictness can again become a factor in the bilateral relationship with the United States.

Even more profound, and more geopolitically relevant, are lingering rifts between Washington and Germany on Berlin's contribution in the military sector. Unlike in the EU context, where Washington's influence is limited, in the security and defense fields the United States very much sees itself as the leading Western nation with the right to criticize openly the lackluster performance of some of its allies. Washington has, for a long time, been critical of Europeans' unwillingness to spend their fair share on defense.[18] Without singling out Germany, the United States has always made it clear that it looks with a particularly critical eye to Berlin. Among the so-called Big Three in the EU—Germany, France, and the United Kingdom—Germany is by far the least active and least potent military player, and the smallest defense spender, even though it has by far the largest economy. Washington, like many others, was shocked when Germany abstained in the UN Security Council vote authorizing a military mission to protect Libyan opposition forces. A few years earlier, American criticism was similarly strong when Germany, contrary to its official claims, seemed to be largely uninterested in developing a more forward-looking new Strategic Concept for the North Atlantic Alliance. So substantial is Washington's disappointment over Germany's passivity that a former U.S. ambassador to NATO has called the country "a drag on NATO," a view shared by many observers in U.S. defense circles.[19] Under President Trump, Washington's discontent with Germany has grown. Trump has made the issue of 2 percent defense spending in NATO (measured against GDP), a goal formally embraced by all NATO member states at the NATO summit in Wales in 2014, the central speaking point, on occasion singling out Germany as a free-rider that does not live up to its duties. Germany, over the past few years, has gradually increased its defense spending and is likely to continue to do so. Yet it is clear that Germany is unlikely to reach the 2 percent goal within the envisioned time frame of 2024. Given the size of Germany's economy, 2 percent would be an actual amount of money too large for German political elites to seriously consider spending. This issue will remain a bone of contention for years to come, just as it already had been in the years before Trump took office.

On trade, the image is reversed. Here it is the U.S. under Trump that blocks progress. Germany, like other European countries, had been a staunch supporter of the Transatlantic Trade and Investment Partnership (TTIP), formerly known as TAFTA. Angela Merkel voiced her support for the project as early as 2005. In 2007, during Germany's EU presidency and largely because of her urging, President George W. Bush, EU Commission President José Manuel Barroso, and Merkel signed the founding document for the Transatlantic Economic Council. This body was charged with sounding out the possibilities of a full agreement across the Atlantic. Its recommendations have led to a new push for TAFTA, culminating in statements by the European Council and President Obama in his 2013 State of the Union address to start negotiations. Since then, significant progress has been made in the negotiation process, but the negotiations had not been concluded by the time President Obama left office. Under President Trump, whose anti–free trade agenda was a key building block of his presidential campaign, TTIP negotiations have not been formally canceled but are essentially frozen. Despite domestic protest and political resistance in Germany against TTIP, the German government remains in favor of the project and hopes to reignite the process at some point in the future. Under President Trump, this is unlikely to happen.

In sum, the biggest source of possible conflict between the United States and Germany lies in Germany's self-imposed role as a reluctant military partner. For a country that still implicitly relies on the American security guarantee for the protection of both its territory and its vital interests around the world, this position will become less and less sustainable in the future. Increased German military exposure on NATO's eastern flank after the Ukraine crisis and in the fight against the so-called Islamic State, have not fundamentally changed the nature of this issue. America will likely be unimpressed by Germany's internal soul-searching over security and defense and will ask for more German contributions, be that in the fight against global terrorism or in possible interventions in Europe's neighborhood. For Germany, which is always more willing to show up for article 5–related military engagement than for global crisis management, this will remain a sensitive issue that could lead to renewed and repeated political conflict with Washington. Overall, Germany will need to invest more, both intellectually and fiscally, in this field if it wants to play a major role in U.S. strategic thinking in the future.

China

Germany established a diplomatic relationship with China in 1972, following the thawing of relations between China and the United States. In 1972, the German trade volume with China was US$274 million. In 2011, it was US$170 billion. Today, Germany's relations with China serve as the prototypical example for how the country positions itself as a global player outside its traditional three-plus-three foreign policy framework: clear focus on the promotion of business interests, few security and defense concerns, clear focus on realpolitik, some references to human rights and democracy issues, and little meaningful dialogue with its partners over a common approach. This approach has served the country well so far, but seems unsustainable in the long run, primarily because of the lack of geopolitical strategic thinking about the rise of Asia and China in particular.

German Chancellor Angela Merkel visited China twice in 2012, accompanied by large business delegations. The purpose of these visits was to strengthen economic ties. Human rights and intellectual property rights issues were largely downplayed. China has overtaken the United States as the number-one foreign investor in Germany, according to statistics from Germany Trade and Invest, the federal republic's economic development agency.[20] About 5,000 German companies currently operate in China, employing 220,000 people, according to the German Chamber of Commerce in China. Seventy-five percent of them belong to the German *Mittelstand*, the midsize, family-owned companies that are the backbone of the German economy.

The "special relationship" (Angela Merkel's words) that has formed between the two countries is based on a fundamental overlapping of interests. Feeling misunderstood and neglected by official Brussels, China now sees influential Germany as the best inroad to Europe. As a report by the European Council on Foreign Relations (ECFR) states, China considers Germany to be the country most useful for its own economic development: "China needs technology and Germany needs markets."[21] Commenting on Germany's relative neglect of human rights issues, the report concludes that Germany believes that the best way to bring about political and social change in China is through close economic ties. This obviously creates two major risks for Germany: an overreliance on China as an export market, which can backfire when demand slows, and the likelihood that through close interaction Germany would build its own strongest future export rival. The latter risk seems a scenario for the more distant future, whereas the former has already materialized as a result of slowing growth in China in 2012.

For some of Germany's Western partners, its robust mercantile China strategy has created uneasiness. After an episode in which Germany tried to prevent an EU Commission antitrust procedure against China over distortions in the solar panel market, a sector with strong German business interests in China, some observers suggested that Germany is ready to undermine EU unity and solidarity in favor of lucrative business possibilities.[22] As Hans Kundnani, coauthor of the ECFR report mentioned, puts it: "There is a danger that Germany pursues its economic interests rather than Europe's strategic interests."[23]

The biggest long-term problem with Germany's China policy is its lack of strategic embeddedness. While it is reasonable to assume that Germany will probably never be a meaningful military player in the Far East, it still depends on geopolitical stability in the region for its imports and exports. It remains to be seen what this means for Germany's foreign and security policy posture and its cooperation with those forces that protect German interests around the globe (such as the United States). It is clear, however, that the American stability services around the world, on which Germany's import and export strategies rely, will probably become costlier over time. This, in turn, will mean that more contributions will be asked of America's allies to free up U.S. resources in the places that only they can be involved in. With its growing strategic business investments in the region, particularly in China, Germany will become entangled in the strategic travails in the Far East one way or another. The discussion about this in Germany has not yet fully started.

Defense

Defense and security policy remains the big weak spot of German foreign policy. While restraint and passivity served the young federal republic well in the postwar era after 1949, it has increasingly become a liability in the two decades since unification. German politicians rightfully claim that the country has come a long way since 1990, and that it has shown some remarkable military readiness in Afghanistan and the Balkans,[24] but Germany is increasingly seen by some of its Western partners as an unreliable ally. A complicated constitutional procedure for troop deployment and an intellectual absence from strategic discussions in NATO and the EU have created an image of a country oblivious to the security realities in the world. Initial caveats in German rules of engagement for its troops deployed as part of NATO's International Security Assistance Force (ISAF) mission in Afghanistan created resentment among some allies. Germany's abstention in the UN Security Council vote on military action to protect Libyan anti-Qaddafi groupings,[25] and Germany's veto of the proposed merger of armaments giants EADS and BAE Systems in 2012, did not improve its image.[26] In sum, it is fair to say that Germany is a big underperformer in all things military. In view of its economic clout and its political influence in Europe, Germany's relevance as a military player is hugely underdeveloped. Increasingly this phenomenon stands in marked contrast to Germany's robust interest-based policies in the business and economics fields.

This contrast can only be explained by German history and the strategic culture the country created for itself after World War II. As mentioned earlier, Germany's strategic culture remains largely unchanged from the one that emerged in the newly established federal republic after the country joined the Western alliance.[27] It is marked by an instinctive rejection of military power as a means of international problem-solving and a strong reluctance even to debate matters of security and defense publicly. This situation is aggravated by the systematic unlearning of thinking in defense and military categories by both the German public and elites. It started during the Cold War, when the United States and other Western allies effectively covered these fields for Germany, and the country has not yet fully recovered from that intellectual disinvestment. Remarkably, historic developments since 1990—the Kosovo War; the attacks of September 11, 2001; Afghanistan; Libya—have not significantly changed Germany's strategic culture. In essence, it is a strategic culture that does not produce any strategy but creates high domestic political costs and high levels of misunderstanding abroad.[28]

With Germany's strategic culture being thus misplaced in today's multipolar and less stable world, and with a steady downward trajectory on defense spending since 1990, the question arises whether Germany is prepared for the security and defense challenges ahead. The answer must be a profound no. Germany has not yet drawn the conclusion from its geopolitical reality as an import- and export-oriented country that it is deeply invested in the geopolitics not only of its neighborhood but also of faraway places such as the South China Sea, the Indian Ocean, the Koreas, Central Asia, and the Sahel. It has not yet managed to understand that it is not immediate threats that guide defense thinking today but more complex security interests. Instead of equipping its armed forces with the means it will need to project power in distant parts of the world, Germany systematically reduces these abilities (such as in its naval posture) or invests in ill-conceived systems (such as the insufficiently sized and problem-ridden military airlift plane Airbus A400M). Instead of driving the development of a more unified EU security and defense policy, Germany has gained a reputation for being one of the biggest obstacles in its way.

Germany's problems in the field of security and defense originate in the fact that its political elites are unwilling to leave the comfortable mindset of a strategic culture that is unsuitable for today's strategic requirements. They are essentially the product of a lack of leadership by those who fear political unpopularity more than the possible ramifications of being ill-prepared for the security environment of the twenty-first century. This risk-averseness cuts through all political parties and camps.

By being so notably absent from the intellectual marketplace over strategic and geopolitical issues, Germany creates uneasiness among its allies and partners. For the economic giant located in the center of the European continent, lacking orientation and depth in this field is a huge source of uncertainty in its neighborhood. It remains to be seen whether the German elites will heed the wake-up call by Polish Foreign Minister Radoslaw Sikorski, who told an audience in Berlin: "I will probably be the first Polish foreign minister in history to say so, but here it is: I fear German power less than I am beginning to fear German inactivity."[29]

Energy

Germany's most important and far-reaching decision in the field of energy policy was the adoption of *Atomausstieg*, the phasing out of civilian nuclear power by 2022. The decision was taken in June 2011, only three months after the tsunami-induced accident at Japan's nuclear power plant in Fukushima. The decision significantly accelerated Germany's nuclear phase-out, which had originally been decided on in 2002 and then was slightly altered in 2010. It came as a surprise to many of Germany's energy partners and neighbors. Quickly, *Atomausstieg* was turned into *Energiewende*, a more comprehensive, long-term master plan to restructure completely Germany's energy production and consumption patterns. The scheme has run into considerable domestic problems, as the structural changes needed to complete the revolutionary plan have turned out to be much larger and much more complicated than anticipated.[30]

It is telling that Germany never considered the substantial side effects its decision would have on its neighbors and partners, all of whom are connected to Germany (and its nuclear power plants) in the highly complex European electricity grid. *Atomausstieg* and *Energiewende*, though enthusiastically welcomed by environmentalists and investors in alternative energies, raised concerns over Germany's reliability as a team player in European energy policy. They have further deepened the suspicion that Germany was turning from *Mustereuropäer*, the model European team player, into a more assertive player with much less hesitance to unilaterally exploit its status as the European economic and political powerhouse.

A second, potentially much more destructive issue in energy policy emerged in 2016 and 2017. The Nord Stream 2 pipeline project, designed to increase the direct transit capacity of Russian gas to Germany, has led to heated discussions in German and European energy circles, and to a German-American dispute, and is seen as the most important strategic issue defining Germany's reliability as a strategic European foreign policy player. The German government, despite heated criticism by foreign governments, the EU, foreign policy experts, and the U.S. government, decided to give its okay to this private energy project. Central European countries, most importantly Poland, see the project as a classic case of German-Russian deal making of strategic importance that is above their heads. They deeply distrust Russia, and some of that distrust is now placed at Berlin's doorstep as well. They believe that cutting transfer countries like Ukraine and others out of the German-Russian gas flow will strategically uncouple Germany from its allies' concerns over Russia. The issue has long ceased to be an energy issue alone. It is now one of geopolitical trustworthiness of Germany. The United States, both under Barack Obama's and Donald Trump's administrations, have sided with the Eastern Europeans on this issue. Despite President Trump blasting the German government at the NATO meeting in July 2018 for backing the new natural gas pipeline link from Russia to Germany,[31] at the time of writing the beginning of the actual construction is imminent. The consortium financing the project—which comprises Gazprom and its five backers, Uniper and Wintershall of Germany, OMV of Austria, Engie of France, and Royal Dutch Shell, the Anglo-Dutch supermajor—is in place.[32] NS2 has obtained all necessary authorizations from Russia, Germany, Finland, and Sweden for construction of the planned pipeline, and found a way around Denmark within their jurisdictions.[33]

Conclusion

The gap between a prevailing German strategic culture that stems from the postwar era and the foreign policy posture demanded from one of the world's most influential and powerful countries is increasingly unbridgeable.[34] Gradually, Germany will have to change, and there are indeed signs of progress. But the adjustment is happening slowly. "The fact that other countries now look to us for leadership has not permeated the corporate culture of our foreign policy apparatus," this author was told in March 2013 by a senior German diplomat. This remains as true in 2018 as it was back then. Germany's continued uneasiness about itself, its passivity, and its reluctance to invest in the foreign policy tools it needs to protect its interests and to remain a predictable, reliable, and useful partner to its allies are reasons for concern both inside and outside the country. Germany will only be able to address these worries once it realizes it needs to become the "servant leader" of Europe,[35] a country aware of its size and importance, conscious of interests, ready to assume its responsibilities, and prepared to serve its partners because that is how it can best serve itself.

NOTES

1. Radoslaw Sikorski, "Poland and the Future of the European Union," speech in Berlin, November 28, 2011 (www.polonia.nl/wp-content/uploads /radoslaw_sikorski_poland_and_the_future_of_the_eu.pdf).

2. For in-depth studies of German foreign policy after 1949, see Lily Gardner Feldman, *Germany's Foreign Policy of Reconciliation: From Enmity to Amity* (Plymouth, U.K.: Rowman & Littlefield, 2012); Christian Hacke, *Aussenpolitik der Bundesrepublik Deutschland*, rev. ed. (Berlin: Ullstein, 2003).

3. See Jan Techau, "No Strategy Please, We're German," in *Towards a Comprehensive Approach: Strategic and Operational Challenges*, edited by Christopher M. Schnaubelt (Rome: NATO Defense College, 2011), pp. 69–93.

4. And it can even be asked whether Germany is the driver or the driven in the crisis. See Jan Techau, "Germany: Europe's Indispensable Pushover?," *Carnegie Europe's Strategic Europe Blog*, March 5, 2013 (http://carnegieeurope .eu/strategiceurope/?fa=51107&lang=en).

5. Germany's campaign to win a permanent seat on the United Nations Security Council is often seen as an example to the contrary. However, this campaign lost all steam after it became clear that its aspiration to gain the seat was not matched by a willingness to contribute to the costs of international crises in any commensurable way, most notably in the case of Libya after the revolt against President Muammar Qaddafi.

6. Russia is Germany's most important supplier of gas and oil. From January to October 2011, Russia supplied 36 percent of oil imported by Germany. See "Germany's Jan.–Oct. Oil Import Bill Up 31.8 Per Cent," Reuters U.K., December 12, 2011 (http://uk.reuters.com/article/2011/12/12/germany-oil-imports -idUKL6E7NC1UG20111212). In 2007, Russia provided 36 percent of imported German natural gas. See the European Commission staff working document, "Accompanying Document to the Proposal for a Regulation of the European Parliament and of the Council concerning Measures to Safeguard Security of Gas Supply and Repealing Directive 2004/67/EC. Assessment Report of Directive 2004/67/EC on Security of Gas Supply," COM (2009) 363, European Commission, July 16, 2009, pp. 33, 56, 63–76 (http://eur-lex.europa .eu/LexUriServ/LexUriServ.do?uri=SEC:2009:0978:FIN:EN:PDF).

7. See Nikolaus von Twickel, "Putin and Merkel Spar over Human Rights and Pussy Riot," *Moscow Times*, November 17, 2012 (www.themoscowtimes.com /news/article/putin-and-merkel-spar-over-human-rights-and-pussy-riot /471588.html).

8. See "Durch Zusammenarbeit Zivilgesellschaft und Rechtsstaatlichkeit in Russland stärken, Antrag der Fraktionen der CDU/CSU und FDP," *Bundestagsdrucksache* 17/11327, November 6, 2012 (http://dipbt.bundestag.de/dip21 /btd/17/113/1711327.pdf).

9. Chancellor Angela Merkel, speech to the United States Congress, November 3, 2009; Chancellor Angela Merkel, speech to the Knesset, March 18, 2008.

10. The concept of *Zivilmacht* was introduced by German political scientist Hanns W. Maull and has become a widely used paradigm to characterize Germany's foreign policy posture. See Hanns W. Maull, "Deutschland als Zivilmacht," in *Handbuch zur deutschen Außenpolitik*, edited by Siegmar Schmidt, Gunther Hellmann, and Reinhard Wolf (Wiesbaden: Verlag für Sozialwissenschaften, January 2007).

11. Martin Beck, Henner Fürtig, and Hanspeter Mattes, "Herausforderungen deutscher Außenpolitik im Nahen Osten," *GIGAfocus*, no. 6 (December 2008) (urn:nbn:de:0168-ssoar-274125).

12. Diana Hodali, "Controversial Arms Exports to Saudi Arabia," *Deutsche Welle Online*, February 13, 2013 (www.dw.de/controversial-arms-exports-to -saudi-arabia/a-16602151).

13. "German Weapons for the World: How the Merkel Doctrine Is Changing Berlin Policy," *Der Spiegel Online*, December 3, 2012 (www.spiegel .de/international/germany/german-weapons-exports-on-the-rise-as-merkel -doctrine-takes-hold-a-870596.html).

14. Philip Stephens, "Settler Policy Imperils Israel's Foundations," *Financial Times*, February 21, 2013 (www.ft.com/intl/cms/s/0/689d27cc-7a98-11e2-9cc2 -00144feabdc0.html#axzz2LplALYaq).

15. "Remarks by President Trump to the People of Poland," Krasiński Square, Warsaw, July 6, 2017 (www.whitehouse.gov/the-press-office/2017/07/06 /remarks-president-trump-people-poland-july-6-2017).

16. "Remarks by President Trump to the 72nd Session of the United Nations General Assembly," New York, September 19, 2017 (www.whitehouse .gov/the-press-office/2017/09/19/remarks-president-trump-72nd-session -united-nations-general-assembly).

17. Mark Landler and Nicholas Kulish, "In Euro Crisis, Obama Looks to Merkel," *New York Times*, June 15, 2012 (www.nytimes.com/2012/06/16 /world/europe/in-euro-crisis-obama-tries-to-sway-merkel.html?pagewanted =all&_r=0).

18. The now-famous farewell speech of U.S. secretary of defense Robert Gates in Brussels sums up the American position on dwindling European

defense resources. Robert Gates, "The Future of NATO," speech delivered at the Security and Defense Agenda Conference, Brussels, June 10, 2011 (www .defense.gov/speeches/speech.aspx?speechid=1581).

19. Joel Shanton, "Germany Is a 'Drag on NATO'— Says Retired U.S. Diplomat," *Public Service Europe*, May 4, 2012 (www.publicserviceeurope.com /article/1889/germany-is-a-drag-on-nato-says-retired-us-diplomat).

20. Harriet Torry, "China Is Leading Foreign Investor in Germany," *Wall Street Journal*, March 19, 2012 (http://blogs.wsj.com/source/2012/03/19 /china-is-leading-foreign-investor-in-germany/).

21. Hans Kundnani and Jonas Parello-Plesner, "China and Germany: Why the Emerging Special Relationship Matters for Europe," *European Council on Foreign Relations (ECFR) Policy Brief* (May 2012) (http://ecfr.eu/page/-/ECFR55 _CHINA_GERMANY_BRIEF_AW.pdf).

22. Stefan Nicola, "Germany Seeks to Prevent China Solar Dumping Case in Europe," *Renewable Energy World*, August 30, 2012 (www.renewableenergy world.com/rea/news/article/2012/08/germany-seeks-to-prevent-china-solar -dumping-case-in-europe).

23. Kundnani quoted in Didi Kirsten Tatlow, "Germany and China: Too Close for Some," *International Herald Tribune Rendezvous Blog*, May 16, 2012 (http://rendezvous.blogs.nytimes.com/2012/05/16/germany-and-china-a -special-relationship/).

24. Cf. German Defense Minister Thomas de Maizière at the Harvard Germany Conference, February 17, 2012.

25. "A Serious Mistake of Historic Dimensions: Libya Crisis Leaves Berlin Isolated," *Der Spiegel Online*, March 28, 2011 (www.spiegel.de/international /germany/a-serious-mistake-of-historic-dimensions-libya-crisis-leaves-berlin -isolated-a-753498.html).

26. Robert Peston, "How Germany Killed the Merger of BAE and EADS," *BBC Business News Online*, October 10, 2012 (www.bbc.co.uk/news /business-19901540).

27. Techau, "No Strategy Please, We're German."

28. Consider as examples the political fallout created by the resignation of German president Horst Köhler over a radio interview on German economic interests abroad in May 2010, and by the German-ordered air strikes on a Taliban-hijacked fuel tanker in Kunduz, Afghanistan, in September 2009.

29. Sikorski, "Poland and the Future of the European Union."

30. Alexander Neubacher and Catalina Schröder, "The Move to Renew-ables: Germany's Nuclear Phase-Out Brings Unexpected Costs," *Der Spiegel Online*, June 6, 2012 (www.spiegel.de/international/germany/germany-s-nuclear -phase-out-brings-unexpected-costs-to-consumers-a-837007.html).

31. Tom DiChristopher, "Behind Nord Stream 2: The Russia-to-Germany Gas Pipeline That Fueled Trump's Anger at NATO Meeting," CNBC, July 11,

2018 (https://www.cnbc.com/2018/07/11/behind-nord-stream-2-the-russia-to-germany-gas-pipeline-that-fueled-t.html).

32. H. T., "Why Nord Stream 2 Is the World's Most Controversial Energy Project," *The Economist*, August 7, 2018 (https://www.economist.com/the-economist-explains/2018/08/07/why-nord-stream-2-is-the-worlds-most-controversial-energy-project).

33. Offshore Energy Today, "Russia: Go-Ahead for Nord Stream 2 Pipeline Construction," August 15, 2018 (https://www.offshoreenergytoday.com/russia-go-ahead-for-nord-stream-2-pipeline-construction/).

34. Germany is consistently ranked among the top ten, or even top five, most powerful countries in the world in various rankings. See, for example, James Rogers and Luis Simón, "World's Fifteen Most Powerful Countries in 2012," *European Geostrategy Blog*, November 29, 2011 (http://europeangeostrategy.ideasoneurope.eu/2011/12/29/worls-fifteen-most-powerful-countries-in-2012/).

35. For a very detailed discussion of the concept of servant leadership as a program for German foreign policy, see Leon Mangasarian, *Führungsmacht Deutschland: Strategie ohne Angst und Anmaßung* (Munich: dtv Verlagsgesellschaft, 2017). See also Jan Techau, "Germany's Responsibility to Europe Is to Become the Continent's Servant Leader," *Global Brief*, February 7, 2012 (http://globalbrief.ca/blog/2012/02/07%E2%9Cgermanys-responsibility-in-europe-is/).

FIVE

Italy

The Middle Country

FEDERIGA BINDI

Italian foreign policy is the result of many different, and at times competing, variables. The country's history, running from the long and glorious Roman era with its pretensions to civilizing all within its orbit to the short run of a fascist unitary state, has resulted in a mixed legacy in foreign policy arenas, especially following 1945. And despite its renown as the birthplace of some of the world's greatest empires, the country is a small player on the world stage.

With its unique geographic location in the middle of the Mediterranean Sea, between East and West, Italy held a privileged geopolitical role during the Cold War—until the collapse of communism in 1989, which left the country without foreign policy direction. Since then, Italy has struggled to redefine itself in the twenty-first century, wary of its fascist history

---

Parts of this chapter draw on my previous work, Federiga Bindi, *Italy and the European Union* (Brookings Institution Press, 2011), chap. 3, "Italy and the EU in Historical Prospective."

while accepting the loss of "great power" status. Although contemporary Italian foreign policy can be characterized at times by striking contradictions, key pillars of foreign affairs have remained consistent since the 1950s.

After Italian unification in the late nineteenth century, Italy joined alliances either as a means of completing its "natural" borders (mostly obtained through World War I) or to please the "best friend" of the day (as in World War II, though that ultimately concluded in disaster and an alliance shift). Under fascism, the short colonial adventure also left its mark in North Africa.

From the end of World War II (1945) to the fall of the Berlin Wall (1989), Italy found itself in a convenient geopolitical position with continued interest and support from the United States while maintaining a good relationship with the then Soviet Union. The latter bond helped to appease the 30 percent of Italian voters who were members of the Communist Party. Post–World War II, the Italian Republic's foreign policy was thus mainly focused on European integration, transatlantic relations, relations with the Soviet Union, the Mediterranean, and more sensitive relations with the former Yugoslavia and Albania. This scenario was considered a "blocked" foreign policy, or a foreign policy in stasis because the country was suspended between the East and the West and domestically between communist and anticommunist political forces. The foreign policy framework, however, suited Italy, a midsize country that could play the role of a "big" Western state, a status confirmed through its participation in the G-7/G-8.

Added to this was the absolute rejection of national interest promotion—a legacy of the fascist period. The concept of national interest was therefore replaced with a vaguer "European interest." In 1994, Silvio Berlusconi, then prime minister, was the first leader to push for a change in this status quo in his first speech to parliament, urging a robust Italian approach to the country's own interests in negotiating within the European Union.[1] That produced an outcry in both Italian public opinion and the media. It would take a few years before the term was again used in public discourse by the former communist leader Massimo D'Alema, when he became prime minister in 1998. Today, a shared consensus exists in the country that national interest should be at the center of both European and foreign policies.

As the Berlin Wall collapsed, so did the Italian domestic political system—itself based on the dichotomy between East (the Communist Party) and West (the Christian Democrats and their allies). No longer a geostrategic partner for the United States or the Soviet Union, Italy found itself deprived of a role, attention, and means. In 1993, former ambassador and historian Sergio Romano wrote:

> Unhappily, the regime is dying, while the position Italy has occupied for the last 45 years is disappearing entirely. That position was an element in a delicate mechanism whose counterweights were European integration, the United States, the Atlantic Alliance and the Soviet Union. . . . Italy no longer knows what it can reasonably expect and lacks the means to obtain its goals. Italy no longer has a foreign policy because its objectives and its instruments have disappeared, all at once.[2]

The parochial Italian leadership had never reflected on how the country's privileged position could easily be lost. The status quo was considered immutable and Italy's role as a big country as deserved rather than the result of peculiar historical and geopolitical variables. Compared to Germany—where the leadership had always operated knowing that reunification of the eastern and western parts of the country would come eventually and had prepared for a new, more assertive German role in the world—the Italian leadership found itself unprepared and unable to elaborate a new paradigm for the country's foreign policy. If the symbol of the new German foreign policy was the fight for a permanent seat on the UN Security Council, the symbol of post–Cold War Italy was the fight *against* a German seat on the Security Council, but masked as a need for a global reform of the Council (admittedly a good point per se).

It took twenty years for the Farnesina (foreign ministry) to begin reflecting on the future of Italian foreign policy. In 2008 Marta Dassù—then a foreign minister adviser—sought to articulate a new approach in a paper, "Rapporto Italia 2020," which for the first time looked at Italian foreign policy in a pragmatic, midterm way. "Rapporto Italia 2020," left unfinished, identified European integration, transatlantic relations, the Balkans, the Mediterranean area and the Middle East, Russia, and energy policy as Italian priorities.[3] As the government changed, however, Dassù's objectives were left on the wayside. When she became deputy foreign minister in 2011, she was unable to finish her own interrupted work.

Italy and the European Union

Italy's loss in World War II led to regime change and a new Republican Constitution, enacted in January 1948. The Christian Democrat leader and prime minister, Alcide De Gasperi, believed that Italy needed to be embedded in multilateral institutions as soon as possible. Italy was thus part of the Bretton Woods Agreement (October 2, 1946) and accepted as a member of the International Monetary Fund (March 27, 1947). Because it had accepted the Paris Peace Treaties of 1947, Italy could take part in the negotiations around the Marshall Plan (thus being a founding member of the Organization for European Economic Cooperation in 1948) and the establishment in 1949 of the Council of Europe. The ratification of the North Atlantic Treaty by Italy's parliament on March 3, 1949, signaled that the country had officially left the World War II shadow behind.

At the time of the Schuman Declaration in May 1950, Italy was a poor, former fascist dictatorship, with an agriculture-based economy and high rates of unemployment. Due to the political uncertainties, foreign financial help was slow to arrive. In the minds of Prime Minister De Gasperi and Foreign Minister Carlo Sforza, membership in the European Coal and Steel Community (ECSC) would secure the newborn Italian democracy: The decision to join the ECSC was supported by many political leaders but opposed by other influential actors, such as the Socialist and Communist parties and the steel industry.

When in Messina, in June 1955, the six ECSC foreign ministers called for further integration among them, the French prime minister, Pierre Mendès-France—fearing large numbers of Italian immigrants—tried to prevent Rome from joining the new organization. However, dramatic international events then provided the necessary impetus for sealing the negotiations: the invasion of Hungary (November 4, 1956) and the nationalization of the Suez Canal (July 20, 1956). Thus, in March 1957 the treaties creating the European Economic Community (EEC) and Euratom (nuclear research and training) were signed in the Italian capital, Rome. In Italy, the invasion of Hungary had a lasting effect also on domestic politics: The Socialist Party (PSI) sharply criticized the USSR's intervention and broke its alliance with the communists, thus becoming pro-European, soon making it a partner in the various government coalitions that characterized Italy in the years to follow. On the other side, the Italian Communist

Party would only begin to change its attitude toward the process of European integration in the 1970s.

When the third Arab-Israeli conflict erupted in October 1973, Italy was especially hard hit by the increase in oil prices, which were affecting all of Europe. The end of the U.S. dollar's convertibility into gold also hit Italy, weakening the national currency, the lira. EEC member states first tried to protect themselves through the "European Monetary Snake"—the precursor of the European Monetary System—beginning in March 1972, but this mechanism was not enough to protect the Italian lira. Once the European Monetary System (EMS) came into force in 1978, Italy was forced to seek a partial opt-out, a decision that earned it the unflattering nickname of European Cinderella.

The political and economic crises that characterized Europe in the 1970s finally ended by the mid-1980s. Meanwhile, European political geography had changed, with the arrival in power of François Mitterrand in France (1981) and Helmut Kohl in Germany (1982). Despite personal and political differences, they were to become the heart of Europe. In Italy, the leading political figure was Giulio Andreotti, who served repeatedly as prime minister and foreign minister in the numerous coalition governments that characterized Italy in the decade and whose skillfulness at negotiation and creating alliances avoided the sidelining of Italian interests. Under Andreotti, Italy reached the peak of its influence in the European Communities and later the European Union.

In 1985 Andreotti was first able to unlock the stalemate preventing Spain and Portugal from signing the accession treaties to the EEC; then, at the European Council in Milan (June 28–29, 1985)—against the United Kingdom and Greece's opposition—he led the European Council into calling for an Intergovernmental Conference (IGC), which negotiated the first major revision of the EEC Treaty—the so-called Single European Act. Serving in the EEC presidency in 1990—right after the fall of the Berlin Wall—Andreotti successfully paved the way for the creation of the euro, ultimately leading to Margaret Thatcher's defeat and resignation at home (November 28, 1990).

The fall of the Berlin Wall (November 9, 1989), however, had lasting consequences on Italian domestic politics and, consequently, on its ability to shape European politics. The end of communism had, in fact, rendered the Italian party system outdated and led to the rise of new political actors such as Forza Italia and the Northern League, as well as post-Communist and post–Christian Democrat parties. Such new parties, however, lacked the credibility of their precursors among their peers. As two successive sets of enlargements—to the north in 1995 and to the east in 2004—also shifted the European geographic balance, Italy progressively drifted away from the EU core.

In March 1994 a right-wing coalition led by Silvio Berlusconi won the elections. For the first time, an Italian government was expressing rather anti-European sentiments. Also, for the first time, Italy was isolated in Europe: none of the government coalition parties belonged to major European political families, and a number of European counterparts objected to the presence of Alleanza Nazionale (the post-fascists) in the government. Silvio Berlusconi learned a hard lesson and devoted much of his energy in the following years to make Forza Italia a member of a major European party, the European People's Party (EEP). The architect of Forza Italia's admission into the EEP was Antonio Tajani, currently the president of the European Parliament.

In 1996, the center-left Olive Tree coalition won the elections. The Prodi I government (headed by Romano Prodi) made a concerted effort to relocate Italy within the European arena. But Prodi's government suffered from the anti-European stance of its post-communist ally, Rifondazione Comunista, which had reverted to the original communist opposition to both European integration and NATO.

Silvio Berlusconi returned to power in 2001, this time with a strong pro-American stance. He tried—with some degree of success—to use his personal relationship with George W. Bush to gain influence in the European arena. Despite all efforts, however, the Italian EU presidency of 2003 was far less successful than previous ones. Without French or German support, Italy faced a deadlock in the negotiations of the so-called Draft Treaty establishing a constitution for Europe, ultimately issuing a statement declaring that negotiations had failed and asking the Irish presidency to continue consultations.

After five years in power, Berlusconi was narrowly defeated in legislative elections. Back in power, Romano Prodi sought to relocate European integration at the center of Italian foreign policy, going back to the "traditional" Christian Democrats' approach to European integration—equating Italian interests with those of all Europe.[4] However, Prodi's narrow majority in parliament did not create the foundations for a long reign, and the Prodi II government fell after less than two years.

May 2008 marked Silvio Berlusconi's return yet again. This time he chose to focus on domestic politics, thus essentially leaving European policy and most foreign policy to the foreign minister, Franco Frattini. By that time, European policy again was a consensual policy in Italy, as a unanimous vote in the Italian parliament to ratify the Lisbon Treaty in August 2008 showed. However, squeezed between a rising Italian public deficit spread and his own sexual scandals, and without the support of the new administration of Barack Obama in the United States, Berlusconi was forced to resign in November 2011.

Following this resignation, a string of unelected prime ministers, mostly chosen for their "credibility" in Europe, took over. Mario Monti (2011–13) and Enrico Letta (2013–14) were two cases in point; accordingly, they both believed EU relations were to be at the top of the government's list. Then, in February 2014, Matteo Renzi became the youngest prime minister in Italian history. Contrary to Monti and Letta, Renzi had no experience in foreign and European policies, and he tended to consider them a dependent variable of domestic politics, with special attention paid to photo-ops with relevant foreign leaders. He skillfully mixed rhetorical references to Europe—he often referred to himself as being part of the "Erasmus generation" (European students who spent at least a term in university in an EU state other than their own on an EU grant), despite never actually having been one—with virulent attacks on dull-witted "European bureaucrats." In fact, his approach to European politics echoed those of Berlusconi in 1994 because of his confrontational approach and his two mantras: Italy has a right to a "leading role in Europe," and "'Europe'" cannot tell Italy what to do." In July 2014, Renzi did not hesitate to cause a diplomatic row when his EU counterparts failed to support his foreign minister, Federica Mogherini, as the EU High Representative (EUHR). In fact, it probably would have better served Italy for Enrico Letta to be named president of the EU Council—as many had suggested. Renzi had resolutely opposed this other appointment—despite the generalized consensus in Europe—based on pure domestic calculations.

Transatlantic Relations

After World War II, the leaders of the main Italian parties—the Christian
Democrat Alcide De Gasperi, the communist Palmiro Togliatti, and the
socialist Pietro Nenni—united to form a coalition government, led by De
Gasperi, which lasted from the end of 1945 to June 1947. However, the condition set by the U.S. government for Italy to participate in the Marshall
Plan was that communists and socialists had to leave the government. The
old films showing Prime Minister Alcide De Gasperi's travel to Washington in 1947 to reassure the American ally of Italy's firm anchorage in the
West are the visual embodiment of the U.S. influence on Italian domestic
politics.[5] In 1948, the CIA determined that the victory of anticommunist
forces in Italy was in the national interest of the United States, which led
to the agency's first covert operation to influence the elections of a foreign
country.

Italy soon became interested in the negotiations of what was to become
the North Atlantic Alliance. France strongly opposed Norwegian membership, but supported Italian participation, which it saw as a guarantee of
better strategic protection of Corsica and Algeria. Great Britain, on the
other hand, opposed Italian participation because of the country's fragile
economic and political situation. The British suggested that Italy should
belong to a Mediterranean pact, separate from the North Atlantic system.

For the United States, Italy represented a serious problem. Geographically speaking, it was not an Atlantic country. Italy was also not expected
to contribute much militarily. Politically speaking, however, the United
States saw Italy's exclusion from the North Atlantic Alliance as potentially
dangerous. Given its former enemy status, an Italy without close ties to
other European countries might assume an isolationist position. Moreover,
with a strong Communist Party, Italy risked being influenced by the Soviet
Union. Italy was therefore included as one of the founding members of the
North Atlantic security system. As part of a comprehensive deal, Norway
also became part of the North Atlantic Alliance.

Domestically, both the communists and socialists opposed membership in the North Atlantic Treaty. The Socialist Party asked—to no
avail—for a popular referendum, and its leader, Pietro Nenni, affirmed
that with the signature of the treaty, "the Third War had been launched."[6]
The Italian Communist Party was, at the time, totally subjugated to the
Soviet Communist Party (PCUS). But even the left fringes of the Chris-

tian Democrats, led by Giuseppe Dossetti and Giovanni Gronchi, were in favor of keeping an equidistant relationship with the two superpowers, the United States and the Soviet Union. They thus favored a neutral, non-aligned Italy and opposed Italy's signing of the North Atlantic Treaty. Since the communists and the socialists were expected to vote against the treaty, De Gasperi desperately needed all of his party's votes in parliament.[7] To garner votes he used Italy's inclusion in the Council of Europe to "sell" Atlantic integration to his own party. In signing the North Atlantic Treaty on April 4, 1949, De Gasperi also underlined its political rather than military aspects.

Since then, transatlantic relations have remained one of the pillars of Italian foreign policy, though—in the last twenty years—with different flavors according to the party in office.

Fast-forward to the 1990s, when the center-left Olive Tree coalition won the elections. The Prodi I government suffered from the antagonistic stance of its post-communist ally Rifondazione Comunista in transatlantic relations. Relations with the United States thus suffered various blows: from Rome's frequent opening to Libya, North Korea, and Iran (all of which irritated Washington); to the Ocalan affair and the Cermis incident; to the negotiations in Rambouillet over Serbia (which some have defined as "critical Atlanticism").[8] The intervention in Kosovo in 1995, supported by both political coalitions in parliament, somehow reversed this trend. The cost in domestic political terms was however high, as both communists and Catholics saw their inherent pacifism challenged. Ironically, Italy's participation in the Kosovo effort took place under the new prime minister—former communist leader Massimo D'Alema—who, like many former communists-turned-democrats, was now eager to please Washington.

After the brief 1996 stint, Silvio Berlusconi returned to power in 2001, this time with a stronger parliamentary majority, giving him more freedom to mold foreign policy than any government before. His staunch pro-American (and pro–G. W. Bush) position was unprecedented in Italy, and this cost the country dearly in terms of relations with traditional European and Middle East partners. According to Filippo Andreatta, that scenario led to an "unbalanced foreign policy in which bilateral relations with the Bush administration took precedent over multilateral relations with Europe, leading to frequent tensions with EU institutions and partners. . . . Most prominent was the support given to the Bush administration's global war on terror after 9/11, which implied significant and unprecedented positions."[9]

Berlusconi focused much of his "personal diplomacy" to build a preferential relation with the Russian president, Vladimir Putin, while at the same time investing in relations with countries like the United Kingdom and Israel. According to Elisabetta Brighi, the government seemed to believe that "a more assertive Italian foreign policy" came via Washington, thus the government equated Atlanticism with nationalism.[10] In reality, Berlusconi used his special relationship with President George W. Bush to gain influence in the European arena and—vice versa—he tried to accredit himself with the American administration as the most reliable European partner.

Relationships with the United States deteriorated again during the Prodi II government (2006–08), whose first move in foreign politics was the withdrawal of Italian troops from Iraq.[11] Now foreign minister, Massimo D'Alema had a rocky relationship with Condoleezza Rice, something that later would also harm his chances to become the first European Union High Representative in 2009.

In May 2008 Silvio Berlusconi once again became head of the government. While he had initially reestablished a more positive relationship with the United States under the Bush administration, with the arrival of President Barack Obama in 2009, Berlusconi lost this "special relationship." Obama was said to be particularly fond of one of Berlusconi's successors, Enrico Letta, with whom Obama shared a similar temperament. Letta, however, left government after just one year, ousted by Matteo Renzi. Renzi idolized the forty-fourth American president, copying his motto "Yes We Can" for his convention, called "La Leopolda," from the venue where it gathered in Florence. Renzi's extreme personalization of foreign policy and skilled use of social media were all focused to give the impression that he had a much stronger relationship with the United States than was the reality. Eager to prove himself to Obama, Renzi went as far as committing to pro-U.S. policies without effective parliamentary scrutiny—the purchase of the F-24 fighter-bombers and Italy's support in Iraq are cases in point.

Russia

The relations between Russia and Italy date back centuries, as any visitor to Saint Petersburg—built by Italian architects centuries ago—can easily see. During the Cold War, Italy viewed itself as a bridge between the East and West and pursued open dialogue and economic partnerships with the

Soviet Union. Substantial Italian investments were made in Russia—the city of Togliattigrad, which was built by FIAT, being a case in point. When the founding treaty of the Council of Europe was signed in May 1949, to please the leftist parties, the Italian government also negotiated a commercial agreement with Moscow, thus initiating what was to become a flourishing cooperation between the two countries.[12]

The fall of the Eastern Bloc in 1989 and the Soviet Union in 1991 caused some policy confusion in Italy but did not fundamentally harm the Russo-Italian relationship. Italy-Russia relations, however, suffered a hit with Russia's controversial decision to occupy and annex the Crimean region while antagonizing Ukraine in its eastern provinces. Italy supported the European consensus that Russia's actions were unlawful and—somewhat reluctantly—participated in the sanction program established by the international community to prevent a wider conflict. Areas like Veneto—where exports to Russia sharply declined—have been very vocal in expressing their discontent with the sanction regime, bringing such discontent into the domestic political arena. Trade and finance relations certainly dipped because of the sanctions, but the ties between the two countries continue to be strong. Russia is Italy's largest supplier of fossil fuels, particularly natural gas, despite cuts in demand in Italy. Both countries have also heavily invested in each other's economies. The mutual investment continues today, and Italy is Russia's sixth largest importer and exporter. Despite the bold declarations in favor of both Russia and its leader, Putin, Italy has continued supporting EU sanctions under the Five Star–Lega government.

Middle East and the Mediterranean

The Mediterranean and the Middle East are natural areas of interest for Italy because of its geographic location near the shores of North Africa. Italy's chief concerns have long been maintaining stability and peace in the wider Mediterranean region, as well as securing safety and durability of its major energy suppliers. How far Italy has pursued these concerns has depended on the government in power and the circumstances. In 2001 and 2003, the Berlusconi government provided troops and logistical support for the U.S.-led invasions of Afghanistan and Iraq in solidarity with Italy's NATO allies. However, as those wars dragged on, Italy withdrew its assets and eventually pulled out in 2006 under Prodi's leadership. Also in 2006,

Italy led the negotiations and peacekeeper intervention in the renewed conflict zone in Lebanon, which successfully prevented a full-blown civil war.
This assured stability and Italian influence in the far Mediterranean and
opened the door for Italian cooperation with Middle Eastern states.[13]

Italy also has a special relationship with Libya. Relations between the two
countries have oscillated over the years but were always important and critical for both. Libya was an Italian colony from 1912 to 1947, following the
1911 occupation. By 1940, 120,000 Italians lived in the country, a number
that dramatically dropped during World War II. By 1962, under the new
Libyan monarchy, there were still some 35,000 Italians living there. When
Muammar Qaddafi took power, however, Italians were brutally expelled,
and the new leader sought compensation for the colonial period.

However, Italy's geostrategic position, its dependence on Arab oil markets, its activism in North Africa, and its only partial subordination to
American pro-Israel policies enabled Rome to collaborate with Libya's Revolutionary Command Council. Italy played a bridge role between Libya
and the West, counterbalancing the spreading Soviet influence within the
Arab world.[14] For instance, Prime Minister Giulio Andreotti in 1978 paid
a visit to Tripoli to soften Libya's resistance to the Camp David Peace
Accords.[15]

At the beginning of the 1980s, with the new administration of Ronald
Reagan, confrontation between Washington and Tripoli rose. Libya was
accused of international terrorism and was included in the list of "rogue
states." Two approaches prevailed in the Western world: the inclusive
approach and the coercive approach. The first one was the one preferred
by Italy: it aimed at preventing the regime from feeling frustrated or
isolated and at moderating Libya's radicalism and unpredictability. The
coercive approach, generally favored by the United States, was mainly based
on economic and diplomatic confrontation, thereby including sanctions
and embargos, and was considered the most immediate way to deal with
Libya. Italy's decision in the first half of the 1980s to let the Reagan
administration install cruise missiles in Comiso jeopardized its relations
with Libya.

A series of events in the 1980s compromised Italy's approach to Middle
Eastern affairs and left the country in an uncomfortable grip. Among these
were the terrorist attack at West Berlin's La Belle Nightclub and the American response, culminating in the bombing of Benghazi and Tripoli (aimed
at destroying Qaddafi's political regime), installation of Libyan missiles on

Italy's southern island of Lampedusa, and the bombing of Pan Am Flight 103 over Lockerbie, Scotland, followed by UN sanctions and embargos.[16]

In the 1990s the recognition of Israel, the weight of UN sanctions, and the increased pressures of domestic opposition—especially in the Benghazi area—led Qaddafi to readdress his relations with the West. Libya's progressive opening to the West began at the end of the 1990s, backed by Italy's diplomatic and political cooperation. Rome's diplomacy helped a country that was struggling to overcome its isolation. It was then that Italy truly embodied its role as a bridge between Libya and Europe. A joint declaration was signed in 1998. Italy acknowledged its colonial responsibilities, and the two governments agreed to set up a Joint Italian-Libyan Company aimed at undertaking joint development projects in Libya. Evidence of Libya's good intentions came in 1998, when it officially became the first country to issue an Interpol arrest warrant against Osama bin Laden, claiming that al Qaeda had collaborated with local radicals. In addition, on April 5, 1999, Libya's decision to hand over the two suspects in the Lockerbie affair brought about both the suspension of sanctions and the implementation of normalization policies with the United States and other European states.[17]

Italian-Libyan relations rapidly upgraded as soon as the sanctions were lifted. By the end of 1999, one-fourth of Italy's petroleum needs were met by Libya, the most economical source available given its geographic proximity. Italy was becoming Libya's largest partner, buying 43 percent of its exports, mostly oil and gas.[18]

The attacks of 9/11 gave Tripoli's leader the opportunity to prove his bona fides in supporting the West in the international battle against terrorism. Qaddafi firmly condemned the terrorist violence and atrocities, assured his support to the United States, even recognizing its right to revenge, and offered the services of the Libyan intelligence network. In 2003 he renounced atomic weapons. At the same time, however, he kept a close eye on human traffickers' use of Libyan coasts as a jumping-off point for African illegal immigrants who wanted to reach Italy and Europe. Migratory issues have thus always been a bit of a thorn in the side for Italy-Libya relations.

Rome has generally been in favor of an integrated approach to immigration, which means both stopping and preventing illegal immigration and encouraging regular flows while promoting local development. Italian governments have long worked to build a model of cooperative security in the Mediterranean area, trying to promote collaboration between naval forces and other competent bodies for rescue operations and joint patrols in the fight against organized crime and illegal migratory flows. Curbing illegal immigration was a major part of negotiations surrounding the Friendship Treaty finally signed by Italy and Libya in 2008. The treaty established mixed Libyan-Italian patrolling and sophisticated electronic surveillance of the Libyan coasts by Italian companies. In exchange, Italy compensated for its colonial past by promising to improve Libya's infrastructure through Italian firms. Each country also pledged to prevent hostile attacks on the other from being launched from each territory.

The treaty had immediate effects with a measurable decrease in illegal immigration, but it was voided by the war in Libya, which began when France attacked Libya in 2011 with the help of the United Kingdom. Prime Minister Berlusconi offered to serve as a negotiator between Libya and the West. A "golden exile" for Qaddafi was discussed. President Obama, meanwhile, was deeply wary of another military venture in a Muslim country. Most of his senior advisers were telling him to stay out. Secretary of State Hillary Clinton, however, persuaded Obama to join the allies in bombing Colonel Qaddafi's forces. According to the *New York Times*, Defense Secretary Robert M. Gates would later say that in a "'51-49' decision, it was Mrs. Clinton's support that put the ambivalent president over the line."[19] Clinton soon set to work to convince Italy to join the war, too, sending personal emissaries to Italy to convince the president and the government to join. Despite a divided foreign ministry over the issue, those in favor of war eventually prevailed with the support of then president Giorgio Napolitano. Italy pushed for strict parameters of the no-fly zone and other military intervention measures under international organizations to ensure that humanitarian intervention was actually taking place and to prevent any one state from unduly influencing the future of the Libyan government.

However, the consequences of the war would be more far reaching than anyone imagined, leaving Libya a failed state and a terrorist haven, as well as a point of departure for the massive numbers of people fleeing the wars in the Middle East and widespread poverty and violence in African states such as Sudan, Nigeria, and others. Having spent significant resources on sea rescues and care of these illegal immigrants, while continuing to bear this burden, Italy sees securing stability across the Mediterranean as a priority.[20] The Lega and Five Star government, under Deputy Prime Minister Matteo Salvini's leadership, has since taken a tougher approach to immigration, including refusing to rescue immigrants at sea—leading to a decrease in the numbers of illegal immigrants coming from the sea.

The Balkans

Italy has a long-standing and tumultuous relationship with its Eastern neighbors. Italy has continued to exert either influence or direct control over the Balkans for centuries, ever since the region was part of the Roman Empire. While contemporary states in the region are aware of this long history, Italian policy in the post–Cold War environment has sought to assert positive aspects of shared history between the region and Italy and foster a warm diplomatic environment.

Before World War I, the newly established Italian kingdom sought to acquire territory in the Balkans, explicitly expressing this intent with the signing of the Triple Alliance Treaty with Germany and Austria-Hungary. This, of course, included much of the territory of the Austro-Hungarian Empire, but Germany and Austria-Hungary were desperate for a third partner to counter Britain, France, and Russia. Amid the chaos of the war, Italy broke from the Triple Alliance, however, and joined the Allies, thus ultimately resulting as a "winner" after the war. The northeastern territories south of the Alps were awarded to Italy, but its territorial claims to the Balkans were stifled by the American president, Woodrow Wilson, who sought to affirm the right to self-determination in the Balkans, resulting in the Yugoslavian state in 1918.

Benito Mussolini's quest to reestablish the glory of the Roman Empire during World War II included reasserting claims in the region and culminated in the occupation of Dalmatia and the war in Albania—both of which were quickly lost following defeat in that war. Soon after, Yugoslavia was granted control over the once-occupied Dalmatian Coast; Yugoslav leader, Josip Tito, then rejected Stalin and joined the nonalignment movement. This proved to be invaluable to Italian security as Yugoslavia provided a buffer state to the communist bloc.

Yet this geopolitical arrangement was not to last. The death of Tito in 1980 and the collapse of the Soviet Union in 1991 contributed to renewed ethnic turmoil in the Balkans. During the Yugoslav civil war (1991–95), Italy sought to maintain good relations with Belgrade (Serbia) while minimizing the violence, but these efforts proved fruitless, and the country was forced to support NATO operations to quell the conflict. During the Kosovo War from 1998 to 1999, Italy begrudgingly allowed its western airbases to be used as staging areas for NATO bombings.

Italy continues to see the Balkans as the bridge between East and West and has heavily invested politically and economically in the area. Some of the finest Italian diplomats—from Fernando Gentilini to Ettore Sequi, Massimo Gaiani, and the current Italian ambassador to the United States, Armando Varricchio—have served in various capacities in the area.

Conclusion

Italy is a midsize country in terms of power and influence in the twenty-first century. Because of its geostrategic position, during the Cold War it retained the status of a big country, sanctioned with its inclusion in the Group of Seven (G-7). The end of the Cold War changed this prominence, although in recent years Italy's location in the Mediterranean region has once again given the country some status, but this has not necessarily translated into influence.

Cuts to the state budget due to unresolved economic issues have also hurt the country's foreign policy strategy. Unable to be a global player, and with a diplomatic staff of just over 2,000, the country has had to choose its priorities. Two main pillars of Italian foreign policy remain European integration and transatlantic relations, closely followed by Russia, the Mediterranean area (especially the migrant problem), and the Balkans.

At times, Italian governments have used relations with the United States to acquire influence within the EU or, vice versa, using Italy's influence in the EU to gain traction in Washington. Notable about past foreign policy is Italy's role during the Cold War as a mostly independent player in the Middle East—a role that has been diminished because the country has joined the United States, often against its own interests, especially in the case of Libya.

NOTES

1. Mario Platero, "L'Italia e l'appuntamento con la Storia," *Il Sole 24 Ore*, May 17, 1994.

2. Sergio Romano, *Guida alla politica esterna italiana* (Milan: Rizzoli, 1993), p. 109.

3. "Rapporto Italia 2020: Le scelte di politica estera," Ministero degli Affari Esteri, 2008, p. 15.

4. In an early speech in front of the Italian parliament (May 18, 2006), Romano Prodi affirmed: "We are convinced that the Italian national interest and the European interest are one and the same. We are convinced that Italy will count—even in relations with its greatest ally—only if it counts in Europe. We will work to put Italy back among the leaders of a new Europe" (www .camera.it). See also "Discorso del premier al Senato prima del voto di fiducia," video, 3:53, July 11, 2017 (www.youtube.com/watch?v=NzP-RfJ8FVE).

5. See www.youtube.com/watch?v=aQLDtPpEds0.

6. G. Scirocco, "Il PSI dell'antiatlantismo alla riscoperta dell'Europa (1948–1957)," in *Atlantismo e Europeismo*, edited by P. Craveri and G. Quagliarello (Soveria Mannelli: Rubettino, 2003), p. 158.

7. V. Capperucci, "La sinistra democristiana e la difficile integrazione tra Europa e America (1945–1958)," in *Atlantismo e Europeismo*, edited by Craveri and Quagliarello, pp. 71–93.

8. Elisabetta Brighi, "Europe, the USA, and the 'Policy of the Pendulum': The Importance of Foreign Policy Paradigms in the Foreign Policy of Italy (1989–2005), *Journal of Southern Europe and the Balkans* 9, no. 2 (August 2007), pp. 99–115.

9. Filippo Andreatta, "La sfida dell'Unione Eurpea alla teoria delle relazioni Internazionali," in *L'Europa Sicura: le politiche di sicurezza dell'Unione Europea*, edited by S. Giusti and A. Locatelli (Milan: Egea, 2008), p. 175.

10. Brighi, "Europe, the USA, and the 'Policy of the Pendulum,'" p. 104.

11. "Prodi: 'Italia fuori dalla guerra Rispetteremo gli impegni per ritiro,'" *La Repubblica*, April 12, 2006 (http://www.repubblica.it/2006/04/sezioni/politica /elezioni-2006-3/via-dall-iraq/via-dall-iraq.html).

12. A. Varsori, *L'Italia nelle relazioni internazionali dal 1943 al 1992* (Rome: Laterza, 1998), p. 74.

13. Maria Elena Amadori, "Italy: the Three Circles Approach of Foreign Policy," *Mediterranean Affairs*, July 19, 2016 (http://mediterraneanaffairs.com /italy-three-circle-approach-foreign-policy/).

14. Karim Mezran and Paola De Maio, "Between the Past and the Future: Has a Shift Occurred in Italian-Libyan Relations?," *Journal of North African Studies* 12 (December 4, 2007), pp. 439–51.

15. Ibid., p. 441.

16. Ibid., p. 442.

17. Luis Martinez, *The Libyan Paradox* (Oxford University Press, 2007).

18. Mezran and De Maio, "Between the Past and the Future," p. 445.

19. Jo Becker and Scott Shane, "The Libya Gamble, Part I: Hillary Clinton, 'Smart Power,' and a Dictator's Fall," *New York Times*, February 27, 2016.

20. "Why Is Italy Seeing a Record Number of Migrants?," BBC.com, November 29, 2016.

SIX

Great Britain's Foreign Policy Dilemmas

KLAUS LARRES

F ormer U.S. secretary of state Dean Acheson's famous and controversial 1962 statement that Britain had "lost an empire and not yet found a role" captured the British dilemma well.[1] This was the case during the Cold War and, as will be seen, it still remains. To the present day, British foreign policymakers continue to view the United Kingdom as a major international power.

The general perception outside the United Kingdom—be it in Washington, Beijing, or Berlin—is somewhat different, however. Even within the European context, Britain was increasingly being left behind even before Brexit. To a large extent this occurred because of a lack of strategic foresight and intelligent decisionmaking and an inability to come to terms with an imperial past and transcend it. In the globalized world of the post–Cold War era and more than seventy years since the end of World War II, Britain continues to flounder and still finds it difficult to find a niche for itself. Yet the country has managed to continue punching above its real weight in global affairs.

This chapter outlines the major features of British foreign policy in the post–Cold War era. Subsequently it considers Britain's national interest in areas such as defense (including NATO issues) and some others. It also looks at the British position toward some international organizations, in particular the European Union. I begin by providing a brief analysis of Britain's Cold War foreign policy in the years from 1945 to 1990, when the country and its foreign policymakers were even more convinced than they were in the post–Cold War years that the United Kingdom naturally belongs to the world's selective club of great powers. Essentially Britain has remained caught in a Churchillian foreign policy framework.[2]

British Foreign Policy during the Cold War

Throughout the Cold War years, London's global influence, as well as Britain's role as an effective international power broker, allowed the United Kingdom to have a disproportionate influence in global politics. The country's network of global connections that went back to the era of empire and British hegemony, Britain's reputation as a trusted ally of the United States, and its military and foreign policy professionalism contributed greatly to the perception that the United Kingdom was much more influential than it really was. London's impressive expertise in all matters of intelligence and counterintelligence, and not least the country's high-quality armaments industry, also played a role.[3]

It makes sense to differentiate between three distinct phases of British foreign policy during the Cold War, as described below.

The Early Cold War Era (1945–56)

During these years Britain benefited from its World War II victor status and continued to be seen as a real world power. However, the domestic and external problems the country had to grapple with were piling up. The establishment of the welfare state, including the beneficial but also very costly National Health Service, and Britain's onerous far-flung commitments abroad greatly overextended the country.

Reliance on the United States was essential to avoid bankruptcy in the early Cold War years. Britain hoped to obtain a generous long-term loan from Washington; the loan it eventually received was much less generous and much more reluctantly extended than London had expected in view of its wartime sacrifices and the new Soviet threat. An early Anglo-American effort to roll back communism was attempted in late 1948. In Albania, the infiltration of Western-trained saboteurs and resistance fighters with the intent to cause uprisings and bring down Enver Hoxha's communist state failed miserably, however. Already Britain's involvement in the Greek Civil War on the side of the anticommunist royalist forces had to be scaled back for economic reasons. Britain's reduction of its commitments abroad led to the dramatically announced Truman Doctrine of March 1947 and Washington's takeover of the fight against communism on a global scale.[4]

Despite Britain's victory over Nazi Germany, Germany continued to be a major headache for British policymakers. As one of the four occupation powers, London had to support the former enemy to prevent widespread starvation and help to reconstruct the German economy and reeducate the German people. Then, in the context of the Korean War, London was persuaded by the United States to agree to the expensive rearmament of the new West German state so that more forces would be available on the European continent if the Red Army were to invade. This latter scenario was seen as a distinct possibility.[5]

Furthermore, despite its economic predicaments and rising nationalist sentiments almost everywhere, Britain somehow still had to find the resources and the will to manage its far-flung colonial interests and military commitments abroad. The independence of India in August 1947, accompanied by a vicious civil war, and the return of Britain's mandate for Palestine (which also led to a major war) to the newly founded UN in 1948 started a process of decolonization that would continue through the 1960s and much of the 1970s. With the peaceful return of Hong Kong to China in 1997, Britain gave up its last major colony. The sun had finally set for good on the empire.[6]

To countenance its diminishing conventional military resources, Britain embarked on the top-secret building of its own atomic bomb in the late 1940s and subsequently its own hydrogen bomb. A first British test explosion occurred in 1954, and an H-bomb was successfully tested three years later. These were major scientific achievements, but they were very costly and essentially unaffordable. However, British policymakers were convinced, as were most American politicians at the time, that relying on nuclear weapons provided the country with much greater "bang for the buck" than the highly expensive upkeep of large conventional armies. Throughout the Cold War years, London actively sought to intensify its partnership with the United States, but trust went only so far. The British did not wish to rely solely on the American nuclear umbrella; they found it much more reassuring to possess "the bomb" themselves. Prestige and Britain's international standing as a great power also seemed to require the possession of nuclear weapons.[7]

London did not see the need to join the continental European countries in the establishment of the supranational European Coal and Steel Community (Schuman Declaration) of 1952 and a few years later refused to participate in the formation of the European Economic Community (EEC). Giving up even a degree of sovereignty to a European entity was anathema in Britain. Anthony Eden, the prime minister, for instance, proclaimed that he felt it in his bones that his country had more in common with the old colonies of Australia, New Zealand, Canada, and South Africa than with its neighbors on the European continent. Already during these early years, the stage was set for Britain's never-resolved dilemma: whether to regard itself as a European country.[8]

The Post-Suez Years (1957–1970s)

During this second phase of Britain's Cold War foreign policy, the country's global influence diminished at an accelerating rate and the European question could no longer be ignored. Britain, France, and Israel's 1956 invasion of Egypt to undo President Gamal Abdel Nasser's nationalization of the Suez Canal proved to be a major disaster that clearly revealed the two European powers' fall from great power status. U.S. president Dwight D. Eisenhower, who had not been consulted, used economic pressure to make Britain abort the recapture of its old Suez Canal military base just a day before it would have been achieved. Without U.S. agreement, it appeared, Britain (and, by implication, France) was no longer in a position to embark on military adventures abroad.[9]

In the aftermath of the crisis, which in London led to the replacement of Eden with a new prime minister, Harold Macmillan, the two European countries drew important but very different lessons. While France came to believe that it had to develop its own power base, including nuclear weapons, since the United States had proved to be an unreliable and difficult ally, the British arrived at the opposite conclusion. The United Kingdom, it seemed, believed it needed to become an indispensable partner to the United States. British global influence could only be maintained, it was concluded in London, if the United Kingdom and the United States walked hand in hand. From Macmillan to Tony Blair and beyond, this belief has been one of the main pillars of British foreign policy in the globalized world of the twentieth and twenty-first centuries. The United States appreciated this. Close relations were soon reestablished after the Suez Crisis. This cooperation could be seen, for instance, in a short-lived deployment of troops by the United States in Lebanon and British paratroops in neighboring Jordan to quell anti-Western uprisings there.[10]

However, the United States had no intention of sharing its global leadership role with the British. The United Kingdom was only consulted and cooperation only occurred when Washington believed this was in its interests. The United States had a much less romantic and a much more hard-nosed approach than the British to the "special relationship." In the second Berlin crisis in the late 1950s, which led to the building of the Berlin Wall in August 1961, and indeed during the dangerous Cuban Missile Crisis of 1962, the British were hardly consulted by the United States. The British prime minister had become a mere bystander to the American-Soviet domination of global affairs.[11]

At the conference in Nassau (the Bahamas) in early 1961, Macmillan even had to beg President John F. Kennedy to sell Polaris missiles to Britain so that his country's own nuclear warheads could be deployed, were this to become necessary. Without the new Polaris delivery vehicle, there was no way that British atomic bombs could have been used.

Soon Britain had little choice but to move closer to Europe. Primarily for economic reasons, but also for political ones, Prime Minister Macmillan applied for admission to the EEC in 1961. French president Charles de Gaulle, who jealously guarded his country's predominant position in European affairs and viewed the Anglo-American "special relationship" with deep suspicion, issued a veto. When the new Labour prime minister, Harold Wilson, applied again in 1967, de Gaulle announced his second veto. It would take the old general's retirement in 1969 and the premiership of Edward Heath (1970–74) to ensure that Britain's third desperate attempt to become a member of the European Community succeeded in 1973.[12]

By this time Britain had moved away somewhat from its close partnership with Washington. Already Prime Minister Harold Wilson had refused to offer British troops to the American war in Vietnam, as had been repeatedly demanded by the U.S. president, Lyndon Johnson. Moreover, in the wake of the sterling crisis in November 1967, Wilson and his chancellor of the exchequer, Roy Jenkins, had concluded that Britain's commitments east of Suez were unaffordable. Two months later Wilson announced that by the end of 1971 Britain would leave its military bases in the Far East and in the Persian Gulf (including its huge naval base in Aden, Yemen). Only Hong Kong would be maintained. London began to rebalance its global commitments and focus more on Europe. The withdrawal from the East did not please the United States, which would have to take over many of Britain's responsibilities there.[13]

Washington, however, had been encouraging the British to focus more on Europe, arguing that if Britain were to become a full member of the European Community (EC), this would actually increase rather than weaken Britain's role in world affairs as well as its importance for the United States. When Edward Heath's pro-European conservative government lost office in early 1974, the succeeding Labour government (again under Prime Minister Wilson) immediately and successfully demanded a renegotiation of the British terms of entry to the EC. In a June 1975 referendum, the British people were asked whether the country should remain a member of the EC (which the government supported); 17.3 million Britons voted in favor and 8.4 million were opposed, a clear 2:1 ratio for "staying in Europe."[14]

By the mid to late 1970s, Britain had given up most of its colonial possessions and military bases abroad. However, the majority of British politicians still regretted the loss of Britain's global role. In their heart of hearts, they deeply resented their replacement as the globe's major power by the United States. They also viewed West Germany's increasing influence on the European continent with great suspicion and a degree of envy. Britain's difficult domestic situation also contributed to the development of a certain beleaguered "bunker mentality" and resentment about the loss of world power status.

Since the mid to late 1960s, Britain's course had been driven by currency crises, economic difficulties, industrial strife, and social unrest. Poverty levels and social deprivation, particularly in the north of the country, were on the increase.[15] Moreover, in 1968, the "Troubles" in Northern Ireland commenced. Since the partition of Ireland in 1916, Northern Ireland—the six northern counties of the island of Ireland (except Donegal)—has been a British province, with 1.5 million inhabitants. In the late 1960s its population was divided approximately 60:40 between British loyalists and Irish nationalists, most of whom desired to bring about a united Ireland. From the late 1960s to the mid-1970s, the conflict became increasingly violent and, in June 1969, brought the deployment of British troops. This intervention, however, soon inflamed the situation further. At the conflict's height, there were almost 35,000 British troops in the province and there was civil war in Belfast, Derry, and many other towns and areas. The regular television news about yet another bomb explosion and yet another shooting in both Northern Ireland and occasionally in England itself only contributed to Britain being seen as in irreversible decline.[16] Throughout the 1970s, the United Kingdom was frequently regarded as the "sick man of Europe." This was confirmed by an International Monetary Fund (IMF) bailout in 1976, which Wilson's successor, James Callaghan, the new Labour prime minister, had to resort to in order to prevent British bankruptcy.[17] This humiliating episode left deep scars.

The Thatcher Years: Revival and Continued Impotence

This was the dire situation Margaret Thatcher faced when the Tories returned to power under her leadership in 1979. With her steely and robust personality, Thatcher had been able to overcome the many hurdles faced by the still patriarchal Conservative Party she would head as the country's first female prime minister. She was also determined to make Britain "great again" with the help of the forces of the free market and a strong anticommunist fervor. U.S. president Ronald Reagan happened to share many of her ideological beliefs, and strong personal links between the two politicians developed. The revival of special relations with Washington reinforced Thatcher's predilection to think in global rather than European terms.[18]

At first, it seemed that Thatcher had managed to strengthen Britain's domestic economy and the country's international standing during her twelve years in office. This perception was misleading. Her radical economic restructuring, including the sacrifice of much of Britain's out-of-date manufacturing industry and expertise and the wide-scale closures of coal mines, caused great social dislocation and hardship. This was especially evident in Wales, the Midlands, and in the north of the United Kingdom, including Scotland. Unemployment skyrocketed during Thatcher's first years in office and only very slowly came down again. Despite Thatcher's economic restructuring efforts, the skills of the country's domestic workforce, and Britain's long-term economic structures, did not improve noticeably. However, by means of a huge deregulation drive she managed to solidify the role of the City of London as the world's major financial center, whose only serious rival at the time was New York City's Wall Street. Soon the

1980s came to be characterized by financial greed and egotistical individual behavior, particularly in the workplace. "There is no such thing as society," Thatcher exclaimed in an interview with the magazine *Woman's Own* in September 1987.[19]

Britain's 1982 victory in the Falklands War against Argentina and the ensuing wave of British nationalism ensured Margaret Thatcher's reelection in a landslide victory in 1983 despite a poor economic record and high levels of unemployment. Thatcher's aim of making Britain "great again" proved unreachable, however. After all, the Falklands War was of more symbolic than real importance. Moreover, without U.S. satellite information about the whereabouts of Argentinian naval forces, victory would likely have been impossible. The United States had initially hesitated to support the British and attempted to mediate as a neutral arbiter before changing its mind. Reagan had priorities other than looking after his British ally. He was much more focused on America's own domestic economy and on overcoming the East-West conflict.[20]

When Reagan began negotiations with the new and progressive Soviet leader Mikhail Gorbachev in 1985, the British and the other European allies were hardly consulted. Bilateral U.S.-Soviet negotiations led to important reductions in the nuclear and conventional armament arsenals of both superpowers. Britain and France, Europe's two nuclear powers, were not invited to participate in the talks. Europe was ignored, despite the fact that short-range missiles were based on European soil and targeted European cities.

By the late 1980s, Thatcher and Reagan (and their spouses) had become personally close, but political relations between the United States and its European allies, including Britain, were strained. Thatcher never overcame her strong anticommunism and for a long time was not convinced that genuine rather than mere tactical change was taking place in the Soviet Union under Gorbachev. Instead, she warned repeatedly that the West needed to be alert and not let itself be seduced by Gorbachev's personal charm and his enormous popularity in Germany and other European countries (which she called "Gorbymania").[21]

By this time Thatcher had already antagonized her European partners with her increasingly strident anti-European rhetoric. She had begun her years in office by insisting on a rebate of Britain's net payments to the EC. Although Thatcher signed the 1986 Single European Act, she had no intention of giving up real sovereignty to the European Commission in

Brussels. She agreed with the elimination of tariffs and improvement of better trade because these measures merely seemed to create a huge free trade area in Europe. Anything else was beyond the pale for Downing Street. The Delors Plan of April 1989 (named for Jacques Delors, president of the EC from 1985 to 1994), which had been developed after the June 1988 European Union (EU) summit in Hanover, was strongly opposed by the British prime minister. The plan foresaw the creation of monetary union and a single currency, and eventually even political union, and thus went far beyond what Thatcher could endorse. Her crudely anti-European 1988 speech in Bruges in Belgium made clear her outright hostility and strong opposition to giving up any British power to a European entity.[22]

The following year, mass demonstrations all over Eastern Europe shook communism to its core. Although in principle Thatcher approved of this anticommunist wave, she was also highly disturbed about a change in the status quo, including Britain's still important role in the Cold War world. When the East Germans rose up and German unification appeared as a distinct possibility by November 1989, Thatcher was aghast. She talked about maintaining two German states for the time being. The German Democratic Republic (East Germany), she said, ought to exist independently as a separate democratic German state for a number of years. Yet the strong and unhesitating support by U.S. president George H. W. Bush for the democratization of Eastern Europe and German unification made Thatcher's position futile. She hoped that Gorbachev would never agree to the unification of the two German states. Thatcher also attempted to enter into an informal anti-German alliance with the French president, François Mitterrand, to undermine the move toward a united German state. Yet Mitterrand and then also Gorbachev realized how unrealistic this was, and eventually both gave their agreement to German unification, despite their strong misgivings. Bush's consistent support for German chancellor Helmut Kohl and the U.S. president's constructive relations with Gorbachev had been decisive. Thatcher was unable to uphold her opposition. In the summer of 1990 she accepted the inevitable and signed on to the unification of Germany, which took effect in early October 1990.[23]

Yet Thatcher's well-known attempts to prevent this outcome, her increasingly unreasonable anti-European tirades, and her ever-greater problems with a deeply divided cabinet undermined her authority, both in the country at large and, even more important, within her own party. Domestically, a new ill-thought-out poll tax was highly controversial and led to vicious street battles between protesters and the police. The Conservative Party became convinced that Thatcher would be unable to win the next elections. The Tories under Thatcher had been trailing the opposition Labour Party for the previous eighteen months in the polls. The gap had widened to almost 14 percent, a dangerously high figure, even considering the unreliability of opinion polls.

Thatcher was also damaging Britain's relations with her close allies in Europe and across the Atlantic. Instead of cooperating with her allies in the momentous events in Eastern Europe, she had managed to antagonize continental Europe's most important country, Germany, and even her relations with Washington had plummeted. Relations with France and Moscow had suffered, too. She had to go, it was concluded on the conservative backbenches and in the conservative central office.[24]

In the annual contest for the leadership of the Conservative Party in mid-November 1990, Thatcher was ousted by her own party. Her former defense minister, the popular Michael Heseltine, threw his hat into the ring. He entered the leadership competition the day after Thatcher's deputy prime minister, Geoffrey Howe, had given a devastating resignation speech in parliament in which he severely criticized Thatcher's European policy as unreasonable and counterproductive.

Heseltine obtained enough votes to force a second round of voting. Thatcher reluctantly resigned instead of standing in a second round, which she may well have lost. Once Thatcher resigned, however, Heseltine lost out in the leadership contest against the much less flamboyant John Major, Thatcher's chancellor of the exchequer. Seen as a safe pair of hands, he became leader of the Conservative Party and succeeded to the premiership.[25]

The Post–Cold War Years

John Major's premiership from 1991 to 1997 must be seen as a transition period in British politics, though quite a prolonged one. His years in office were characterized by continued division between the pro- and anti-European factions both in Parliament and in his cabinet. He and his chancellor of the exchequer, Norman Lamont, also suffered from financial humiliation when the country's economy proved to be too weak to sustain Britain's membership in the European Exchange Rate Mechanism. The country was ejected from this forerunner of the European Monetary Union on September 16, 1992. Although in April 1992, Major had won an entirely unexpected reelection victory against Labour Party leader Neil Kinnock, both his contemporaries and the subsequent scholarly literature have had few kind words about Major's accomplishments.[26]

Major, however, set in motion the Northern Irish peace process. It led to the negotiation of the Good Friday Agreement in 1998 under his successor, which largely resolved the conflict. Yet British policy related to the war in Bosnia in the early to mid-1990s and Major's inability to control his ministers and impose his authority on Britain's policy toward the EU undermined his government. In the midst of much controversial discussion in August 1993, Major managed to persuade a majority of the House of Commons to ratify the Maastricht Treaty, however. The treaty would turn the EC into the EU and foresaw the establishment of a monetary union and a common European currency. Although the prime minister had obtained opt-out clauses for his country on a number of social and judicial EU clauses, many of his Euroskeptic ministers and backbenchers never forgave Major for what they saw as his betrayal of British sovereignty.[27]

Tony Blair's election as British prime minister in a landslide victory in May 1997 was greeted with relief. There was widespread jubilation that the Major government had been put out of its misery. The Labour Party was returned to power after more than two decades in the wilderness. Not surprisingly, expectations were running high in almost all respects. The 1997–2007 Labour governments led by Tony Blair and then by Gordon Brown from 2007–10 have defined Britain's role in the early twenty-first century.

The New Labour Era

When Tony Blair was swept into office in 1997, the country seemed to have been infused with new energy and optimism. There was tremendous hope at No. 10 Downing Street that Britain could creatively contribute to shaping the post–Cold War world. Not least, the new Blair government was keen to grasp the forces of globalization and run with them.

However, two decades later, Tony Blair is among Britain's most maligned and unpopular politicians.

The economic policies of the governments led by Blair and his successor, Gordon Brown, are now regarded as complete failures. The New Labour era is frequently interpreted as a time of missed opportunities and unwise falling back to old policies. Regarding foreign policy, it was above all Tony Blair's fateful decision to invade Saddam Hussein's Iraq alongside U.S. president George W. Bush that has had profound repercussions. There was much domestic and global opposition to the war, and the fact that no proper UN authorization had occurred for the invasion did not help. Thus, by late 2002, it appeared that Blair was refocusing his foreign policy on the "special relationship" with the United States while neglecting everything else.[28] Although this assessment is quite justified, there is of course more to the New Labour years and Britain's post–Cold War foreign policy than the Iraq War. It makes sense to review Blair and Brown's foreign policy under the following two rubrics: (1) New Labour's foreign policy principles and (2) Blair's European policy and his attempt to act as a bridge between Europe and the United States.

FOREIGN POLICY PRINCIPLES. Tony Blair's foreign policy priorities fell within the realm of liberal internationalism, emphasizing the value of building international institutions to prevent global anarchy. The importance of democracy and normative values, such as social justice, are also emphasized for the workings of the international system in contrast to, for instance, old-fashioned secret diplomacy. Traditionally the Labour Party's liberal internationalism also refers to an antimilitaristic foreign policy with an emphasis on disarmament, collective security, and firm control of the international arms trade.[29]

Throughout New Labour's period in office, and in particular during the first five years, the principles of liberal internationalism and the extent to which they ought to be adhered to were vigorously debated among Labour parliamentarians. The invasion of Iraq in 2003 and the pursuit of a very different realpolitik by the Blair government put a certain stop to these debates. In this, as in many other respects, the 2003 invasion of Iraq was a real turning point in British foreign policy that can be compared in its significance to the fateful Suez adventure in 1956.

In its 1997 election manifesto, the Labour Party declared that it wished to return Britain to the heart of Europe, though Blair had no intention of joining the envisaged eurozone without a referendum. Nothing much was said about Britain's role in the European Common Foreign and Security Policy area. Instead, Blair emphasized that Britain's defense policy continued to be based on NATO and the country's independent nuclear deterrent. But the Labour Party emphasized a new moral dimension of the country's foreign policy: If elected, Blair intended to ban the production and use of all antipersonnel landmines, and he wished to draw up new rules for Britain's extensive arms exports. The Labour Party also declared that it would again establish an independent ministry of international development (under the Tories, an Overseas Development Administration had been part of the Foreign Office bureaucracy). In addition, Blair professed his wish to support the reform of the UN and pay more attention to the British Commonwealth. The Labour Party also intended to "make the protection and promotion" of human rights a central part of its foreign policy, though exactly how human rights were to be defined and prioritized remained unclear. Blair came out in support of the establishment of an International Criminal Court for dealing with genocide, war crimes, and crimes against humanity. The 1997 manifesto also emphasized the importance of paying more attention to global climate change. It intended to reduce Britain's output of carbon dioxide by 20 percent by 2010. On the whole, the Labour manifesto declared that Britain ought to be "a leading force for good in the world."[30]

Less than two weeks after Labour's election victory, the new foreign secretary, Robin Cook, set out the four main goals of the Blair government's foreign policy approach. He spoke of security, prosperity, quality of life, and mutual respect. With respect to the last principle, mutual respect, Cook emphasized that his country had "a national interest in the promotion of our values. . . . Our foreign policy must have an ethical dimension and must support . . . democratic rights." The new foreign secretary said that "the Labour government will put human rights at the heart of our foreign policy" and emphasized that it was the purpose of his mission statement to supply "an ethical content to foreign policy." The statement, he explained, "recognizes that the national interest cannot be defined only by narrow *realpolitik*."[31]

Cook's emphatic statement was sold as a radical departure. However, it soon clashed with the reality of British foreign relations in the contemporary world. Over time it made the foreign secretary seem like a hypocrite and exposed him and his foreign policy to ridicule. By the year 2000–01, references to an "ethical foreign policy" had been quietly dropped. In a 1999 speech he gave in Chicago, Tony Blair emphasized the notion of a "just war," such as NATO's campaign in Kosovo, which was "based not on any territorial ambitions but on values." He declared that the world needed "new rules for international cooperation" and that people were "witnessing the beginnings of a new doctrine of international community." In the post–Cold War world, the prime minister believed that "our actions are guided by a more subtle blend of mutual self-interest and moral purpose in defending the values we cherish. In the end, values and interests merge." Deciding when not to observe the principle of noninterference and when to "get actively involved in other people's conflicts" was highly difficult. Blair suggested "five major considerations." First, it had to be investigated whether we are "sure of our case." Second, ask whether all diplomatic options have been exhausted. "We should always give peace ever chance," he pronounced. Then consider whether there were military operations that could realistically be pursued. Fourth, ask "Are we prepared for the long term?" rather than just focusing on exit strategies. And last, ask "Do we have national interests involved?"[32]

These were noble and in the abstract highly laudable principles. Four years later, however, it did not take British public opinion long to apply Blair's five conditions to the Iraq invasion. The Blair government's action was found wanting and in violation of its own rules of engagement. Henceforth the Blair government's foreign policy principles were derided and viewed with great cynicism. Blair's political and moral authority would never recover.

BLAIR'S EUROPEAN POLICY. When Blair became prime minister in early May 1997, he was regarded as the most pro-European prime minister since Edward Heath. His speeches as leader of the opposition and the Labour Party's 1997 election manifesto were viewed as strongly pro-European. Most of his European initiatives took place during his first term in office.[33] It is this period that is emphasized in the considerations that follow.

Soon after moving into 10 Downing Street, Blair announced that he wished to open a new chapter in Britain's relations with Europe. In a speech in the German town of Aachen, where he received the Charlemagne Prize (the *Karlspreis* in German) in May 1999, he said that it was his objective that "over the next few years Britain resolves once and for all its ambivalence toward Europe: I want to end the uncertainty, the lack of confidence, the Europhobia. I want Britain to be at home with Europe because Britain is once again a leading player in Europe. And I want Europe to make itself open to reform and change too. For if I am pro-European, I am also pro-reform in Europe."[34]

Already during the election campaign of 1997, Blair had emphasized that he not only wanted to pursue a more constructive policy toward Europe but also claimed a leadership role for Britain. "We will lead a campaign for reform in Europe," he said. "But to lead means to be involved, to be constructive, to be capable of getting our own way," and "we will stand up for Britain's interests in Europe," and "we cannot shape Europe unless we matter in Europe."[35] The new prime minister did not just wish to benefit from Europe economically; he also wished to catapult Britain into a decisive position with regard to the European policymaking process in Brussels.

Soon, Blair embarked on a rather more constructive European policy.[36] In June 1997, just over a month after his election, he signed the Amsterdam Treaty and thus also accepted the social chapters of the Maastricht Treaty, which his predecessor had strictly refused to adhere to. Still, the new Labour government continued to insist on the provision of a national veto in areas such as security policy, immigration, and taxation. In 1998, the Blair government managed to obtain parliamentary approval for anchoring the European Convention on Human Rights in British law. In the same year, Blair and Jacques Chirac, the French president, signed the Saint-Malo Agreement, which on the basis of close Anglo-French security cooperation laid the foundation for the European Security and Defense Policy (ESDP).

The process of expanding the EU by admitting many of the former communist states was concluded with the EU summit in Nice in December 2000. Blair supported this process vigorously. Many institutional reforms that were later achieved, such as those incorporated in the Lisbon Treaty of 2007, went back to proposals made by Blair during his early years in office. Already in March 2000, Blair influenced the ambitious goals of the Lisbon EU summit, which inaugurated the Lisbon process. At the beginning of his premiership, Blair firmly intended to adopt the euro and abolish Britain's own currency, the pound sterling. Yet he grew increasingly cool toward this idea. Both within his own cabinet and in the population at large, there was a clear lack of support for replacing the pound with the euro. Chancellor of the Exchequer Gordon Brown personally did not view the adoption of the euro positively; it ran counter to British interests, he believed. The statement in the 1997 election manifesto was meant seriously. It said that "any decisions about Britain joining the single currency must be determined by a hard-headed assessment of Britain's economic interests."[37]

Moreover, due to enormous domestic pressure, the Labour government promised the British people that a referendum would be held on the adoption of the euro. By the end of Blair's second term in office, the issue was off the table.

Blair was genuinely convinced that the policy of confrontation toward Europe that had characterized the Thatcher and Major years needed to be abandoned. Instead, London needed to find close allies in order to succeed with its ideas for reforming Europe in a constructive way. In the literature, this is often referred to as Blair's "step change." It occurred simultaneously with Blair's "new bilateralism" in 1998. The prime minister encouraged his ministers to establish good relations with their respective counterparts in the continental European governments. Although this was a sensible idea, it soon developed into a strategy of selective cooperation, as it appeared that the British ministers were only interested in cooperating with those of their European counterparts who shared their ideas and plans. This is often referred to as the first signs of a growing lack of enthusiasm for Blair's European policy (at least when compared with his first year in office).[38]

Above all, it soon became clear that London was only interested in cooperation if Britain could obtain a leadership role. This even applied to the Anglo-French partnership in the defense field, which in the context of the disastrous European policy in the wars in Bosnia and Kosovo had led to the Saint-Malo Agreement in 1998. It was Tony Blair who had taken the initiative to arrive at this important agreement, which was meant to increase the EU's military capacities for autonomous security policy activities without, however, questioning the existence and integrity of NATO. Blair and French president Jacques Chirac agreed on the creation of a rapid European Reaction Force (ERRF), which was meant to be 60,000 strong and operative by the year 2001. With this initiative European security policy received much-needed attention, including the promise of significant resources. Yet once again, the objectives were overly ambitious; there was an air of unreality surrounding the whole Saint-Malo initiative that turned out to be prophetic.[39]

After all, even during Blair's first term—and despite his many pro-European activities and initiatives during his first few years in office—it soon became clear that the he was not interested in giving up British sovereignty in important respects. The British prime minister instead pursued a rather pragmatic course of action intended to combine supranational and traditional national competencies. Thus, Blair's European policy was clearly pragmatic. His at times close cooperation with conservative counterparts such as French president Chirac and Prime Ministers José María Aznar of Spain and Silvio Berlusconi of Italy was based on his pragmatism. Jean Monnet's objective of "ever closer union," as it appeared already in the 1957 Treaty of Rome, was not shared by Blair. In fact, he believed this was an unrealistic objective.[40]

In a speech in Warsaw on October 6, 2000, it became obvious that despite all his pro-European utterances, Blair was still thinking in traditional terms about Britain's European policy. Blair enthusiastically supported the expansion of the EU and the inclusion of the Eastern European states. He also referred to Britain's role in Europe and the future institutional setup of the EU. He emphasized that it was time "to overcome the legacy of Britain's past." Still, at the same time he referred to his country's traditionally close relations with the United States, which he believed were advantageous for the EU. "Our strength with the United States," he explained, "is not just a British asset, it is potentially a European one. Britain can be the bridge between the EU and the U.S."[41]

In the course of the election campaign of 2001, Blair could justifiably refer to some successful initiatives and demonstrate that he had indeed managed to turn Britain into a constructive and appreciated partner within the European Union. Blair, however, had not succeeded in turning the British into a more pro-European nation. He kept emphasizing that his pro-European policy by no means meant that he had turned away from the close alliance with the United States. He rejected the notion that Britain had to decide between Europe and the United States. "We shall remain the USA's firm ally and friend; but we are not going to turn our backs on Europe," he pronounced.[42] This was the high point of Blair's pro-European phase, though it was still firmly rooted in Britain's traditionally close relations with the United States.

During his second and third terms in office (2001–05; 2005–07), Tony Blair was unable to continue his careful pro-European policy. The terrorist attacks on September 11, 2001, in the United States, and Blair's decision to join President George W. Bush in the invasion of Iraq in March 2003, made this impossible. Bush's "war on terror" and the war in Afghanistan further strengthened Blair's relationship with Washington.[43] The hostile attitude of Germany and France toward the war in Iraq and much of Europe's only lukewarm support of the war on terror, including the war in Afghanistan, drove a wedge between Blair's Britain and the EU. Blair had an increasingly antagonistic relationship with the German and French leaders. His close cooperation with U.S.-friendly governments such as Poland and several other Eastern European countries, as well as with Aznar's Spain and Berlusconi's Italy, undermined Blair's good standing and credibility in most other European capitals. U.S. secretary of defense Donald Rumsfeld's differentiation between the countries of "old" Europe that were opposing the Iraq War and the nations of "new" Europe, which referred to the pro-American governments in Eastern Europe, Italy, Spain, and Britain, increased the deep division between Blair and the continental European countries.[44]

By 2003–04, not much was left of the ambitious "new doctrine of international community" that Blair had emphasized in his Chicago speech in 1999. The Iraq War did indeed hinder and delay the further development of a more coherent European continent. While George W. Bush in Washington observed this with satisfaction, Blair's European policy lost all credibility when he joined Bush in the violent toppling of Saddam Hussein.

When Blair resigned as prime minister in late June 2007 to make way for his designated successor, Gordon Brown, Blair's foreign policy had failed in many important respects. Brown, who always had been more Euroskeptical than Blair, made no attempt to introduce the euro in Britain. A referendum would have clearly failed to obtain the support of the British people. Brown himself did not believe in the project in any case. However, Brown pushed the Lisbon reform treaty of 2007 through Parliament, insisting that the changes called for in this treaty were not so substantial that a referendum was required. Ratification by the House of Commons was sufficient, he declared.[45]

Soon the global economic and financial crisis came to preoccupy the Brown government. Although Brown succeeded in keeping the crisis under control and preventing a worst-case scenario, his personal standing and his fortunes as prime minister never recovered from the onslaught of the crisis. After all, as Tony Blair's chancellor of the exchequer for the previous ten years, Brown had overseen the creation of the excesses of the housing market, Britain's economic bubble, and the City of London's profligate behavior, all of which greatly contributed to the Great Recession in the United Kingdom. In the general election of 2010, Brown was voted out of office.[46] After more than twelve years in power, the Labour Party was replaced by

David Cameron and Nick Clegg's Conservative–Liberal Democrat coalition government, the first coalition in Britain since the collapse of Winston Churchill's national government in 1945.

Outlook: The Road to Brexit

Owing to the global economic and financial crisis—the Great Recession of 2008–12—the new U.K. government that came to office in May 2010 pursued a policy of restraint. Austerity and retrenchment was the approach of the new ministers to cope with the crisis. The members of the Conservative–Liberal Democrat coalition government, led by Prime Minister David Cameron and Deputy Prime Minister Nick Clegg, had little taste for attempting to creatively shape the post–Cold War world. Regarding Britain's foreign policy, the coalition government also looked backward, resorting to London's traditional approaches. Not least, the new government was keen on once again emphasizing the "special relationship" with the United States. Relations with the EU, however, deteriorated further. The prime minister's own Euroskeptical attitude and pressure from his backbenchers led him to refer frequently to the possibility of a British exit from the EU. Then, in a January 2013 speech, he announced that a referendum on continued British membership in the EU would take place if his party managed to win the next election. One of the questions the British would be asked to address was whether Britain should exit the twenty-eight-member organization it had joined forty years ago.[47] It made sense when the Cameron government soon began to further intensify Britain's bilateral relationships, and not just those with Washington.[48]

The coalition government entered into a closer relationship with France, largely for financial reasons. Both countries could no longer afford their still comparatively significant military arsenals. This led to intensified cooperation in nuclear technology questions in particular. Along with an ever-greater skepticism, if not outright hostility, toward the EU, the coalition government also discovered the Commonwealth again and emphasized Britain's links with its former colonies, not least in the economic and trade sphere. Naturally London attempted to use its long-standing links with India, its former crown jewel colony, to embark on more constructive trade relations. Like all Western countries, Britain was also keen on intensifying relations with China and Southeast Asia.[49]

While many of these policies made sense, they did not represent particularly creative or innovative steps. Neither did they indicate a new departure in Britain's foreign relations. Instead, Cameron's foreign economic policy consisted of a policy of delusion considering that Britain's most important export market by far was Europe. Membership in the Single Market and the customs union gave Britain real clout and genuine economic advantages that no other market could rival, including the American or Chinese markets.

Similar to the Obama administration in Washington and most continental European governments, London was glad to have ended its costly military engagement in Afghanistan. Although the United Kingdom cautiously supported developments in the Arab Spring in general and viewed them with sympathy, this was largely restricted to rhetorical support. Like all Western countries, the United Kingdom also strongly condemned the civil war in Syria but refused to get drawn into the conflict militarily. Due to skillful maneuvering of Labour leader Ed Miliband, Cameron lost a decisive parliamentary vote in August 2013. This encouraged the Obama administration in Washington to also defer a decision by asking Congress to decide whether it wished to declare war on the Syrian president Assad. This, however, weakly shifted responsibility to a gridlocked Congress that unsurprisingly failed to take action.[50]

Russia and Iran's increasing engagement in Syria was criticized by the United Kingdom as by most other Western countries. The same applied to Russia's annexation of Crimea in March 2014 and its hidden invasion of eastern Ukraine, which led to the imposition of severe sanctions on Russia. Yet the coalition government was too preoccupied with domestic and European affairs to play much of a role in the negotiations that led to the Minsk II cease-fire agreement of February 2015. It was the German chancellor and the French president, together with Russian president Vladimir Putin, who were the driving forces behind the agreement. The U.K. prime minister and foreign secretary were not among the parties who negotiated the complex deal.[51]

Similarly, the counterrevolution in Egypt was at first viewed skeptically in London, but this quickly changed once it became clear that the replacement of democratically elected President Mohamed Morsi of the Muslim Brotherhood in July 2013 by military leader Fattah el-Sisi had positive results for Western policy. El-Sisi's forceful and ruthless suppression of all domestic dissent turned Egypt once again into a comparatively stable pro-Western country. Little criticism of el-Sisi's undemocratic rule and repressive methods could be heard in London or elsewhere in the West. There was also very little appetite in London to become militarily involved in prolonged and intensive antiterrorist campaigns to fight al Qaeda and the new rising threat of the Islamic State in the Middle East or elsewhere. Humanitarian intervention generally took a backseat.[52]

One of the exceptions to this reticence to become engaged militarily was the short-term air force engagement in Libya in 2011. In cooperation with France, with the United States playing a less dominant role in the background while supplying crucial military equipment and ammunition, the Western engagement led to the toppling of Libyan strongman Muammar Qaddafi. This, however, caused a power vacuum in the country that in turn led to a vicious civil war. The West, however, withdrew and washed its hands of Libya and, in due course, Yemen and partially Iraq.

The days of Western leadership in international affairs clearly seemed to be over. Britain was no more interested in nation-building in the Middle East than were the United States or France. Leading from behind, if leading at all (a slogan inadvertently coined by one of President Obama's officials), was also quite appropriate to the conduct of Prime Minister Cameron's foreign policy. A more benign voice has explained, however, that under both Prime Ministers Brown and Cameron a "cautious pragmatism" dominated. It replaced Prime Minister Blair's preference for the "proclamation of grand strategic ambition."[53] It was certainly true that the absence of the latter was received with much relief by most Britons. Still, the euphemistic term "cautious pragmatism" in fact refers to a lack of international engagement and the near-absence of an important British voice in global affairs during much of David Cameron's years in office. It must be questioned whether this really served the best interests of the country.

While Cameron's foreign policy was unspectacular, to put it mildly, his major flaws and mistakes concerned Britain's domestic and European policy. Twice he risked the country's unity. He agreed to the request of a referendum on Scottish independence without specifying the necessity of a two-thirds majority as a minimum requirement for independence. A simple majority would be sufficient. The referendum, which took place on September 18, 2014, proved a nail-biting cliff-hanger, and during the last few weeks of the campaign, the likelihood of a victory for the independence movement in Scotland became a realistic prospect. The government had good reason to panic. Cameron threw all of his government's resources into the campaign to keep Scotland within the United Kingdom. This included dramatic visits to Scotland by members of the royal family. In the end, Cameron was lucky. A narrow majority of voters in Scotland decided to reject independence and stay within the United Kingdom. Unity had just about been preserved: 55.3 percent of people voted against independence while 44.7 percent voted in favor of Scottish independence.[54]

Two years later, Cameron was less fortunate. The referendum on exiting the EU (Brexit) on June 23, 2016, resulted in an overall small majority voting for the United Kingdom to leave the European Union: 51.9 percent favored leaving the EU while 48.1 percent wanted to remain in the EU.[55] There were many reasons why so many Briton's voted in favor of leaving the EU. These included the formidable anti-European integration resentments that had accumulated over decades in the United Kingdom and the virulent long-standing anti-EU rhetoric of the majority of the British media, in particular the press organs owned by Rupert Murdoch.

Still, decisive too was the influx of refugees to continental European countries (in particular to Italy, Greece, Austria, and not least Germany) and the perceived danger that many of these people would join the large number of Eastern Europeans who had been flocking to the United Kingdom—or so it seemed. The vote was thus strongly influenced by anti-foreigner resentment—or as some scholars have put it politely, "anti-immigration populism,"[56] particularly in England outside London and in Wales. For in London, Scotland, and Northern Ireland, the "remain voters" obtained a clear majority in the referendum, but due to the negative vote in England and Wales the overall outcome resulted, as noted, in a small majority for the "leave" vote.[57] Incidentally, there also was a demographic dimension to the vote. Older white men voted overwhelmingly to leave the EU while the younger generation, those under thirty years of age, saw their future in a Britain well integrated into the EU. They voted overwhelmingly in favor of staying in the EU.

On the day of the failed referendum Cameron announced his resignation, and he retired within a couple of months, once his successor had emerged. Cameron, possibly one of Britain's most untalented prime ministers ever, was succeeded by the former home secretary Theresa May. Although having been one of Cameron's "remain" friends, she had played a dubious and cautious role during the referendum campaign, hedging her bets and making sure she would not offend the "leave" forces. She also was careful not to give Boris Johnson, the former mayor of London and her strongest though quite unpopular rival, the chance to succeed Cameron. May made Johnson foreign secretary and thus a member of her team. She did not wish to create a strong rival outside her cabinet.[58]

The new prime minister now had the difficult task of negotiating an exit deal with the EU as well as a new relationship with Britain, either within or without the Single Market and customs union. This soon came to be referred to as a "soft" or "hard" Brexit. May triggered article 50 of the EU treaty for leaving the EU on March 29, 2017. She now had exactly two years to negotiate the exit terms and a new post-Brexit relationship with Brussels and the twenty-seven remaining EU members. May and her Brexit minister, David Davis, however, proved to be quite inept in their new roles.[59]

Moreover, May soon made her life a lot more difficult by calling a snap general election on June 8, 2017. The opinion polls had shown a favorable outcome, and May wanted to strengthen her overall majority to be able to negotiate with the EU from a much stronger position, both externally and domestically. At least that was what she said when dissolving Parliament only two years after the last election.

It backfired badly, however. May only very narrowly won the elections, with the Labour Party under its new chairman, left-winger Jeremy Corbyn, increasing its vote significantly. Instead of adding to the Conservative Party's seats in the House of Commons, the Conservative vote plummeted, leaving May with just a precarious three-seat majority. Only after she negotiated a deal with the highly conservative and religiously fundamentalist Northern Irish Democratic Unionist Party (DUP) to tolerate her government and vote with it on a case-to-case basis was she able to form a new though weak government.[60] Only when the DUP's ten seats were added to the Conservative's three-seat majority was May able to preside over a small but functional overall parliamentary majority.

This naturally meant that the Northern Irish problem was again at the forefront of British politics. The DUP insisted that no new hard border should be established between the Republic of Ireland and Northern Ireland, whatever the outcome of the Brexit negotiations would be. While in principle this was also the view of Theresa May, in practice it proved to be a difficult problem to surmount because after the United Kingdom's departure, the new external border of the EU would now be the external border of the Republic of Ireland. The question arose of whether the border between Ireland and Northern Ireland could continue to be an open, invisible border even when the United Kingdom decided not only to leave the EU but also the Single Market and the customs union. Yet the re-introduction of a hard border was not acceptable to anyone, certainly not to Sinn Fein, the Irish nationalists. Any such development threatened to lead to the resumption of the violent Troubles in the North of Ireland.

Ever since the Brexit vote, British policy has been in disarray. The May government has turned out to be highly disorganized. It also proved to have little aptitude to agree on a coherent negotiation strategy toward the EU. Consequently, negotiations between the British team, led first by Brexit secretary David Davis and then by Dominic Raab, and the EU chief nego-tiator Michel Barnier, a former French foreign minister, have made little progress. But the deadline of March 29, 2019, when Britain will have to leave the EU, needs to be met—unless the government and/or Parliament change their mind.

The decision by the U.K. government to honor the narrow referendum decision of June 2016 has led to a major change in the United Kingdom's relations with the outside world. Brexit may prove to be a major milestone in U.K. history. Britain's standing and influence in global affairs has al-ready suffered a great deal.

NOTES

1. Dean Acheson made this statement on December 5, 1962, during a speech at the U.S. Military Academy in West Point. See, for example, Con-stantine A. Pagedas, *Anglo-American Strategic Relations and the French Problem, 1960–63: A Troubled Partnership* (London: Frank Cass, 2000), p. 245.

2. Klaus Larres, *Churchill's Cold War: The Politics of Personal Diplomacy* (Yale University Press, 2002).

3. See Klaus Larres, "Britain and the Cold War, 1945–1990," in *The Oxford Handbook of the Cold War*, edited by Richard H. Immerman and Petra Goedde (Oxford University Press, 2013), pp. 141–57.

4. Robert Frazier, "Did Britain Start the Cold War? Bevin and the Tru-man Doctrine," *Historical Journal* 27 (September 1984), pp. 715–27.

5. Anne Deighton, *The Impossible Peace: Britain, the Division of Germany, and the Origins of the Cold War* (Gloucestershire: Clarendon Press, 1990).

6. Denis Judt, *Empire: The British Imperial Experience from 1765 to the Present* (New York: Basic Books, 2003).

7. Lawrence Freedman, *Britain and Nuclear Weapons* (New York: Macmil-lan, 1980).

8. Stephen George, *An Awkward Partner: Britain in the European Commu-nity*, 3rd ed. (Oxford University Press, 1998); Klaus Larres with Elizabeth

Meehan, eds., *Uneasy Allies: British-German Relations and European Integration since 1945* (Oxford University Press, 2000).

9. Keith Kyle, *Suez* (New York: Macmillan, 1992).

10. John Dumbrell, *A Special Relationship: Anglo-American Relations from the Cold War to Iraq*, 2nd ed. (Hampshire, U.K.: Palgrave Macmillan, 2006).

11. Kitty Newman, *Macmillan, Khrushchev, and the Berlin Crisis, 1958–1960* (Abingdon, U.K.: Routledge, 2007); L. V. Scott, *Macmillan, Khrushchev, and the Cuban Missile Crisis* (New York: St. Martin's Press, 1999).

12. Jacqueline Tratt, *The Macmillan Government and Europe* (New York: St. Martin's Press, 1996); Piers Ludlow, *The European Community and the Crises of the 1960s: Negotiating the Gaullist Challenge* (Abingdon, U.K.: Routledge, 2006).

13. John Darwin, *The Rise and Fall of the British World System, 1830–1970* (Cambridge University Press, 2009).

14. For precise details, see David Butler and Uwe Kitzinger, *The 1975 Referendum* (London: Macmillan, 1976).

15. Matthias Matthijs, *Ideas and Economic Crisis in Britain from Attlee to Blair* (Abingdon, U.K.: Routledge, 2010); Nickolas Tiratsoo, ed., *From Blitz to Blair: A New History of Britain since 1939* (London: Weidenfeld & Nicolson, 1997).

16. Tim Pat Coogan, *The Troubles: Ireland's Ordeal, 1966–1996, and the Search for Peace* (Boulder, Colo.: Rinehart, 1996).

17. Kathleen Burk and Alec Cairncross, *Goodbye-Great Britain: The 1976 IMF Crisis* (Yale University Press, 1992).

18. For a good and still very readable biography, see Hugo Young, *The Iron Lady* (New York: Farrar Straus Giroux, 1989).

19. The magazine article was published on September 23, 1987. For the full text of the interview, see www.margaretthatcher.org/document/106689.

20. See Richard Aldous, *Reagan and Thatcher: The Difficult Relationship* (New York: W. W. Norton, 2012); Nicholas Wapshott, *Ronald Reagan and Margaret Thatcher: A Political Marriage* (New York: Sentinel, 1997).

21. For a good account of Thatcher's increasingly suspicious sentiments of both Reagan and Gorbachev, and the Europeans, see her memoir *The Downing Street Years* (New York: HarperCollins, 1993) and the memoirs of two of her closest advisers: George R. Urban, *Diplomacy and Disillusion at the Court of Margaret Thatcher: An Insider's View* (London: I. B. Tauris, 1996); Percy Craddock, *In Pursuit of British Interests: Reflections on the Foreign Policy under Margaret Thatcher and John Major* (London: John Murray, 1997).

22. For Thatcher's increasing Euroskepticism, including the Bruges speech, see Klaus Larres, "Margaret Thatcher and German Unification Revisited," in *The Revolutions of 1989*, edited by Michael Gehler, Wolfgang Mueller, and Arnold Suppan (Vienna: Austrian Academy of Sciences, 2013). See also

Klaus Larres, "Schwierige Verbündete: Margaret Thatcher, John Major und die Politik Helmut Kohls," in *Deutsche Europapolitik Christlicher Demokraten (1945–2009)*, edited by H. J. Küsters (2013).

23. Larres, "Margaret Thatcher and German Unification Revisited"; Larres, "Schwierige Verbündete."

24. See Larres, "Schwierige Verbündete."

25. Ibid.

26. For a good biography of John Major, see Anthony Seldon, *Major: A Political Life* (London: Weidenfeld & Nicolson, 1997); see also John Major, *The Autobiography* (New York: HarperCollins, 1999).

27. See Anthony Forster, *Britain and the Maastricht Negotiations* (London: Macmillan, 1999); Alasdair Blair, *Dealing with Europe: Britain and the Negotiations of the Maastricht Treaty* (Farnham, U.K.: Ashgate, 1999).

28. See Con Coughlin, *Tony Blair and the War on Terror* (Ecco, 2006); James Naughtie, *The Accidental American: Tony Blair and the Presidency* (Public Affairs, 2004); Peter Lee, *Blair's Just War: Iraq and the Illusion of Morality* (Hampshire, U.K.: Palgrave Macmillan, 2012); David Coates, *Blair's War* (Cambridge: Polity, 2004).

29. See Rhiannon Vickers, *The Labour Party and the World* (Hampshire, U.K.: Palgrave Macmillan, 2011).

30. Ibid. See also Iain Dale, ed., *Labour Party: General Election Manifestos, 1900–1997* (Abingdon, U.K.: Routledge, 1998).

31. Quoted in Mark Phythian, *The Politics of British Arms Sales since 1964: "To Secure Our Rightful Share"* (Manchester University Press, 2010), pp. 289–301.

32. See Colin Tyler, "Citizenship, Rights, and Tony Blair's Doctrine of International Community," in *Globalization, Citizenship, and the War on Terror*, edited by Maurice Mullard and Bangole Cole (Edward Elgar, 2007), pp. 124ff.

33. See Stephen Wall, *A Stranger in Europe: Britain and the EU from Thatcher to Blair* (Oxford University Press, 2008).

34. Tony Blair, "Speech in Aachen," May 20, 1999 (www.number10.gov.uk /output/page1334.asp).

35. See Dale, *Labour Party: General Election Manifestos, 1900–1997*, p. 348.

36. See Julie Smith, "A Missed Opportunity? New Labour's European Policy, 1997–2005," *International Affairs* 81, no. 4 (2005), pp. 710ff.

37. Quoted in Matthijs, *Ideas and Economic Crisis in Britain*, p. 163.

38. See Smith, "A Missed Opportunity?," pp. 709–11.

39. See Anne Deighton, "The European Security and Defence Policy," *Journal of Common Market Studies* 40/4 (2002), pp. 719–41.

40. See Philip Stevens, "The Blair Government and Europe," *Political Quarterly* (2001), pp. 67–75.

41. For Blair's Warsaw speech of October 2000, see www.number-10.gov /uk/output/page3384.asp.

42. Quoted in Smith, "A Missed Opportunity?," p. 714.

43. See, for instance, Benedict Dyson, *The Blair Identity: Leadership and Foreign Policy* (Manchester University Press, 2009), pp.70ff.

44. See, for instance, Lee, *Blair's Just War*; see also Dieter Dettke, *Germany Says No: The Iraq War and the Future of German Foreign and Security Policy* (Woodrow Wilson Center Press, 2009); John Kampfner, *Blair's Wars: A Liberal Imperialist in Action* (New York Free Press, 2003).

45. See Gordon Brown, *Beyond the Crash: Overcoming the First Crisis of Globalization* (New York: Free Press, 2010).

46. Ibid. See also the various articles in Matt Beech and Simon Lee, eds., *The Brown Government: A Policy Evaluation* (New York: Routledge, 2010).

47. Nathaniel Copsey and Tim Haughton, "Farewell Britannia? 'Issue Capture' and the Politics of David Cameron's 2013 EU Referendum Pledge," *Journal of Common Market Studies* 52 (Annual Review) (2014), pp. 74–89.

48. See Philip Gannon, "The Bridge That Blair Built: David Cameron and the Transatlantic Relationship," *British Politics* 9, no. 2 (2014), pp. 210–29. For a good account of Cameron's domestic and foreign policies, see the chapters in Anthony Seldon, Mike Finn, and Illias Thoms, eds., *The Coalition Effect, 2010–2015* (Cambridge University Press, 2015).

49. Seldon, Finn, and Thoms, *The Coalition Effect*.

50. See James Strong, "Interpreting the Syria Vote: Parliament and British Foreign Policy," *International Affairs* 91, no. 5 (September 2015), pp. 1123–39. See also Klaus Larres, "Obama's Mixed Foreign Policy Balance Sheet," *The National Interest*, October 18, 2016 (http://nationalinterest.org/feature/obamas -mixed-foreign-policy-balance-sheet-18089).

51. European Parliament, "Ukraine after Minsk II: The Next Level Hybrid Responses to Hybrid Threats?," Briefing, March 16, 2015 (www.europarl.europa .eu/RegData/etudes/BRIE/2015/551328/EPRS_BRI(2015)551328_EN.pdf).

52. See Timothy J. Oliver, "Interventionism by Design or Failure: The Coalition and Humanitarian Intervention," *Political Quarterly* 86, no. 1 (January–March 2015), pp. 110–17.

53. Oliver Daddow, "The Use of Force in British Foreign Policy: From New Labour to the Coalition," *Political Quarterly* 84, no. 1 (January–March 2013), pp. 110–18.

54. See Steven Erlanger and Alan Cowell, "Scotland Rejects Independence from United Kingdom," *New York Times*, September 18, 2014.

55. For a precise map of the results, see www.telegraph.co.uk/politics/0 /leave-or-remain-eu-referendum-results-and-live-maps/.

56. See Mathew Goodwin and Caitlin Milazzo, "Taking Back Control? Investigating the Role of Immigration in the 2016 Vote for Brexit," *British Journal of Politics and International Relations* 9, no. 3 (June 2017), pp. 450–64.

57. See the interesting discussion in Robert Saunders, "A Tale of Two Referendums, 1975 and 2016," *Political Quarterly* 87, no. 3 (July–September 2016), pp. 318–22. See also Oliver Craig, *Unleashing Demons: The Inside Story of Brexit* (London: Hodder and Stoughton, 2016).

58. See Tim Shipman, *All Out War: The Full Story of How Brexit Sank Britain's Political Class* (London: William Collins, 2016).

59. See John Armour and Horst Eidenmueller, *Negotiating Brexit* (Baden-Baden: Nomos, 2017).

60. For a breakdown of the available parliamentary votes for May, see Guy Faulconbridge and Costas Pitas, "What Is British PM May's Working Majority?," Reuters, June 28, 2017.

SEVEN

Spain

Foreign Relations and Foreign Policy

JOAQUÍN ROY

After the demise of the Francisco Franco regime, Spain saw that its position in the world was rather weak.[1] Consequently, the Spanish government adopted a frantic agenda of actions that provided a practical illustration of the Spanish saying *Apuntarse a todo* ("Sign up for everything"). In practice, that meant that at the initial stage of Spain's democratic rebirth, Madrid even insisted on belonging to the movement of nonaligned countries. That was an odd choice, because for decades Spain had been attached to the security and defense strategy of the United States through military agreements that allowed Washington to establish air and naval bases in Spanish territory. In any event, Spain's record of membership in international

For their part in the development of this chapter, I would like to thank Federiga Bindi, who generously invited me to participate in the conference "The EU Foreign Policy under the Lisbon Treaty," and Maxime Larivé, Beverly Barrett, and María Lorca, who provided bibliographical and editing assistance and updated economic data.

organizations was noteworthy. Spain ratified the UN Universal Declaration of Human Rights and became a member of the Council of Europe in 1977, joined the North Atlantic Treaty Organization (NATO) in 1981, and acceded to the European Community (EC) in 1986. Spain's mediation role was recognized at the Middle East Peace Conference, convened by the United States in Madrid in 1991, and in the Mediterranean process, founded by the EU and its southern partners in 1995. The establishment in Barcelona of the General Secretariat of the Union for the Mediterranean, which resulted from that process, is a legacy of Spanish diplomacy.

The record of Spain's membership in the European Union has proved to be truly impressive.[2] In the 1920s, José Ortega y Gasset remarked that "Spain is the problem and Europe is the solution," and in recent decades Spain has been pursuing the European solution to the problems that he espoused. During the second part of the Franco regime, Spain tried to cope with the democratic requirements set by the EC, but because Spain was a dictatorship, they were politically impossible to meet at the time. When Spain became a member of the EC in 1986, the country was ready to join the effort to develop the institutions of the EC and helped to strengthen EC staff resources with experts and scholars from Spanish universities and publishing networks.[3] Simultaneously, the best and the brightest of Spain's government cadres joined the EC's expanded institutions, taking on positions of responsibility in decisionmaking bodies.[4] In the 1960s, the Franco regime had crafted the popular tourism slogan "Spain is different!" Yet, by 1986, Spain was not different. It was a European country like any other, returning to its natural state after a long hiatus.

In time, prominent Spaniards joined the EC staff and chaired EU institutions.[5] When the process of drafting the EU's Constitutional Treaty was announced, rather than regarding it as an obligatory task, Spain embraced the mission. Spain in turn received considerable benefits through resources, in the form of development aid and infrastructure financing, provided by the EC to help the weakest of the European regions. From an index of 60 percent of the European median in 1986, Spain's income today is in the range of 105 percent, with some regions surpassing 125 percent. From being a country that was a net receiver of aid from the EC, Spain is today a net payer. However, due to Spain's economic growth, aid has been vanishing. As a result, since the global financial crisis that developed in 2008 there has been considerable alarm among officials responsible for public works and infrastructure projects.

Regional Relations

Relations with the rest of Europe and the United States have monopolized the attention of Spain's governments since the rebirth of Spanish democracy. However, that does not mean that Spain has forgotten other parts of the world. When Spain emerged from isolation, the government adopted an ambitious policy of normalization of international relations, beginning with the country's three closest neighbors. Spain has a record of excellent relations with France and Portugal. The fact that Spain and Portugal acceded jointly to the EU was a sign of the coordination of economic and political policies in the two countries. The imperial confrontation between France and Spain was long gone; in recent years, competition has been limited to certain French interests resisting, for economic reasons, Spain's membership in the EU. With respect to their joint fight against the Basque terrorist group Euskadi Ta Askatasuna (ETA), bilateral cooperation between Spain and France has been very satisfactory. Spain and the United Kingdom have systematically avoided allowing the issue of Gibraltar, an anomaly in the post–World War II trend toward decolonization, to become a serious obstacle to their mutual cooperation. While it remains a sensitive topic with respect to both the issue of sovereignty and concerns about money laundering and contraband, London and Madrid can be considered very close allies in multiple scenarios.

A standard description of Spain's geographic location has been taught to Spanish students since time immemorial. "Spain," the lesson says, "is bounded on the north by France, on the east and south by the Mediterranean Sea . . . and on the west by Portugal." Seldom was there an explicit reference to the U.K. colony of Gibraltar, and Morocco was not considered a "neighbor" in the strict sense. Strategic, social, and economic arguments dictate that Morocco is actually the most important of Spain's neighbors in terms of migration issues, the difficulty of reaching trade agreements, and the two countries' claims and counterclaims of territorial sovereignty over the Spanish cities of Ceuta and Melilla, which are located on the coast of Morocco.

France

An enemy over long periods of history and an ally when convenient, France has not been a worry of Spanish regimes and governments of any form since Napoleonic times. The impressive Pyrenees border has reinforced the mutually beneficial, civilized coexistence of France and Spain. Trade and investment have replaced dynastic and political ambitions in both countries, and Spain's membership in the EU has, with a few exceptions, put an end to animosity and envy. The attractiveness to the French of Spain's "exotic" culture has meshed with the fascination of the Spanish with France's distinguished cuisine. Since the rebirth of democracy, the goal of Spanish governments has been to adhere to the joint overall strategy of Germany and France within the European Union. Both countries are important sources of investment in Spain and consumers of Spanish exports, and they account for a good part of the tourism trade in Spain. Trade disputes over competition from Spanish products just before Spain acceded to the EU (and more recently as a result of the economic crisis) have been the only source of discomfort in the Madrid-Paris relationship. Both conservative and socialist French governments have interacted very well with Spain's right and left governments. As mentioned, the sensitive issue of ETA terrorists taking refuge in France has been resolved by the decisive cooperation of Paris in curtailing terrorist activities in France and detaining criminal suspects, devoid of France's traditional independentist posture.

Portugal

Spain and Portugal, the two Iberian countries, share geography, history, similar languages and social and religious attitudes, a romantic nostalgia for imperial colonial hegemonies, and a sense of loyal cooperation in facing a common European destiny. Although Spain has been presented in other parts of the world as a model for national political transformation, Portugal can claim precedence over Spain in getting rid of its autocratic regime. In April 1974, the Portuguese peacefully toppled (through the "Carnation Revolution") the remains of the Oliveira Salazar government, the oldest fascist-leaning dictatorship in Europe. This feat took place well over one year before the end of the Franco regime in Spain.

Paradoxically, the two nations' coexistence, devoid of animosity and war (a common occurrence in Europe's violent history), can be explained by the fact that both nations have evolved since the Middle Ages (Portugal is the oldest European nation-state) at a respectful mutual distance. Not even the accidental fact that Portugal was part of Spain for dynastic reasons during the reign of Phillip II gave rise to Portuguese anti-imperialist feelings toward Spain. The only remaining source of Portuguese resentment is a small city called Olivenza (in Spanish) and Olivença (in Portuguese), located along a disputed section of the border between the two countries. Portugal lays a de jure claim to it, but it has been administered de facto by Spain since 1801.

Happy with forging historical alliances with other European powers, especially Britain, Portugal has evolved peacefully. It has entered into an economic relationship with Spain in which Spain has been the leader, capturing large shares of trade and industry without causing notable Portuguese resentment. The Portuguese consider the relationship an unavoidable phenomenon. It is questioned only by small economic interests and some Portuguese intellectuals, although in recent times, a fraction of Portugal's right-wing parties has used the Spanish economic hegemony to capture votes, with dubious results.

As in the case of political relations between France and Spain, Portugal's socialist and conservative governments have had an excellent rapport with ideologically diverse Spanish governments. The two countries are so intertwined that the Nobel Prize–winning writer José Saramago once suggested that Portugal's future was to become an autonomous region of Spain.[6] Still, interstate expressways and railways in Portugal are not at the level of those in Spain, and the current financial crisis has led to the termination of plans for a high-speed train line between Madrid and Lisbon.[7]

Gibraltar

The return of Gibraltar to Spain's sovereignty has remained a foreign policy goal of all Spanish governments since the Treaty of Utrecht gave control to the British in 1713. Francisco Franco closed the frontier between Spain and Gibraltar in 1969. Since then, Spain's democratic governments have engaged in calmer but persistent negotiations with London on the issue. Spain's membership in NATO added to the diplomatic difficulties because Spain claimed that Gibraltar was a NATO naval base, something denied by the British government. The most delicate issue is sovereignty. While Gibraltar's 30,000 residents are opposed to becoming Spanish citizens, implementing an innovative joint sovereignty has been suggested as an alternative to continuing with Gibraltar's status as a British colony. The end of the United Kingdom's membership in the European Union has updated this alternative.

Morocco

Morocco has continued to be a leading priority in Spanish policy for reasons besides migration, which has made Spain the main destination of Moroccan workers and a stepping stone into Europe for sub-Saharan illegal immigrants. An important concern is the highly sensitive issue of the Spanish cities of Ceuta and Melilla, which are located on the Moroccan coast on territory claimed by Morocco. A vestige of the old Spanish protectorate and historical presence in North Africa, the two cities are a permanent part of the bilateral agenda, but both governments are committed to not crossing the dangerous line of confrontation, as happened in 1957 when Moroccan irregulars backed by the Moroccan army forced Spain to leave the small enclave of Sidi Ifni. In 1975, during the last days of the Franco dictatorship, the Moroccan authorities staged the so-called Green March to Spanish Western Sahara and forced the partition of the territory between Mauritania and Morocco. Eventually, Morocco ended up occupying all the territory, which led to calls for independence by the residents and claims by neighboring Algeria that its sovereignty was being violated.

Morocco has maintained that the Spanish enclaves of Ceuta and Melilla are integral parts of Morocco's sovereign national territory. Because the two North African towns and their offshore islands had belonged to the Spanish crown for centuries and both were administered as integral parts of Spain and had predominantly Spanish populations, Spain insisted that they remain Spanish. When Spain joined the EC in 1986, Ceuta and Melilla were considered Spanish cities and European territory, and the two cities claimed to be candidates for financial assistance from the EC's Regional Development Fund. Spain also hoped that its membership in NATO, while providing no security guarantee to Ceuta and Melilla, might make Morocco's King Hassan II less likely to move against the territory, since it belonged to a NATO member. However, Spanish demands for the return of Gibraltar have consistently reinforced Moroccan ambitions to regain Ceuta and Melilla.

The Western Hemisphere

Spain's relations with the subregions and countries of the Western Hemisphere can be subdivided into those with the United States and Canada, with Latin America, and with the Caribbean. Due to the greater historical importance to Spain of the United States and Latin America, including the Spanish Caribbean countries, special attention is given to relations with those countries.

The United States: Sleeping with the Hegemon

Spain's relations with the United States offer a contrast between contemporary diplomatic declarations and the historical record. While officials consistently claim that the two countries have been steady allies since U.S. independence, the historical evidence shows that Spain and the United States often took different sides, remained distanced from and indifferent to each other, and, at times, went to war with each other. The exceptions to that norm are the heralded help that Spain gave to the United States during its struggle for independence and the steady alliance of the two since the signing of the successive treaties and expanded mutual defense agreements between Francisco Franco and Dwight Eisenhower.

During the early years of Spain's democratic rule, the focus of the government was on consolidating the country's parliamentary system. Foreign policy issues received less attention. However, disagreement persisted between the governing Unión de Centro Democrático (Union of the Democratic Center, or UCD) and the opposition PSOE (Partido Socialista Obrero Español, or Spanish Socialist Workers' Party) over Spain's relations with NATO and with the United States. When Leopoldo Calvo Sotelo replaced Adolfo Suárez as prime minister in 1981, he launched a vigorous campaign to gain approval for Spain's membership in NATO. Shortly after that was accomplished, a new executive agreement was signed in July 1982 with the United States on the use of bases in Spain. This agreement was one in a series of renewals of the basic 1953 security arrangement providing for U.S. use of strategic naval and air bases on Spanish soil in exchange for U.S. military and economic assistance.

Many Spaniards still resented the presence of U.S. bases in Spain, recalling the widely publicized photograph of U.S. president Eisenhower embracing Franco when the first agreement on the bases was signed. There were occasional popular protests against such reminders of U.S. support for the dictatorship, including a demonstration during President Ronald Reagan's 1985 visit to Spain. The Socialists had consistently advocated a more neutralist, independent role for Spain. When they came to power in October 1982, Felipe González pledged a close examination of the defense and cooperation agreements with the United States. A reduction in the

U.S. military presence in Spain was one of the stipulations included in the referendum held in 1986 on Spain's continued membership in NATO. Accordingly, the prime minister announced in December 1987 that the United States would have to remove its seventy-two F-16 fighter-bombers from Spanish bases by mid-1991. Spain also informed the United States in November 1991 that the bilateral defense agreement, which the Spanish population overwhelmingly rejected according to opinion polls, would not be renewed. Nevertheless, in January 1988, Spain and the United States reached in principle a new base agreement to last eight years. The new military arrangements called for a marked reduction of the U.S. presence in Spain and terminated the U.S. military and economic aid that had been tied to the defense treaty.[8]

Latin America: Between Colonial Legacy and the Future

Spain has maintained a "special relationship" with its former colonies in Latin America.[9] To a large extent, Spain's diplomatic strategy vis-à-vis Latin America is exemplified by the establishment of the Ibero-American Community.[10] A modernized version of the traditional *Hispanidad*, it is based on the links among Spain, Portugal, Central and South America, and parts of the Caribbean (Cuba and the Dominican Republic) through language, commerce, history, and culture. In this context, Spain has shared its experience of political transition from dictatorship to democracy while respecting ideologically different regimes and opting for an approach to the region that reflects the overall programs of the European Union. Spain's general strategies emphasize regional economic integration, poverty reduction, respect for human rights, and political consolidation. In recent years, however, the Spanish government as well as the EU has been testing a more country-specific approach, giving some countries priority over others.

When the Spanish Socialist Workers' Party came to power in 1982, Latin America became even more important to Spanish interests. The Spanish government implemented generous development aid programs for Latin America, and the two Spanish commissioners in Brussels who were charged with EU relations with the region, Abel Matutes and Manuel Marín, brought Latin America to the attention of the EU's international development agencies. Spain spearheaded the EU's new Latin American policy by promoting peace, democracy, and regional economic and political integration, in particular in Central America, a region riddled with internal conflict. While the U.S. government was skeptical about this novel European involvement, in time Washington welcomed the support in areas where U.S. influence was lagging. On balance, Spain's involvement has been very positive.

During José María Aznar's two terms as prime minister (1996–2000 and 2000–04), Spanish relations with some Latin American countries (Mexico, Venezuela, and Cuba, especially) became tense for different reasons. However, relations were exceptionally good with others, like Colombia, the Dominican Republic, and most of the Central American republics. With the victory of José Luis Rodríguez Zapatero in the 2004 general elections, the scenario changed. Relations with Venezuela got better, a move that was not taken well in Washington. Relations with Brazil and Chile were substantially strengthened, specifically as part of ambitious investment in sensitive and profitable areas such as communications, banking, and transportation.

In more recent years, friction developed with Argentina due to disagreements over Spanish investments and the populist measures taken by the administrations of former president Néstor Kirchner and his widow and successor, Cristina Kirchner. With Chile, relations were excellent under the coalition (*Concertación*) formed by the Christian Democrats and the Socialists, and they continued to be very good with a conservative president, Sebastián Piñera, and again with Michelle Bachelet, who became president in 2014. The same can be said with respect to Uruguay, Peru, and most especially Colombia, a country that has enjoyed as much attention from Zapatero's government as from Aznar's and more recently from Prime Minister Mariano Rajoy, leader of the Partido Popular (People's Party). Certain tensions have developed with the countries of ALBA (Alianza Bolivariana para los Pueblos de Nuestra América, or the Bolivarian Alliance for the Americas), which was led by Venezuela's late president, Hugo Chávez, because of populist measures or postures that have threatened Spanish investments. The indigenous anti-imperialist attitude of Evo Morales in Bolivia has affected the legal status and security of Spanish firms there.

In the Caribbean, the Dominican Republic has for decades been a model of economic and political cooperation with Spain, which provided the republic with both investment and developmental aid. In fact, Spain was the main actor in promoting the country's accession to the African, Caribbean, and Pacific Group of States (ACP). As a result, the Dominican Republic has received an impressive volume of development aid from the EU. All Spanish

governments since democracy was reinstated have backed social and economic development programs in Central America, contributed with funds
and military assistance to EU or UN peacemaking and peacekeeping programs, and generously supported democratic consolidation in the region.

A separate chapter on Spain's foreign policy should be dedicated to Cuba.
Spain's relationship with this former colony should be considered very
special. Within the EU, Spain has led important and unusual diplomatic
overtures toward the Castro regime. Spain has maintained close diplomatic,
social, and economic relations with Cuba in spite of political changes in
both countries. In addition, Spain took the initiative in opposing a U.S. decision curtailing trade (the Helms-Burton Act) while sponsoring EU measures detailing preconditions for deeper political relations and cooperation
on development programs, as expressed in the Common Position, to be met
by the Cuban government. Under the Aznar and the socialist governments,
Spain supported and led the policy of "constructive engagement," in tune
with the general EU emphasis on maintaining open lines of communication.[11] In 2013, Madrid endorsed a new EU plan to reinforce the EU-Cuba
relationship and contributed to approve the end of the Common Position
and the signing of a new cooperation agreement.

The Rest of the World

In recent years, Spain has expanded its rather limited historical presence
in the sub-Saharan region. For obvious reasons, Madrid has maintained an
interest in its only former colony, Equatorial Guinea. In spite of the harsh
dictatorial nature of the regime, Spain has continued a steady flow of investment and trade operations. Close relations with countries like Senegal,
Mauritania, and Mali have helped in controlling illegal immigration to the
Canary Islands.

Spain has been considered a solid partner in political mediation in the
Middle East. Spain generally has had no disagreements with very different
regimes in the region, although it was late in recognizing the state of Israel
and it has provided steady support for Palestinian claims of statehood. The
Arab countries have been a strategic priority for Spain because they are a
source of oil and natural gas, and several Arab countries are important investors in Spain. When the Iraq War exploded, the Spanish government,
led by Prime Minister Aznar, sent a small military unit to join the U.S.-led
coalition. However, after the defeat of Aznar's party in the 2004 election,
the new president, José Luis Rodríguez Zapatero, abruptly withdrew the

troops, causing a major upset in the administration of George W. Bush. In contrast, Spain has participated in the NATO-led Afghanistan operation since its inception, maintaining a steady number of soldiers, a hundred of whom have been killed in action and in terrorist attacks.

Despite its early colonial presence in the Philippines, Spain was a latecomer in the Far East, and it has been trying to expand its historically modest relations with East Asian nations. The People's Republic of China and Japan are Spain's main countries of interest in the region. Thailand and Indonesia have been Spain's main allies in the important Association of Southeast Asian Nations (ASEAN). As have many other European states, Spain has expanded trade and investment in South Korea and Malaysia and even in Vietnam. Lately, India has become a center of Spanish business activity and diplomacy. Relations with Australia and New Zealand have been cordial and profitable.

Global Presence

Some aspects of foreign relations have become a priority on the Spanish global agenda, calling for a combination of "hard power" and a special brand of "soft power" that involves defense and military matters as well as economic, trade, and development assistance. All of these sectoral activities have to be taken into account in the context of Spain's membership in the European Union.

The North Atlantic Treaty Organization

As mentioned earlier, during the first years of the Spanish political transition to democracy there was almost unanimous backing for Spain's accession to the EC. However, consensus was not that clear with respect to NATO. Its geographic position made Spain a valuable partner for the alliance, as it was during the last decades of the Franco regime. Advocates for membership thought that Spain's strategic geographic location was an argument in favor of membership because it would make the country an obvious target in any major conflict unless it had allied support. They also maintained that integration into NATO would guarantee the badly needed modernizing of Spain's armed services as well as secure an adequate national defense. A corollary hope was that NATO membership would reorient the focus of army leaders away from reactionary preoccupations and toward defense of the West. Politically neutralizing the resentful military after the attempted coup of 1981 allegedly was part of the deal to join both the EC and NATO.

However, several Spanish political groups, particularly the socialist and the communist parties, did not agree that full membership would serve the country's defense and foreign policy aims. They thought that it would raise the level of tension between the world powers and make Spain a more likely target in any future conflict with the Soviet Union. Opponents of NATO membership claimed that NATO would be of no help with one of Spain's primary worries, the cities of Ceuta and Melilla, located as they are in North Africa, outside the protective geographic zone of the North Atlantic Treaty. They also maintained that NATO would be of no benefit to Spain in recovering Gibraltar, because it could be assumed that NATO members would support Britain. Another factor influencing those who opposed Spain's entry into NATO was resentment of the United States, the principal supporter of the Franco regime.

Although Prime Minister Adolfo Suárez had announced Spain's intention of applying for NATO membership, his UCD government remained openly divided. After Suárez resigned in 1981, his successor, Leopoldo Calvo Sotelo, gave priority to joining NATO. In his view, Spain's entry into NATO would speed up negotiations for integration into the EC. In December 1981, the Spanish congress approved membership over the opposition of the large leftist sector, which protested that NATO membership had been pushed through Parliament, violating a prior consensus. The PSOE organized an aggressive negative campaign, and Felipe González, the party's leader, made the NATO issue a major feature of his electoral campaign in 1982, promising a popular referendum on withdrawal. However, González later had second thoughts and found reasons to delay the referendum; eventually he advocated a positive vote for limited membership. With 60 percent turnout, 52.6 percent of the voters supported Spain's continued membership while 39.8 percent opposed it. The following year, in a move seen as emphasizing the European aspect of the defense system, González applied for Spanish membership in the Western European Union (WEU). In 1988, Spain and Portugal were formally invited to join the organization.

International Defense and Military Cooperation

As outlined already, since the end of Spain's military activity in Europe and the country's defeat in the Latin American wars of independence, Spain's armed forces had been absent in all the major conflicts of the last century, with the exception of a brief intervention in Russia during World War II. Spanish soldiers were used only in North Africa and as an internal force to support the Franco regime. Since the normalization of the army after Spain became a member of NATO, the Spanish military (fully professional once the draft was terminated) has participated in an array of peacemaking and peacekeeping missions as well as in programs to train the armed forces of countries in need of democratic order and political consolidation. In June 2011 Spain approved the Spanish Security Strategy (Estrategia Española de Seguridad, or EES)[12] and created the Spanish Security Council, which succeeded the traditional National Defense Council and marked a shift to a broad interpretation of security that is not limited to military matters.[13] In this understanding, internal and external security are meshed. While the UN is considered a permanent framework for any Spanish military action, NATO membership entails obligatory military missions. The EU needs to be considered a permanent point of reference for any type of alliance. This strategy is in perfect tune with that of other EU nations, especially the United Kingdom and France.

In the last two decades, more than 100,000 Spanish soldiers have served in more than fifty missions on four continents, especially in the former Yugoslavia, the Middle East, and Central America.[14] Forty thousand of them have served in Bosnia, making the mission a success story in international cooperation. Spanish troops also have served in Operation EUFOR Althea in Bosnia, and they are an integral part of the International Security Assistance Force (ISAF) in Afghanistan. They have participated in the UN Interim Force in Lebanon (UNIFIL), in the European Union's Atalanta operation to fight piracy off the coast of Somalia, and in the program to train Somalia's security forces. The number of Spanish troops abroad now totals more than 3,500.

However, all Spanish military operations have been at risk of decreased effectiveness because of the global economic crisis. As a result of EU demands for drastic cuts in government spending, Spain has abandoned large investments in weapons systems. Alternative options include reselling some of the more important arms to other countries to generate revenue for new investment.[15]

The Economy

The first two decades of Spain's membership in the EU were very beneficial economically. Spain became the eighth-largest economy in the world. Its prosperity lasted until 2007, and during that time growth was spectacularly fast.

The strength of the euro—a European integration success—provoked a reduction of interest rates, propelling growth to levels that were unsustainable without the necessary infrastructure reform. A sudden increase in prices and wages caused a large external deficit and an increase in the external debt, which was necessary to level the external imbalance. The 2008 global financial crisis and the explosion of the housing market bubble hit the country hard.

In May 2010, the government admitted that Spain also was suffering the impact of the global crisis, and under pressure from the EU, the United States, and the International Monetary Fund, the government took drastic economic measures. The aim was to avoid the fate of Greece, to salvage the welfare state system, and to maintain the euro and the EU itself—a primary preoccupation of Spain and Brussels.

Even during the current crisis, some economic sectors seem brighter than others. One is the tourism industry. Even before the rebirth of Spanish democracy, tourism had been a major economic sector, making it crucial to the country's stability. The World Travel and Tourism Council has announced that in 2017 Spain was the second most popular tourist destination, thus overtaking the United States, now ranked third.[16]

Trade and Investment

Spain has experienced a considerable increase in its export activity in the past decade. It is worth noting that activity picked up particularly after 2002, when the euro was fully introduced, physically as well as nominally (see figure 7-1). Nonetheless, the global financial crisis has had a brutal impact on Spain.[17] Between 2007 and 2008, Spain's exports reached the highest level in history; however, the crisis had a significant negative effect on exports, which dropped to levels that were close to those reported at the beginning of the twenty-first century. More recent trends and data show that the export sector experienced a considerable increase during the second decade of the

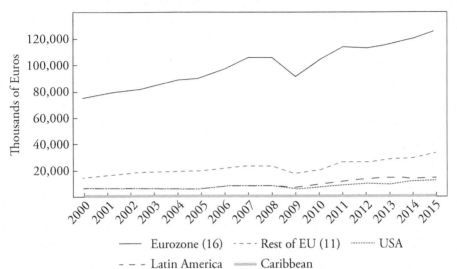

FIGURE 7-1. **Spanish Exports (Merchandise)**

new century, a trend that has continued since. Spain's import activity, however, has remained higher than export activity and actually increased during the expansionary phase of the business cycle. Nevertheless, import activity peaked in 2007 (see figure 7-2). Afterward, it suffered a drop, in line with the economic slowdown, but has recovered in the second decade of this century, thereby having a very positive effect on Spain's trade balance.

Spanish overall foreign investment was impressive until 2007, dropping in 2008 because of the financial crisis (see figure 7-3). It is noteworthy that the majority of investments have taken place within the European Union. However, investments in Latin America increased proportionally, making Spain the number-one investor in some countries of the Southern Cone, ahead of the rest of Europe and the United States.[18]

International Cooperation and Development Aid

Spain is a leader in the field of cooperative development, targeting poverty and hunger in the world as an integral part of its foreign policy. Programs reflect more than a strategy to increase income and purchasing power.

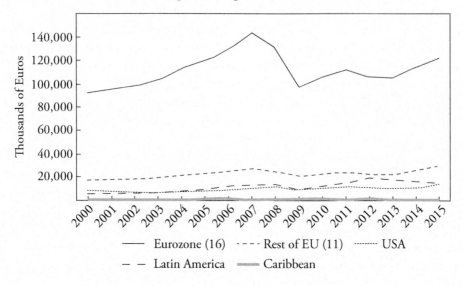

FIGURE 7-2. **Spanish Imports (Merchandise)**

Eurozone (16)　　Rest of EU (11)　　USA

Latin America　　Caribbean

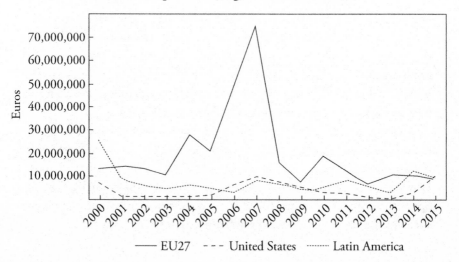

FIGURE 7-3. **Spanish Foreign Direct Investment**

EU27　　United States　　Latin America

Defense of human rights, environmental conservation, gender equality, and respect for cultural diversity are also integral parts of Spain's foreign policy, which enjoys a broad consensus not only in government circles but also in the realm of the autonomous communities and among local entities and the civilian population at large through active nongovernmental organizations funded by public and private sources.

A review of Spain's development assistance over the last two decades reveals that its emphasis has oscillated between the preference of the Partido Popular (PP) for giving aid in the context of Spanish investment and the priority given by the Spanish Socialist Workers' Party to programs emphasizing social issues. At the time, it remained to be seen what the PP policy would be in the event of the predicted electoral victory in the fall of 2011. No major changes were contemplated by the new government. Subsequent facts confirmed that prediction. In any event, both strategies have suffered from the impact of the serious financial crisis and budget cuts by the Spanish government.

Conclusion

In general, reviews of Spain's foreign policy since the recovery of democracy claim that it has been rather stable. Only some concrete exceptions (for example, the initial disagreement over membership in NATO) are part of the official record. However, closer analysis reveals that Spain's foreign policy has shown several important inconsistencies caused by major serious reversals in the internal political framework. The fact is that a crucial chapter of foreign policy under Prime Minister José Maria Aznar was the backbone of the electoral victory of José Luis Rodríguez Zapatero in 2004 and his two terms in office. The terrorist attacks in Madrid, on March 11, 2004, were a retaliation by al Qaeda for the intervention of Spanish armed forces in Iraq and the close relationship between Aznar and George W. Bush. The major reason for the defeat of the People's Party in the national election a few days later was the faulty handling of the crisis: The government accused ETA terrorists of the attack. Foreign policy played a major role in the change of government and was evident in the first term of the Zapatero mandate (2004–08), surviving until what appeared to be the exhaustion of PSOE government control in the summer of 2011, when new elections were called. With the return of the PP to power, foreign policy was set to stay on the radar, but the priority given to economic and financial matters reduced the attention given to overseas activities.

The alternative PSOE foreign strategy was composed of innovative measures and decisions, among them the design of the Alliance of Civilizations (with the full backing of the UN), in contrast with Bush's "war on terror." At the same time, the government announced an increase in the volume of Spain's foreign aid in order to reach the 0.7 percent of GDP set in the UN Millennium Development Goals. Moreover, Zapatero joined the conservative–social democratic alliance formed by France and Germany, in contrast to Aznar, who linked Spain with the United States and the United Kingdom. On top of that, a new defense policy favored a European security arrangement, downsizing defense links with NATO and the United States.

During Zapatero's administration the government gave priority to individual rights (equality) and social rights (welfare and immigrant conditions). The foreign record, however, shows that the same passion has not been quite equally applied. Some areas (poverty, clean water supply) were stressed while others (same-sex marriage and abortion) were deemphasized, especially in Latin America. Imposing conditions on the delivery of aid was not at the top of the agenda. The same prudent approach defines Spain's asylum policy, which shows a cautious attitude. This profile is obvious in the content of the *Plan Director*,[19] where the key terms are "good governance" and "institutional strengthening."

The explosion of the Arab crisis and subsequent Arab Spring revealed an array of contrasting and sometimes embarrassing Spanish policies dealing with autocratic regimes in North Africa and the Middle East, and the same can be said of relations with Spain's last three colonies, Cuba, Morocco, and Equatorial Guinea. Experts point out the lack of coordination in aid policies and the absence of clear documentation of the progress of Spanish political actions and commercial activities. This diplomatic pattern is especially important when one considers the country's past authoritarian legacy in dealing with less-than-democratic regimes.

The relatively positive situation of Spain in today's international scene, which makes the country a suitable partner for alliances and compromises, shows that single disputes with other countries are rare—vestiges of historical factors that seem to be very difficult to correct. With a few exceptions, they have not been a cause for drastic disagreements, although confrontations have occurred.

In conclusion, a central question remains: Are Spain's foreign policy and global relations in tune with the overall international behavior of the European Union and its most important member states? The answer is, in general terms, a solid "yes." Only minor corrections to foreign policy can be detected in certain scenarios and on peripheral issues. These do not make Spain a "different" country. The only dimensions of Spain's foreign policy that could be considered peculiar in the EU context are "special relationships" with other countries that reflect the lasting impact of a shared history or geographic constraints. These special relationships would not make the country today an uncomfortable candidate for membership in the European Union, as they did not in 1986 when Spain's accession took place.

In fact, the specifics of Spanish policy are complementary to the overall minimal EU "foreign policy." Where the EU as a whole cannot reach, Spain can contribute toward the collective success, and on scenarios and issues in which Spain does not have the capacity to act, membership in the EU enables the Spanish government to have a say. The establishment of the European External Action Service (EEAS) is proof of this thesis in practice. Spain can draw on its extensive network of close diplomatic relations with and development aid to countries of Latin America to help mediate crises in the region. The same can be said, to a lesser extent, of Spain's links in the Middle East and North Africa.

Taking into account current world circumstances, a careful assessment of Spain's foreign policy must accept that Zapatero's policies were in part designed and executed to redress the actions taken by Aznar, who in turn reversed the consensus that had existed during the Felipe González administration. The PP leader, Jose María Aznar, opted to follow Bush's agenda, based on hard power. The Aznar period was an exception in recent Spanish history. Zapatero was elected to recover a space for Spain in the EU and the world scene inspired by the effectiveness of soft power. However, that strategy was formed under rather optimistic circumstances and did not take into serious consideration the possibility that the coming years might not present economic conditions as positive as the ones that existed in 1994–2008. This new setting affected the role of the government of Popular Party Prime Minister Mariano Rajoy, which had to work under financial constraints and forced dedication to domestic issues. With the PP's return to power in 2011, a period of certain instability was generated when in the elections of 2015 Rajoy did not obtain a majority to rule, a problem that was replicated in a second try in 2016. The traditional two-party system was reformed by the appearance of additional groups (left-leaning Podemos and centrist Ciudadanos). To avoid a third attempt, the conservatives and socialists made a deal to allow Rajoy to govern with a parliamentary minority. However, Mariano Rajoy fell over a corruption scandal involving members of his party, leading the way for a new socialist (PSOE) led by Pedro Sanchez.[20]

In realistic terms, Spain will always have to accept the fact that while the EU is in trouble and decisions are harder to reach due to the EU's intergovernmental nature, particular members still have a decisive say. The reality is that Madrid (under any government) has to follow guidelines from Berlin or Paris or both. And that may be in Spain's best interest, although the country may accept it only reluctantly. In any event, Spain has to recognize that the EU is not the same as in the last stages of the previous century. Enlargement and dramatic globalization have made the EU very different.

This uncertain picture will develop in a global scene that may be very different from the one that currently exists. The EU will not be the same as the one facing today's economic and social challenges. New powers are emerging, calling into question the continued leadership of the United States in international affairs. Nationalism is threatening some of the fundamentals of the EU, under the pressure of uncontrolled immigration, while the United States under the Donald Trump administration is engaging in a new international strategy. Spain will then have to choose wisely, balancing its own national interests and values in the realm of foreign policy.

NOTES

1. For a review of classic books on Spain's foreign policy, see Rafael Calduch, *La política exterior española en el siglo XX* (Madrid: Ediciones Ciencias Sociales, 1994); Kenneth Maxwell and Steve Spiegel. *The New Spain: From Isolation to Influence* (New York: Council on Foreign Relations Press, 1994); Juan Carlos Pereira, *La política exterior de España: De 1800 hasta Hoy* (Barcelona: Ariel, 2003, 2010); Benny Pollack and Graham Hunter, *The Paradox of Spanish Foreign Policy: Spain's International Relations from Franco to Democracy* (London: Pinter, 1987).

2. For a selection of classic and recent books on Spain in the EU, see the following: Ramón Tamames, *La larga marcha de España a la Unión Europea* (Madrid: Edimadoz, 1999); Esther Barbé, *La política europea de España* (Barcelona:

Ariel, 1999); Raimundo Bassols, *España en Europa: historia de la adhesión a la CE, 1957–85* (Madrid: Política Exterior, 1995); Angel Viñas, *Al servicio de Europa: Innovación y crisis en la Comisión Europea* (Madrid: Universidad Complutense, 2006); Francesc Granell, *Veinte años de España en la integración Europea* (Barcelona: Real Academia de Ciencias Económicas y Financieras, 2006); Joaquín Roy and María Lorca-Susino, eds., *Spain in the European Union: The First Twenty-Five Years (1986–2011)* (Miami: European Union Center/Jean Monnet Chair, 2011).

3. For an additional selection of the classic textbooks and standard reference works on the EU, developed and used in Spanish universities, see Victoria Abellán and Blanca Vilà, *Lecciones de Derecho Comunitario Europeo* (Barcelona: Ariel, 1993); Francesc Morata, *La Unión Europea: Procesos, actores, y políticas* (Barcelona: Ariel, 1998); Araceli Mangas and Diego J. Liñán Nogueras, *Instituciones y derecho de la Unión Europeas* (Madrid: McGraw-Hill, 1996); and Donato Fernández Navarrete, *Historia y economía de la Unión Europea* (Madrid: Centro de Estudios Ramón Areces, 1999).

4. Angel Viñas, "Las políticas comunitarias: una visión interna," *Información Comercial Española*, vol. 831 (July–August 2006); Francesc Granell, *Catalunya dins la Unió Europea: Política, economía, i societat* (Barcelona: Ediciones 62, 2002).

5. Viñas, "Las políticas comunitarias."

6. Miguel Mora, "Portugal, ¿comunidad autónoma?," *El País*, July 17, 2007.

7. On the joint experience of Spain and Portugal as members of the EU, see Joaquín Roy and Aimee Kanner, *España y Portugal en la Unión Europea* (México: Universidad Autónoma de México, 2001); Joaquín Roy and Aimee Kanner, "Spain and Portugal in the European Union," in *The European Union and the Member States: Cooperation, Coordination, and Compromise*, edited by Eleanor E. Zeff and Ellen B. Pirro (Boulder, Colo.: Lynne Rienner, 2001), pp. 235–63; Sebastián Royo and Paul Christopher Manuel, *Spain and Portugal in the European Union: The First Fifteen Years* (London: Frank Cass, 2003).

8. For the latest and possibly most complete account of the relationship between Spain and the United States in the context of the rebirth of Spanish democracy, see Charles Powell, *El amigo Americano: España y Estados Unidos: de la dictadura a la democracia* (Madrid: Galaxia Gutember, 2011).

9. For a selection of studies on Spain's relations with Latin America, see Celestino del Arenal, *España y América Latina 200 años después de la Independencia: Valoración y perspectivas* (Madrid: Marcial Pons and Real Instituto Elcano, 2009); Celestino del Arenal, *La política exterior de España hacia Iberoamérica* (Madrid: Ed. Complutense, 1994); Juan Carlos Pereira and Angel Cervantes, *Relaciones diplomáticas entre España y América* (Madrid: Fundación Mapfre América, 1992); Carlos Rama, *Historia de las relaciones culturales entre España y la América Latina: Siglo XIX* (México: Fondo de Cultura Económica, 1982).

10. For a selection of studies on this special dimension, see Celestino del Arenal and Alfonso Nájera, *España e Iberoamérica: De la Hispanidad a la Comunidad Iberoamericana de Naciones* (Madrid: CEDEAL, 1989); Celestino del Arenal and Alfonso Nájera, *La Comunidad Iberoamericana de Naciones: Pasado, presente y futuro de la política iberoamericana de España* (Madrid: CEDEAL, 1992); Castor M. Díaz Barrado, *Perfiles de la Comunidad Iberoamericana de Naciones* (Madrid: Casa de América, 1994); Paul Isbell, Carlos Malamud, and Federico Steinberg, *Iberoamérica: Realidad frente a mito: De Guadalajara 1991 a Salamanca 2005* (Madrid: Real Instituto Elcano, 2005); Roberto Mesa, *La idea de Comunidad Iberoamericana: Entre la utopía y la historia* (Madrid: CEDEAL, 1989); Joaquín Roy and Albert Galinsoga, *The Ibero-American Space: Dimensions and Perceptions of the Special Relationship between Spain and Latin America* (University of Miami/University of Lleida, 1997).

11. For a complete review of the relations between Spain and Cuba, see Joaquín Roy, *The Cuban Revolution (1959–2009): Its Relationship with Spain, the European Union, and the United States* (New York: Palgrave McMillan, 2009).

12. For complete text and analysis, see Barcelona Centre for International Affairs (CIDOB), *The Spanish Security Strategy (EES): Everyone's Responsibility* (Barcelona: CIDOB, 2011).

13. Javier Solana, "España ante el nuevo mundo," *El País*, March 28, 2011; "Más seguridad," editorial, *El País*, June 28, 2011.

14. Ignacio Fuente Cobo, *La cooperación militar española en los países iberoamericanos* (Madrid: Centro Superior de la Defensa, 2007).

15. Jesús Núñez Villaverde, "Mal momento para una buena noticia," *El País*, June 25, 2011.

16. Katrina Pirner, "Spain Surpasses US as World's Second Most Popular Tourist Destination," South EU Summit, April 17, 2018 (https://www.southeusummit.com/europe/spain/spain-surpasses-us-worlds-second-popular-tourist-destination/).

17. Francesc Granell, "Spain's Management of the Economy since 1986," in *Spain in the European Union*, edited by Roy and Lorca-Susino, pp. 193–210.

18. For examples of research on investment in Latin America with Spanish participation, see William Chislett, *La inversión española directa en América Latina: retos y oportunidades* (Madrid: Real Instituto Elcano, 2003); William Chislett, *Spanish Direct Investment in Latin America: Challenges and Opportunities* (Madrid: Real Instituto Elcano, 2003); Félix Martín and Pablo Toral, eds., *Latin America's Quest for Globalization: The Role of Spanish Firms* (Burlington, Vt.: Ashgate, 2005); Pablo Toral, *The Reconquest of the New World: Multinational Enterprises and Spain's Direct Investment in Latin America* (Aldershot, U.K.: Ashgate, 2001); Joaquín Roy, "The Latin American Image of Spain in the Aftermath of Recent Investments," in *Latin America's Quest for Globalization*, edited by Martín and Toral, pp. 287–305.

19. Ministerio de Asuntos Exteriores y de Cooperación, "Plan Director de la Cooperación Española: 2009–2012," December 2009 (http://www.aecid .es/galerias/publicaciones/descargas/libro1_PlanDirector_LR.pdf), and "Plan Anual de Cooperación Internacional," 2010. Special attention should be given to a review in Ignacio Molina, "Hacia una renovación estratégica de la política exterior española," *Informe Elcano* (Madrid: Real Instituto Elcano, 2014) (www .realinstitutoelcano.org/wps/portal/web/rielcano_es/publicacion?WCM _GLOBAL_CONTEXT=/elcano/elcano_es/publicaciones/informe-elcano -15-renovacion-politica-exterior-espana).

20. Silvia Amaro, "Spain Has a New Government but Political Instability Is Not Over," CNBC, June 5, 2018.

EIGHT

From Soviet Satellite to Regional Power

Poland after 1989

MICHELA CECCORULLI AND SERENA GIUSTI

After the 1795 Partition of Poland by Austria, Prussia, and Russia, the country did not reappear on the European map until the end of War World I in 1918. Reborn following World War I, Poland had a democratic regime for a few years but rapidly turned into a dictatorship. In 1939, it was once again subjugated and split, this time by Nazi Germany and the Soviet Union. It has been estimated that 5 million Poles died between 1939 and 1945, when World War II ended. Poland then came under control of the Soviet Union. When the country rid itself of its Soviet legacy in 1989, it looked westward to break with the past and to accelerate the process of transforming itself into a democracy and a market economy. Like other former Soviet satellites, Poland was determined to reconnect with the Western mainstream and develop into a "normal country."

The process of transformation in the area was preceded by the rediscovery of a Central European identity, which helped to boost the argument that the Central European countries were more European than the Eastern

European countries and therefore should join the Euro-Atlantic community before the others. The idea of Central Europe as a particular region
was reinforced by an intellectual vision that considered regional identity
superior to parochial nationalism and a potent deterrent against chauvin-
ism and minority tensions.[1] In the early 1990s, the European Community
(EC, then European Union, EU, after the entry into force of the Treaty
on the European Union) was pushing for a regional framework of cooperation (the Visegrad Group) as a preliminary stage in the process of European integration. However, political elites in Poland and the other
Central European countries (CECs) considered it an obstacle on their way
to Brussels and opted for a preferential bilateral relationship with the EU.
Accession to NATO and the EU was the main goal of post-1989 Poland.

Having succeeded in achieving membership in both organizations, in
1999 and in 2004, respectively, the country has aspired to play a leading
role ever since. The political leverage that Poland has acquired arose from
various factors: sustained economic growth; credible leadership (especially
between 2007 and 2014); the diplomatic capacity to reconcile with past enemies and at the same time to build a network of new partners; a strategy
for dealing with the troubled Eastern European neighborhood; solid experience in the field of democratization; and finally, a deep-rooted national
identity.

Poland, a successful model of the EU's transformative power, has rapidly become a front-runner and a regional power in Europe. Poland's credibility and authority are however menaced as a consequence of democratic
deterioration since the Law and Justice Party (PiS) won the 2015 parliamentary elections and returned to rule the country after the short-lived
government of 2005–07. There is concern in particular for laws designed
to control the media, limit civil liberties, politicize the civil service, and
attack judicial independence. These are likely to be declared unconstitu-
tional. As a result, the government is engaged in a blatantly illegal effort to
subjugate the Constitutional Tribunal. In the meantime, the European
Commission triggered to apply article 7 of the Treaty on European Union
that would suspend certain rights deriving from the application of the treaties.[2] Furthermore, the European Commission (June 2017) launched infringement procedures against Poland, along with the Czech Republic and
Hungary, for noncompliance with their obligations under the 2015
Council Decisions on relocation.[3] This escalation of tension between Warsaw and Brussels, along with the country's alignment with the EU's most

Euroskeptic members, Hungary and the United Kingdom, risks marginalizing Poland within the EU.

Poland's Membership in NATO and the EU

In the aftermath of the Cold War, the foreign policy of the Central European countries was essentially shaped by their will to "return to Europe," which became the manifesto and essence of the 1989 revolts of Soviet satellites against communism and Soviet domination.[4] After the dissolution of the Warsaw Pact in 1991, the Conference on Security and Cooperation in Europe (CSCE) was still considered a viable security provider.[5] During the Soviet era, prominent dissidents who were active in pan-European peace and human rights movements had believed that only the withdrawal of the United States from Western Europe and of Soviet troops from Central Europe—with the consequent dissolution of both the Warsaw Pact and NATO—would put an end to the East-West confrontation. The neutrality option was also seen as a way of eschewing bloc policy rather than directly opposing NATO. Accordingly, in 1989 the CSCE was still regarded as a desirable framework for developing a pan-European security regime and avoiding a Soviet military reaction, which would be plausible if Eastern European countries joined NATO. The attempted coups d'état of 1991 and 1993 in Russia, as well as the electoral success of left-wing and right-wing parties with neo-imperialist agendas, showed the frailty of Russia's democratization process and the unpredictability of its foreign policy.

With the wars in Yugoslavia in the 1990s, the European security environment appeared to worsen further and Poland adopted a more realistic outlook, coming to see NATO as the only guarantee of its security and independence.[6] The year 1994 marked a significant stage in the process of drafting the Partnership for Peace program, which became an important instrument in preparing for Poland's accession to NATO in 1999. The December 1994 NATO summit made it clear that "the enlargement of NATO will complement the enlargement of the EU, a parallel process that also, for its part, contributes significantly to extending security and stability to the new democracies of the East."[7] However, when NATO made the decision in 1997 to admit new members (including Poland, Hungary, and the Czech Republic), it was clear that the reasoning and dynamics of the two organizations differed.

Poland did not join the EU until 2004, after a demanding, multidimensional process of transformation. Unlike most of its ex-communist neighbors, which opted for a gradual transition to capitalism, in 1990 Poland already had adopted the so-called shock therapy approach, under the guidance of Finance Minister Leszek Balcerowicz. Price controls were removed, markets were fully opened to foreign trade, the zloty was made convertible, privatization began, and subsidies to state-owned industries were abolished. Although those changes were considered among the reasons for Poland's future outstanding economic performance, at the time such radical reforms produced widespread social discontent, which brought the post-communists back to power in the 1993 elections. After a short, sharp slump in which GDP shrank by almost 15 percent, growth resumed in 1992—and it has not stopped since.

Accession to the EU further boosted the country's economic growth, thanks to huge inflows in the form of mainly (but not only) structural funds under the Cohesion Policy.[8] EU funds have strongly contributed in particular to modernization of the infrastructure system, to regional development (Poland being the most decentralized country in Central and Eastern Europe), and to a reduction of the income gap between new members of the EU and long-standing ones.[9] All of this led World Bank economist Marcin Piatkowski to conclude in early 2014 that Poland "has just had probably the best 20 years in more than one thousand years of its history."[10]

Poland has also benefited from having the largest internal market among the Central and Eastern European countries (CEECs). Significant increases in domestic demand have safeguarded Poland from the worst effects of Europe's recent economic crisis. Performing far better than other countries,[11] the state of the Polish economy vis-à-vis the economic crisis has been determined in part by the floating exchange rate. While Poland's limited connections to international and European financial markets are part of the explanation, one cannot overlook the role of sound macroeconomic policies based on free trade, fiscal discipline, and more integration at the European level in reducing the likelihood of transmission effects. Not only has Poland outperformed all other European economies in recent years, but it has also distinguished itself from many other large emerging markets, like Russia, Brazil, and Mexico. Although for the new member states there is no possibility of "opting out," having committed to the full adoption of the *acquis communautaire*, no timetable has been fixed. There has been a tendency to a soft approach in consideration of a tension between the Maastricht criteria for low inflation and limited budget deficits and the need for transition economies for public investment. In addition, opinion polls reveal a public that is skeptical about the euro and the possible benefits, especially as consumer goods prices are expected to raise.

Poland and the EU's Foreign Policy

Relying on its economic strength, Poland has rapidly come to be a highly proactive member of the EU. When it held (for the first time) the presidency of the Council of the European Union, from July 1 to December 31, 2011, Poland insisted that the EU build its own competitive advantage and speak with one voice in leading international fora.[12] Poland believes that the global balance of power is shifting in favor of developing countries and that the shift will change the global market structure as well as the way that countries cope with financial, environmental, energy, food-related, technical, and epidemiological risks.[13] Furthermore, Poland emphasized the role of the Cohesion Policy as the paramount investment tool in efforts to reach the Europe 2020 objectives and the role of innovation as a source of growth.

The first important change in Poland's foreign policy can be observed in improved relations with Germany. Poland shares a 456-kilometer (283-mile) border with Germany, a fact that has caused trouble in the past, but today that closeness (despite minor issues) is likely to have a positive effect on Poland's status on the regional and international stage. There is a clearly observable trend toward not only economic but also security coordination between the countries. Poland's affiliation with Germany has been quite strong and has encompassed a variety of matters at various levels. Poland is ever more relevant to Germany, which is now ready to recognize its strategic importance in attracting Central and Eastern European states toward the eurozone.[14]

Together with improved relations along its western border, Poland has contributed to reinforcement of the EU's Ostpolitik by promoting the Eastern Partnership (EaP)—a policy launched in 2009 dedicated to strengthening relations with the post-Soviet states of Armenia, Azerbaijan, Belarus, Georgia, Moldova, and Ukraine, with specific attention given to externalities produced with regard to Russia and the reconfiguration of the whole EU-Russia partnership. Sharing its own experiences in its transition to democracy, Warsaw has prompted a bolder European policy of democracy promotion in both the eastern and the southern neighborhoods. Generally, the new EU members from Central and Eastern Europe retain important comparative advantages in democracy promotion with regard to the Middle East and North Africa because they were not colonial powers in the region, unlike some EU member states, such as France, Italy, and the United Kingdom.[15] Taking into account Central and Eastern European members' transition experience and the possible bottom-up changes in the eastern neighborhood, Poland proposed the creation of the European Endowment for Democracy (EED), a new instrument for democracy promotion launched in August 2013.[16] The goal of the EED is to foster and encourage democratization and to promote deep, sustainable democracy in countries undergoing political transition. Its initial, although not exclusive, focus is on the European neighborhood. The EED will undertake short-term, actor-oriented activities; its task is to select those actors from both civil and political society that are most able to produce change in their country.[17] For Poland, the EED is also a way to reconcile its interests in Eastern Europe and to assert its influence in the Mediterranean, where its involvement so far has been very modest.

As Poland has become a more self-reliant country, it has further encouraged the EU with regard to developing a common defense policy. In Warsaw's view, following the progressive U.S. disengagement from Europe, the EU must think strategically and enhance its self-defense capability and military might as a way to complement the transatlantic security system.[18] This is all the more relevant when looking at Russia's last moves and given the coming into power of a less accommodating government vis-à-vis the former Soviet Union. Poland is deeply committed to supporting development of the European Security and Defense Policy (ESDP), especially after Donald Trump's administration has shown signs of disengagement from NATO and consequently from European security. Part and parcel of this policy is the strengthening of subregional arrangements that have a security component, such as the Visegrad Group (Poland, Hungary, the Czech Republic, and Slovakia) and the Weimar Triangle (Poland, France, and Germany). Poland maintains that command structures and instruments (with specific reference to EU battle groups, potentially the Visegrad and Weimar groups) should be strengthened along with participation in crisis management operations.[19] In particular, in the 2007 National Security Strategy (but also in the 2014 strategic document), Poland committed to provide men and instruments for EU stabilization, peacekeeping, humanitarian, rescue, and training missions.[20] Today, Poland has already participated in the completed operations EUFOR Concordia and EUPOL Proxima, in the former Republic of Macedonia; operation EUPM, in Bosnia and Herzegovina; EUJUST THEMIS, in Georgia; EUFOR RD Congo; and EUFOR Chad/CAR.[21]

Poland's support for an EU defense policy, one that does not create exclusive clubs of more powerful states, can be inferred from the relevance attached to the European Defense Agency (EDA), which is considered fundamental in developing the EU's defense capabilities.[22] The Polish political elite supports the intensification of EU-NATO talks and cooperation in the security realm and strongly emphasizes the need to envision joint solutions in order to avoid duplicating efforts. The political elite also promotes discussions between the Allied Command Transformation and the EDA.

Many observers see Poland's support for a European defense policy as a new direction in the country's foreign policy.[23] In the past, the accommodation of Russia by some European states, notably France and Germany, raised doubts about their commitment to meeting Poland's security needs. That was the reason behind Poland's unconditional backing of NATO's out-of-area operations (the first of which took place in 1999 with the bombing of Serbia). To some other observers, closeness with the United States was automatic, given the emphasis on "hard security," a similarly confrontational approach toward Russia, and the reliability of a distant superpower with global interests.[24] However, the strategic U.S. move away from the European continent, the ambiguous policy on missile defense, and the so-called reset approach that the United States undertook with Russia have led Poland to take a cooler stance toward the United States.

Poland: The Staunchest U.S. Ally in Europe?

Elsewhere in this book, in chapter 10, David Cadier stresses how misplaced was the division made some ten years ago between an "old" and a "new" Europe—the latter referring in particular to the Central European states, which, in the words of Donald Rumsfeld, the former U.S. secretary of defense, had become the new "center of gravity" in NATO Europe. While crucial, the relationship between Poland and the United States is much more nuanced than it might seem. Cadier is right when he says that Poland's Atlanticism is more "strategic" than "normative."

Along with economic and energy collaboration[25] and the shared objective of democracy promotion, cooperation on security and defense matters is a big part of the U.S.-Poland relationship.[26] Poland's defense cooperation with the United States—which ranges from joint training exercises to establishment of a U.S. air detachment in Poland, use of F-16 aircraft by the Polish air force (allowing interoperability of the aircraft of the two countries), and cooperation between the countries' defense industries—has two main priorities: to improve transatlantic ties and to provide visible evidence of U.S. engagement and presence on the ground.

The basis of the relationship is the 2008 Declaration on Strategic Cooperation, which offers a long-term perspective on cooperation between the two countries. Among other things, the declaration provides for installation of a ground-based ballistic missile defense system as part of a U.S. missile defense shield to counter the proliferation of weapons of mass destruction and related delivery systems.[27] Although plans to install the system have changed somewhat since Barack Obama came to power, his presidency launched the European Phased Adaptive Approach (EPAA) system (September 2009), intended to protect the European continent against short-, medium-, and long-range missiles from the Middle East (for example, from Iran).[28]

NATO's participation in the U.S. system would contribute to the development of a common missile defense system for the NATO alliance, strengthening the commitment to NATO's traditional tasks.[29] Preserving the traditional and core aim of the alliance—that is, collective defense—is fundamental to Poland. In that regard, the new NATO Strategic Concept—which was adopted in Lisbon in 2010, reaffirming the centrality of article 5—espouses Poland's strategic interests, especially after Russia's provocative moves. Preserving the alliance's collective defense mission would render members equally safe and secure and ultimately increase their propensity to participate in out-of-area operations,[30] to which Poland has made a large contribution over the years.

Poland considers NATO "the chief multilateral instrument" of its security policy, in both the political and the military spheres.[31] Poland strongly supports the accession of Moldova, the Western Balkans, and the South Caucasus to NATO, underlining its full commitment to overseeing their political and economic transformation.[32] Moreover, Poland wholly supports strengthening partnership with nonmember states.[33] In the past, testifying to what was an increasingly pragmatic approach to foreign policy,

Poland acknowledged that NATO could not but engage Russia on specific challenges such as developments in Afghanistan, a possible nuclear missile threat from Iran, reinforcement of the nonproliferation regime, and a reopening of discussions about Conventional Forces in Europe (CFE).[34] Yet, following Russia's increasingly assertiveness in Ukraine and in the post-Soviet space and given the Law and Justice party being in power, Poland has been pressing NATO to bolster the eastern flank. As a result, Poland appreciated the decision of the NATO Summit in Warsaw (July 2016) that committed the alliance to strengthening its military presence in the east, with four battalions in Poland, Estonia, Latvia, and Lithuania on a rotational basis—which was to be in place by 2017. However, President Trump's refusal to explicitly endorse article 5 in his speech (May 25, 2017) in Brussels is alarming to Poland, which might, as a reaction, be convinced to commit more to the EU's projects for sharpening a common defense.

Poland and Russia: Between Reconciliation and Mistrust

During the Soviet era, Russia was portrayed as the antithesis of Europe; in the words of the Czech writer Milan Kundera, it was "another civilization, the radical negation of the modern West."[35] Kundera hinted at the Soviet variant of Russia that exerted oppressive control over the countries of Central Europe. On the other hand, Mikhail Gorbachev defended the place of Russia in Europe: "We are Europeans. Old Russia was united with Europe by Christianity The history of Russia is an organic part of the great European history."[36] The post–Cold War system preserved the bulk of the Western institutions (NATO and the EU) while marginalizing Russia, which was confronting a deep economic, political, and social crisis, even a crisis of identity. Russia's weakness allowed Poland not only to join to the Euro-Atlantic community but also to evolve as a more self-confident country. Nevertheless, in the first years of its membership in the EU, Poland opposed reconciling with Russia, which under President Vladimir Putin had returned to being assertive. The posture of President Lech Kaczyński's Law and Justice Party (PiS) in particular was confrontational, calling for limiting Russian influence in the former Soviet satellites and demanding an apology and compensation from Russian leaders for mistakes of the past. During the government of Lech Kaczyński's brother, Jarosław Kaczyński (2006–07), Poland vetoed opening negotiations for the renovation of the

Partnership and Cooperation Agreement (PCA) between Brussels and Moscow.

With the advent in 2007 of the government of Donald Tusk, a member of the Civic Platform (PO) party, emphasis was put on building a constructive relationship with Russia. The Polish government dropped the objection raised by the previous government to Russia's bid to join the Organization for Economic Cooperation and Development (OECD) and the veto on EU-Russia negotiations on the PCA; in return, Moscow lifted its ban on Polish meat imports. In 2008, a new government-sponsored forum for intellectuals and historians from both countries was established to improve dialogue on the tormented history of Polish-Russian relations. Called the Polish-Russian Group on Difficult Matters, it discusses, among other topics, the Polish-Soviet war following the Bolshevik Revolution, the Soviet occupation of eastern Poland in September 1939, and the mass murder of thousands of Polish officers by Soviet security forces at Katyn in 1940.

During negotiations to enter the EU, Poland had proposed acting as special interlocutor in Brussels talks to build bridges between the EU and Russia and countries in Eastern Europe—which were to remain on the fringe of the European integration process[37]—and decided to press the EU toward a more effective Ostpolitik. Fearing for the destiny of countries sandwiched between the enlarged EU and a resurgent Russia, Warsaw aimed at emancipating them from Russia's influence. Consequently, the Kremlin reacted negatively when in June 2008 Poland and Sweden proposed boosting the eastern dimension of the European Neighbourhood Policy (ENP)—the sequel to the grand 2004 enlargement—which was designed to bolster relations with the nearest countries of Eastern Europe, the southern shore of the Mediterranean, and the south Caucasus. The Eastern Partnership was conceived as a way of engaging with six former Soviet republics (Ukraine, Moldova, Belarus, Georgia, Azerbaijan, and Armenia) after Russia blocked Georgia's and Ukraine's path to NATO. Although Poland and the EU presented the EaP as a "civilizational" project, it rapidly assumed the features of a geopolitical one. The Kremlin has tried to oppose it, as the Ukrainian crisis has shown.

Relations between Brussels and the Kremlin worsened as a consequence of the August 2008 five-day war between Moscow and Tbilisi, after which the sovereign territory of Georgia was reduced following the

Russian-facilitated secession of two of Georgia's formerly autonomous regions, Abkhazia and South Ossetia. Poland was among the countries advocating an extraordinary meeting of the European Council to adopt sanctions against Russia. French President Nicolas Sarkozy, serving as the president of the EU, succeeded in persuading Georgia and Russia to agree on a ten-point peace plan. Russia's military intervention in Georgia, along with the pressure brought to bear by Poland, boosted the launch of the EaP in May 2009.

In March 2009, Polish-Russian relations finally benefited from the U.S.-Russian policy of the "pressing the reset button." The global financial crisis offered Washington and Moscow an opportunity to cut military expenses and to cooperate on a number of salient issues, such as Iran, Afghanistan, and European and regional security. In a new spirit of reconciliation, Prime Minister Tusk and his Russian counterpart, Putin, agreed in 2010 to hold a joint ceremony to mark the seventieth anniversary of the Katyn massacre.[38] President Kaczynski did not take part in that ceremony, having decided instead to participate in a separate commemoration, along with many senior members of his party and the president of the Polish Central Bank. However, the plane that he was flying in crashed near Smolensk, in Russia, and he and all his companions died. Russia's concern and assistance following the airplane accident were warmly received in Poland. Both the Russian president and prime minister addressed the Polish nation, characterizing the accident as a tragedy for both nations. *Katyń*, the previously banned, Oscar-nominated movie directed by Andrzej Wajda, was finally aired immediately after the accident on Russia's main TV channel.[39]

With the eruption of the Ukraine crisis, relations have become tense again. Because the Kremlin has been meddling in Ukrainian domestic politics, Poland has advocated for strong sanctions against Russia and a more consistent NATO presence on the eastern flank of the alliance. Poland, like the other EU members, has condemned Russia's annexation of Crimea and supported finalization of the Association Agreement with Kiev. Besides committing the country to the EU's values (democracy, human rights, and the rule of law, as well as free market principles, sustainable development, and effective multilateralism), the Association Agreement provides for Ukraine's gradual integration into the EU internal market through deep and comprehensive free trade.

Beyond Europe: Widening Economic Relations

Poland's trade relations are well developed and for the most part involve neighboring states, even though there have been efforts to shift away from traditional patterns in recent years. The EU is the primary market for Polish exports. Not only trade integration but also financial services integration has been remarkable, favoring foreign direct investments (FDIs) in the fast-growing state. According to the International Monetary Fund, Poland's bilateral trade with the eurozone reached 40 percent of GDP in 2011, with the major partners being Germany, France, Italy, the United Kingdom, and, in recent years, the Netherlands.[40] Germany is Poland's main trade partner, although bilateral trade is less than it was two decades ago. Foreign direct investments come mainly from Germany and France and recently from the Netherlands, while Polish companies account for a substantial amount of FDIs, primarily in Italy, Luxemburg, and Germany's financial services sector. However, both Polish FDIs in Russia and Ukraine and Russian and Ukrainian FDIs in Poland are weak.[41]

In recent years, the drive to seek new markets, accelerated by the economic crisis and new energy requirements, has pushed Poland to look more closely at Eastern Europe, Russia, and the Commonwealth of Independent States (CIS). Poland's borders with the Russian Federation, Ukraine, and Belarus are worth paying attention to considering trade with these countries, the likelihood of labor or seasonal migration to and from Poland, and the socioeconomic development of the area in general.[42] Accordingly, Poland has searched for ways to facilitate cross-border movement with Ukraine (in 2009 and 2011), Belarus (in 2010), and Russia (in 2012).

Being the country with the largest reserves of shale gas in Europe, Poland might also become an energy supplier for Eastern European countries looking for more independence from Russia.[43] Warsaw supported development of the Nabucco natural gas pipeline, which was to run from the Caspian Sea via Turkey, thereby avoiding Russia and Ukraine. The pipeline was meant to help diversify gas sources for the EU and reduce its dependence on Russia for energy as well as on Ukraine as a transit country. The Nabucco project was in competition with the South Stream plan pushed by Russian gas powerhouse Gazprom and Italy's Ente Nazionale Idrocarburi (ENI), which also aimed to pump Caspian supplies to Europe.

To make up for the reduced foreign investment experienced in the first years of the global financial crisis, Poland has tried to attract investments

from Arab countries and direct them toward the so-called special economic areas—that is, the scarcely populated areas in the eastern part of
Poland that would benefit from efforts to attract investors.[44] With the aim
of diversifying its portfolio of trade partners, Poland has recently strengthened its relations with China. China sees Poland as a gateway to Central
and Eastern Europe and the EU market and considers it attractive for investments because of its relatively cheap, well-qualified, and competent
workforce. Chinese trade volume exceeded US$10 billion in 2008 and
reached US$14.8 billion in 2013, for a 3 percent year-on-year growth rate.
Poland is exporting more to China, and China is investing more in Poland. Negative views of China are gradually diminishing in Polish society.
Fewer and fewer people see China solely as an undemocratic regime: there
is growing acceptance of the image of China as a new superpower that is
dynamic, globally projected, and relatively peaceful. The future evolution of the Polish-Chinese partnership, however, depends not only on Chinese domestic politics but also on U.S. engagement in Europe and the
course of Beijing-Moscow relations.

Conclusion

Since 1989, Polish foreign policy has progressively become more proactive,
assertive, and pragmatic. Warsaw has used the EU tactically to pursue its
own interests and to acquire more leverage within the EU and Central and
Eastern Europe. Poland's Atlanticism seems to have turned out to be quite
pragmatic, with Warsaw adopting a more equidistant position between the
United States and the EU. Poland's strong support for strengthening
Europe's defense is a case in point. This attitude is strengthening since
Trump became president of the United States.

Poland's mounting relevence is due in part to its formidable economic
performance, which is an "important element of foreign policy."[45] As a matter
of fact, Poland has embarked on implementing an impressive slate of reforms, the full benefits of which are still to be seen. The Polish leadership
has put forward an ambitious strategy for accomplishing foreign policy
goals and has domestic public opinion on its side. Poland has revived regionalism as a means of advancing the CEC's interests and strengthening
Poland's role in the EU. There has been a dramatic reassessment of relations with countries that once were considered hostile, such as Germany

and Russia. And yet Poland is looking carefully at Russian moves on the regional landscape. Recently, the war in Georgia and the annexation of Crimea (Ukraine) have persuaded Warsaw to review its more lenient posture toward Russia. Poland also has encouraged regional cooperation with the near abroad through the EaP in order to dilute potential instabilities in the periphery and create a buffer with Russia. Hence, Poland has emphasized its role as a bridge between the West and Eastern Europe and Russia and has made the promotion of democracy a new part of its external projection. Increasingly aware of its geo-economic and geostrategic relevance, Poland does not disregard relations with other states such as China, seeing them as possibly contributing to Poland's development and weight at the regional and international levels. Poland's future performance and potentialities might, however, be put at risk by the political conduct of the Law and Justice Party that is already causing concern among the international community.

NOTES

1. On this subject, see M. Croan, "Lands in Between: The Politics of Cultural Identity in Contemporary Eastern Europe," *Eastern European Politics and Societies* 3, no. 2 (Spring 1989), pp. 184–90.

2. See D. Kelemen, "Poland's Constitutional Crisis," *Foreign Affairs*, August 25, 2016.

3. Despite the European Commission's repeated calls for action, these three countries remain in breach of their legal obligations and have shown disregard for their commitments to Greece, Italy, and other member states; see European Commission, "Relocation: Commission Launches Infringement Procedures against the Czech Republic, Hungary and Poland," press release, June 14, 2017 (http://europa.eu/rapid/press-release_IP-17-1607_en.htm).

4. A. Michnik, *Letters from Freedom* (University of California Press, 1998), p. 150: "For now two roads lie open before my country [Poland] and our newly freed neighbors: one road leads to nationalism and isolationism, the other to a return to our 'native Europe'"; Chancellery of the Prime Minister of the Republic of Poland, "A New State for New Challenges," Warsaw, May 1998, p. 8: "Poland wants to return to Europe, to Europe's vital traditions, its trade, and its international role"; A. Smolar, "From Opposition to Atomization," *Journal of Democracy* 7, no. 1 (January 1996): "'Returning to Europe' or 'becoming a normal society' became the watchwords of most of the leaders who came from the ranks of the democratic opposition to communism."

5. The name was changed from Conference on Security and Cooperation in Europe (CSCE) to the Organization for Security and Cooperation in Europe (OSCE) in December 1994.

6. The U.S. secretary of state, James Baker, defined the CSCE as the "conscience of the continent" but emphasized that only NATO could maintain peace in Europe. J. Baker, "The Common European Interest: America and the New Politics among Nations," *U.S. Department of State Dispatch*, September 3, 1990, p. 37.

7. Communication from the Ministerial Meeting of the North Atlantic Council, M-NAC-2(94)116, Brussels, December 1, 1994 (www.nato.int/docu /comm/49-95/c941201a.htm).

8. For the period 2007–13, inflows reached €68 billion, the largest amount among receiving members. Poland will once again get the biggest portion (€106 billion) in the next multiyear budget (2014–20).

9. Crespo Cuaresma and others, "Drivers of Convergence in Eleven Eastern European Countries," Policy Research Working Paper 6185 (Washington: Poverty Reduction and Economic Management Department, World Bank, August 2012).

10. M. A. Orestein, "Six Markets to Watch: Poland," *Foreign Affairs*, January/February 2014.

11. S. Giusti and L. Tajoli, "The Pros and Cons of 'De Facto' Polish Opting-Out of the EMU," in *Europe in Crisis*, edited by L. S. Talani (London: Palgrave, 2016), pp.181–201.

12. Ministry of Foreign Affairs, Republic of Poland, "Programme of the Polish Presidency of the Council of the European Union," July 1, 2011–December 31, 2011 (Warsaw).

13. Council of Ministers, "National Development Strategy 2020: Active Society, Competitive Economy, Efficient State," Attachment to Resolution No. 157 of the Council of Ministers of September 25, 2012 (Warsaw).

14. M. Baranowski and T. Kleine-Brockhoff, "The Complexity of Relations between Germany and Poland," Publiserviceeurope, February 7, 2012.

15. This important factor, among others, regarding Central and Eastern European democracy assistance in the Arab countries is emphasized in Kristina Mikulova and Benedetta Berti, "Converts to Missionaries: Central and Eastern European Democracy Assistance in the Arab World," Carnegie Endowment for Democracy, July 30, 2013 (http://carnegieendowment.org/2013/07/30/converts -to-missionaries-central-and-eastern-european-democracy-assistance-in -arab-world/ggvh).

16. On this topic, see E. Fassi and S. Giusti, "Supporting the Unsupported: The European Endowment for Democracy and the Promotion of Democracy in the EU's Neighbourhood," *International Spectator*, December 2014.

17. According to article 2, "The direct beneficiaries of the Endowment's activities may include: pro-democratic movements and other pro-democratic actors in favor of a pluralistic multiparty system on democratic ground; social

movements and actors; civil society organizations; emerging leaders, independent media and journalists (including bloggers, social media activists, etc.), nongovernmental institutions, including foundations and educational institutions functioning also in exile; provided that all the beneficiaries adhere to core democratic values, respect international human rights standards and subscribe to principles of nonviolence."

18. Council of Ministers, "National Development Strategy 2020," p. 12.

19. Ibid., p. 15.

20. "National Security Strategy of the Republic of Poland," 2007 (Warsaw), p. 11.

21. Ministry of Foreign Affairs, Republic of Poland, "EU and NATO Operations" (www.msz.gov.pl/en/foreign_policy/security_policy/eu_nato_operations /eu_and_nato_operations).

22. *Polish Defense Yearbook*, vol. 3 (Warsaw: Magnum X Publishing House, 2012).

23. C. M. O'Donnell, "Poland's U-Turn on European Defence: A Missed Opportunity?," Policy Brief (Brussels: Centre for European Reform, 2012).

24. I. Samson, "Assessment of Visegrad Cooperation from a Security Perspective: Is the Visegrad Group Still Vital in the 'Zeros' of the 21st Century?," in *Visegrad Cooperation within NATO and CSDP*, V4 Papers, no. 2, edited by C. Törő (Warsaw: Polish Institute of International Affairs, 2011), p. 25.

25. U.S. multinational companies have devoted attention to Poland's reserves of shale gas in particular.

26. However, a hot issue remains that of visa requirements to enter the United States. Poland is not part of the Visa Waiver Program, which includes "old" EU members.

27. "Declaration on Strategic Cooperation between the United States of America and the Republic of Poland," Council on Foreign Relations, August 20, 2008 (www.cfr.org/poland/declaration-strategic-cooperation-between-united -states-america-republic-poland/p16991).

28. See Missile Defense Advocacy Alliance, "European Phased Adaptive Approach (EPAA)," October 2018 (http://missiledefenseadvocacy.org/missile -defense-systems-2/missile-defense-systems/policy-coming-soon/european -phased-adaptive-approach-epaa/).

29. B. Górka-Winter and M. Madej, "NATO Member States and the New Strategic Concept: An Overview" (Warsaw: Polish Institute of International Affairs, May 2010), p. 81.

30. "Insider View: Head of the Polish National Security Bureau Stanisław Koziej on Poland's Defense Modernization," *Central Europe Digest*, March 1, 2013 (www.cepa.org/sites/default/files/Past_CED_Issues/Central%20Europe %20Digest,%20March%201,%202013-.pdf).

31. Council of Ministers, "National Development Strategy 2020," p. 14.

32. Ibid., p. 15.

33. "National Security Strategy of the Republic of Poland," p. 10.

34. Samson, "Assessment of Visegrad Cooperation from a Security Perspective," p. 32.

35. M. Kundera, "The Tragedy of Central Europe," *New York Review of Books*, April 26, 1994, pp. 34, 37.

36. M. Gorbachev, *Perestroika: New Thinking for Our Country and the World* (London: Fontana, 1988), p. 190.

37. See Sherman W. Garnett, "Poland: Bulwark or Bridge?," *Foreign Policy*, no. 102 (Spring 1996), pp. 67–68; K. Pełczyńska-Nałęcz and M. Kaczmarski, *Polityka wschodnia UE i rola Polski w jej kształtowaniu po rozszerzeniu w 2004 r* [EU's Eastern Policy and the Role of Poland in Its Development after the Enlargement of 2004] (Warsaw: Osrode Kstudiow Wschodnich, 2009).

38. The Katyn massacre was a mass execution of Polish nationals by the Soviet secret police in spring 1940 on the orders of Soviet leader Joseph Stalin. The Soviet Red Army had taken the Polish prisoners after invading eastern Poland in September 1939. For decades, Moscow had blamed the Nazis for the massacre, but in 1990, under perestroika, admitted that Stalin had ordered it. The massacre further embittered Poland's relations with Moscow, which has refused to consider the massacre as genocide and has been reluctant to prosecute any living henchmen.

39. P. M. Kaczyński, "Pain in Poland," *CEPS Commentary*, April 10, 2013.

40. "Republic of Poland: Selected Issues," IMF Country Report 12/163 (Washington: International Monetary Fund, July 2012).

41. "Republic of Poland: 2014 Article IV Consultation," IMF Country Report 14/173 (Washington: International Monetary Fund, July 2014).

42. GUS Central Statistical Office, "Border Traffic and Movement of Goods and Services at the European Union's External Border on the Territory of Poland in 2011," *Statistical Information and Elaborations* (Warsaw).

43. The enthusiastic first estimates by the U.S. Energy Information Administration on Polish shale gas, which predicted a prosperous future based on gas revenues, have since been revised. According to the Polish Geological Institute, Polish shale gas resources could be as low as 346.1 to 767.9 billion cubic meters. Those numbers would still guarantee profits for the shale gas industry, and the Polish Ministry of the Environment has issued numerous licenses for the exploration of hydrocarbons from unconventional sources in order to correct and verify the data from the preliminary survey.

44. C. Tonini, "La ricetta polacca contro la recessione [Poland's Anti-Recession Recipe]," *East 30*, June 27, 2013, pp. 8–12.

45. Council of Ministers, "National Development Strategy 2020," p. 56.

NINE

Danish Foreign Policy

From Pastry to Bloody Denmark?

JONAS PARELLO-PLESNER

D anish, what are you writing about?" an American friend asked with a puzzled look, referring to this chapter on Danish foreign policy. "Well, it's not a chapter on the *pastry!*" I replied. While most Americans know what a Danish pastry is, fewer know anything about Danish foreign policy. And it is not just Americans. British politicians have a tradition of dismissing Denmark as irrelevant. Horace Walpole lamented Britain's reduction to "as insignificant a country as Denmark or Sardinia" at the end of the eighteenth century,[1] and in September 2011, a member of the British Labour Party exclaimed, "We are not bloody Denmark!"[2]

Nevertheless, Denmark, a small country situated at the northern tip of the European continent, does carry out a full-fledged foreign policy. The trends in Danish foreign policy have been shaped by history and geography as well as by the conditions encountered by any small state with limited room to maneuver in the international system. Nevertheless, Denmark has sought to make a small but clear mark in global politics in several specific policy areas.

This chapter starts with some of the historic facts that have shaped the Danish foreign policy outlook, such as lost wars, unsuccessful attempts to maintain neutrality, and Nordic attachment versus European integration. Then it looks at Denmark's foreign policy after the Cold War, when Denmark was freed from the traditional small-state security dilemma. The Soviet Union had dissolved, and Germany, the traditional danger on Denmark's southern border, was now—even if unified—firmly bound by both the European Union and the country's continued pacifism. The chapter also examines Denmark's membership in the EU and the Danish decision to stay out of parts of EU cooperation, such as the euro, defense, and legal affairs. Denmark's evolving relations with the United States, Russia, China, and India are discussed, as are Denmark's ambitious diplomatic efforts with respect to climate change and energy efficiency.

Denmark's post–Cold War security situation gave rise to a newfound activism in Danish foreign policy throughout the 1990s. During the last decades, that activism took a stronger military bent, moving Denmark beyond the blue helmets of UN peacekeeping missions and foreign aid— two traditional tenets of Danish policy—and into the wars in Iraq and Afghanistan.

Today, global developments like terrorism, poverty, climate change, fragile states, piracy, and cyberattacks are what Denmark perceives as threats to its freedom and prosperity, although Russia's threatening posturing also raises concerns. And Denmark's efforts have been noticed beyond its borders. American political leaders, including former president Barack Obama, have remarked that Denmark "punched [well] above its weight."[3]

Denmark's activist foreign policy was galvanized in particular by Prime Minister Anders Fogh Rasmussen during his tenure from 2001 to 2009. Fittingly, Rasmussen went on to become secretary general of NATO from 2009 to 2014, the first Dane to hold that position.[4] Rasmussen was succeeded by another Rasmussen, Lars Løkke, who was prime minister from 2009 until 2011 and then returned to power after elections in the summer of 2015.

In power from October 2011 to June 2015, the Social Democrat–led government with Helle Thorning-Schmidt as prime minister continued the active stance in Danish foreign policy. Denmark took part in the air campaign in Libya in the spring of 2011, with broad parliamentary support, and also provided logistical support for the French-led operation in Mali in January 2013. In 2013–14 Denmark took part in eliminating Syria's chemical weapons by providing a transport ship. Also in 2014, Denmark joined the American-led coalition campaign against the terrorist group the Islamic State of Iraq and Syria (ISIS) in Iraq with fighter planes, military trainers, and special forces. Following Russia's aggression against Ukraine from 2014 onward, Denmark has within NATO stepped up contributions to reassurance-measures for enhanced protection of the Baltic countries. These efforts show a continued ambition for Denmark to add its contribution to international problem-solving, including on the military side.

Historical Background

In any country distinct historical factors shape the nation's current perceptions and foreign policy outlook. In the case of Denmark, a few in particular deserve to be highlighted: the country's history of lost wars, its long-standing respect for international norms and cooperation with international institutions, strong transatlantic ties through NATO, and its membership in the European Union.

A Diminished Power

Three centuries of lost military battles have reduced Denmark to its current size. Gone to Sweden are the provinces of Scania, Hallandia, and Blekinge, which gave Denmark its profitable control of both sides of the Sound of Oresund and controlled access to the Baltic Sea. Gone is the double monarchy of Denmark and Norway, which was split up at the Vienna Congress in 1814 after Denmark sided with Napoleon's France. Gone to Germany are the majority of the provinces of Schleswig and Holstein, territorial control of which led to several wars with Germany in the mid-nineteenth century.

Denmark was left at its current size of 44,000 square kilometers.[5] That reduction in size led to a new degree of homogeneity, with national identity, language, and territory fitting nicely into the mold of the modern nation-state. In contrast, the earlier Danish kingdom had been highly influenced by German-speaking elites, such as the von Bernstorff family who were talented foreign ministers in the eighteenth century and Bernhard Ernst von Bülow in the nineteenth century. The latter began as Danish ambassador to Germany and later switched state allegiance to become foreign minister of Germany because it was a far more powerful position to serve a united Germany than a diminished Denmark.

International Cooperation

Early on, Denmark worked to uphold international legal norms and institutions. The border with Germany was settled by referendum in 1920—a democratic novelty at the time. Sovereignty disputes with Norway regarding the east coast of Greenland were settled by presenting the issue to the Permanent Court of International Justice. These took place back in the 1930s, around the same time as the toothless League of Nations faltered as a global organization trying to solve differences peacefully among nations.

Denmark also became a founding member of the United Nations and has stayed attached to international institutions as a matter of principle and out of a sense of self-preservation.[6] As a small state, Denmark has found membership in and strengthening of international institutions to be crucial, both to seek protection against the whims of powerful states (and supporting equal rules for small and big alike) and to promote global free trade. Free trade remains vital for a small, export-oriented economy. Seafaring has been a hallmark of the country since the time of the Vikings and in modern times has achieved worldwide reach with the nautical icon and shipping giant Maersk. Faithful to that tradition, Denmark has worked for the free and unhindered circulation of goods in both the World Trade Organization (WTO) and in the EU. Denmark has been pushing for a transatlantic free trade deal between the EU and the United States, the so-called Transatlantic Trade and Investment Partnership (TTIP), which is more uncertain than ever with Donald Trump as U.S. president and trade frictions on tariffs instead dominating the agenda.

Transatlantic ties became a pillar of Danish foreign policy with the onset of the Cold War. They replaced an earlier—often unsuccessful—policy of neutrality, a principle that remained fundamental for another Nordic country, Sweden, for much longer.[7] In Denmark's case, neutrality was shed in return for membership in NATO in 1949 and for a certain "mini special" relationship with the United States based on U.S. overflight rights and access to bases in Greenland, which were especially vital during the Cold War. Transatlantic ties have been strong since then, particularly since Denmark has demonstrated a consistent willingness to contribute to international challenges in the post–Cold War era.

Development assistance has been another pillar of Danish foreign policy, even well before Harvard's Joseph Nye began referring to it as one essential component of soft power. Despite not having a large-scale colonial past for which to atone, Denmark has for decades distributed more than the UN international aid target of 0.7 percent of its yearly gross national income (GNI) to developing countries. This commitment has meant Denmark is engaged in affairs far beyond its geographic borders, with long-lasting ties to beneficiary countries such as Tanzania. It has also been a vehicle for reaching beyond Denmark's Western allies and linking up with partners in the developing world.

In recent years, this development tradition has fostered so-called stabilization programs to employ both military and civilian capacities in helping fragile states, combining experience from hard security operations (in Denmark's case, in Iraq and Afghanistan) and development experience to help meet the challenges of nation-building and reconstruction. The ongoing refugee crisis is likely only to amplify the need for nation-building and good governance along European rim countries.

Denmark and the European Union

Historically, Denmark has oscillated between engagement in a growing European reality and its Nordic aspirations, the latter based on a deeper sense of cultural and linguistic affinity. Nonetheless, attempts at a Nordic Union, including on common foreign and security policies, had already failed in the lead-up to Denmark's NATO membership in 1949 and again in the late 1960s. Nordic cooperation has instead remained functional but intergovernmental, mostly limited to less sensitive areas of policy.

As an alternative, Denmark followed the United Kingdom and Ireland into the European Community (EC) in the accession wave of 1973, which brought the EC to nine members. Denmark's initial engagement with the EC, and its successor, the EU, has been primarily pragmatic, based on market openings in the internal market. Danish voters have been less convinced than southern and Benelux member states about the vision of an ever-closer union, having three times said *nej* (no) to advancing European integration, first in 1992 with the Maastricht Treaty. That led to a second referendum, which resulted in a "yes" vote after including several Danish opt-outs, still in place today, concerning defense, legal, and monetary affairs. In a separate referendum on the euro in 2000, Danish voters opted for keeping the national currency, the Danish crown. Most recently, in

November 2015, Danish voters rejected changing the opt-out on legal affairs into an opt-in model similar to the United Kingdom.

Attitudes on the EU have thus been split—not so much between political parties as between the political elites and the population. Most parties in Parliament favor further EU integration—although the euro crisis is putting a dent in their enthusiasm—yet the Danish people, when consulted, are more prone to step on the brakes. Still, the British exit referendum (so-called Brexit) has increased EU support in the population. Very few want to follow the exit route, although there is sadness in Copenhagen to see the expected departure of the United Kingdom. Denmark and the United Kingdom share the free trade, light-touch regulatory and transatlantic approach also inside the EU.

However, in contrast with the response in many other European countries, including founding members such as France, the 2004–07 "big bang" enlargement of the EU, which integrated eastern European countries, found large-scale popular support in Denmark. Moreover, that enlargement process was both initiated (in 1993) and concluded (in 2002) when Denmark was hosting the rotating presidency of the EU. That gave rise to the Danish presidency catchphrase, "From Copenhagen to Copenhagen." However, continued European enlargement is no longer appealing to Danes, particularly with regard to Turkey (although they would look favorably at fellow Nordic state Iceland).

There is an ongoing commitment by the majority of Danish political parties to abolish the Danish opt-outs, yet successive governments have so far failed to find an opportune moment to do so. The rejection in the 2000 referendum on joining the euro and the referendum on legal affairs in 2015 will stick in political memory. The euro crisis makes it less likely that any referendum on the euro will pass.

The opt-out on legal affairs matters for Denmark's capacity to take part in joint European cooperation such as Europol, which tracks transnational crime in the European area. Changing the opt-out would have remedied that. Following the "no" vote, the Danish government negotiated a bilateral agreement with the EU to continue working with Europol. The opt-out on defense matters limits Denmark from taking part in military operations under the EU flag and in the development of the European defense policy, shortened as PESCO, which French President Macron is giving a big push forward. For example, the Danish soldiers who took part in the NATO missions in Macedonia and Bosnia had to be withdrawn in 2003 and 2004, respectively, when the missions were placed under the auspices of the EU. Abolishing this opt-out would secure Denmark the full spectrum of options for participating in all forms of military engagement with the UN and NATO, as well as EU missions.

Danish Foreign Policy after the Cold War

Denmark has found itself in a privileged position since the end of the Cold War, confronting no direct, conventional threats. The fall of the Soviet Union, combined with the anchoring of a reunified Germany in the EU, has left Denmark with no large neighbors of whom to be wary, although the ominous direction of Russian foreign policy in the near abroad could alter that in the years to come.

Denmark, thus unleashed after the Cold War, started pursuing a much more active foreign policy. For example, Denmark was actively engaged in promoting early diplomatic recognition of the Baltic states after they separated from the Soviet Union. Denmark felt an affinity with these countries in terms of geography, history, and size, and it pushed other, more reluctant European powers on this question. Consequently, Denmark lobbied hard for the early inclusion of these countries in the Council of Europe, NATO, and the European Union.

Denmark also was actively engaged in the Yugoslav wars of the 1990s. The failure of Europe to prevent atrocities like the massacre of Srebrenica was a wake-up call, and it kick-started Denmark's move toward more robust military engagement abroad, particularly to avoid humanitarian catastrophes. In that vein, Denmark, led by a Social Democratic government, participated in the NATO engagement in Kosovo in 1999 to protect the civilian population, notwithstanding the fact that it was not possible to pass a UN resolution to legitimize the intervention, normally seen as a benchmark for warranting international legitimate action. With that, a new, more active version of Danish foreign policy—one that did not restrict itself to peacekeeping but moved to armed peacemaking—emerged.

Danes Are Also from Mars

This active foreign policy initiated in the 1990s by the Social Democratic government got a new twist when the Liberal Conservative government came into power in November 2001 and Prime Minister Anders Fogh

Rasmussen coined the term "activist foreign policy." That policy was reality-tested by the U.S. government's unfolding reaction to the terrorist attacks of September 11, 2001.

Denmark strongly supported the UN-authorized intervention in Afghanistan and early on supplied both troops and development assistance. Denmark, like other NATO nations, withdrew from its combat role in 2014. Prior to that and for several years, Denmark had over 700 battle troops on the ground in Afghanistan's difficult province of Helmand. Danish troops have suffered one of the highest per capita death tolls, with forty-three deaths. Yet Denmark has also combined its military actions with long-term development assistance and annual contributions of approximately US$85 million. Danish soldiers and security personnel take as much pride in helping to establish or reopen girls' schools and training the local security forces as they do in degrading the Taliban's military capabilities. Even after the withdrawal of combat troops in 2014, Denmark maintains military trainers to train and assist the Afghan National Security Forces (ANSF).

The other U.S.-led war of the last decade, the invasion in Iraq in 2003, was more divisive in Denmark, as it was across Europe. Under most circumstances, Denmark prefers to see no contradiction between its strong Atlantic ties and its aspirations to help build a common European foreign policy, yet when compelled to choose, the Danish government decided to join the Americans in Iraq.

Thus, when the government had to make a choice between "Venus and Mars," as Robert Kagan famously put it, Denmark went by a narrow parliamentary majority with the god of battle—and the Americans—and entered Iraq in 2003.[8] The government's decision was disputed then and has been ever since. Denmark maintained soldiers in the country until 2007.

When a Social Democratic coalition government was in office from 2011 to 2015, its government manifesto emphasized a break with the previous government's decision to engage in Iraq. Thus, a pledge was made to secure a two-thirds majority in parliament before engaging in future military interventions, and the government established a commission on the Iraq War. However, it did not rule out involvement overseas in "responsibility to protect" cases, where international action may be warranted even without a UN mandate.

And when reality-tested with transatlantic ties, the Social Democratic government in August 2013 supported a U.S.-initiated military response, without a UN mandate, to the use of chemical weapons by Syria's regime against its own people. In the end, President Obama didn't carry through with the initially announced military response to Syria. Instead, in one of the whims of foreign policy, an unexpected opening arose to eliminate Syrian chemical weapons, although the Syrian regime of Assad hid some chemical agents, which became evident in the following period through their use against the Syrian population. In this endeavor, Denmark provided a ship to transport chemical components out of Syria. The United States undertook final destruction of most of the chemical components at sea.

Then, unexpectedly in 2014, approved by the Social Democratic government but with comfortable parliamentary support, Danish soldiers were back in Iraq but in a new role as trainers for the Iraqi army to thwart the advances of the terrorist organization, ISIS. This renewed Danish engagement, even in historically contested Iraq, is a testimony to Denmark's strong transatlantic ties. There is a strong connection and commitment to the United States. Even in 2013, when the Edward Snowden revelations about alleged illegal surveillance in Europe turned relations with U.S. core allies such as Germany sour, it did not dent the strong bond in Denmark. In 2016, Denmark was again the maritime lead with a transport ship on a U.S.-supported mission to remove and destroy Libya's remaining chemical stockpile.

What's in a Cartoon?

Another defining moment for Danish foreign policy was the crisis unleashed in mid-2005 by the publication of satirical cartoons in the Danish daily *Jyllands-Posten*. It sparked angry popular reactions in Muslim countries, particularly but not exclusively in the Middle East.

The outrage brought home to Danish policymakers and the population that today there is no purely local news. It also brought home the significant role played by nonstate actors in international affairs. The global village had a practical meaning and a direct impact on Danish foreign policy. The Danish government perceived its response to the cartoon crisis primarily as a defense of internal rights, particularly freedom of expression. Muslim ambassadors in Denmark and elsewhere demanded that the Danish government issue an apology for the drawings, which it refused to do, arguing that it could do no such thing on behalf of a free press. There was support in large parts of Europe for its position, although some governments, like that of the United Kingdom, kept very quiet.

Denmark and the cartoons became a proxy for popular anger in Muslim countries about broader international issues such as the Iraq War and for pent-up rage at the West in general and the United States in particular. Denmark was thus a convenient "soft" target for repressive governments in the Middle East, which allowed their people to vent their anger in public demonstrations. In 2011, throughout the Arab Awakening, the same popular anger instead unseated several of the same authoritarian regimes.

The Danish government insisted that it could not interfere with an independent newspaper's editorial decisions. However, Prime Minister Anders Fogh Rasmussen did distance himself later from "hurting people's [religious] feelings" and drawing satirical cartoons with religious subjects.[9]

Fogh's government had ruled since 2001 with a parliamentary majority secured by the far-right People's Party, which has an uneasy relationship with Islam in Denmark and has consistently demanded tighter immigration policies. The cartoon crisis inevitably inflamed the debate about immigration and multiculturalism inside Denmark.[10] The crisis also put a dent in Denmark's perception of its image abroad. Many Danes imagine that they are associated with a positive image overseas, based on a combination of substantial development assistance (for example, Denmark is the largest per capita contributor to the Palestinian authorities), no large-scale colonial past, windmills, LEGO bricks and bicycles, and H. C. Andersen's fairy tales such as "The Little Mermaid." There was, therefore, national surprise and consternation at the popular outburst against Denmark, which included the burning of embassies in Damascus and Tehran and a short-lived boycott of some Danish goods.

Since the cartoon crisis, Denmark has increased its engagement in the Middle East, opening new embassies in the region and enlarging funding for its Arab initiative, which focuses on supporting reform in areas such as women's rights in Arab and North African countries. The crisis has had lasting effects on the threat level in Denmark and the individual security of some people in Denmark, as demonstrated in 2010 by a plan to assassinate the already heavily protected cartoonist Kurt Westergaard and by foiled plots against *Jyllands-Posten*, the newspaper that first printed his drawings. After the cruel assassinations of the French satirical magazine *Charlie Hebdo*'s cartoonists in January 2015, Denmark was in February 2015 also hit by homegrown but ISIS-inspired terrorism, which targeted a freedom of speech event and the synagogue in the center of Copenhagen. The Danish cartoon crisis thus further imprinted the threat of international terrorism on Danish foreign policy and society. Still, it hasn't made the government timid about, for example, joining the coalition against ISIS in 2014, notwithstanding the potential terror blowback it might entail.

Green and Efficient

Denmark has a long record of engagement with environmental issues as well as a national dedication to energy efficiency. The oil crisis of the 1970s sparked a move in Denmark toward renewable energy (through windmill development) and enhanced energy efficiency. Denmark has succeeded in growing economically without increasing its energy consumption.[11]

Consequently, climate change—and an international approach to curbing it—is a Danish priority, although this has gotten harder with President Trump in the White House. Denmark expended much effort securing and hosting the Copenhagen Climate Change Conference in 2009, although the outcome did not live up to Danish or European (or anyone else's) expectations. Instead, the summit came to herald a new world order, with China and other emerging countries showing clearly that they are not succumbing to the customary compromises established by established powers.

That setback did not deter Denmark. The campaign to put sustainable energy at the center of global cooperation continues. From 2010, Denmark has put its mark on the international agenda through the Global Green Growth Forum. The initiative aims at fast-tracking the transition to sustainable growth worldwide by gathering stakeholders from business, civil society, and governments. The country has its own national ambition to become independent of fossil fuels by 2050.[12]

In the international arena, the EU's climate negotiations have been led by a Dane, Connie Hedegaard, the EU's commissioner for climate change (from 2010 to November 2014), who in Durban in December 2011 was instrumental in persuading China and other large emitters to commit to a legally binding deal to reduce carbon emissions. In addition, the Danish presidency of the European Union in early 2012 had "Green Europe" as one of its catchphrases.

Finally, with the Ukraine crisis, Denmark has pushed energy efficiency for Ukraine as part of the solution to wean Ukraine off Russian oil and gas.

International Governance

Denmark has for some time been preparing for a changing world order. The Danish government undertook a globalization analysis already in 2006. It challenged Denmark to look beyond the confines of Europe and the United States. This challenge has been reinforced by the strong export component in Denmark's economy, which demands that Danish companies continuously seek new growth markets.

Consequently, Denmark has welcomed the advent of emerging economies—both the BRICS (Brazil, Russia, India, China, and South Africa) and the Next Eleven[13]—because it represents a positive contribution to world growth and new export opportunities. The government has launched specific strategies for targeting BRICS and other emerging markets. On trade, the direction is clear: For a small export-oriented economy, growth markets are no longer solely in Western nations. Economic diplomacy is the buzzword.

The worrying issue for Denmark in this new emerging world order is the gradual move toward informal international forums like the G-20, BRICS, and the climate change–related group BASIC (Brazil, South Africa, India, and China). Denmark wholeheartedly supports international solutions reached through rule-based institutions like the UN, the World Trade Organization, World Health Organization, International Atomic Energy Agency, and United Nations Framework Convention on Climate Change, yet realizes that global deals such as those on trade, nuclear nonproliferation, and climate change seem harder and harder to broker.

At the same time, Denmark recognizes that new threats such as terrorism, piracy, and pandemics (witness the fight against Ebola in 2014, which necessitated assistance from the U.S. military above and beyond the UN-led efforts) are not well covered or addressed by those institutions and that new mechanisms of governance are needed. Still, Denmark prefers these to be rule-based and inclusive.

With respect to piracy, Denmark, as a seafaring nation with a large shipping industry, has been taking an active part in the UN-authorized, NATO-led counter-piracy operations in the Gulf of Aden outside the coastal waters off Somalia. This novel security threat is not adequately addressed by international organizations. Sparked by the frustration of the Danish navy when Danish patrol boats had to release pirates because there was no adequate legal mechanism for prosecuting them, Denmark began pioneering a legal framework for prosecuting acts of piracy.[14] Here, the traditional state-centered concept of sovereignty clashes with a new type of transnational and borderless crime, or crime originating in a de facto failed state like Somalia.

Relations with Emerging Powers

Denmark has sought to strengthen bilateral relations with emerging powers. In the case of China, Denmark was one of the first Western countries to recognize the People's Republic, having had diplomatic relations with China dating back to 1950. Denmark's overall policy is one of engagement with China while aiming for gradual change through the power of example and practical cooperation. Building on this long-standing relationship, Denmark in recent years has actively sought Chinese cooperation on issues such as climate change as well as programs to improve the rule of law and human rights in China—issues that matter to Denmark in its relationship with China. In spite of some friction on human rights, Denmark signed a strategic partnership with China in 2008 to expand cooperation in a range of fields, from climate change to expanded economic relations and university cooperation. At the time, Denmark was the smallest EU member state to enter into such a partnership, which had been reserved for heavyweights like Germany, France, and the United Kingdom. Denmark has also been trying to engage China on foreign policy issues such as cooperation in Africa on development assistance, where the massive influx of Chinese no-strings-attached investments affect the conditions for Danish development assistance. The bilateral results of that endeavor have so far been limited, as they have been on human rights.

Inside the EU, Denmark has been a staunch supporter of free trade with China and has opposed using defensive trade measures. On the EU arms embargo against China, Denmark was skeptical of lifting it in the initial phases (2003–05), particularly because of the lack of improvement in human rights in China. In the strategic partnership communiqué from 2008, Denmark just repackaged the agreed EU language stating that Denmark would "work toward lifting" the EU arms embargo against China.[15]

Denmark has tried to Europeanize its policies on China. Yet divisions inside the EU make it difficult to toe a common line. An example is the issue of meeting with the Dalai Lama. Denmark had a tradition of accepting such meetings at a political level; however, there is no common EU line on it, making it easier for China to direct its anger at individual countries.

Just as other European powers did, Denmark succumbed to China's "soft sanctions" following a Dalai Lama visit and meeting with then prime minister Lars Løkke Rasmussen in spring 2009. In December 2009, the diplomatic skirmish ended in a written statement from the Danish government promising to oppose "Tibetan independence," which implicitly created Chinese expectations that future Danish prime ministers would decline personal meetings with the Dalai Lama. That seemed to come true when, in February 2015, the Dalai Lama passed by Copenhagen without meeting the top echelons of the Danish government. Furthermore, Hu Jintao's state visit in 2012 was tarnished by allegations that the Danish police curbed pro-Tibetan demonstrators' rights. All in all, the combination of China's growing strength and a lack of European unity makes it more difficult for a small state like Denmark to impact Chinese policy.

With India, Denmark again had a bilateral head start, through a relationship shaped by its long-standing development assistance, which was phased out in 2005. The current relationship is focused on commercial diplomacy, though a bilateral criminal extradition case has occupied the bilateral bandwidth and has frozen official relations. The then Danish ambassador had already, during his tenure in Gujarat, developed ties with Narendra Modi, who is now prime minister of India, yet it still took time to bypass the bureaucracy's entrenched refusal to talk with Denmark until an extradition takes place. India takes less of a security and foreign policy interest in Denmark, as is the case with India's relations with the EU more broadly.

Like most European countries, Denmark has had a long relationship with Russia, all the way back to intermarriage between the Danish royal family and the czars. In a 2007 study, the European Council on Foreign Relations (ECFR), an independent think tank, classified Denmark as among the "frosty pragmatists" inside the EU with respect to relations with Russia.[16] The study cited feuds over events such as the Chechen Congress, held in Copenhagen in 2002, as well as the row the same year over the supposed Chechen "terrorist" Akhmed Sakaviev, when Denmark refused to proceed with his extradition. After 2007, a period of rapprochement followed. In a smaller ECFR-study based on interviews with Danish foreign policy elites in 2010, no one classified Russia as an enemy. Instead, all interviewees classified Russia as a partner.[17] This more forthcoming attitude was reciprocated: Russia undertook a state visit to Denmark in April 2011, and Queen Margrethe paid a return visit in September 2011. The aim was to enhance business cooperation and investment promotion. A decision was also taken in 2010 to let one of Russia's natural gas pipelines to Europe pass through Danish territorial waters.[18]

Then came 2014 and Russia's aggressive and illegal annexation of Crimea and ensuing destabilization of Eastern Ukraine through separatist proxies. Since then, relations with Russia have been deteriorating. Denmark supported the several rounds of sanctions on Russia enacted by the EU in close lockstep with the United States. For Denmark, Russia's actions have violated fundamental international norms. It is particularly troubling for a smaller country in Europe to witness the stronger nation bully the weaker. In 2018, there is much more political concern about possibly letting a Russian Nordstream II pipeline pass through Danish waters. Still, Russia is not perceived as a territorial threat to Denmark in the way the Baltic states acutely feel it.

Denmark's Foreign Policy: 2018

"Events, events"—this is how British Prime Minister Harold Macmillan allegedly explained foreign policy. The years 2014, 2015, and 2016 were eventful ones. Russia shook the foundations of the post–Cold War security architecture in Europe, creating new uncertainties and demand for NATO deterrence. In the Middle East, the ongoing unraveling—in particular the sectarian strife in Syria and Iraq but also in Libya and Yemen—placed terrorism on center stage. The Islamic State resurgence in Iraq threatened traditional borders and the purported success of the fight against terrorism. The flow to the Middle East of foreign fighters, including from Denmark, creates new threats and dilemmas for years to come. Simultaneously, flows of refugees and migrants put strain on Europe's borders and on Denmark. With Trump's election in 2016, it puts new uncertainty into how the transatlantic relations will evolve in the coming years. Claus Grube, state secretary in Denmark's Ministry of Foreign Affairs until 2013, had no qualms in 2010 writing in the annual Foreign Policy Yearbook that "Denmark has never been more secure than it is today."[19] But such a sentiment might not stand with the same degree of certainty these more recent years.

Now, Danish security strategy is conducted in a more complex and unpredictable environment. Global developments like terrorism, poverty, climate change, fragile states, and piracy threaten Danish freedom and prosperity. In Europe, the security architecture is challenged by Russia. Denmark seeks to cooperate internationally to do its share to minimize the potential impact of these global threats.[20] In that vein, Denmark has participated actively in military campaigns, including NATO operations—for example, conducting flight missions in Libya during the spring and summer of 2011, in the French-led mission in Mali in 2013, and with the U.S.-led coalition in Iraq against ISIS from 2014 onward.

Denmark's policy is essentially aimed at achieving what Carl Bildt, the former Swedish minister for foreign affairs, has termed "flow security," in which "good" flows of products, technology, legal immigration, and communication go unhindered in a globalized world and "bad" flows of crime, counterfeit goods, pandemics, and terrorism are kept at bay.[21]

In 2016, former ambassador to the United States Peter Taksøe-Jensen delivered a report on the future of Danish foreign policy titled "Danish Diplomacy and Defense in Times of Change." According to the report, Denmark needed to prioritize its national interests better and focus on them. Among these is the Arctic, where the Kingdom of Denmark through Greenland is an Arctic nation and where there is a link to the United States with the American air base at Thule in the far north of Greenland.

Conclusion: Denmark's Future

So, in a sense the British Labour representative's remark quoted in the introduction about "bloody Denmark" fits the narrative of this chapter, although not as he intended. Denmark has transformed itself away from its image as a symbol of pacifism, defense soft-pedaling, and NATO foot-dragging back in the 1980s to become a tough hedgehog, with spikes, a mini–United Kingdom ready to commit forces in Iraq, Afghanistan, and Libya in defense of global norms.

So far, so good for Denmark's active foreign policy, yet there are challenges to maintaining an active foreign policy. The reduction in defense budgets is such a challenge. Denmark remains capable of punching above its weight militarily, yet it is only starting to increase its defense budget. In NATO, the United States has been warning allies that the "insurance premium" has gone up with Russia's new bellicose behavior. The military spending of NATO members in Europe is enshrined in the 2 percent spending criteria, which dictates that European countries should field a larger share of the costs for European security. Denmark's military spending hovers around 1.1 percent of its GDP, although the government in 2018 launched a solid increase over the next years.[22] President Trump's pressure on the issue puts extra heat on. Nevertheless, output is still there. In 2014 Denmark managed on then shrinking budgets to contribute to the ISIS campaign with fighter planes, to field a transport plane and health workers in the fight against Ebola, and to enhance Baltic air policing to reassure NATO allies.

For years, Denmark has been reorienting its military and civilian capacities toward an expeditionary role abroad to secure fragile states far from Danish borders. But the reemergence of Russia as a potential territorial threat in Europe questions that priority, particularly when Denmark may be faced with the trade-off of classical territorial defense in the years to come.

In the Arctic, unsettled boundary claims remain between the Kingdom of Denmark (on Greenland's behalf) and Russia around the North Pole. Denmark strives to maintain the Arctic as a conflict-free, cooperative zone, yet if Russia's swashbuckling behavior moved to the far North, that could demand a new posture. Nonetheless, the quest for seafaring access and natural resources is likely to intensify in the coming decades, demanding a renewed focus on protection and Danish capabilities in the Arctic.

Denmark's international influence also may be diminished by the international governance shift from rule-based institutions such as the UN to more informal groupings like the G-20, in which Denmark has only a very indirect voice through the EU. Denmark retains an ambition to create a stronger European voice in the world. However, if Denmark still seeks to "punch above its weight," and if the EU continues to "punch below its weight," the EU will hardly be a Danish ambition-amplifier. Here the fallout from Brexit, euro uncertainty, and the handling of the refugee crisis will have an impact on how influential Europe can be and how much Denmark can expect to be heard through the EU. In the coming years, the EU could possibly evolve rapidly into a kind of "core Europe," with the eurozone as its center, and this could mean that Denmark must make some uncomfortable choices, particularly as its natural partner, the United Kingdom, moves to the outside.

NOTES

1. Quoted in Joseph S. Nye Jr., *The Future of Power* (New York: Public Affairs, 2011).

2. BBC News, "Labour Apologises to Belgians and Danes over West Slur," September 22, 2011 (www.bbc.co.uk/news/uk-politics-15021503). Yet as the British newspaper *The Times* reported, Danish fighter jets trumped the Royal Air Force in the air campaign in Libya; see Deborah Haynes, "Denmark's Top Guns Trump RAF in Libya," *The Times*, September 29, 2011.

3. This has been a popular saying by top U.S. political leaders, including former president Obama here quoted in 2011; see "Obama: Denmark Punching Above Its Weight," CPH Post Online, March 15, 2011 (cphpost.dk/news /international/obama-denmark-punching-above-its-weight.html).

4. The nomination of Anders Fogh Rasmussen as NATO secretary general was the coronation of his government's active Danish foreign policy, which had left behind its subservient small-state diplomacy; see interview in Mads Kastrup, "Fogh: Derfor sagde jeg ja til Nato," *BT*, March 14, 2010 (www.bt.dk /politik/fogh-derfor-sagde-jeg-ja-til-nato).

5. It is substantially larger if the territory of Greenland, still part of the Danish kingdom, is included.

6. Denmark's early entry into the United Nations was due, for the most part, to the singular acts of the Danish ambassador in Washington, Henrik Kaufmann, who was following a separate line of diplomacy since the formal Danish government was largely collaborating with German occupation forces.

7. The Danish policy of neutrality was successful during World War I, when Denmark remained neutral. During World War II, Denmark's neutrality was unsuccessful since the country ended up being occupied by Germany.

8. Robert Kagan, *Of Paradise and Power: America and Europe in the New World Order* (New York: Knopf, 2003).

9. Prime Minister Anders Fogh Rasmussen, speech, February 3, 2006 (www.stm.dk/_p_7519.html).

10. See also Hans Branner, "Muhammed-krisen og den nye dobbelthed i dansk udenrigspolitik," in *Streger i et forvirret billede*, edited by Jesper Linell (Copenhagen: Den Nye Verden, 2006).

11. See the "Danish example" on energy, economic growth, and carbon dioxide emissions explained at the Danish Ministry of Climate Change (https:// efkm.dk/publikationer/).

12. "Energy Strategy 2050," February 2011 (http://www.stm.dk/multimedia /Energistrategi_2050.pdf), and the current government's work program from 2016 (www.regeringen.dk/regeringsgrundlag/).

13. Both terms were coined by Jim O'Neill of Morgan Stanley. The countries of the Next Eleven are Bangladesh, Egypt, Indonesia, Iran, Mexico, Nigeria, Pakistan, Philippines, South Korea, Turkey, and Vietnam.

14. Although piracy has a long lineage and at times had government backing, as with Francis Drake and the British Crown, handling it within a group of sovereign states is a novel approach.

15. "Joint Statement between the Government of the People's Republic of China and the Government of the Kingdom of Denmark on the Establishment of a Comprehensive Strategic Partnership," http://kina.um.dk/en/about -denmark/sino-dk-relations/denmarks-china-policy/~/media/Kina /Documents/Other/CSPjointstatement.pdf.

16. Mark Leonard and Nicu Popescu, *A Power Audit of EU-Russia Relations* (London: ECFR, 2007), p. 43.

17. Unpublished background study by Jonas Parello-Plesner and Emma Knudsen on Denmark's foreign policy, conducted as part of background research, in Ivan Krastev and Mark Leonard, *The Spectre of a Multipolar Europe* (London: ECFR, 2010).

18. The Nord Stream route crosses the exclusive economic zones of Russia, Finland, Sweden, Denmark, and Germany, as well as the territorial waters of Russia, Denmark, and Germany.

19. Claus Grube, "The International Situation and Danish Foreign Policy 2010," in *Danish Foreign Policy Yearbook 2011*, edited by Nanna Hvidt and Hans Mouritzen (Copenhagen: Danish Institute of International Studies, 2011), p. 24.

20. For further information, see testimony on the Danish government's written security policy delivered to the Danish parliament, January 14, 2014 (www.ft.dk/samling/20131/redegoerelse/r7/1321850.pdf).

21. Carl Bildt, "Common Challenges Ahead," speech, Helsinki, March 4, 2010.

22. See Danish Ministry of Defense, "Ny aftale for Forsvaret 2018–2023," press release, January 28, 2018 (http://www.fmn.dk/nyheder/Pages/ny-aftale -for-forsvaret-2018-2023.aspx).

TEN

The Foreign Policy of the Czech Republic

Domestic Politics Back with a Vengeance

DAVID CADIER

The Czech Republic is facing, today, a more challenging international environment and a more pressuring European context that it has ever experienced since its accession to the EU in 2004 or, even, its return to independence in 1989. The international normative and legal orders are increasingly contested by the rising ambitions of new powers and by the return of nationalist tendencies across the board. In the United States, which since 1989 had been regarded by Czech elites as providing both a strategic compass and a cultural model for they own country, the new president has expressed views on NATO and Russia that are antithetical to Czech Republic's long-held positions. The EU and Russia are profoundly at odds with each other since the outbreak of the Ukraine crisis, and Prague is said to be one of the targets of Moscow's attempts to influence the internal politics of member states. The EU has itself been confronted by several internal trials, such as terrorist attacks, the rise of populism, the refugee crisis, and the exit of the United Kingdom (which was regarded in Prague as a like-minded country inside the bloc). The European context is not only challenging but also pressuring, in the sense that the EU integration project very much stands at a crossroads and individual member states will have to make decisive choices in this regard. Germany and especially France are pushing for deeper integration around the eurozone core, and the prospect of a "multi-speed Europe" (with countries having different status and levels of integration) is becoming more likely. The Czech Republic is not a member of the eurozone, and its population remains widely opposed to adopting the common currency, but its high dependency on Germany in terms of trade and investments also means that remaining outside of these new integration frameworks—if they materialize—could turn out to be costly for its domestic economy. The Czech Republic teamed up with its Central European partners from the Visegrad Group in refusing to take in refugees and in rejecting the relocation quotas previously agreed on at the EU level by member states. In response, the EU Commission has launched an infringement procedure against Poland, Hungary, and the Czech Republic.[1] At the same time, though, on topics other than migration, Prague has been—like Bratislava— wary to avoid being too closely associated with the populist governments in power in Warsaw and Budapest, which find themselves in open confrontation with the EU institutions over their domestic reforms eroding the rule of law. As all these examples illustrate, Czech foreign policy faces significant challenges and dilemmas; it very much finds itself at a critical juncture.

Anticipating the Czech Republic's choices in this context appears particularly difficult, however. No clear direction has emerged in Czech foreign policy over the past years; if anything, this policy has in fact often been characterized by its indetermination and paralysis, mainly due to political infighting.[2] As emphasized by a former senior Czech diplomat, who served in the EU Commission and as ambassador to NATO, the "ambiguity of Czech positions" weakens the country and causes "unease among its allies over the extent to which it can be relied upon."[3] This sense of confusion is only reinforced by the fact that some of Prague's recent decisions go in the opposite direction of what had come to constitute the country's traditional foreign policy stance since 1989. The previous emphasis on human rights and democracy promotion, which had for long constituted a defining feature of Czech foreign policy, is increasingly being replaced by a more pragmatic and trade-oriented approach: While the Czech Republic used to be known as the staunchest critic of the Cuba regime in the EU, it recently singularized itself by being the only EU country that kept its embassy open in Syria and even somehow improved its trade relations with the Syrian regime of Bashar al-Assad in spite of the war raging in the country. Similarly, while two presidents of the Czech Republic, Václav Havel and Václav Klaus, had cultivated privileged relations with Washington, the former regarding the United States as a political model and the latter as an economic one, current Czech president Miloš Zeman came to ban the U.S. ambassador from Prague Castle in April 2015 after he had criticized Zeman for being the only EU leader to attend the World War II commemorations in Moscow. Finally, following an opposite evolution than that of the EU mainstream, the Czech Republic stood among the member states wishing to impose sanctions on Russia after the Russo-Georgian War of 2008 and among those rather reluctant to impose them following Russia's 2014 intervention in Ukraine, although Moscow's responsibility in the outbreak of the latter conflict was much greater than in the former.

This evolution prompts the following questions: What drives Czech foreign policy, and what prompted the changes noted above in particular? Are these changes the mark of a profound change of direction in Czech foreign policy or simply punctual contradictions resulting from domestic politics spilling over into foreign policy? What are Prague's diplomatic priorities and foreign policy preferences at the EU level? How is the Czech Republic likely to position itself in the changing international and European contexts? This chapter purports to shed some light on these questions by contrasting Czech foreign policy then and now. It begins by presenting the historical background, domestic sources, and past traditions in this policy. It then focuses in turn on three issue areas of key importance for Prague in EU foreign policy—namely, relations with the United States, relations with Russia, and policies toward the Eastern neighborhood—and traces the evolution of Czech positions on these dossiers. The conclusion summarizes the findings and discusses the likely future direction of Czech foreign policy.

Historical Background, Domestic Context, and Czech Foreign Policy Traditions

In 1989, after decades of seeing its foreign policy determined by outside factors, the Czech Republic was led to radically rethink its foreign policy in a peculiar regional context. The collapse of the bipolar geopolitical configuration left a security vacuum in Central Europe, a heterogeneous region that had been embedded in the frame of successive empires (whether Habsburg or Soviet). To protect and consolidate their newly regained statehood, the Czech Republic and other Central European countries have strived to anchor in the novel continental architecture in which the EU and NATO served as the two pillars. In the 1990s, Czech foreign policy was almost exclusively devoted to joining these two organizations.

The process of laying the foundation for a new foreign policy coincided domestically with a period of national reconstruction. The strategic need to anchor the country in regional security structures, and the ontological need to reestablish the state in its Western identity, came together in the "return to Europe" paradigm. The Czech Republic did *return* to Europe eventually by completing its accession to both NATO in 1999 and the EU in 2004. As such, it achieved the overarching foreign policy objective that monopolized its attention and resources for fifteen years. This irremediably created a void in Czech foreign policy thinking. As the political class grew disinterested in—and largely tuned away from—foreign policy matters once these memberships had been achieved, this void has been filled by a small number of foreign policy entrepreneurs, who shaped the diplomatic course of the country.

Two figures have dominated Czech politics in the two decades following the return to independence: Václav Havel and Václav Klaus. Havel, who served as president from 1989 to 2003 after having been the leader of the dissidence (the underground intellectual opposition movement to the communist regime), played a crucial role in molding the ideological basis of Czech foreign policy. His aura facilitated relations with Western powers and institutions. He made foreign policy his *domaine reserve*, and he did not hesitate to impose his own choices, even sometimes against public opinion or government members' positions, on the topic of reconciliation with Germany. Havel's imprint has been profound and perennial, because he and his advisers essentially laid the foundations of the country's foreign policy (and oversaw it through most of the 1990s). Translating dissidents' philosophy into international relations, he established, for instance, the human rights and democracy promotion pillar in Czech foreign policy.[4] It became a cornerstone of Czech diplomacy that was promoted as a specialization at the EU level.[5] Havel's foreign policy positions should not simply be summed up to this aspect, however, as is too often done. He was also a convinced Atlanticist and a firm believer in the European project.

This last aspect in particular distinguishes him from the other prominent political figure of that period, Václav Klaus, who was prime minister between 1993 and 1997 and then president from 2003 to 2013. Klaus manifested much less interest in foreign policy and, one could add, less diplomatic abilities. Nevertheless, because he had a durable impact on the Czech political debate, installing notably at its core a strong attachment to the free market economic model and a sense of sovereign exceptionalism feeding a skeptical attitude toward the EU integration process, he influenced the domestic context in which foreign policy was formulated, as well as the country's international image. This is true not just about his ideological orientation but also his governing practice: Klaus was known for using the presidential springboard to voice his personal views in a provocative manner. He did not hesitate, for instance, to draw a comparison between the EU and the old Soviet Union *inside* the European Parliament or to travel to conferences abroad to promote his book refuting climate change theories. As will be illustrated below, his successor, President Miloš Zeman, has adopted a comparable maverick posture in foreign policy since he took office.

In the 2000s, a third group of foreign policy entrepreneurs came to occupy key positions in the Czech foreign policy system. These entrepreneurs could be designated as Atlanticists (they were also sometimes referred to as "hawks" in the Czech debate). In addition to a strong pro-American orientation and a critical stance toward Russia, they assumed the democracy promotion agenda from Havel and reproduced Klaus's lukewarm approach to the EU. Sociologically, this group is mainly composed of former dissidents who have turned hawkish as well as policymakers who specialize in strategic affairs. Both strands had been socialized to American worldviews in the 1990s and enjoy strong links with the U.S. epistemic and policymaking communities. The leading figure of this group, Alexandr Vondra, minister for European affairs between 2007 and 2009 and minister of defense between 2010 and 2012, fits both profiles: He is a former member of Charter 77 and was ambassador to the United States around the time of NATO accession. This group's imprint was notably manifest on certain key decisions in the 2000s—such as support for the U.S. invasion of Iraq in 2003, participation in the Ballistic Missile Defense scheme conceived by the George W. Bush administration, or the tough reaction to the Russo-Georgian conflict of 2008—that led the Czech Republic to be closer, in EU foreign policy debates, to Poland and the Baltic states than to Slovakia and Hungary. The influence of the Atlanticists progressively decreased after the early 2000s, however, due to generational change and as a new Social Democratic government that came into power in 2014, sidelining some key figures.

In examining the domestic context, it is important indeed to distinguish between the foreign policy elite and the political class. The latter is rather inconsistent and largely inconsequential in terms of foreign policy doctrine, but it affects foreign policy practice nonetheless. International issues rank very low on parties' and politicians' agendas; they occasionally pick on some issues to score points in the domestic political debate but rarely articulate a coherent vision in international affairs. In the 2000s, the two main parties—the Civic Democratic Party (ODS) and the Czech Social Democratic Party (ČSSD)—have adopted declamatory postures when in the opposition but have, by and large, followed similar foreign policy lines when in government. Similarly, ANO, a party that emerged in the early 2010s and entered government by forming a coalition with the ČSSD following the 2013 legislative elections, did not have any section on foreign policy in its program. Václav Klaus, the former president, and Miloš Zeman, the current president, have further complicated the picture by voicing singular views and adopting stances antagonistic to the government. Overall, the strategic course of the country in international affairs has long been set by the foreign policy elite while domestic politics mainly played a mediating role, by derailing, paralyzing, or boosting specific policies. For instance, the two preferences that have been installed at the heart of Czech foreign policy after 1989, Atlanticism and democracy promotion, have been mainly pushed by the foreign policy and strategic elites but not endorsed to the same extent by the political class or public opinion. After 2013, however, divisions within the party leading the governing coalition, the ČSSD, and the growing influence of other political actors with populist inclinations led foreign policy to be overtaken by domestic politics. The ČSSD found itself consumed by political infighting between its pro-European faction and its members advocating a more sovereign and conservative orientation.[6] Two political figures capitalized on this situation and filled the rhetorical gap on international affairs: Zeman, who himself is a former member of ČSSD and retains a power of nuisance in the party, and Andrej Babiš, the current prime minister and leader of ANO, the party that won the legislative elections of October 2017. Both politicians resorted to populist strategies and discourse—in the context of the refugee crisis in particular—that led for the foreign policy elites to be less audible.

Significant Actors and Regional Focus:
The Case of the United States

Among non-EU actors, the United States is by far the most significant for the Czech Republic. Maintaining a strong and functional transatlantic link has been the cardinal priority of Czech foreign policy since the 1990s, pursued within multilateral frameworks such as the EU and NATO, as well as through constant endeavors to upgrade bilateral ties with Washington where possible. Throughout the 2000s, the Czech Republic stood out as one of the staunchest Atlanticists in Europe, with successive governments not hesitating to go against public opinion in supporting U.S. policies. In more recent years, Czech Atlanticism has become much less vocal but remains largely unquestioned.

A sustained American military presence in Europe has long been seen by Czech policymakers as a way out of the geopolitical dilemma that placed the country between two overly powerful neighbors (Germany and Russia) and that, historically, often determined the fate of their country. Czech support for the U.S. campaign in Iraq, a region beyond its traditional zone of geopolitical interest, can be understood in these terms. The rationale was to follow the Americans in the Middle East in order to try to preserve U.S. involvement in Middle Europe.[7] Yet Prague's allegiance to Washington does not derive solely from security considerations: A significant share of the country's elite regard the United States as a political and economic model. Washington is also praised for its role in pushing for the Czech Republic's integration into NATO and for its proactive democracy promotion agenda. In other words, for Czech foreign policy elites, Atlanticism has been normative and not just strategic. This was notably manifest in the discussions around the Czech Republic's participation in the U.S. Ballistic Missile Defense (BMD) project envisaged by the Bush administration. In the early to mid-2000s, the Czech Republic and Poland were to participate in the Bush administration's plan for a third BMD site by hosting on their soil a radar station and ten interceptor missiles, respectively. The first negotiations began in 2002, they became official in 2007, and in the summer of 2008 the first agreements were signed.[8] For the Czech foreign policy elites, their country's participation in the BMD system amounted to an upgrade of its strategic status: The opportunity to get even a few American boots on Czech soil was welcomed as an additional security guarantee. But some of the advocates of the project also cast it in identity terms, presenting it as a way to strengthen the country's anchor in the Euro-Atlantic civilization as well as its Western identity. In fact, Prague did not ask for any material compensation in return for hosting the BMD and seemed content merely with the opportunity to strengthen its alliance with Washington. This clearly contrasted with Poland's utilitarian and business-minded approach to the BMD negotiation. The domestic opposition to the project was much smaller in Poland than in the Czech Republic, and thus it should have been easier to sell internally. Yet Warsaw asked for much more from Washington in return for hosting components of the system, such as financial and technical assistance in modernizing its army and the deployment of several Patriot missiles on its territory. In other words, in contrast to the Czech stance, Polish Atlanticism seemed more strategic than normative.[9]

In the Czech Republic, the foreign policy and security elites, the center-right parties of the governing coalition, and the mainstream media were overall supportive of their country's participation to the BMD system. The majority of the population, an active share of civil society, and political parties outside government were opposed to it, however. The ČSSD, which was the main opposition party at the time, decided to capitalize on popular discontent; contrary to most foreign policy issues in this period, what came to be designated in Czech debates as the "radar" thus became heavily politicized.

This party and other opponents from both the political class and civil society criticized the BMD project for unnecessarily putting the Czech Republic at risk and for encroaching on its sovereignty. Opposition parties delayed the ratification of the July 2008 agreement in the lower house of parliament, where the governing parties did not have a majority. In September 2009, anyway, the new U.S. administration of President Barack Obama announced that it was dropping the project in light of its financial cost and technical uncertainties.

For this decision and other features of its positioning in international affairs (such as the "reset" with Russia or the "pivot" to Asia), the Atlanticist coterie in the Czech Republic largely resented the foreign policy of the Obama administration, for it was not corresponding to their preestablished ideological conceptions. This transpired in the "Open Letter to the Obama Administration" of July 2009, signed by preeminent political figures from Central and Eastern Europe, including Alexandr Vondra and Karel Schwarzenberg, who had been the two most influential decisionmakers in Czech foreign policy since Václav Havel.[10] The text bemoaned "that Central and Eastern European countries were no longer at the heart of American foreign policy" and warned against taking the region's stability and Atlanticist inclination for granted. In other words, the initial reaction of Czech foreign policy elites to Obama's attempt to "normalize" relations with Central Europe—that is, to bring those relations in line with the region's geopolitical value for U.S. international strategy—was to criticize the new stance rather than try to adapt to it. This tends, again, to emphasize the normative (or ideological) rather than strategic texture of their Atlanticist stance. The text was not explicitly endorsed by the caretaker government in power in Prague at the time and was criticized by many Czech analysts, but its publication and the cancellation of the BMD plan affected Czech-U.S. relations for several months.

In light of the party's previous positions, questions lingered as to how much the ČSSD-led government, which took office in January 2014, would affect Czech policies toward the United States. Overall, while seeking to distinguish itself from the legacy of political figures such as Vondra and Schwarzenberg, the new team did not fundamentally put into question the country's transatlantic leaning. In the context of the debate on the "strategic reassurance" to be provided to NATO's Eastern members following Russia's actions in Ukraine, Prime Minister Bohuslav Sobotka made remarks that clearly contrasted with earlier goals pursued through participation in the BMD project. He declared that, contrary to Poland or the Baltic states, the Czech Republic was not calling for a reinforcement of NATO military presence on its territory or in Europe more generally.[11] The statement must in part be read as a posturing move in domestic politics rather than as a genuine foreign policy orientation, however: It was rather inconsequential at the strategic level because such deployment was not contemplated by the Atlantic alliance anyway and was mainly seeking to echo the public's deep-rooted aversion to the stationing of foreign troops on national soil. In fact, many internal political actors criticized this declaration, including President Zeman, who is not positioning himself as an Atlanticist.[12] What is more, a few months later, while preparing for an official visit to Washington, Sobotka reaffirmed that the Czech Republic sees "the transatlantic bond as the foundation of [its] security policy."[13] Similarly, the election of Donald Trump did not fundamentally alter the course of Czech policies toward the United States. Some commentators from the press and civil society have criticized the political program of the new American president while, by contrast, Zeman has declared his admiration for it. Overall, according to a study comparing EU member states reactions to Donald Trump's election, "the image of the U.S. in the Czech Republic remains little changed."[14]

Relations with Russia

Russia is another important non-EU actor for Czech foreign policy. On this issue, divisions among internal players have been more salient than on relations with the United States. The Czech position has been more complex and more nuanced than what is accounted for in international media, where the country is depicted either as irremediably fearful of Russia because of its history or as amenable to the Kremlin's positions because it is crippled from within by Russia's influence.

From an economic point of view, Czech-Russian relations have been steady and consequential. On the political and rhetorical side, by contrast, they have often been rocky. While relations were good in the years immediately after the Velvet Revolution, they deteriorated over the question of the Czech accession to NATO. A period of cordial normalization followed in the early 2000s, but a new period of tension emerged around the American BMD plan and, more broadly, Russia's new assertiveness in regional affairs. In 2007, Moscow regularly denounced the BMD scheme and went as far as threatening to point its missiles at Prague and Warsaw. Czech policymakers responded by castigating Russia's "neo-imperial" attempts to regain control of its former sphere of influence. Nevertheless, these condemnations were mainly rhetorical and very rarely obstructed diplomatic channels.

In the Czech Republic, declarations on Russia quite often serve, indeed, domestic political objectives. The Russian question is highly polarizing internally, more than in most European countries, and it is thus crucial to understand how the various domestic preferences compete and how this configuration affects Czech foreign policy. The Atlanticist stream of the foreign policy elites, the ODS party, an important share of the mainstream press, and several nongovernmental organizations (NGOs) and think tanks are highly critical of the Kremlin and often present Russia as a threat to national security. They have often used Russia as a straw man in domestic political discourse: The Mirek Topolánek government (2006–09) had, for instance, used Russia as justification for the BMD project, but also, more surprisingly, as a reason to ratify the Lisbon Treaty.[15] By contrast, the ČSSD, the business community, and a share of the population are more inclined, traditionally, to see Russia as an economic partner. President Zeman for his part sometimes adopts, in a provocative style similar to that of his predecessor, positions that are overtly pro-Kremlin, largely endorsing, for instance, Vladimir Putin's account of the Ukraine crisis. This position allows him to appeal to the share of Czech voters who are more positively inclined toward Russia and demonstrate his independence from the government.

While in the past they were mainly shaped by the foreign policy elite, Czech policies toward Moscow have been increasingly influenced by domestic political dynamics; they sometimes seem more dictated by these dynamics than by Russia's actions themselves. The difference between Prague's reactions to the Russo-Georgian conflict of 2008 and to the Ukraine crisis of 2014 is particularly illustrative in this regard: Contrary to the other EU member states, the Czech Republic adopted a more hawkish position on the former than on the latter. In 2008, Czech government elites condemned Russia as the aggressor and joined member states such as Poland, the Baltic states, and the United Kingdom in demanding EU sanctions against Moscow.[16] By comparison, neighboring Slovakia, whose geographic and historical situation vis-à-vis Russia is similar to that of the Czech Republic, adopted a different stance on the conflict: Bratislava pointed to Tbilisi's responsibility in initiating hostilities and joined the group opposed to sanctions (including Germany, France, Italy, the Netherlands, and Greece).[17] The latter group eventually prevailed, and no sanctions were imposed in 2008.

In 2014, following Russia's annexation of Crimea and its support for armed groups in Eastern Ukraine, the EU progressively imposed a set of economic sanctions on Russia. In the internal EU debates on these sanctions, the Czech Republic has often counted among the member states opposed to these sanctions or calling for their lifting.[18] More specifically, Prague has been oscillating between reluctantly supporting sanctions as an incarnation of EU unity and implicitly calling them into questions. This lack of clarity stemmed from deep divisions at the highest state level, where the three principal figures at the time defended divergent positions, although they were (or had been) members of the same political party (ČSSD). Then Prime Minister Sobotka had adopted a reserved attitude toward sanctions, not officially calling for their removal but pointing to their negative effects on Czech businesses and seeking specific exemptions. Then Foreign Minister Lubomir Zaorálek and his team had been the most critical of Russia and advocated sanctions in the name of the EU mainstream. Finally, President Zeman has called for the lifting of sanctions, presenting the conflict in Ukraine as a "civil war" in which Russia was not involved.[19] Outside the governing circle, the ODS and most of the media have called for tougher sanctions and military cooperation with Ukraine, while the Czech citizenry sees the Ukraine crisis as a threat to European security but remains divided on the issue of sanctions.[20]

In reviewing these positions, it is important, however, to distinguish between rhetorical posturing and concrete policy decisions: President Zeman might be a vocal critic of sanctions and regularly expresses his views at home and abroad, but when the Czech Republic has to vote in the European Council on the continuation of EU sanctions on Russia, the decision rests with the government.

Priorities and Niches in the EU's Common Foreign and Security Policy: The Case of the Eastern Neighborhood

In the early 2000s, promoting further EU enlargement eastward ranked high among the foreign policy priorities of the Czech Republic and other Central European member states. The rhetorical commitment to that objective remains—the Czech 2011 foreign policy white book (*Conceptual Basis of the Foreign Policy of the Czech Republic*) listed, for instance, "strengthening the European integration of Eastern Europe" as one of the country's priority inside the EU—but the actual level of engagement in realizing has largely faded. Not only is the prospect of such enlargement increasingly unlikely in the medium term, in light of both the EU's internal dynamics and of the regional context, but Visegrad countries have themselves become much less warm to the idea.[21] This is especially true of the Czech Republic.

In the late 2000s, as EU membership was not readily available for states like Moldova or Ukraine, the Visegrad countries invested instead in the

eastern dimension of the European Neighborhood Policy (ENP). More specifically, they supported the creation and development of the Eastern Partnership (EaP), a program that aims at fostering the economic integration
and political association of six post-Soviet states with the EU.[22] Poland, in
particular, played a crucial role in providing the conceptual basis for the
policy and in working toward its adoption at the EU level, supported in that
endeavor by the other Visegrad countries. The Central European investment in the EaP has been serving multiple goals. Being geographically close
to—and retaining historical, socioeconomic, and societal links with—the
post-Soviet neighborhood, Central European countries have an acute interest in the region's stability and economic development. In addition, the
effort by Central European member states to tip the ENP geopolitical spot-
light eastward has also been serving intra-EU objectives: It is a means to
carve for themselves a niche of specialization within the Common Foreign
and Security Policy (CFSP) structures and thereby to increase their agenda-
setting capacities in Brussels. The Visegrad countries can indeed claim a
certain expertise both on the post-Soviet region and on the process of
democratic transition.

In the case of the Czech Republic, the diplomatic attention to, and
EU-level activism for, the Eastern neighborhood has been unequal, how-
ever.[23] The region, with the exception of Belarus, was largely bereft of
Prague's foreign policy radar until the mid-2000s. Prague's reaction to the
2004 Orange Revolution in Ukraine was very limited, for instance. In 2007,
however, the Czech Republic presented in the framework of the Visegrad
Group a proposal on how to develop an eastern pillar within the ENP.[24]
Later on, it supported the Polish initiatives that led to the creation of the
EaP, which was in fact launched in Prague in May 2009 under the aegis of
the Czech EU presidency. Two factors prompted this new foreign policy
activism toward the Eastern neighborhood. First, this new diplomatic priority was successfully pushed internally by policy entrepreneurs from the
Atlanticist foreign policy elite and the NGO sector: the former saw it as a
mean to roll back Russia's influence in the Eastern neighborhood, and the
latter as a way to promote democracy in the region.[25] Second, the Czech
Republic was keen to find a flagship project for its EU Council Presidency
role in 2009 and in increasing its specialization and influence within EU
structures more generally. The influence of these two factors is confirmed
by the fact that with the Czech EU presidency being over and the internal
influence of the Atlanticist foreign policy elite receding, Prague's diplomatic

attention and level of activism toward the region has diminished. In that sense, Czech foreign policy seems more closely aligned than before with the attitude of the population: 62 percent of Czechs oppose, indeed, further EU enlargement.[26]

Conclusion

During the 2000s, the Czech foreign policy process was largely deserted by the political class once NATO and EU accession were achieved. In that decade, as noted by a long-term observer of Czech politics, foreign policy has never been among the top-five priorities of any of the successive governing coalitions.[27] Instead, diplomatic and strategic elites played a key role in shaping the policy choices of the country.

As this chapter has shown with reference to Czech policies toward the United States, Russia, and the Eastern neighborhood, this state of affairs has recently been somehow reversed, however. The foreign policy elite is no longer able to steer Czech foreign policy as it used to, and the influence of its Atlanticist branch in particular has decreased. Conversely, domestic political considerations and partisan infighting have increasingly affected foreign policy decisions. This is salient not just in the three issue areas analyzed, but also with regard to Czech EU policies. For instance, outgoing Foreign Minister Zaorálek, who since 2014 had been regarded as one of moderate and pro-European voices on the Czech political scene, engaged in March 2017 in an unexpected rant against the EU and its institutions—in all likelihood to be in a better position to compete with the populist-leaning President Zeman and Prime Minister Andrej Babiš.[28] Czech commentators abundantly criticized his declarations, pointing out that they risked weakening the country's position in the EU by conveying an image of unpredictability and short-termism.

Foreign policy cannot, obviously, be summed up—or simply grasped—based on rhetorical statements. Several Czech initiatives at the EU could be mentioned, and more generally, Prague's balancing act—at once using the Visegrad Group as a punctual coalition platform on certain topics and avoiding association with the governments in power in Warsaw and Budapest—shows that it increasingly conceptualizes its national interests in European terms. What is more, the *politicization* of Czech foreign policy amounts, in fact, to a *normalization* to a certain extent. The conditions in which Havel laid the groundwork for Czech foreign policy, as well as his aura and vision, were exceptional. The momentum following the Czech Republic's accession to the EU and NATO, in which Atlanticist policy entrepreneurs were able to tilt the country's foreign policy in a certain direction, took place in a markedly different European and international contexts. For the Czech Republic, as for all the other member states, the choices to be made at the EU level are much more pressing now than a decade ago. Following the Brexit vote and the election of Donald Trump, Atlanticism has lost much of its shine and operability in this context, at least in the way it was previously defined.

The structural influence of domestic politics on foreign policy is common to any country; emphasizing it simply invites one to pay closer attention to political parties and to how they relate to foreign policy matters. The lack of schooling and vision of the political class in international affairs is hardly a pattern confined to the Czech Republic. What appears more detrimental in the case of the Czech Republic and several other European countries, though, is the absence of a political party setting forward a positive agenda and, most important, a sense of ownership about the EU.

NOTES

1. See "EU Takes Action against Eastern States for Refusing to Take Refugees," *The Guardian*, June 13, 2017.

2. This is the main conclusion of the 2016 edition of an annual assessment of Czech foreign policy conducted by a local think tank. Vít Dostál and Tereza Jermanová, eds., *Agenda for Czech Foreign Policy 2017* (Prague: Asociace pro Mezinárodní Otázky/AMO, 2017).

3. "Interview: Confusing Czech Foreign Policy Worries Allies," *European Security Journal*, May 25, 2017 (www.esjnews.com/interview-karel-kovanda).

4. On Havel's ideas and on its imprint on Czech foreign policy, see Jacques Rupnik, "In Praise of Václav Havel," *Journal of Democracy* 21, no. 3 (2010), pp. 135–42; Ondřej Ditrych, Vladimír Handl, Nik Hynek, and Vít Stříteský, "Understanding Havel?," *Communist and Post-Communist Studies* 46, no. 3 (2013), pp. 407–17; Rick Fawn, "Symbolism in the Diplomacy of Czech President Vaclav Havel," *East European Quarterly* 33, no. 1 (1999), pp. 1–19.

5. David Cadier and Kristina Mikulova, "European Endowment for Democracy: Institutionalizing Central and Eastern European democracy promotion model at the EU level?," in *Democratization of EU Foreign Policy? The*

Role of New Member States, edited by B. Berti, K. Mikulova and N. Popescu (Abingdon, U.K.: Routledge, 2015), pp. 83–101.

6. Dostál and Jermanová, *Agenda for Czech Foreign Policy 2017*, p. 14.

7. Jacques Rupnik, "America's Best Friends in Europe: East-Central European Perceptions and Policies towards the U.S.," in *With US or Against US: Studies in Global Anti-Americanism*, edited by Tony Judt and Denis Lacorne (New York: Palgrave, 2005), p. 99.

8. See Nikola Hynek and Vít Střitecký, "The Rise and Fall of the Third Site of Ballistic Missile Defense," *Communist and Post-Communist Studies* 43, no. 2 (2010), pp. 179–87.

9. David Cadier, "Après le retour à l'Europe: convergences et contrastes dans les politiques étrangères des pays d'Europe centrale [After the Return to Europe: Convergences and Contrasts in the Foreign Policies of Central European Countries]," *Politique Etrangère* 3 (September 2012), pp. 573–84.

10. "An Open Letter to the Obama Administration from Central and Eastern Europe," *Gazeta Wyborcza*, July 16, 2009. Neither Vondra nor Schwarzenberg were in power at the time of the letter's publication, but both resumed key governmental positions just a few months after (as minister of defense and minister of foreign affairs, respectively).

11. "Slovak PM Follows Czechs in Ruling Out Foreign NATO Troops," *Reuters*, June 4, 2014.

12. "PM Draws Fire for Saying Czech Republic Will Not Call for NATO Troop Increase," *Radio Prague*, June 4, 2014.

13. Bohuslav Sobotka, "Beyond Ukraine: NATO Solidarity in a Time of Crisis," *Foreign Policy*, August 18, 2014.

14. Jeremy Shapiro and Dina Pardijs, "The Transatlantic Meaning of Donald Trump: A U.S.-EU Power Audit," *European Council on Foreign Relations (ECFR) Power Audit* (September 2017), p. 19.

15. "Czechs Must Choose Lisbon or Russia, says PM Topolánek," *Radio Prague*, November 20, 2008.

16. Karel Schwarzenberg, "Ruská invaze je zlom," *Respekt*, August 18, 2008.

17. Cadier, "Après le retour à l'Europe."

18. Richard Youngs, *Europe's Eastern Crisis: The Geopolitics of Asymmetry* (Cambridge University Press, 2017), pp. 72 and 95.

19. "Putin's Ally in Prague Castle," *EUobserver*, February 16, 2015.

20. In a Public Opinion Research Centre (CVVM) poll conducted in October 2014, 73 percent of the respondents characterized the Ukraine crisis as a risk for European security, 41 percent supported EU sanctions on Russia, while 39 percent disagreed with them. See Jan Adamec, "Less than Half of Czechs Agree with the Sanctions against Russia, Says the Latest CVVM Survey," *Visegrad Revue*, October 24, 2014.

21. Vladimir Bilčik, "Foreign Policy in Post-Communist EU," *International Issues and Slovak Foreign Policy Affairs* 19, no. 4 (2010), pp. 3–17.

22. The six countries concerned are Armenia, Azerbaijan, Belarus, Georgia, Moldova, and Ukraine.

23. Petr Kratochvíl and Ondřej Horký, "Eastern Promises? Czech Ambiguity in the European Neighbourhood," in *The Quest for the National Interest: A Methodological Reflection on Czech Foreign Policy*, edited by P. Drulák and M. Braun (Frankfurt am Main: Peter Lang AG Internationaler Verlag der Wissenschaften, 2010), pp. 71–86.

24. Elsa Tulmets, "Preparing the EU Presidency: The Czech Contribution to the Project of 'Eastern Partnership,'" *Polish Quarterly of International Affairs* 4 (2008), p. 79–98.

25. David Cadier and Monika Sus, "Modalities of Think Tanks' Involvement in Foreign Policy Making: A Comparative Analysis of the Czech Republic and Poland," *The International Spectator* 52, no. 1 (March 2017), pp. 116–31.

26. EU Commission, "Europeans' Views on the Priorities of the European Union," Eurobarometer 86 survey, December 2016 (http://ec.europa.eu /COMMFrontOffice/publicopinion/index.cfm/Survey/getSurveyDetail /instruments/STANDARD/surveyKy/2137).

27. Martin Ehl, "Letter from Prague," *Carnegie Europe*, January 30, 2015 (http://carnegieeurope.eu/strategiceurope/?fa=58860).

28. "Zaorálek: Volný pohyb osob za prací v EU musíme mít pod kontrolou [Zaorálek: The Free Movement of Workers in the EU Must Be Regulated]," *Hospodářské noviny*, March 20, 2017.

PART II

The Cold War Superpowers
in a Hot World

Russia's Staunch Foreign Policy in a Wavering Landscape

SERENA GIUSTI

For centuries Russian foreign policy has been marked by expansion, militarization, and border defense. The identity of Russia itself has been forged by the country's capacity to spread out and conquer new territories. While Russia under the czars was long one of the key players in European diplomacy (and also had a strong interest in expanding eastward), under Soviet rule it became a superpower whose ideological and geopolitical influence extended throughout the world. Soviet foreign policy took on a global dimension due to the bipolar nature of the international system, within which Russia and the United States struggled for dominance. The system revolved around the two superpowers, and it relied for its survival on the doctrine of nuclear deterrence based on mutual assured destruction. There were, however, several shifts in alliances as some countries passed from one sphere of influence to the other; other countries were able to maintain nonaligned status.

The Kremlin, following the centuries-old strategic logic of Russian imperialism, kept strict control over the Eastern European countries (the so-called satellites) in order to use the region as a buffer against possible military attack by the major Western powers.[1] Unlike other empires, the Soviet Union did not fall because it was defeated in war but because the political and economic model on which it was based failed. The bipolar system crashed after the satellites rejected the Soviet legacy for full sovereignty, and the Soviet Union itself imploded quite unexpectedly.

Even the international relations theory of realism failed to forecast the end of the rivalry between the great powers, the unilateral Soviet withdrawal from its sphere of influence, and the rise of nationalism. Russia no longer controlled an imperial hinterland in Europe, and it no longer was confronted with a zero-sum relationship with the United States. As Ilya Prizel pointed out, "Within the short space of three years the Russian people have seen the ideology that dominated their polity for seven decades delegitimized. Worse still, they have lost the vast territories that for centuries [they] considered their own and have witnessed the disappearance of an imperial status that has been part and parcel to Russia's national being since at least the sixteenth century."[2]

President Vladimir Putin declared the demise of the Soviet Union the "greatest geopolitical catastrophe of the century," and its messy and lingering effects still reverberate at both the regional and the international level.[3] The end of the Soviet polity resulted in a multidimensional domestic transformation during which the country was forced to engage in a complex process of redefining itself and constructing a new identity.[4] Consequently, in the early 1990s Russian foreign policy was rather muddled and mostly reactive. Three main competitive approaches to defining and prioritizing national interests—liberal Atlanticist, centrist, and Eurasian—emerged.

The liberal Atlanticist school advocated that Russia, as part of Western culture and civilization, relinquish the idea that it was a unique state entrusted with a messianic mission. Accordingly, Russia's salvation and its ability to modernize rested primarily on its capacity and will to reconnect with the Western mainstream (Europe and the United States).[5] This approach implied that Russia would renounce its traditional sphere of influence and cooperate with Western institutions to ensure the stabilization and normalization of the former communist countries. Russia would seek integration with the Euro-Atlantic community and prominent international organizations. In economic and security terms, this integrationist approach called for overcoming the historical rivalries and conflicts that constituted Russia's legacy by developing harmonious relations with major regional and global actors.

The centrists supported the deepening of Russia's relations with its Western partners, on a fully equal basis, while recognizing Russia's Asian and Turkish roots. The centrists also believed that Russia should play a pivotal role in global affairs while maintaining some kind of influence over the former Soviet republics. In the centrist narrative, Russia's foreign policy was to be defined as a point of equilibrium, which could vary between building fruitful relations with the West, reinforcing links with the Community of Independent States (CIS), and building strategic partnerships in Asia.

The Eurasian school remained faithful to the belief that Russia, located at the crossroads between Europe and Asia, represented a distinct civilization and should preserve its unique identity. As Jeffrey Mankoff explains, "Eurasianism ranges from the imperial and aggressive to various attempts at synthesizing the traditional antipodes of Westernizers and Slavophiles into a kind of Third Way."[6] The Eurasians believed that the Soviet Union's implosion was due neither to a dysfunctional economic system that was unable to grow and compete with the rest of the world nor to the revolt of both the satellites and the republics but to a conspiracy against Moscow. They were in favor of a strong state (*derzhavniki*) capable of defending the country's prerogatives against Western demands. The best alternative for Russia would be to play the role of bridge between a united Europe and the Asia-Pacific region. According to this school, Russia could not keep its status as a great power without establishing order in Eurasia, where Moscow would become the cornerstone of a widening Eurasian community.[7]

While mirroring well-rooted traditions in Russia's foreign policy, these approaches have been rediscovered in contemporary Russia under Vladimir Putin, and the leadership has copiously borrowed from them to channel their current interests.

The EU and Russia: A Troubled Partnership

The first phase of Russia's foreign policy was oriented toward the West. With the collapse of the Soviet Union and the loss of its immense prestige throughout the world, Russia became a weak and disoriented country.[8]

President Boris Yeltsin (1991–99) and his foreign minister, Andrei Kozyrev, advocated a new system of values, incorporating the supremacy of democracy, human rights, freedom, and legal and moral standards—values on which Western societies were based. They supported the gradual participation of Russia in Western organizations and its integration into the world economy; they also asked international financial institutions for economic assistance in dealing with the effects of the dramatic 1997–98 financial crisis. Russia's leadership looked also to the West as a security provider because tensions along the country's new borders threatened to involve it in conflicts that could destabilize the ongoing domestic reform process.

From the beginning, the Russia-EU relationship has been problematic. As Vladimir Baranovsky noted, "Geographically, Europe and Russia are overlapping entities. Half of Europe is Russia; half of Russia is in Europe. However, politics, in contrast to geography, does not necessarily take this as axiomatic—either in Europe or in Russia."[9] Under the Cold War regime, Europe's interaction with the Soviet Union was mediated by the United States, which provided security to the Western European countries through NATO. With the advent of Mikhail Gorbachev's perestroika, the Soviet Union undertook an unexpected opening toward the West, including Europe's institutions.

The first step in the "normalization" of relations between Brussels and Moscow, which encompassed Moscow's adaptation to EU legislation, was the signing in 1994 of a Partnership and Cooperation Agreement (PCA). The agreement—which entered into force only in 1997, after the end of the Chechen War—was established for an initial period of ten years, with an automatic annual extension unless either party withdraws from the agreement. The PCA could be classified as an entry-level agreement that does not envision Russia's membership in the EU but endorses the interest of both parties in developing further mutual cooperation. PCAs are agreements that include the European Communities (EC) pillar of the EU as well as the second and third pillars, Common Foreign and Security Policy and Justice and Home Affairs.[10] At the Saint Petersburg summit in May 2003, the EU and Russia agreed to reinforce their cooperation by creating over the long term four "common spaces" based on their shared values and interests: the Common Economic Space; the Common Space of Freedom, Security and Justice; the Common Space of External Security, including crisis management and nonproliferation; and the Common Space of Research and Education. The Moscow summit in May 2005 developed the instruments to put the common spaces into effect by creating "road maps" with specific required objectives and actions. The Russia-EU relationship has generally been conducted at the top political level.

In a few years, however, the relationship deteriorated. The main causes of tension were the alleged Western support for the so-called Color revolutions (Georgia 2003, Ukraine 2004, and Kyrgyzstan 2005); the recognition of Kosovo's independence in 2008 by two-thirds of EU members; EU engagement in the post-Soviet space through its 2004 European Neighborhood Policy (ENP); and finally the launch in 2009 of the Eastern Partnership (EaP), which is aimed at tightening the relationship with six countries of Eastern Europe and the South Caucasus (Armenia, Azerbaijan, Belarus, Georgia, Moldova, and Ukraine)

Some improvements in relations between Moscow and Washington (for example, the "reset policy" in 2009) softened for a while the traditionally hostile position toward Russia of countries like Poland and the Baltic nations, with positive implications for the EU's policy toward Russia. In particular, the overall political climate seemed to be soothed with the rapprochement between Moscow and Warsaw that occurred following the tragic plane crash at Smolensk in April 2010 in which the Polish president and ninety-six of the country's top political and military leaders died. They had been traveling to Katyn to commemorate the Soviet massacre of Polish officers there during World War II.

An important and, on paper, very promising step in the relationship between the EU and Russia has been the Partnership for Modernization (PfM), which was launched during the Rostov-on-Don summit (May 31–June 1, 2010). The PfM has been presented as pursuing a common agenda to advance the EU and Russian economies and to bring their citizens closer while contributing to global recovery and stronger international economic governance. It is primarily a flexible framework for promoting reforms, enhancing growth, and increasing competitiveness in the priority areas of innovation, medium-size enterprises, alignment of technical regulations and standards, and intellectual property rights. Implementation of activities entails the involvement of various actors, institutional and private, with both an economic-financial and a political mission. The partnership is more open than other EU cooperative programs to the involvement of informal actors and better suited to blurring the boundaries between the public and private spheres. The PfM—which could have promoted progressive convergence, homogenization, and multilevel cooperation between EU and Russia—has instead remained mostly unexploited.[11]

New tensions erupted in March 2011 when UN Security Council Resolution 1973, which authorized military action in Libya to protect civilians, was applied more broadly by France and Great Britain to effect regime change. Russia, along with Brazil, China, Germany, and India, abstained. The Kremlin claimed that the action was a pretext for NATO to intervene in an internal conflict. However, the issue that creates the most conflict has been competition over the post-Soviet space. Regardless of the European Commission's reassurances that the EaP would be developed in parallel with the strategic partnership with Moscow, the member states (Poland and Sweden) promoting the EaP and the timing (one year after the war in Georgia) have led Russia to suspect that it is a less-than-neutral policy. Although the European Neighborhood Policy does not offer participants membership in the EU, its economic, political, and social dimensions were perceived by Moscow as an attempt to carve out a Western sphere of influence in Russia's traditional backyard.[12] The Kremlin responded by proposing to the ENP countries membership in Russia's Customs Union, an integration project similar to the EaP in its approach but not in its ends.

It was in this climate of mounting competition between Brussels and Moscow for "control" of the post-Soviet space that violent protests in Kiev's Maidan Square in November 2013 led rapidly to regime change in Ukraine. In reaction to the annexation of Crimea and violation of Ukraine's sovereignty and territorial integrity by Russian armed forces, the EU canceled the summit with Russia and decided not to hold regular bilateral summits. Moreover, restrictive measures were adopted—for example, certain individuals were prohibited from traveling to the EU—followed by economic sanctions targeting Russian state-owned banks and forbidding the export of technologies needed by Russia's oil and defense industries. President Putin immediately reacted by signing a decree that imposed an embargo for a one-year period on imports of most agricultural products whose country of origin had either "adopted the decision on introduction of economic sanctions in respect of Russian legal and (or) physical entities, or joined the same."

Because the EU and Russia are highly interdependent, economic confrontation damages both. Trade between the two—which showed steep growth until mid-2008, when the trend was interrupted by the global financial crisis—resumed again in 2010 and reached record levels in 2012;

however, it is now falling. Russia is the third trading partner of the EU, and the EU is the first trading partner of Russia. Russia is the EU's most important single supplier of energy products, accounting for over 25 percent of the EU consumption of oil and gas. In turn, Russia's economy remains highly dependent on the export of energy raw materials, and the EU is its most important destination.

The terrorist attacks in Paris and Brussels convinced Western leaders to cooperate with Russia in the fight against the Islamic State. However, the Kremlin decision to intervene militarily in Syria, the first time outside the borders of the former Soviet Union since the end of the Cold war, soon divided and angered the international community. The Kremlin intervention in Syria, nominally aimed at hurting the Islamic State, has rather helped to keep Bashar al-Assad in power while prompting tens of thousands of Syrians to flee. The international community has condemned Russia, especially after heavy bombardments in Aleppo in the fall of 2016, but the European Council (October 2016) failed to impose further sanctions against Russia. Western hostility toward the Kremlin's behavior in Syria (even though Russia is a strategic actor for any cease-fire that could lay the foundation for a peace process in Syria) has persuaded the country to pragmatically reapproach Turkey. It seems that Russia is skillfully exploiting any EU's weakness and division for advancing its interests in various geopolitical scenarios.

Russia's Return to the Post-Soviet Space

When Vladimir Putin became president in 2000, his foremost priority was to restructure the economic foundations of the country to bring about economic recovery and to restore Russia's international dignity. Drawing on the immense new wealth generated by oil and gas exports as well as on his ability to recentralize political power, Putin explicitly committed his government to regaining Russia's status as a great power. Putin's conception of the process for developing Russia's foreign policy followed a linear sequence: first, strengthen the Russian state politically and economically; second, restore Russia's international status; third, act assertively on the international scene.[13] In fact, his two first presidencies (2000–04; 2004–08) sought "to legitimize Russia's new role and to project its power through economic as opposed to traditional political-military means."[14]

Accordingly, one way for Russia to tighten control of its neighborhood has been to push for more economic integration. In his speech at the Foreign Ministry in summer 2013, Putin reaffirmed Russia's commitment to economic integration at the regional level, calling the "deepening of the integration" of former Soviet territory the "heart of our foreign policy."

Until at least the 2013 crisis in Ukraine, Russia pursued not a neo-imperial but a post-imperial strategy. However, as other stakeholders (in particular the EU, through the EaP) became more dynamic in the "near abroad,"[15] the Kremlin reacted accordingly.[16] As Roger Kanet rightly noted, in many circumstances Russia has shown flexibility and a willingness to take a "soft policy" approach—for example, taking a liberal approach to governing Kaliningrad and participating as a "neutral arbitrator" within the Organization for Security and Cooperation in Europe (OSCE) Minsk Group in the conflict over Nagorno-Karabakh.[17] The Kremlin also reinforced cultural links with former Soviet republics by financing educational, linguistic, and social programs and promoting the process of institutionalization of different kinds of regional organizations (for example, by forming the Collective Security Treaty Organization and the Customs Union).

However, Putin has not hesitated to resort to coercive means to attain his ends, especially through the political use of energy pricing, as in the case of Ukraine, a country recalcitrant to join the Customs Union.[18] Russia's energy strategy is based on the gradual reduction of subsidies for oil and gas exports to its neighbors, accompanied by implicit foreign policy signals (for example, offers of membership in regional organizations and financial aid) to encourage them to remain politically committed to the Kremlin's perspectives. "As a result, Russian foreign energy policy has developed into a potent mix of political revanchism (policies directed at the recovery of territory and power) and quasi-liberal economic adjustments."[19] Access to energy had been a strong implied incentive for Ukraine not to align with the West; however, it did not bring the results intended by Moscow. The consequent Russian annexation of Crimea and backing of separatists in Eastern Ukraine mark a new level of intervention, one involving the use of force to attain power and geopolitical goals. That intervention has produced serious tensions between Russia and both the EU and the United States, which, as mentioned, agreed in August 2014 on a package of sanctions that were further extended.

Russia, the United States, and NATO:
From Reconciliation to Collision?

Since the end of the Cold War, Russia-U.S. relations have been shaped by two elements: "emotions" (and related self-images, stereotypes, misperceptions, distrust, and recriminations) and concrete interests. During the U.S. hegemony over the international system, Russia had been very collaborative and worked with Washington on various delicate dossiers, including Iraq, German unification, Eastern Europe's new course, and the USSR's nuclear arsenal. The vision of U.S. president George H. W. Bush of a "new world order" was founded on a stable partnership with Moscow, which shared the aim of establishing a common security community stretching from Vancouver to Vladivostok. The terrorist attacks in New York City and Washington on September 11, 2001, in particular, provided an extraordinary and unexpected opportunity for Russia to rebrand itself as a close ally of the United States in the fight against international terrorism. In 2002, the Russia-NATO Council was established with the aim of promoting cooperation of the parties on several issues: terrorism, military affairs, Afghanistan (including Russia's transport of nonmilitary freight for the International Security Assistance Force and efforts to fight local drug production), industrial concerns, nonproliferation, and others.

Nevertheless, the relationship stiffened when the United States decided on military intervention in Iraq (2003) and supported the Color revolutions in the post-Soviet space. At the April 2008 NATO summit, U.S. president George W. Bush's proposal to extend NATO membership action plans to Georgia and Ukraine (which was blocked by France and Germany) and to build missile defense installations in Eastern Europe (which was later shelved by Barack Obama's administration) turned the relationship into an overt confrontation. But it was the five-day Russia-Georgia war in August 2008 that brought relations between the Kremlin and Washington to their lowest point since the dark days of the Cold War.

However, the election of Barack Obama marked a new cooperative phase based on the premise that Russia had to be treated as a sui generis entity, not equated with a country in transition toward the Western mainstream.[20] In 2009, knowing that Russia was vital to U.S. security interests in the most critical geopolitical scenarios,[21] the new administration launched the "reset policy," inspired on both sides by a strong dose of pragmatism. Among the positive outcomes of the reset policy were New START (Strategic Arms Reduction Treaty); the reduction by half of the number of strategic nuclear missile launchers and a new inspection and verification regime; NATO-Russia dialogue on antiballistic missile defense; the Russian president's participation in the NATO Lisbon summit in 2010; and creation of the U.S.-Russia Bilateral Presidential Commission.

The new friendly climate was very soon replaced by another wave of mistrust and conflict. Putin's highly contested reelection (2012), the row over the missile defense system in Europe, approval of the Magnitsky Act (scrapping the controversial and outdated Jackson-Vanik amendment),[22] NATO's military intervention in Libya, and divergent approaches to the situation in Syria became the stumbling blocks that triggered and revealed the exhaustion of the reset policy. In the meantime, Russia was perceived as a less strategic actor than it had been before. The UN proved ineffective in dealing with most recent major crises (for example, Iraq, Iran, and Afghanistan),[23] so even Russia's seat on the Security Council (a vestige of the Cold War period) partly lost its relevance, especially after the council's failure to prevent a bloody civil war in Syria.[24] Russia has firmly invoked the UN as the only actor entitled to mediate to find a solution to international conflicts, preventing in this way any military intervention carried out by other powers that disregards the precepts of international law. Nevertheless, Russia itself did not respect international law when it annexed Crimea and engaged in the "hybrid" military penetration in Donetsk and Donbass in Ukraine. Russia's behavior in Ukraine has unsettled Eastern European members of NATO and created a debate in the West about the strength of NATO's commitment to defend its members (article 5). That has resulted in both stronger reassurances and preparation of a readiness action plan that envisions enhancing intelligence and awareness capabilities, more high-intensity military exercises, prepositioning equipment and supplies further east, and improving the capacity of the NATO Rapid Reaction Force. President Donald Trump reaffirmed (June 2017) the long-standing U.S. commitment to come to the defense of any NATO members that are attacked, after he refused to do so while visiting the alliance headquarters in Brussels (May 2017).[25]

At the moment, it is quite difficult to predict how Russia-U.S. relations will evolve now that Trump has become president, since he is acting in an impulsive and erratic way. However, it is quite clear that fundamental differences between the two actors on a number of dossiers—Syria, Ukraine, Iran—will remain very much in place. Those differences show that pragmatism alone is not enough to overcome reciprocal mistrust and conflicting visions of world politics.

Losing Energy Leverage?

For Russia, which holds the world's largest proven reserves of natural gas and is among the top-ranking oil producers, energy is not simply about commercial interests. Energy has been an extraordinary political tool in the efforts of the country to return to its status as a great power, allowing it to continue to exert its influence in the post-Soviet space. The EU's dependence on Russian energy gives Russia leverage not only on most of the EU member states but also on transit countries like Ukraine.[26] Energy became a divisive topic in Washington-Brussels relations and among the EU member states after two competitive pipeline projects gained momentum: Nabucco, sponsored by the United States and the European Commission, and South Stream, a joint venture of Gazprom and Italian-owned ENI, joined by France and Germany.

South Stream is a pipeline that was proposed to transport Russian natural gas to the Black Sea, from there to Bulgaria, and from Bulgaria to Italy and Austria. The project, which would have partly replaced the planned extension of Blue Stream from Turkey through Bulgaria and Serbia to Hungary and Austria, was seen as a rival to the planned Nabucco pipeline.[27] The Nabucco pipeline (also referred as the Turkey-Austria gas pipeline) was proposed to transport gas from Turkey to Austria, thereby diversifying natural gas suppliers and delivery routes to Europe. The viability of supplies for this project were uncertain. The main supplier was expected to be Iraq, in cooperation with Azerbaijan, Turkmenistan, and possibly Egypt, but no agreement had been reached with those countries.[28]

After the latest crisis in Ukraine, the EU has finally committed itself to diversifying its energy supplies and lessening its dependence on Russia, which is already chasing alternative clients, particularly in Asia, where it has concluded important agreements with China (for example, a thirty-year energy agreement, estimated to be worth $400 billion, was reached in spring 2014). After a volatile increase that occurred during the Arab Spring, Russia had to confront the decreasing price of energy. It is already cutting gas prices to Europe, and Gazprom revenue expectations are starting to decline. The weakening global price of oil is the newest factor in the game. U.S.

shale gas developments are an accelerating game changer. In addition, demand in the eurozone ought to be weaker given stuttering growth there, while perceptions of political risks in the Middle East are improving and supplies from war-torn Libya and Iraq are holding up better than expected.

New Horizon: Asia

As its relations with the Euro-Atlantic community have worsened, Russia has been reinforcing its cooperation with a variety of other partners. In 2015, Russia created, together with Kazakhstan, Kyrgyzstan, Belarus, and Armenia, the Eurasian Economic Union (EAEU) with the purpose of overcoming trade barriers and promoting integration in a fragmented space. The EAEU is currently seeking to finalize a free trade deal with Iran in an attempt by Russia and its fellow members to deepen ties with the country. Despite alleged economic reasons for regional integration, EAEU primarily responds to Russia's interest to strengthen its own global influence. Russian leadership sees the organization as "a platform for structuring relations with the EU, ASEAN [Association of Southeast Asian Nations] and China in regard to the Belt and Road Initiative."[29]

Putin is cultivating the idea of extending Russia's geopolitical sphere of influence to include the Asia-Pacific region, and the proposed broad economic union would constitute a *trait d'union* between the Asia-Pacific region and Europe. As Dmitri Trenin notes, "Moscow understands the importance of the rise of Asia, and of China in particular, and is seeking to find ways to develop its eastern provinces, which otherwise risk tilting, economically, toward the great neighbor across the river."[30]

Moscow also is weaving relations with Japan, India, South Korea, and Vietnam. Russia's foreign policy clearly notes that "global power and development potential is now more dispersed and is shifting to the East, primarily to the Asia-Pacific region."[31] Russia also believes that the progressive institutionalization and politicization of the BRICS (Brazil, Russia, India, China, and South Africa) will contribute to increasing the multipolarity of the international system while strengthening Russia's status as an economic and political power. President Putin has described the group as "a key element of the emerging multipolar world" whose members "advocate the creation of a more balanced and just system of global economic relations." Russia is willing to consolidate the BRICS as both an economic and a political force to counterbalance U.S. power in particular. Especially after its exclusion from the 2014 G-8 summit during the Ukraine crisis, Russia considered the BRICS launch in July 2014 of a $100 billion development bank and an emergency reserve fund a great success. That was the group's first major step toward reshaping the current West-dominated international financial system.

The diplomatic success of the BRICS depends mainly on the future of Moscow-Beijing relations, which at the moment are quite promising.[32] Moscow and Beijing share similar views on the most critical issues, such as the turbulence in the Middle East, Iran's nuclear program, cross-border security, and the North Korean nuclear issue. China and Russia, as North Korea's neighbors, have the common goal of resuming the six-party talks and urging North Korea to return to the negotiating table. According to Leon Aron, "the path taken by Putin's Russia and Xi [Jinping]'s China seems to be based on a tacit division of the world into spheres of influence between the two powers, where Moscow recognizes Chinese influence in Africa and the Pacific in exchange of Beijing's recognition of Russian primacy on the Eurasian mainland, Middle East included."[33]

Russia is also keen to make economic deals with Latin America, and its forgiveness of Soviet-era debt should stimulate investment in energy exploration off Cuba. Given the reluctance of the United States to allow Russia to build Global Navigation Satellite System (GLONASS) navigation stations on U.S. soil, the Kremlin now plans to build them in the region, possibly in Nicaragua, Cuba, or Brazil. Russia also is ready to become a security guard to "protect against possible provocations," presumably by the United States, at a Chinese-led project to build a canal between the Pacific and the Atlantic across Nicaragua. However, it is Argentina that Moscow sees as an especially promising partner. In contrast to the Chinese expansion to Latin America, which is concerned almost entirely with economics, Russia's engagement is increasingly intertwined with its geopolitical agenda.[34]

Finally, increased access to the Arctic—with its energy and mineral resources, new fisheries, and shortened sea routes—and to rivers flowing north to the Arctic is pushing Russia to become a maritime state. Russia will no longer be susceptible to geographic isolation or encirclement. At the same time, these changes will require Russia to become more closely integrated into global commercial and financial networks, to welcome international business involvement, and to participate in international bodies that harmonize international shipping, safety, security, and environmental regulations.

Africa: A Potential Partner in Russia's Portfolio

Russia's interest in Africa lies primarily in the continent's economic potential. It is rich in natural resources, and its population of over 1 billion can serve as a market for Russian goods and services. Although Russia never had African colonies, it has had a long history of interaction with the continent. Russian and African approaches to international affairs are devoid of any antagonism. As a matter of fact, on many issues their positions are common or fairly close. Despite this favorable background, so far Africa has not been considered a priority for Russian foreign policy. However, its status might rapidly change if the Kremlin's relations with the West deteriorate further.

President Putin has already shown a renewed interest in the continent, especially as far as the northern shores of the Mediterranean and South Africa are concerned. South Africa's inclusion in BRICS became a stimulus for strengthening the African vector. Moscow's return to Africa often is regarded as a response to China's growing presence in the continent. Although Russia is not able to compete with China in exporting cheap goods, it maintains its paramount position as an arms exporter.

Recently, Russia has been strengthening military-technical cooperation with a number of African countries. In 2012, Russia's overseas arms sales reportedly exceeded $14 billion, and around 80 percent of the sales were accounted for by the state intermediary agency Rosoboronexport. The Stockholm International Peace Research Institute (SIPRI) reported in December 2011 that Russia accounted for 11 percent of the volume of major arms supplied to sub-Saharan Africa.[35] Russia's arms trade with African countries is part of a broader strategy to create economic links and gain influence in the region. The arms trade itself is significant, but it can also feed into other economic arrangements.

Conclusion

Contemporary Russian foreign policy has been determined by both history (Russia's self-image as a great power) and the sense of frustration that the country felt after the implosion of the Soviet system, which was accompanied by a deep economic slump. Once Russia returned to its place among the great powers, thanks to its energy revenues, its priority has been to consolidate its international role and expand its influence in strategic areas.

The Kremlin is strengthening its leverage by widening its network of partners and creating new organizations. With respect to Western states and institutions, Russia is pursuing the related objectives of modernization (by importing knowledge from outside) and integration into the global economy; it also intends to carry more weight in all venues that have a significant impact on the international system. Russia manages relations with the rest of its partners according to a pragmatic "economization" approach and exploits some strategic partnerships, such as the BRICS group, to acquire more influence over global affairs and thereby counterbalance U.S. power. However, Russia's global power aspirations seem to be limited inasmuch as the Russian economy lacks advanced technology and depends on growing exports of raw materials. Furthermore, Russia's leverage in responding to crucial crises has not proved determinant, reducing its importance vis-à-vis that of other prominent international actors.

The greatest novelty of Russia's foreign policy resides in its use: Until Dmitri Medvedev's presidency foreign policy had been generally considered a dependent variable of domestic politics. When public support for leadership started plummeting, foreign policy became a key element in maintaining a large national consensus and strengthening the role of the president. There is a clear inclination toward "sovereignization,"[36] exploiting foreign policy for domestic purposes, notably for rallying the reluctant public around the flag. However, it is to be seen whether this option would still be viable if a new wave of protests were to rise, or especially if the economic situation were to deteriorate. Russians generally expect their country to assume a strong leadership role in the world, just as they oppose global leadership by either Europe or the United States. They conceive of the external projection of their country in traditional terms, mainly as a means of defending national interests rather than promoting values. Despite the extent of anti-Western propaganda, the majority of Russians have a rather positive view of the West. Those who are unsympathetic toward Putin's regime hardly assume a critical stance on its management of external relations. Both Putin's supporters and his opponents, an aggregate of anti-Western nationalists and pro-Western liberals, respectively, subscribe to the Kremlin's foreign policy agenda. As Krastev stressed, "So when it comes to foreign policy, we should expect that a democratic Russia will also be a nationalistic Russia, not unlike other regional powers like Turkey."[37]

From that standpoint, Russia's control over the near abroad is crucial, as the muscular behavior of the Kremlin in Ukraine proves. While rejecting any international intervention designed to effect regime change in its neighborhood, Russia wants to reaffirm its leadership in the region. Control over the near abroad is seen as a necessary credential for being recognized as a major pole in a multipolar international system. This strategy is clearly colliding with that of the Euro-Atlantic community, which has decided to punish Russia for its annexation of Crimea and its meddling in the southern regions of Ukraine. In response, Russia is widening and deepening its friendship with other relevant actors in the international system. However, for both geopolitical and economic reasons, it would be very costly for either the West or Russia to allow their relationship to deteriorate into a permanent conflict. The war in Syria has further deepened the West-Russia divide, showing, however, that Russia is an indispensable interlocutor in many different geopolitical scenarios. The initial attempt by U.S. president Trump to have a far more sweeping strategic realignment with Russia has vanished quickly, as there is still a low level of trust between the two countries, which pursue quite different and sometimes clashing political agendas.

NOTES

1. Peter Sherman, *Russian Foreign Policy since 1990* (Boulder, Colo.: Westview Press, 1995), p.10.

2. Ilya Prizel, *National Identity and Foreign Policy* (Cambridge University Press, 1998), pp. 239–40.

3. Vladimir Putin, *State-of-the-Nation Address*, April 25, 2005.

4. Jeffrey Mankoff, *Russian Foreign Policy* (Lanham, Md.: Rowman & Littlefield, 2012), p. 11.

5. In Boris Yeltsin's view, any narrowly defined relationship between Russia and its former satellites based on the country's continuing dominance would have been an obstacle to Russia's economic reform and the process of political liberalization. The supporters of a pro-Western foreign policy downgraded the importance of the "near abroad" (the newly independent countries), seeing Russia's future in Europe as part of an integrated community. See F. Stephen Larrabee and Theodore W. Karasik, *Foreign and Security Policy Decisionmaking under Yeltsin* (Santa Monica, Calif.: RAND, 1997); and Heinz Timmermann, "Russian Foreign Policy under Yeltsin: Priority for Integration into the 'Community of Civilized States,'" *Journal of Communist Studies* 8, no. 4 (1992), pp.163–85.

6. Mankoff, *Russian Foreign Policy*, p. 67.

7. Leszek Buszynski, *Russian Foreign Policy after the Cold War* (Westport, Conn.: Praeger, 1996), p. 11.

8. Stephen Sestanovich, "Inventing the Soviet National Interest," *National Interest*, no. 20 (Summer 1990), p. 2.

9. Vladimir Baranovsky, "Russia: A Part of Europe or Apart from Europe?," *International Affairs* 76, no. 3 (2000), p. 443.

10. See C. Hillion, "Institutional Aspects of the Partnership between the European Union and the Newly Independent States of the Former Soviet Union: Case Studies of Russia and Ukraine," *Common Market Law Review* 37 (2000), pp. 1211–35.

11. During Dmitri Medvedev's presidency (2008–12), foreign policy became instrumental in the overall plan for modernizing the country. It was seen as an opportunity to diversify Russia's economy and overcome its culture of "legal nihilism." Medvedev called on external actors to help with the country's mission and affirmed that the effectiveness of other nations' foreign policy would be measured by their contribution to the improvement of living standards in the country. The Russian political elite, however, do not consider modernization as a holistic process. Rather, they envision a process of conservative, partial modernization limited to the economic sphere. The state structure and institutions as well as Russia's hybrid form of democracy will persist. Selective changes will take gradually, as compatible with the stability of the country.

12. The EU also has mediator status in talks over Transnistria, a border control mission in Ukraine and Moldova, and a monitoring mission in Georgia.

13. Serena Giusti and Tomislava Penkova, "From Ideology to Pragmatism: The New Course of Russian Foreign Policy," *World Affairs* 12, no. 4 (Winter 2008), p. 15.

14. Angela E. Stent, "Restoration and Revolution in Putin's Foreign Policy," *Europe-Asia Studies* 60, no. 6 (August 2008), p. 1089.

15. The near-abroad countries, Russia's post-Soviet neighbors, are less foreign and less fully sovereign than states in the "far abroad"; therefore relations with them cannot be simply classified as foreign policy. See Mankoff, *Russian Foreign Policy*, p. 219.

16. Leon Aron asserts that "under the Putin Doctrine, the pursuit of regional hegemony has acquired a new dimension: an attempt at the 'Finlandization' of the post-Soviet states, harkening back to the Soviet Union's control over Finland's foreign policy during the Cold War. In such an arrangement, Moscow would allow its neighbors to choose their own domestic political and economic systems but maintain final say over their external orientation." Leon Aron, "The Putin Doctrine," *Foreign Affairs*, March 8, 2013.

17. Roger E. Kanet, *Russia: Re-Emerging Great Power* (New York: Palgrave Macmillan, 2007), pp. 144, 147.

18. The pressure on Ukraine had been especially strong but not fully efficacious. While Ukraine refused (quite unexpectedly) to sign an Association Agreement with the European Union in late 2013 that also promised to give a significant fillip to the Ukrainian economy, it also refused to enter the Moscow-led Customs Union. Ukraine had already been embroiled in several rows with Russia over gas siphoning and gas prices, occasionally interrupting supplies to Europe, which gets around a quarter of its gas from Russia. Before the crisis in Ukraine erupted, weaker demand for steel (a key export and a major source of revenue for Ukraine) and the country's unsuccessful attempts to restart cooperation with the International Monetary Fund (which had demanded unpopular economic reforms in exchange for unfreezing its loans to Kiev) were pushing Ukraine to cut a deal with Russia to reduce the burden of its burgeoning gas bill. Russia affirmed on numerous occasions that it could cut gas prices for its neighbor if Ukraine joined the Customs Union or ceded control of its gas pipeline network to Gazprom. In December 2013, Russia agreed to lend Ukraine $15 billion and to slash the price of gas from $400 to $268 per thousand cubic meters as a reward for the Ukrainian president, Viktor Yanukovych, ditching of the Association Agreement with the EU. That move, however, did not prevent protests from degenerating into rioting.

19. Amelia Hadfield, "Energy and Foreign Policy: EU-Russia Energy Dynamics," in *Foreign Policy, Theories, Actors, Cases,* edited by Steve Smith, Amelia Hadfield, and Timothy Dunne (Oxford University Press, 2008), p. 327.

20. Russia has a very peculiar notion of democracy: Political legitimacy is derived mainly from the leadership's ability to satisfy people's expectations rather than by a bottom-up democratic process. Russians are more sensitive to the output than the input aspect of their polity. Russia's leadership maintains that the form of democracy adopted and the timing of adoption cannot be standardized; instead, they need to be adjusted to the national context. Russia has its own set of values. Those values are democratic, but they have emerged from Russia's unique historical experience, and they are distinct from what the West recognizes as democracy. The Kremlin rejects the "unlawful" use of soft power and human rights campaigns that risk destabilizing sovereign states through the manipulation of public opinion.

21. Mankoff, *Russian Foreign Policy,* p. 91.

22. The law bars Russian officials implicated in the detention and death of corporate lawyer Sergey Magnitsky from entering or keeping assets in the United States. It also allows Washington to add any Russian official seen as a human rights offender to a kind of "blacklist."

23. Moscow has stopped support for even the weakened version of sanctions against Iran that it previously voted for in the UN Security Council; as

for Syria, Moscow has vetoed three times U.S.-backed resolutions calling for sanctions against Bashar al-Assad's regime.

24. Russia's strenuous opposition to any kind of intervention has in the end helped the United States to avoid the complex regional implications of the Syrian crisis. In the case of Libya, in contrast, NATO's intervention did not have major consequences beyond the country's perimeter. Although Moscow was not able to persuade Bashar al-Assad to relinquish power, it mediated discussions with Damascus on eliminating chemical weapons. However, conflict in Syria is far from a solution, and the escalation of tension between Moscow and Washington has become reinvigorated after the United States, the United Kingdom, and France launched more than one hundred missiles against what they say were Syrian chemical weapons facilities in response to a chemical weapons attack in a Damascus suburb (April 2018). This came at a time when relations between Russia and the West had plunged to their worst level in decades, following the poisoning in March of an ex-spy in England that the United Kingdom blamed on the Kremlin. As a consequence, the United States and many European countries decided to expel Russian diplomats accused of being spies.

25. See Peter Baker, "Trump Commits United States to Defending NATO Nations," *New York Times,* June 9, 2017 (www.nytimes.com/2017/06/09/world/europe/trump-nato-defense-article-5.html?_r=0).

26. Russia is the main supplier of crude oil and natural gas and has emerged as the leading supplier of solid fuels. In 2012, some 33.7 percent of EU-28 imports of crude oil were from Russia, slightly below the shares recorded for 2010 (34.7 percent) and 2011 (34.8 percent). Russia became the principal supplier of solid fuels in 2006, overtaking South Africa. By contrast, Russia's share of EU-28 imports of natural gas declined from 45.2 percent to 29.5 percent between 2002 and 2010, but increases in 2011 and 2012 reversed that trend (http://epp.eurostat.ec.europa.eu/statistics_explained/index.php/Energy_production_and_imports).

27. The project was undermined by Russia's military intervention in Ukraine and subsequent Western sanctions that made it difficult to raise financing, so in December 2014 Putin decided to abandon the pipeline. Furthermore, since much of the gas that Russia sells to Europe transits through Ukraine, a new pipeline that bypassed Ukraine would reduce Russia's leverage over Kiev.

28. On the pros and cons of the two projects, see P. K. Baev and I. Øverland, "The South Stream versus Nabucco Pipeline," *International Affairs* 86, no. 5 (2010), pp. 1075–90.

29. On this topic, see Rilka Dragneva and Kataryna Wolczuk, "The Eurasian Economic Union: Deals, Rules, and the Exercise of Power," Chatham House Research Paper, May 2017 (www.chathamhouse.org/sites/files/chathamhouse

/publications/research/2017-05-02-eurasian-economic-union-dragneva-wolczuk
.pdf).

30. See Dmitri Trenin, "The Putin Doctrine," *Carnegie Endowment for International Peace*, February 1, 2013 (http://carnegieendowment.org/2013/02/01
/putin-doctrine/fn1a).

31. Ministry of Foreign Affairs of the Russian Federation, "Concept of the Foreign Policy of the Russian Federation, Approved by President of the Russian Federation, V. Putin on February 12, 2013" (http://www.mid.ru/en
/foreign_policy/official_documents/-/asset_publisher/CptICkB6BZ29
/content/id/122186).

32. In geopolitical terms, China and Russia are by far the strongest powers of the club's five members. With a combined population of almost 1.5 billion people over an area of 26,805,203 square kilometers, equal to roughly 18 percent of the world's land area, the People's Republic of China and the Russian Federation together could become a formidable regional actor capable of dominating Eurasia and projecting its influence over the entire globe.

33. Aron, *The Putin Doctrine*.

34. See D. Vakulenko, "Putin Extends Influence in Latin America," *Journal of Political Risk* 2, no.10 (October 2014) (www.jpolrisk.com/putin-extends
-influence-in-latin-america/).

35. P. D. Wezeman, S. T. Wezeman, and L. Béraud-Sudreau, "Arms Flows to Sub-Saharan Africa," SIPRI Policy Paper 30 (December 2011) (http://
books.sipri.org/files/PP/SIPRIPP30.pdf).

36. See Trenin, "The Putin Doctrine."

37. Ivan Krastev, "Would Democratic Change in Russia Transform Its Foreign Policy?," *Open Democracy*, February 7, 2013 (www.opendemocracy.net
/od-russia/ivan-krastev/would-democratic-change-in-russia-transform-its
-foreign-policy).

TWELVE

The Foreign Policy of the United States

Indispensable No More?

JUSSI M. HANHIMÄKI

Can America be fixed?" So asked Fareed Zakaria in January 2013. Or, he wondered, will the United States go the way of Japan, with an economy that fails to grow owing to the inability of its dysfunctional political system to deliver necessary reform? Will America fail to retool to meet the challenges of the twenty-first century?[1] Barack Obama, in his second inaugural address on January 21, 2013, echoed none of this pessimism. "A decade of war is now ending. An economic recovery has begun," the forty-fourth president proclaimed. "America's possibilities are limitless, for we possess all the qualities that this world without boundaries demands: youth and drive; diversity and openness; an endless capacity for risk and a gift for reinvention."[2]

Six years later these citations still sum up much of the debate about the present state and future status of the United States. On the one hand, we have the dreaded prospect of a diminished America, a country that saw its power and influence peak in the first two post–Cold War decades. While

China and other emerging markets continue growing, the United States and the "West" appear to be in decline. The future of the liberal international order looks bleak. "Belief in an authoritarian version of national destiny is staging a powerful comeback," Edward Luce puts it. "Western liberalism is under siege," he adds.[3] On the other hand, we have the vision of a United States that, like many times in the past, has been through some hard times but is about to rebound. In fact, many would argue it already has. The United States boasts historically low unemployment: 3.8 percent on June 1, 2018 (the lowest since 2000). In the past few years, the Dow Jones Industrial Average (DJIA) has reached new record after new record. America's GDP growth is at the healthy 3.5 percent. As of the end of 2018, the recovery that Barack Obama promised a decade ago is a reality.[4]

Is America's future a gradual descent into relative insignificance, similar to the trajectories of so many great powers and empires of the past? Or have we simply witnessed another resurgence of U.S. power and influence? Decline or renewal? That is the question.

However, it may be the wrong question. Discussing American decline (or lack thereof) is a very old topic among the pundits and talking heads that crowd television shows, the Internet, and the pages of influential journals. In 2011, one participant in that ongoing debate even felt compelled to insist that "this time" the decline of the United States was "for real."[5] In fact, it has been "real" since 1945. As anyone who has studied U.S. history knows, the American economy has been in relative decline ever since the end of World War II. But it has also grown, in absolute terms, over the same period. Decline and growth at the same time! Go figure.[6]

Perhaps the more appropriate question is: Will the United States successfully adapt to the changing circumstances of the twenty-first century? Despite the disturbing antics of the Donald Trump administration—from the proliferation of insulting tweets from POTUS to exiting from the Paris climate agreement and snubbing traditional allies at NATO and G-7 summits—I will cautiously but firmly answer: yes. I will go further and maintain that the United States does not actually need to make dramatic adjustments in its foreign policy in the near term because its major national interests and goals remain, by and large, unchanged. This is particularly true for American national security policies. In essence, safeguarding American primacy as a desirable and realistic goal remains the fundamental goal of U.S. policymakers. The means by which different administrations pursue this central goal mutate and even—as is evidently the case if comparing Trump with Obama—contradict each other. The bottom line, though, is simple: structural continuity trumps (pun intended) efforts to radically shift the overall course of U.S. foreign policy.

The chapter is divided into two main parts. It will first briefly survey the evolution of U.S. foreign policy in the decades following the end of the Cold War. In the second part I explore several of the key issues facing the United States in the near and medium term. I discuss, in particular, the U.S. relationship with Russia, China, the Middle East, and Europe.

American Primacy in the Post–Cold War World

On May 27, 2010, the Obama administration released its *National Security Strategy* (NSS). The document was striking in two ways. On the one hand, it was a clear effort to distinguish the Obama doctrine from the much-reviled and simplistic George W. Bush doctrine of unilateralism with its heavy reliance on U.S. military power. On the other hand, the continuity from Bush was notable. For example, Obama may have stopped using the term "war on terror," but he still identified defeating al Qaeda as a central mission for U.S. national security policy. The importance of alliances and the significance of economic development were not new in the 2010 Obama NSS; they were simply phrased in a somewhat different manner than the 2002 and 2006 Bush strategies.[7] In fact, one could go further back and see an essential continuity in U.S. foreign and national security policy through-out the post–Cold War era. The nature of that continuity can be summed up simply as the maintenance of American primacy in a liberal international order.

Illusions of Omnipotence

The United States emerged from the Cold War victorious, prosperous, and confident. The collapse of the Soviet Union was interpreted as proof of the superiority of liberal capitalism over totalitarian socialism. While the former Soviet Union disintegrated and faced economic collapse and political turmoil, the American economy remained robust and entered, during the 1990s, a period of almost unprecedented and seemingly endless growth. Meanwhile, the broad-based international support for the U.S.-led military operation to oust Iraq from Kuwait was evidence of the fact that most of the world looked up to the United States as a protector of the principles of collective security. This was America's "unipolar moment," Charles Krau-thammer announced in 1990. The United States was "bound to lead," Joseph Nye echoed.[8]

The confident tone remained a trademark of the 1990s. At the start of his second term, President Bill Clinton spoke about a world in which "more people than ever embrace our ideals and share our interests" and promised "to bring America fifty more years of security and prosperity." He summed up this position in his second inaugural in January 1997: "America stands alone as the world's indispensable nation."[9] In 2000, delivering his last State of the Union address, Clinton further upped the ante of hyperbolic rhe-toric: "Never before has our nation enjoyed, at once, so much prosperity and social progress with so little crisis and so few external threats."[10]

Many scholars shared the optimism of policymakers in the unparalleled power of the United States. The previous gloom about American decline—expressed most famously in Paul Kennedy's 1987 book *Rise and Fall of Great Powers*—disappeared, causing Michael Cox to wonder, in 2001, "Whatever happened to American decline?"[11] Instead of fretting about de-cline, policy-oriented scholars, in digesting the sudden, and unanticipated,[12] disappearance of the Soviet Union wondered what the United States should do with its victory. For while America may have been bound to lead in the 1990s, there was no clear answer to an important and nagging question: Lead toward what end? Here scholars and policymakers disagreed as much as ever before. In the 1990s, however, the Clinton administration came under much criticism for what many judged a directionless conduct of America's external affairs. Clinton was variously described as the president who considered "foreign policy as social work" and, despite his rhetoric, presided over the "end of idealism" in American foreign policy. Interest-ingly, Clinton was also charged with being a "new moralist on the road to hell" whose conduct was clouded by "fatal distraction[s]." He was even called the "bully of the free world."[13]

In the minds of most observers today, however, the real "bully" was Clinton's successor. In 2000, George W. Bush had famously promised a "humble" foreign policy. Circumstances prevented that. September 11, 2001, is unlikely to be remembered as a moment that changed the course of world history. But the terrorist attacks did provoke a chain reaction from the United States that reflected the country's status as the self-appointed indispensable nation. Instead of humility, the United States appeared keen on brushing aside any advice, domestic or foreign, to use restraint. The Bush administration acted unilaterally for the most part, alienating most of its allies while projecting its awesome military power to Afghanistan and Iraq. The niceties of international law were blithely ignored, and scandals about rendition and the use of torture tarnished the U.S. image. There was much talk about a Bush revolution in foreign policy and the doctrine of pre-emption (or preventive military attacks) when the administration unveiled its *National Security Strategy* papers in 2002 and 2006. Much of this was misguided and, in hindsight, even unnecessary. Military action in Afghani-stan, for example, could be justified at the time as a necessary act; that the consequence would be open-ended engagement in a country that had already been ravaged by more than two decades of war was, to put it mildly, a result of shortsightedness. The war in Iraq, by contrast, created a multitude of long-term problems that linger on a decade-and-a-half after Bush declared that mission "accomplished" in 2003. The outpouring of global good-will toward the United States after 9/11 was squandered in a matter of two years.[14]

However, as historians Melvyn Leffler and John Gaddis have pointed out, the charge that the United States was doing something extraordinary by acting unilaterally was misplaced. When national security has been at stake, America's multilateral moments have been few and far between.[15] Moreover, the administration's reaction to Bush's immense global unpop-ularity in the wake of the Iraq War was perfectly rational. In his second term, the forty-third president began to reach out and repair damaged re-lations with traditional European allies. His image was so badly tarnished, though, that only the election of Barack Obama in 2008—whose promise of "change" electrified audiences around the world—finally ended the anti-American moment in international relations.[16]

The Obama "Reversal" and the Trump Shock

Change was, though, a relative thing. In January 2009, Barack Obama moved into the White House burdened by unrealistically high expectations. Many expected that the forty-fourth president would reverse course, bring back thousands of Americans from a mishandled war, and dazzle the world with his winning diplomacy. He would make America respected again, not (just) because of its military prowess but by using the irresistible appeal of the American dream, of which he was such a shining example. Soft power was "in"; hard power was "out." Unilateralism was a thing of the past. Obama's inauguration was one of the highest-rated media events around the globe in early 2009. Almost overnight, the negative view of the United States that had become commonplace during the Bush presidency was gone. In December 2009, Obama visited Oslo to pick up that year's Nobel Peace Prize "for his extraordinary efforts to strengthen international diplomacy and cooperation between peoples."[17]

For all the talk about change, however, much remained the same. Barack Obama could not, it turned out, walk on water. The Obama administration's priorities were, as they had to be, *American* priorities: protecting U.S. national security and reviving the U.S. economy. In fact, one of the striking things about the first years of the Obama administration was the degree of continuity. To be sure, the administration wound down America's involvement in Iraq; in 2011, the last U.S. troops left the country. This was, however, a continuation of the gradual withdrawal that the Bush administration had announced in the fall of 2008. Moreover, while the Iraqi "war of choice" was (temporarily) ending, the Obama administration escalated the U.S. commitment to the Afghan "war of necessity" by deploying additional troops to Afghanistan and ordering a series of deadly strikes against targets in Pakistani territory. The spectacular killing of Osama bin Laden on May 2, 2011, brought some closure to many Americans (and others) who had been touched by the attacks of September 11, 2001. But the global war on terror—even if no longer officially called that—entered its second decade in Obama's third year in office. Indeed, as the Islamic State of Iraq and Syria (ISIS) surged in power and influence during Obama's second term, several thousand U.S. troops were redeployed to Iraq.[18]

Of course, not all of Obama's foreign policy efforts were related to fighting wars. America's standing among its European allies certainly improved after 2009. There was the signing and ratification of the New START Treaty in 2010. Some, albeit lackluster, efforts were made to repair America's difficult relations with the Muslim world—a task made more complicated by the Arab Spring of 2011.[19] All such efforts can, however, be seen as part of a long-term continuum of U.S. foreign policy. Even some of the rhetoric remained unchanged. At the beginning of his administration Obama pledged that his top priority would be to protect the American people while remaining "true to our values and ideals" and used some Kennedy-like rhetoric to remind any terrorist network "that our spirit is stronger and cannot be broken. You cannot outlast us, and we will defeat you."[20] That the Bush administration had chosen security over values was a charge heard repeatedly from its critics. Yet there was little to suggest that either Bush or Obama, or indeed Clinton before them, ever faced such a binary choice. When Obama pledged to ensure American security, defeat terrorism, and uphold American ideals, he sounded much like his predecessor (if a bit more eloquent). Nor did the new administration suddenly abandon America's right to act preemptively. Upon accepting the Nobel Peace Prize, the forty-fourth president maintained, "I—like any head of state—reserve the right to act unilaterally if necessary to defend my nation." He went on to defend the idea of humanitarian intervention by saying that "force can be justified on humanitarian grounds."[21] In short, on occasion the United States might have to intervene militarily either to defend its security or to end blatant and widespread attacks on civilian populations. Ideally such interventions were to be blessed by the international community, but a moment might arrive when this would not happen.

Rather than a radical departure with the past, Obama's foreign policy was a mixture of the Clinton administration's emphasis on multilateral engagement and democratic enlargement and the Bush Doctrine's assertions about the American need to reserve for itself the right to take unilateral military action. Most notably, the central goal—the maintenance of American primacy—was an undiluted part of Obama's agenda. Much like his predecessors, Obama was not shy about stating that his administration operated on the premise that "just as America helped to determine the course of the twentieth century, we must now . . . shape an international order capable of overcoming the challenges of the twenty-first century."[22]

It is worth remembering, however, that unlike his two immediate predecessors, Barack Obama entered office in an atmosphere of global doubt about the United States' ability to lead the world. America, in 2009, was no model state for others to emulate. Besieged by an economic crisis generally considered the worst since the Great Depression and an international security posture many regarded as a classic case of imperial overreach, the United States appeared unprepared for the challenges of the twenty-first century. Worse, the internal political divisions within the United States almost drove the country over the fiscal cliff in late 2012. Only a last-minute compromise postponed any real decision on America's interminable debate about the right levels of government spending and tax rates. Economic troubles, security dilemmas, political gridlock. Not a promising beginning for a second presidential term. The Obama campaign did not talk much about "change" during the 2012 elections.

Four years later, however, things looked rather different. In his 2016 State of the Union address, Obama pointed to a list of achievements and transformations, including job growth and declining deficits. Those arguing that the U.S. economy was in decline were, in Obama's words, "peddling fiction." He heralded a number of achievements in foreign policy: the Iran nuclear agreement and the arguably successful struggle against ISIS. Most of all, however, Obama emphasized the need "to mobilize the world to work with us." Alliances and international cooperation were to be the keys to defeating transnational security threats like terrorism, countering climate change, and boosting economic recovery. Underlying all this was a basic message: America was on the rebound, the Great Recession was behind us, and the United States was on the right track. The message resonated with large swathes of the American (and international) public.[23] However, while Obama's personal popularity was on the rise, November 2016 produced one of the most unexpected political shocks in recent American history. With a campaign promising to "Make America Great Again," Donald J. Trump triumphed. He relentlessly attacked the Obama administration's record and ("crooked") Hillary Clinton as emblematic of such failures. While often devoid of substance, Trump's victory was immediately seen as a major watershed in American history: the promise of change (again) beat continuity.[24]

At the time of this writing, the Trump administration has been in office almost two years. Hence it is worth examining what has changed in terms of U.S. foreign policy. The short answer is: less than meets the eye. For notwithstanding all the noise about fake news and the proliferation of 140- or 280-character messages, and despite U.S. withdrawal from the Iran nuclear agreement, the possibility of a trade war with China, apparent diplomatic breakthrough on the Korean peninsula, and even the imposition of tariffs on traditional allies, Donald Trump's foreign policy has not, at least not yet, fundamentally transformed the United States' relations with the rest of the world. Continuity, not change, remains the fundamental characteristic of American foreign policy.

American Geopolitics in a Globalized World

We may live in a globalized world of disappearing borders, rapid communications, and uncontrollable transnational forces. But it would be counterfactual to assume that such "old-fashioned" notions as national security or geopolitics no longer matter. Among U.S. foreign policy circles, thinking about the world in regional terms and interpreting the world through the lens of the nation-state still prevail over "thematic" approaches. Whether during the Obama years or after, discussions of America's role in the world tend to focus on the state and prospects of U.S. relations with key countries or regions in the world: Russia, China, Europe, the Middle East. In 2018, with the resurgence of nationalism as a key theme in presidential rhetoric, the tendency to equate foreign policy with the sum of relations with other nations has, arguably, become even stronger.[25]

U.S.-Russian Relations: The Reset Roller Coaster

Is the Cold War making a comeback? So it may appear from the tense situation between the two countries that still maintain, by a wide margin, the largest nuclear arsenals in the world. The late 2012 passage by the U.S. Congress of the Magnitsky Act, which boldly criticized Russia's human rights record, was considered by Moscow to be evidence of America's "vindictive desire" to damage Russia's global reputation. "Apparently, Washington has forgotten what year this is and still thinks the Cold War is going on," the Russian foreign ministry announced in early December 2012. A few weeks later, President Vladimir Putin signed into law a bill that prohibits Americans from adopting Russian children. "The country will not be humiliated," Putin told journalists in explaining his action, thus openly drawing a link between the two laws. "Increasingly we are plunging into a new Cold War," predicted Professor Stephen Cohen of Princeton University.[26]

Beyond the saber rattling that surrounded the passage of these two, now largely forgotten laws, old Russian-American disagreements and tensions abound. The Syrian Civil War, North Korea, the Russian annexation of Crimea, and the U.S. missile shield program in Europe are but a few examples of the many issues that have inflamed relations between Moscow and Washington in the last decade. Much like in 2009, when the newly inaugurated Barack Obama touted his firm intention to "reset" relations with Russia, in 2017 the incoming Trump administration appeared keen to move beyond the Cold War mindset. Candidate Trump had asked, repeatedly, why improving relations with Moscow could possibly be considered a negative development and refrained from criticizing President Putin. However, by 2017, widely confirmed reports of Russian meddling in U.S. elections, including the indictment of Trump's former campaign manager Paul Manafort (and the earlier resignation of National Security Adviser Michael Flynn), have essentially frozen the likelihood of a Trump-Putin détente. As further proof of the continued tension in Russian-American relations—regardless of who occupies the White House (or holds power in Moscow)—new sanctions on Russia were announced in late October 2017. In 2018, the tit-for-tat expulsion of Russian and American diplomats—which followed a nerve agent attack in England against a former Russian spy, Sergei Skripal—highlighted the continued tensions between Washington and Moscow.[27]

For anyone hoping for a "real" reset, the record of Russian-American relations from 2009 to 2018 gives some glimmers of hope. After many years of fruitless campaigning, Russia, for example, became a member of the World Trade Organization (WTO) in 2012. The New START Treaty was signed in April 2010 and entered into force in early 2011, forecasting a 50 percent reduction in both sides' strategic nuclear arsenals by 2021. Although Russia may be opposed to further sanctions on Iran, it supported four sets of UN Security Council resolutions to this effect before 2012. Moscow has, at least on the surface, been supportive of the Trump administration's efforts vis-à-vis North Korea. Russia has collaborated with NATO on Afghanistan. In short, while problems tend to make headlines far more frequently than successes, the reality of the Russian-American relationship in 2018 is a far cry from that during the Cold War years. Indeed, one could even argue that, no matter what its internal political situation, Russia's economic integration into the liberal world order is progressing, and the nuclear arms race has given way to a regime of reduction and nonproliferation, jointly sponsored by Moscow and Washington.

The July 17, 2018, Trump-Putin Helsinki summit and its immediate aftermath illustrated the bifurcated nature of the Russian-American relationship. At a much-criticized press conference in Helsinki, Trump appeared to be in total disagreement with his country's intelligence community, denying any possibility of Russian interference in the 2016 U.S. elections. Almost all observers, Republicans and Democrats alike, agreed with Senator John McCain's view that Trump's performance had been "one of the most disgraceful performances by an American president in memory." Trump may have seen the meeting as a possibility of launching into a Nixon-like détente; instead he was seen as having been humiliated in front of the world by an autocratic Russian leader. True to form, Trump almost immediately backpedaled, claiming that his remarks had been misrepresented. Most famously, instead of saying that there was "no reason it would have been Russia" that meddled in the 2016 elections, Trump said he had meant to say there was "no reason it would *not* have been Russia."[28]

In all likelihood, American policy toward Russia will remain bifurcated, driven by the ideals embedded in the American political system and the need to protect and advance American interests. There is little new here. Already during the Cold War years, the United States navigated cooperation and conflict with its main adversary, the Soviet Union. Nuclear agreements were signed and trade agreements were made even as the Cold War warriors engaged in proxy wars (from Vietnam to Afghanistan), propaganda campaigns, and economic warfare. The passing of laws such as the Jackson-Vanik Amendment, which did not permit the Soviet Union (or later Russia) to enjoy most-favored-nation status with the United States as long as it employed restrictive emigration policies, was vehemently criticized by Moscow. But such laws did little to prevent a summit from taking place or a nuclear arms agreement from being signed.[29]

One should not, in fact, confuse the present tensions or attempts at détente between Moscow and Washington with those that existed during the Cold War era. The Russia of the Putin era is, simply, not of the same caliber as the USSR. Notwithstanding its nuclear machinery and cyberwarfare prowess, Russia presents no immediate threat to American interests but can rather be viewed as a potentially useful partner for various U.S. policy initiatives (from nuclear nonproliferation to stabilizing Central Asia). In these and a number of other areas, Russia is for the United States part of the solution rather than the source of the problem. Whether Americans fear Moscow's meddling in their elections or Russian leaders find criticism of their domestic politics objectionable is symptomatic of the two countries' respective situations in the global pecking order of the twenty-first century: the United States as the self-appointed spokesperson of an idealized liberal world order and Russia as the reluctant quasi-member of that order harking back to an earlier era of national greatness. The bilateral relationship is likely to remain what it has been for some time: full of frosty rhetoric aimed at domestic audiences combined with limited cooperation on a number of substantive issues.[30] Under Trump, American policy may occasionally tilt toward the latter. But condominium and close cooperation are as unlikely as a renewed Cold War.

The Chinese Colossus and America's Pivot

At the same time as the celebrations of Barack Obama's reelection were under way in the fall of 2012, the People's Republic of China (PRC) went through its own political transition. Characteristically, the process lacked the drama of the exit polls and minute-by-minute reporting so prevalent in U.S. politics. Xi Jinping took over the reins of leadership, succeeding Hu Jintao as the head of the Communist Party's politburo. "Change" was not talked about, but the principle of "strict discipline" did get a mention. By December 2018, Xi's position as the top leader had been strengthened to the point that he is customarily referred to as the most powerful Chinese leader since Deng Xiaoping (and sometimes even compared to Mao). China's remarkable economic growth, sustained for several decades, has not only produced the notion of the Chinese dream (to match the American one) but the prospect of the PRC bypassing the United States as the largest economy in the world, which seems enough to guarantee the Chinese Community Party's hold on power for the foreseeable future.[31]

Regardless of who occupies the White House, China's economic success prompts jealousy and frequent complaints about unfair trading practices and currency manipulation (highlighted during the 2016 U.S. presidential campaign). The consistent annual increases in Chinese defense expenditures (in 2012–16, for example, the PRC's spending doubled) and its tense relationship with a number of neighbors and regional players—most notably but not limited to Japan, South Korea, the Philippines, Taiwan, and Vietnam—has caused much speculation about Beijing's imperial designs. Although in 2013 the United States spent approximately five times as much on defense as the PRC, some worried that a combination of possible American defense cuts and continued Chinese spending increases would, in the next decade, erase Washington's military superiority—something that the Trump administration appears determined to avoid. The Obama administration's so-called pivot to Asia that effectively began in the fall of 2011 reflected the gradual shift in the focus of America's national security policy that has come about as a result of China's continued rise.[32]

Some find the (explicit or implicit) assumption that China represents a growing threat to American interests foolhardy. In the spring of 2012, for example, Henry Kissinger chastised the Obama administration for assuming that Chinese policies were geared toward creating a "Sinocentric bloc" that would exclude the United States. While calling for a more cooperative approach to China, Kissinger warned against reviving Cold War–era strategic thinking with modern-day China playing the role of the Soviet Union. "The U.S.-Chinese relationship should not be considered as a zero-sum game," Kissinger wrote, adding, "nor can the emergence of a prosperous and powerful China be assumed in itself to be an American strategic defeat." Robert Ross agreed, calling the Obama administration's pivot "unnecessary and counterproductive."[33]

There is little doubt that the Sino-American relationship has replaced the Soviet-American relationship as the most important bilateral relationship on the globe. In the past decade there has been much talk about the "G-2." And there are many observers who seem convinced that, as Kissinger frets, the general American attitude is to view China as a strategic threat. Only a liberalized China could be a real partner with the United States. China ruled by the Communist Party can never be a true member of an American-led liberal world order.

In the end, this is a relationship that, most observers would agree, is simply "too big to fail." Both countries have the capacity to inflict significant economic damage on the other (for example, 66 percent of the U.S. trade deficit is with China). Both can cause serious security dilemmas for the other. But at the same time, the likelihood that either of the two will openly challenge the other on fundamental issues is limited. How else to explain the fact that the U.S. Congress, no matter the jingoism that we sometimes hear about a need to protect American workers from unfair Chinese competition, is relatively silent on China's human rights record? Many, in fact, express confidence that China has perfected a nondemocratic model that may well augur ill for the idea that liberal democracy is the ultimate way of organizing a successful long-term future.[34]

President Trump's visit to China in November 2017 was a sobering reminder of the limits of American interest in trying to change China's internal political system or even its economic practices. In marked contrast to his bombastic election rhetoric about China, Trump effectively "congratulated" the PRC for having taken advantage of the economic opportunities of the liberal international order. Perhaps more tellingly, the forty-fifth president refrained from criticizing China's human rights record. Apparently, a "bromance" of sorts was gradually emerging between the leaders of China and the United States.[35] But then, a few months later and all the way through the first half of 2018, Trump announced a series of tariffs against China, ranging from solar panels and dishwashers (January) to steel and aluminum (March). China appeared ready for the challenge, drawing up long lists of retaliatory tariffs. By May, confusion reigned, with some analysts warning of an impending trade war and others arguing that much of the tough talk was exactly that, talk. In late May, one analyst put all the talk of trade wars into a longer-term perspective, noting that "Chinese and American . . . leaders have been arguing and rejiggering their economic relationship at almost every point over the past 20 years."[36]

Whatever its internal political evolution, China does present a potentially massive headache for American policy planners. If China's economy slows down, the strains on its choreographed stability are likely to increase. Given China's economic connectedness with much of the rest of the world, the impact on global growth would be significant. Such problems present, however, a medium- and long-term challenge. What we can expect from the United States is continued engagement with Beijing and an effort to strike a balance between firm support of key allies in the Far East (such as Japan and South Korea) and noninvolvement in the ongoing territorial disputes that put such allies on a path toward confrontation with China. In recent years, this has been most evident in the context of the South China Sea, where the Chinese have flexed their muscles to an unprecedented degree, intimidating other regional players (the Philippines, Vietnam, Taiwan, Malaysia. and Brunei, among others) with naval patrols and by constructing artificial islands that it claims have belonged to China for millennia. Although many of the nations subject to the PRC's coercive action are American allies, the Trump administration—much like the Obama administration before it—has chosen not to risk a direct military confrontation over the question. Instead, the president offered, while visiting Vietnam on November 12, 2017, to "mediate" the dispute. This was, if anything, an indication that a year after being elected on the promise that he would be tough on China, Trump has become adverse to any possibility of a real confrontation with Beijing.[37]

Enter the North Korean drama. The road to the June 2018 Singapore summit between Trump and Kim Jong-un was paved by Beijing in two meetings (in March and May) between the North Korean leader and China's Xi Jinping. To be sure, there is much speculation about the relationship between Pyongyang and Beijing. Yet it is difficult to imagine that North Korea would be willing to give up its nuclear weapons merely as a result of Donald Trump's threats. It is far more likely that Chinese security guarantees and promises coupled with increased trade (and aid) convinced Kim that he had something to gain by agreeing to the Singapore meeting.

The simple fact is that the United States and China actually share a number of security and economic interests. In 2018 some of this has been lost behind tough talk and angry tweets. Yet it is blatantly clear that neither side would end up "winning" a full-scale trade war. Both Beijing and Washington would benefit from an "opening to North Korea." And neither is ready to go to war over disputes in the South China Sea. Occasional tension and harsh rhetoric are likely to continue. The United States— whoever is in charge—is likely to challenge the PRC on matters of trade or human rights as it has done over the past several decades. But this hardly implies a major transformation of the most significant bilateral relationship in the world. There is unlikely to be a sudden "China Reckoning" as suggested by Kurt Campbell and Ely Rather in 2018.[38] Rather, expect a long process of recalibration as the economic, domestic, and security policies of the United States and the People's Republic of China continue their uncertain coexistence.

The Arc of Instability: Is America Part of the Problem?

Aside from large countries like Russia and China, much of American foreign policy revolves around the unstable region that Zbigniew Brzezinski, former national security adviser, dubbed the "arc of crisis" in the late 1970s. The Arab Spring and its unresolved consequences; the wars in Afghanistan, Iraq, and Syria; the rise and apparent decline of ISIS; the ongoing Israeli-Palestinian standoff; and the withdrawal of the Trump administration from the 2015 Iran nuclear agreement (the Joint Comprehensive Plan of Action)— the region provides a cacophony of problems that, for mere mortals, appear unsolvable. Domestic American pressures (such as the so-called Jewish lobby) and external expectations add to the complications facing any U.S. administration in trying to come up with a winning strategy for even one of these issues. Sadly, the future holds few positive prospects for the many conundrums that complicate U.S. Middle East policy.

Take the Israeli-Palestinian conflict. Given all the other regional issues, the Obama administration clearly placed the decades-long search for a solution on the back burner. To be sure, the United States has tried on numerous occasions, including during Obama's first term, to bring the

Israeli and Palestinian leaders together. But domestic imperatives, the uncertainties created by the Arab Spring, the ongoing civil war in Syria, and
the U.S. efforts to pressure Iran into abandoning its nuclear weapons all
conspired to make any significant move toward a two-state solution impossible. In early 2013, instead of moderating their policies, Israel approved the building of new settlements, a major obstacle on any road map
for peace. One can ascribe much of the subsequent deadlock to the fact
that the conservative Likud Party's leader, Benjamin Netanyahu, has held
the premiership since 2009 and shown little interest in a two-state solution. With Donald Trump in the White House, it is even more difficult to
see any major breakthroughs in this intractable conflict: The relocation of
the U.S. embassy from Tel Aviv to Jerusalem prompted a new wave of
unrest in Gaza in May 2018. In fact, the time may have finally arrived to
acknowledge the obvious: no matter who is in power in Washington, the
United States will not be the player who provides the solution to a conflict
that has just "celebrated" its fiftieth anniversary (if the 1967 war is considered the starting point).[39]

There are no real bright spots in other areas of U.S. Middle East policy.
The winding down of two "American" wars, in Iraq and Afghanistan, were
high on Barack Obama's to-do list in January 2009. To an extent he kept
his promise. Most troops did come home from Iraq by October 2011. At
home this retreat has been explained as a moderately successful nation-
building exercise. The reality, however, quickly turned out to be different.
While the war in Iraq, which Obama had always criticized as the "wrong"
war, was over as far as U.S. troop deployments were concerned, the region
was quickly enmeshed in another terrifying nightmare. ISIS—under the
leadership of Abu Bakr al-Baghdadi—stepped into the vacuum of power created by the withdrawal of American troops, the weakness of the new Iraqi
state, and the turmoil surrounding the Syrian Civil War. The upshot was
that during Obama's second term in office, the United States was deeply
involved in another war on Iraqi territory, conducting thousands of air
strikes against ISIS targets. In December 2016—five years after the proclaimed end of Operation Iraqi Freedom—there were 5,000 U.S. troops in
the country. While ISIS was, by 2017, in retreat, the number of American
troops had also gone up to approximately 7,000. There is a strong whiff of
continuity here—indeed going back all the way to 2003.[40]

While the repercussions of the Iraq War fester, withdrawal from
Afghanistan never truly happened. In 2009 there was the "Obama surge." By

2011, about the same time as Osama bin Laden was killed by U.S. Navy Seals in Pakistan, approximately 100,000 American troops (out of a total 140,000 foreign troops) were operating in Afghanistan. However, in 2018, the country that is sometimes called the graveyard of empires appears no closer to security and stability than at the time of Obama's election in 2008. The Taliban insurgency is alive and well, with rates of violence having gradually grown during Obama's presidency. To be sure, U.S. troop levels came down significantly during Obama's second term: By 2016, there were "only" 8,400 American soldiers in Afghanistan. But, in a classic statement promising more of the same, Obama warned against further withdrawals in July 2016: "It is in our national interest—after all the blood and treasure we have invested—that we give our Afghan partners a chance to succeed." A year later, in August 2017, Donald Trump announced the deployment of (an unspecified number of) further U.S. troops. He came uncharacteristically close to his predecessor by emphasizing that "a hasty withdrawal would create a vacuum for terrorists, including ISIS and al Qaeda."[41]

The war in Afghanistan gave rise to a new acronym: AfPak. The long-term American (and NATO) presence in Afghanistan had the consequence of expanding the theater of operations into the tribal regions of neighboring Pakistan. It was here, after all, that Osama bin Laden was hiding until he was killed in early May 2011. Many American drone attacks have hit targets on Pakistani territory, causing civilian casualties and straining the U.S.-Pakistani relationship. As a consequence, the route toward a peaceful solution in Afghanistan has become increasingly complicated. The challenge in the next few years for the United States is not only to help the Afghan government pacify the country internally but also to create a broad regional framework that includes a growing group of stakeholders: the government of Ashraf Ghani, parts of the Taliban, Pakistan, and a diverse group of interested actors (including Russia and Iran). The troubles in AfPak are likely to continue for years to come with unpredictable consequences throughout the region.[42]

Dealing with Afghanistan, Iraq, and the Israeli-Palestinian conflict would be enough for any administration. But these issues are only part of an increasingly crowded regional agenda. There is the lingering impact of Syria's yet unresolved civil war and the effects of ISIS's brutality. There is the perennial challenge of Iran and its regional rivalry with Saudi Arabia, hardly made simpler to handle following Trump's decision to withdraw from the Iran nuclear deal in May 2018. Add to these a host of other issues, ranging from the continued instability of Lebanon to the fragility of other states in the region (such as Yemen), and the inbox of Secretary of State of Mike Pompeo is likely to be crowded with unresolvable problems for the short, medium, and, should he stay in office longer than his predecessor, Rex Tillerson, long term. Indeed, it may be time to confront the common wisdom that assumes that the United States can provide solutions to many— indeed, any—of the conundrums in the Middle East. It bears remembering that the search for American-brokered solutions in the Middle East has been an ongoing part of U.S. diplomacy since the early 1970s, when William P. Rogers and Henry Kissinger, as secretaries of state, engaged some of the same players (Egypt, Israel, Syria, and Iran, among others) that still hold important keys to solving, as well as exacerbating, regional security problems.

In the end, during the Trump administration the United States is likely to remain at least as engaged in the Middle East as it has been since the 1970s. The pressures, from home and abroad, are too strong for any U.S. administration to disengage from the region. Just do not expect American-made solutions to the many problems of the arc of instability.

Transatlantic Troubles

While the Middle East and the Far East have become the geopolitical focus of the United States in recent decades, Europe seems to have disappeared from the horizon. Transatlantic relations and European security, once central to American foreign policy, seem to matter little in Washington. Since the 1970s there has been a gradual erosion in the significance of what was, in the decades following World War II, the most important cooperative relationship for both the United States and its partners in Western Europe. In the past two decades America has gone increasingly global while Europe has focused on building and—especially since the United Kingdom's Brexit vote in June 2016—maintaining the European Union. Transatlantic cultural differences (especially the so-called God gap) have widened. U.S. military interventionism, especially the war in Iraq in the early twenty-first century and Donald Trump's apparent willingness to risk a transatlantic trade war, have only exacerbated preexisting tensions. As a consequence, as Mary Nolan put it some years ago, "for neither Europe nor the United States will the twenty-first century be [as] transatlantic as the twentieth was."[43]

During the Obama presidency, the declining significance of transatlantic relations for U.S. foreign policy was confirmed. To be sure, the Obama administration came into office with an outpouring of goodwill from Europeans, who were relieved to be past what they considered the nightmare years of George W. Bush. One cannot dispute the fact that transatlantic relations at the beginning of Obama's second term were as good as they have been in the twenty-first century. In 2008, European publics loved Obama, because he *was* so different, in every conceivable way, from Bush. There may not have been any major substantive change in U.S. policy toward Europe. Yet four years later, most Europeans sighed in collective relief when Obama was reelected. Whether this was merely a question of imagery—poor press for Obama's opponent, Mitt Romney—rather than substance, we will probably never know. What is quite clear, however, is that in contrast to his predecessor or successor, Europeans had a love affair with Obama. In 2016 his approval rates in both France and Germany, for example, approached 90 percent.[44]

It would be a mistake, however, to assume that Obama's popularity in Europe was an outgrowth of a substantial overhaul in U.S. policy. American *interests* and the global leadership role that the United States plays (or desires to play) had not changed. Continuity has tended to outflank change as much in transatlantic relations as in any other fields of U.S. foreign policy. The lack of Bush-era angst made it easier, to be sure, for many European nations to contribute more to the NATO operations in Afghanistan after 2009 and to side with the United States on such issues as the sanctions regime toward Iran. In 2011, Americans and Europeans cooperated on Libya, with some seeing that as an example of a more robust European contribution. In reality, the NATO intervention in Libya confirmed the well-known structural gap between U.S. and European military capabilities. There was, Secretary of Defense Robert Gates warned in June 2011, a "very real possibility of collective military irrelevance" in the future lest Europeans began spending more on defense.[45]

Gates was saying nothing particularly unusual or counterfactual. The United States continues to shoulder the bulk of the bill, providing the great majority of the logistical and intelligence resources that are necessary for any effective military operation. Europeans, by contrast, play the role of minor supporters or, in some cases, critics of a U.S.-dominated agenda. While Americans grumble that there is no true transatlantic burden-sharing in

the security field, Europeans retort that they are too often expected to follow Washington's lead blindly: There is no true sharing of power when it
comes down to making decisions. The situation is likely to remain the
same as long as the transatlantic structural imbalance in defense spending
prevails. And, despite Donald Trump's repeated claims that "Europe must
do more"—with Germany singled out as a particularly delinquent free-rider
at the July 2018 NATO summit in Brussels—the situation is unlikely to
change radically during his presidency. No one, it seems, is projecting that
the Europeans will collectively increase their spending significantly. Although all have pledged to meet the 2 percent target (as in the proportion
of their respective GDP's to be spent on defense) by 2024, in 2016, only
four European countries (Britain, Estonia, Greece, and Poland) did so.
More fundamentally, even if there is a "Trump effect" of increased European defense spending, the transatlantic gap is likely to persist as the
United States under Trump will continue to keep military expenditures at
roughly 4 percent of GDP (in fact, after several years of decline, U.S. defense expenditures grew in 2016). In 2017–18, this meant that out of total
NATO defense spending, Europeans continue to account for less than
one-third.[46]

The age-old question of burden-sharing is related to other complicat-
ing issues for the future of transatlantic relations. The U.S. pivot toward
Asia and China, the management of NATO's withdrawal from Afghanistan,
containment of Iran's nuclear program, NATO strategy in Syria, or how
to deal with Russia are all issues on which Americans and Europeans rarely
see eye-to-eye. There is, though, very little that is new about any of these
potential conflict spots if placed in the historical context of transatlantic
relations. NATO's past is filled with transatlantic disagreements over "out-
of-area issues" (mainly crises in the Middle East) and over the proper policy toward the Soviet Union/Russia. Since the Vietnam War, Europeans
have worried about the United States shifting its strategic focus away from
the Old Continent.[47]

Beyond security issues, the future of transatlantic relations hinges on
economic questions. The fate of the euro remains uncertain, made no
clearer with domestic developments in key countries like Italy. Britain's
Brexit vote in the summer of 2016 has raised a host of complicated issues
regarding the future of transatlantic trade and, indeed, the European project itself. Doubts about the future of European integration have been further elevated by the rise of nationalism and populism across the continent,

fueled in part by the arrival of roughly a million refugees fleeing Syria's civil war. At the same time, the current political climate makes the possibility of a long-anticipated transatlantic free trade agreement (the Transatlantic Trade and Investment Partnership, TTIP) uncertain at best. This, despite the evident case in favor of the TTIP. The European Union (if considered as one unit) remains America's largest bilateral trading partner. In fact, as Daniel Hamilton and Joseph Quinlan put it, "No commercial artery is as large as the one tying the United States and Europe together."[48] Indeed, the past decade has underlined this transatlantic economic interconnectedness. Beneath the cloud of recent anti-integrationist, anti–free trade rhetoric, the numbers (trade, investment, employment) indicate that transatlantic economies have not only bounced back from the "dark days" of the Great Recession but have done so largely in tandem.

One should not, of course, assume that there is something inevitable and unbreakable about the transatlantic relationship. As long as Donald Trump remains in the White House, American policy toward its traditional allies is likely to remain unpredictable at best, Trump's refusal to endorse the closing communiqué of the June 2018 G-7 Summit being but one example of his many unsettling acts. But it is also worth keeping in mind that the recurrent conflicts and temper tantrums that appear in headlines pale when set against the realities of common interests and shared goals. Inflammatory rhetoric and dismissive commentary are not irrelevant and cannot be ignored. But neither are they necessarily a reflection of fundamental differences. For one thing that is rather obvious about the history of the transatlantic relationship—even during the Cold War—is the recurrence of "crises." And yet, somehow, the relationship has endured and even thrived. Conflicts have illustrated, time and again, the strength of the transatlantic community. Or, to put it in the simplest possible way: common American and European interests have not suddenly ceased to exist.

Change and Continuity

There is no doubt that the world is changing rapidly and that the United States, the once seemingly omnipotent superpower, will need to adapt to global transformations—shifts in economic and military power in particular—if it is to maintain its preeminent position. Obituaries for the age of American primacy are being written repeatedly alongside the treatises that purport to demonstrate how the twenty-first century will be a Pacific century. More broadly speaking, the liberal international order that emerged in the post–World War II era under U.S. guardianship is in danger of unraveling unless emerging countries like China are incorporated into existing structures of governance and cooperation. To an alarming extent the world is indeed "in disarray," as Richard Haass summed it up in 2017.[49]

There is, though, an additional consideration that needs to be taken into account when projecting future scenarios: Such forecasts rely on interpretations of existing trends. In 1901, for example, Theodore Roosevelt forecast that the century just opening would be "the Pacific century" (Karl Marx had done so already some decades earlier). Japan was widely expected to take over as the world's number-one economic power in the 1970s and 1980s; the decline of the Japanese model might appear inevitable in retrospect, but it seemed impossible back in 1979 when Ezra Vogel published his best-selling *Japan as Number One*. In 2018, in the same issue of *Foreign Affairs*, one respected analyst referred to the liberal international order as a "myth," while others waxed lyrical about its resilience.[50] To be sure, one can find any number of "correct" predictions to counterbalance these retrospectively mistaken ones (Alexis de Tocqueville comes to mind). The only useful lesson to be drawn may simply be to predict, as the authors of *Global Trends* did in 2012, that the world will move toward any number of possible futures but that assuming one of them to pan out exactly is folly. Disappointing it may seem, but we just do not know—we never have known—what the future holds.[51] One should, thus, be mindful of the "confident" and "scientific" predictions about the future that we are confronted with day in and day out. Their shelf life is often limited, driven by an incessant need for labeling and, often, the authors' desire to be "policy relevant."

Take the notion of "the rise of the rest" that was all the rage among policy analysts in the wake of the economic and financial crisis of 2007–08. The emerging powers, Stewart Patrick maintained in 2010, would present a major strategic challenge for the United States as the world was entering "a chaotic era" and American policymakers needed to "recalibrate their aspirations for multilateral cooperation and reexamine long-standing assumptions about the United States' role in the world."[52] Only two years later the tone of the debate began to shift. Ruchir Sharma pointed out that "the rest" were slowing down. The biggest of them—the so-called BRICs (Brazil, Russia, India, China, and South Africa)—Sharma pointed out, had all experienced declining growth rates after 2007, raising questions about the inevitability of the tectonic shift in global economic power—from the West to the rest—that was supposedly happening before our very eyes. More generally, the idea that there was (or is) an entity that can be called "the rest" (or "the Global South," for that matter) is starting to look increasingly like a case study in sloganeering (not unlike the notion of the third world) that has limited relevance in the real world. In fact, the countries of the emerging markets (another shorthand term that, if deconstructed, means little) have different economic, political, and social structures that result in varied growth rates. Nor—as the consumer warnings in most financial instruments advise us—is past performance a guarantee of future earnings; the once seemingly irresistible growth of the American economy in the late 1990s did, after all, grind to a halt in the early twenty-first century. Brazil appeared to be unstoppable in the early 2000s, but in 2013 its growth rates were roughly those of the United States. Indeed, as Sharma categorically put it: "The new global economic order will probably look more like the old one than most observers predict. The rest may continue to rise, but they will rise more slowly and unevenly than many experts are anticipating."[53]

If this is indeed the case, the future of the liberal international order, and America's central role within it, looks far less bleak. Notwithstanding the many obvious problems and challenges that face the United States, the United States commands a formidable military machine and an economy that far outweighs any other in its global influence. Equally important, America enjoys a network of bilateral and multilateral relationships that give it the flexibility necessary to adapt to the challenges of the globalized world. It still remains possible for the United States to "pivot" one way while maintaining close ties elsewhere and intervening, militarily or otherwise, in yet other regions. It is this unique flexibility that will make it possible for the nation to maintain a preeminent position even in the globalized and fragmented world of the early twenty-first century. Donald Trump may have managed to damage America's credibility with his particular mannerisms. But one should also take heart of the fact that the actual foreign policy changes his administration has so far implemented have been, at best (or worst), limited. As in so many times past, despite the inauguration of a new president and Donald Trump's seemingly obsessive need to shock the world, there has not been a complete transformation on "big ticket" items (Russia, China, the Middle East, Europe). And where transformation has taken place—as in the case of North Korea—it is difficult to argue that the Trump administration has made the world a more perilous place. Like it or not, there has been far more continuity than change.

Ultimately, for better or worse, it means that even with Donald Trump in charge, the United States remains an indispensable guarantor—or at minimum a central player in the reconfiguration—of the international order in the twenty-first century.

NOTES

1. Fareed Zakaria, "Can America Be Fixed?" *Foreign Affairs* 92, no. 1 (January/February 2013), p. 22.

2. Barack Obama, "Inaugural Address," January 21, 2013 (www.whitehouse.gov/the-press-office/2013/01/21/inaugural-address-president-barack-obama).

3. Edward Luce, *The Retreat of Western Liberalism* (London: Little, Brown, 2017), p. 11.

4. U.S. Department of Labor Statistics, June 18, 2018 (https://data.bls.gov/timeseries/LNS14000000).

5. Niall Ferguson, "Complexity and Collapse: Empires on the Edge of Chaos," *Foreign Affairs* 89, no. 2 (March/April 2010), pp. 18–32; Gideon Rachman, *Zero-Sum Future: American Power in an Age of Anxiety* (New York: Simon & Schuster, 2011). "This time it's for real" is from Gideon Rachman, "Think Again: American Decline," *Foreign Policy*, no. 184 (January/February 2011), pp. 59–63. For an entertaining exchange of views, see Rudyard Griffiths, ed., *The End of the Liberal Order? Niall Ferguson vs. Fareed Zakaria* (London: Oneworld Publications, 2017).

6. This point has been made repeatedly by Geir Lundestad. See, for example, Lundestad, *The Rise and Decline of the American 'Empire': Power and Its Limits in Comparative Perspective* (Oxford University Press, 2012). See also Dana H. Allin and Erik Jones, *Weary Policeman: American Power in an Age of Austerity* (London: International Institute for Strategic Studies, 2012).

7. Barack Obama, *National Security Strategy*, White House, 2010 (http://nssarchive.us/national-security-strategy-2010/).

8. Charles Krauthammer, "Unipolar Moment," *Foreign Affairs* 70, no. 1 (1990/1991), pp. 23–33; Joseph Nye, *Bound to Lead: The Changing Nature of American Power* (New York: Basic Books, 1991). See also Hal Brands, *Making the Unipolar Moment: U.S. Foreign Policy and the Rise of the Post–Cold War Order* (Cornell University Press, 2016); Jeffrey A. Engel, *When the World Seemed New: George H. W. Bush and the End of the Cold War* (New York: Houghton Mifflin, 2017).

9. "More people share . . ." and "fifty more years" are from "Excerpts from the State of the Union Address," February 4, 1997, in Philip Auersweld

and John Garofano, eds., *Clinton's Foreign Policy: A Documentary Record* (New York: Kluwer Law International, 2003), p. 53. "Indispensable nation" is from William J. Clinton, "Inaugural Address," January 20, 1997 (www .presidency.ucsb.edu/ws/index.php?pid=54183). This phrase is usually attributed to Secretary of State Madeleine Albright. In fact, Albright did use it on several occasions, but the "ownership" goes to Clinton (or rather his speechwriters).

10. "Excerpts from the State of the Union Address," *Clinton's Foreign Policy*, p. 84.

11. Paul Kennedy, *The Rise and Fall of Great Powers* (New York: Vintage, 1987); Michael Cox, "Whatever Happened to American Decline? International Relations and the New United States Hegemony," *New Political Economy* 6, no. 3 (2001), pp. 311–40. A few years later Cox would follow up by wondering whether decline was back. Cox, "Is the United States in Decline—Again?," *International Affairs* 83, no. 4 (2007), pp. 643–53.

12. On this point, see Michael Cox, "Why Did We Get the End of the Cold War Wrong?," *British Journal of Politics and International Relations* 11, no. 2 (2009), pp. 161–76.

13. Michael Mandelbaum, "Foreign Policy as Social Work," *Foreign Affairs* 75, no. 1 (January/February 1996), pp. 16–32; Stephen Schlesinger, "The End of Idealism," *World Policy Journal* 17, no. 1 (Winter 1998–99), pp. 31–41; Alvin Z. Rubinstein, "The New Moralists on a Road to Hell," *Orbis* 40, no. 2 (Spring 1996), pp. 31–41; Richard N. Haass, "Fatal Distraction: Bill Clinton's Foreign Policy," *Foreign Policy* (Fall 1997), pp. 112–23; Garry Wills, "Bully of the Free World," *Foreign Affairs* (March/April 1999), pp. 50–59.

14. See Ivo Daalder and James Lindsay, *America Unbound: The Bush Revolution in Foreign Policy* (Brookings Institution Press, 2003); Robert Draper, *Dead Certain: The Presidency of George W. Bush* (New York: Free Press, 2008); Jacob Weisberg, *The Bush Tragedy* (New York: Random House, 2008); Fred Kaplan, *Daydream Believers: How a Few Grand Ideas Wrecked American Power* (Chicago: Wiley, 2008); David Calleo, *Follies of Power: America's Unipolar Fantasy* (Cambridge University Press, 2009).

15. John Gaddis, *Surprise, Security, and the American Experience* (Harvard University Press, 2005); Melvyn Leffler, "9/11 and American Foreign Policy," *Diplomatic History* 29, no. 3 (June 2005), pp. 395–413; Melvyn Leffler, "September 11 in Retrospect," *Foreign Affairs* 90, no. 5 (September/October 2011), pp. 33–44.

16. On this point, see Jussi Hanhimäki, "The Obama Administration and Transatlantic Security: Problems and Prospects," in *The Routledge Handbook of Transatlantic Security*, edited by Jussi Hanhimäki, Georges-Henri Soutou, and Basil Germond (London: Routledge, 2010), p. 273.

17. Norwegian Nobel Committee, "Announcement of the Nobel Peace Prize for 2009," October 9, 2009 (http://nobelpeaceprize.org/en_GB/laureates /laureates-2009/announce-2009/).

18. See Jussi M. Hanhimäki, "Between Primacy and Decline: America's Role in the Post–Cold War World," in *International Relations since the End of the Cold War: New and Old Dimensions*, edited by Geir Lundestad (Oxford University Press, 2013), pp. 203–06.

19. For a highly positive account of Obama's first year in office, see Jonathan Alter, *The Promise: President Obama, Year One* (New York: Simon & Schuster, 2010).

20. Barack Obama, "Inaugural Address," January 20, 2009 (www.presidency .ucsb.edu/ws/index.php?pid=44#ixzz1NxViKbXo).

21. Barack Obama, "A Just and Lasting Peace," Nobel Lecture, December 10, 2009 (http://nobelprize.org/nobel_prizes/peace/laureates/2009/obama -lecture_en.html).

22. Ibid. See also Hanhimäki, "Between Primacy and Decline," p. 206.

23. Barack Obama, "State of the Union Address," January 12, 2016 (https:// obamawhitehouse.archives.gov/the-press-office/2016/01/12/remarks-president -barack-obama---prepared-delivery-state-union-address).

24. For a recent account of the 2016 election, see Rachel Bitecofer, *The Unprecedented 2016 Presidential Election* (New York: Palgrave, 2017).

25. To date, there are few academic studies on Obama's overall foreign policy record. See, though, Martin S. Indyk, Kenneth G. Lieberthal, and Michael O'Hanlon, *Bending History: Barack Obama's Foreign Policy* (Brookings Institution Press, 2012); Derek Chollet, *The Long Game: How Obama Defied Washington and Redefined America's Role in the World* (New York: Public Affairs, 2016); Colin Dueck, *The Obama Doctrine: American Grand Strategy Today* (Oxford University Press, 2015); and David Rothkopf, *National Insecurity: American Leadership in an Age of Fear* (New York: Public Affairs, 2016).

26. Putin cited in Simon Shuster, "Why Has Russia Passed a Bill to Ban U.S. Adoption of Russian Orphans?," *Time*, December 20, 2012.

27. See James Goldgeier, "A Realistic Reset with Russia," *Policy Review* 156 (August/September 2009), pp. 15–26; Emma Ashford, "Why New Russia Sanctions Won't Change Russia's Behavior," *Foreign Affairs Snapshot*, October 31, 2017; Daniel Fried, "When Diplomats and Spies Must Go," *Foreign Affairs Snapshot*, April 3, 2018.

28. "See How Trump's Stand Has Shifted since Helsinki," *CBC News*, July 21, 2018.

29. See Jussi M. Hanhimäki, *The Rise and Fall of Détente: American Foreign Policy and the Transformation of the Cold War* (Washington: Potomac Books, 2013), pp. 43–59, 77–99.

30. See Angela Stent, "U.S.-Russia Relations in the Second Obama Administration," *Survival* 54, no. 6 (December 2012–January 2013), pp. 123–38; Ivo H. Daalder, "Not Quiet on the Eastern Front," *Foreign Affairs* 96, no. 6 (November/December 2017), pp. 30–38.

31. Tania Branigan, "Xi Jinping Takes Reins of Communist Party and Military," *The Guardian*, November 15, 2012; "The World's Most Powerful Man," *The Economist*, October 14, 2017.

32. See Xenia Dormandy, *The Next Chapter: President Obama's Second-Term Foreign Policy* (London: Chatham House, 2013), pp. 36–41.

33. Henry Kissinger, "The Future of U.S.-Chinese Relations," *Foreign Affairs* 91, no. 2 (March/April 2012), p. 48; Robert S. Ross, "The Problem with the Pivot," *Foreign Affairs* 91, no. 6 (November/December 2012), p. 70.

34. See Eric X. Li, "The Life of the Party: The Post-Democratic Future Begins in China," *Foreign Affairs* 92, no. 1 (January/February 2013), pp. 34–46; Mira Rapp-Hooper, "What China Wants from Trump," *Foreign Affairs Snapshot*, November 7, 2017. For a broad historical overview of China's engagement with the outside world, see Odd Arne Westad, *Restless Empire: China and the World since 1750* (New York: Basic Books, 2015).

35. For a brief analysis on Trump's visit to China, see Joohee Cho and Karson Yiu, "China, South Korea Grapple with Trump Trip Effect," *ABC News*, November 15, 2017.

36. Zachary Karabell, "Why the US-China 'Trade War' Remains a War of Words," *Wired*, May 30, 2018.

37. On Trump's mediation offer, see Saphora Smith, "Trump Offers to Mediate in South China Dispute," *NBC News*, November 12, 2017. See also Robert A. Manning and James Przystup, "Stop the China Sea Charade," *Foreign Policy*, August 17, 2017.

38. Kurt Campbell and Ely Ratner, "China Reckoning: How Beijing Defied American Expectations," *Foreign Affairs* 97, no. 2 (March/April 2018), pp. 70–81. See also "Did America Get China Wrong? The Engagement Debate," *Foreign Affairs* 97, no. 4 (July/August 2018), pp. 183–95.

39. The literature on the topic is vast, but see, for example, Daniel C. Kurtzer and others, *Peace Puzzle: America's Quest for Arab-Israeli Peace, 1989–2011* (Cornell University Press, 2013); William B. Quandt, *The Peace Process: American Diplomacy and the Arab-Israeli Conflict since 1967*, 3rd ed. (Brookings Institution Press, 2005); and Lawrence Freedman, *A Choice of Enemies: America Confronts the Middle East* (New York: Public Affairs, 2009). On Obama, see "Obama's Record on Israeli-Palestinian Peace," *Foreign Affairs Snapshot*, October 5, 2016; on the Trump administration, see Shalom Lipner, "Is Trump Ruining the U.S.-Israeli Relationship?," *Foreign Affairs Snapshot*, October 5, 2017.

40. The literature on ISIS is rapidly growing. For recent insights, see Mohammad-Mahmoud Ould Mohamedou, *A Theory of ISIS: Political Violence and Transformation of the Global Order* (University of Chicago Press, 2017); and Fawaz A. Gerges, *ISIS: A History* (Princeton University Press, 2017).

41. Barack Obama, "Remarks on United States Military Strategy in Afghanistan," July 6, 2016 (www.presidency.ucsb.edu/ws/?pid=117881); Trump cited in Daniel Byman and Steven Simon, "Trump's Surge in Afghanistan," *Foreign Affairs Snapshot*, September 18, 2017.

42. Ahmed Rashid, *Descent into Chaos: The U.S. and the Disaster in Pakistan, Afghanistan, and Central Asia* (New York: Penguin, 2009); Ahmed Rashid, *Pakistan on the Brink: The Future of America, Pakistan, and Afghanistan* (New York: Viking, 2012); Seth G. Jones, *In the Graveyard of Empires: America's War in Afghanistan* (New York: W. W. Norton, 2010).

43. Mary Nolan, *The Transatlantic Century: Europe and America, 1890–2010* (Cambridge University Press, 2012), p. 9.

44. Anne Perkins, "Europe Loved Obama. Trump's Excesses Remind Us Precisely Why," *The Guardian*, January 11, 2017.

45. Robert Gates, "The Security and Defense Agenda (Future of NATO)," speech in Brussels, June 10, 2011 (www.defense.gov/speeches/speech.aspx?speechid=1581).

46. Michael Mandelbaum, "Pay Up, Europe," *Foreign Affairs* 96, no. 5 (September/October, 2017), pp. 108–14; "Military Spending by NATO Members," *The Economist*, February 17, 2017. For global military spending, see the Stockholm International Peace Research Institute (SIPRI) website: https://www.sipri.org.

47. For general discussions of the history of transatlantic disagreements, see Geir Lundestad, *The United States and Western Europe since 1945: From "Empire" by Invitation to Transatlantic Drift* (Oxford University Press, 2005); Jussi Hanhimäki, Benedikt Schoenborn, and Barbara Zanchetta, *Transatlantic Relations since 1945: An Introduction* (London: Routledge, 2012); and Nolan, *Transatlantic Century*.

48. Daniel Hamilton and Joseph Quinlan, *The Transatlantic Economy 2017* (Brussels: American Chamber of Commerce to the European Union, 2017).

49. Richard Haass, *A World in Disarray: American Foreign Policy and the Crisis of the Old Order* (New York: Penguin, 2017). See also John Ikenberry, *Liberal Leviathan: The Origins, Crisis, and Transformation of the American World Order* (Princeton University Press, 2012).

50. Daniel Deudney and G. John Ikenberry, "Liberal World: The Resilient Order," *Foreign Affairs* 97, vol. 4 (July/August 2018), pp. 16–24; Graham Allison, "The Myth of the Liberal Order: From Historical Accident to Conventional Wisdom," *Foreign Affairs* 97, vol. 4 (July/August 2018), 124–33.

51. Ezra Vogel, *Japan as Number One: Lessons for America* (Harvard University Press, 1979); *Global Trends 2030: Alternative Worlds* (Washington: National Intelligence Council, 2012). See also Mathew J. Burrows, *Global Risks 2035: The Search for a New Normal* (Washington: The Atlantic Council, 2016), and, as a useful reminder of the poverty of prediction, Josef Joffe, *The Myth of America's Decline: Politics, Economics, and a Half-Century of False Prophecies* (New York: Norton, 2013).

52. Stewart Patrick, "Irresponsible Stakeholders? The Difficulty of Integrating Rising Powers," *Foreign Affairs* (November/December 2010), pp. 44–53. See also Stewart Patrick, "The Evolving Structure of World Politics," in *International Relations since the End of the Cold War*, edited by Lundestad, pp. 25–29.

53. Ruchir Sharma, "Broken BRICs," *Foreign Affairs* 91, no. 6 (November/December 2012), p. 7.

THIRTEEN

Conclusion

The Unbearable Weight of History and the End of Transatlantic Relations?

FEDERIGA BINDI

Ever since the Greeks, as Thucydides recalls in *The History of Peloponnesian War*, the European continent has experienced different versions of balance of power. Codified in the 1648 Peace of Westphalia, bringing peace after the Thirty Years War, the principle of Balance of Power effectively lasted until World War II. In 1620, as the Thirty Years War was beginning, the *Mayflower* set sail for what was to become the United States. Its first president, George Washington, in his 1796 Farewell Address, warned against becoming embroiled in the entangling alliances of European balance-of-power politics: "History and experience prove that foreign influence is one of the most baneful foes of republican governments. . . . The great rule of conduct for us in regard to foreign nations is in extending our commercial relations, to have with them as little political connections as possible. . . . Europe has a set of primary interests which to us have none; or a very remote relation. Hence she must be engaged in frequent controversies, the causes of which are essentially foreign to our concerns. . . . In relation to the still subsiding war in Europe . . . our country, had a right to take, and was bound in duty and interest, to take a neutral position."[1]

In 1823, in the aftermath of successful independence movements in Latin America, President Monroe articulated in an address to Congress the so-called Monroe Doctrine. While his intent was to block European powers from intervening in hemispheric affairs, in 1904 President Theodore Roosevelt advanced a "Corollary" proclaiming a general right of intervention for the United States in the Western Hemisphere, after the United Kingdom, Germany, Italy, and other countries imposed a naval blockade on Venezuela when the country defaulted on its debt, an action that Roosevelt saw as a violation of the Monroe Doctrine.[2] In fact, the United States had already intervened in Haiti (1902) and Panama (1903); following the Corollary, it established a financial protectorate in the Dominican Republic (1905) and invaded Cuba (1906), thus initiating a long streak of both direct and indirect American interventions in Central and Latin America. Separated by an Ocean, however, until World War I the United States never took any actions in Europe.

Teddy Roosevelt was the first president who completely identified America's national interest with balance of power and insisted that the country make its influence be felt globally.[3] As World War I unfolded, Roosevelt asserted that a German victory would threaten American security. His successor, however, saw foreign policy in completely different terms. Woodrow Wilson believed in what we would define today as soft power: U.S. "unselfishness" and ability to play the honest broker. Wilson believed in American moral exceptionalism, in America's obligation to serve as a beacon of liberty for the rest of mankind, in the moral superiority of democracies, and that foreign policy should reflect the same moral standards as personal ethics.[4] As the sinking of the Lusitania became the proximate cause of America's declaration of war, the war was described as a struggle between good and evil, with the "Kingdom of Heaven" opposed to the "Kingdom of Hung-land,"[5] a strategy that would be used later by President Truman in asking Congress for financial assistance to Europe. The idea of moral superiority of the American democracy, conjugated with the legacy of the U.S. interventions in both World War I and World War II, in fact proved to be the most important tools of America's soft power and public diplomacy narrative.

In the 1990s, after the end of the Cold War, U.S. dominance came to be perceived in Washington almost as a birthright. The Clinton administration worked to preserve U.S. power through a series of maneuvers aimed at rewarding countries that had accepted a subordinate position and co-opting those that had not.[6] Foreign aid, military deployments, and other initiatives started to be increasingly designed to strengthen liberal regimes and punish autocrats.[7] The Clinton administration adopted a fairly combative approach to international trade and economics generally: it took advantage of the United States' strong position to negotiate NAFTA and employed harsh tactics to conclude the Uruguay Round of the GATT negotiations.[8]

In the 1980s, an extreme version of the presumption of American global leadership had been put forward by William Kristol, Richard Perle, Paul Wolfovitz, Dick Cheney, and others who—linking back to Teddy Roosevelt—advocated for American "greatness" and leadership in the world, not necessarily to make the country safer, or the world better, but for the sake of leadership itself.[9] As this group got into leadership positions in the G. W. Bush administration, Wilson's idea of U.S. moral superiority conjugated with Teddy Roosevelt's right to intervene, leading to the Bush Doctrine and the 2002 *National Security Strategy*,[10] which asserted a right of first strike: the United States should not wait until attacks occur to retaliate, but rather seek out plotters and strike preventively.[11] As 9/11 prompted a strong and virtually unanimous response from policymakers and legislators across the aisles, the war on terror became the new, defining focus of U.S. foreign policy, playing the same role anticommunism had played during the Cold War.[12]

The European Union

The creation of the European Communities meant the discarding of the principles established by the Peace of Westphalia, creating the conditions for the longest period of peace the continent has ever experienced. Although the European Union has developed a proper foreign policy only in the last decades, the foreign policy of its member states have to be viewed, above all, against the background of their EU membership. To be fair, each country has interpreted and used its membership in distinctive ways.

For Germany, it has primarily been a matter of economic leadership. The 2008 economic crises gave Germany a major role within the EU and internationally, especially in relations with the United States, though the two countries had diametrically opposed economic policy receipts on how to deal with it. Germany's economic power, however, has not been matched by a similar leadership in the EU's Common Foreign and Security Policy or in Common Security and Defense Policy. In these fields, Germany is more of a reactive player. Berlin has however used, on occasions, the EU vehicle to conduct foreign policies that would have otherwise been impossible, such as the involvement in the Iran nuclear deal, or the sanctions on Russia after the annexation of Crimea.

Similarly, for former fascist dictatorship Italy, the Communities provided a golden opportunity to get a new seat at the table. Italy played a leading role in the 1980s to 1990s, and was instrumental for both the Single European Act and the Maastricht Treaty. The end of the Cold War, however, had lasting consequences on Italian domestic politics; together with the two successive sets of enlargements—to the north in 1995 and to the east in 2004—Italy lost its centrality and its ability to shape European politics, as the lack of European solidarity on the issue of illegal immigration is clearly showing.

Different is the case of France, the country at the origin of the Communities, including the failed attempt to create a European Defense Community (EDC) in 1952. Since the outset, France has always had an interest in using the EC/EU to amplify its global role. From Charles de Gaulle's opposition to British EEC membership, to Emmanuel Macron's role in approving the Permanent Structured Cooperation (PESCO) in December 2017, the strategy has never substantially changed. As the only EU nuclear power and UN Security Council Permanent Member after Brexit, France will recuperate in the security domain the prominent role it had in the early days of European integration. How much France will want to invest and push on EU foreign policy and security, however, will become clear in mid-2019, when the new EU institution leaders will nominated: If France is really invested in more EU defense and security policies, and wants PESCO to succeed, it needs to take the lead and have a French candidate nominated to the post of European Union High Representative (EUHR).

On the other side of the Channel, London did not see the need to join the ECSC in 1952 and the EEC in 1957, as it still perceived the United

Kingdom as a colonial empire. Soon, however, Britain had little choice but to move closer to Europe, primarily for economic reasons, but also for political ones: Washington had been arguing that if Britain were to become an EEC member, it would increase it prominence in world affairs, as well as its importance for the United States. The United Kingdom has been active in the field of European defense, but on the condition of having a leadership role, and essentially with the main purpose of undermining— rather than strengthening—EU cooperation. Regardless of political affiliation, leaders also kept emphasizing the "special relationship" with the United States, a belief that concurred with the calling of the Brexit referendum. Ever since the Brexit vote, however, British policy has been in disarray, and the Theresa May government has proved unable to execute a coherent negotiation strategy. Against hopes that the United States would at least remain involved in EU defense, the United Kingdom announced its withdrawal from the prospected leadership of the EU battalion in 2019.

Denmark shares the United Kingdom's free trade and transatlantic approach, and thus its engagement with the EEC/EU has been primarily pragmatic, based on market openings in the internal market. Attitudes on the EU are still split, though Brexit has raised EU support among the population. While the majority of Danish political parties wish to abolish the Danish opt-outs, successive governments have so far failed to do so. The opt-out on defense matters, however, prevents Denmark from taking part in military operations under the EU flag. Abolishing this opt-out would secure Denmark the full spectrum of options for participating in all forms of military engagement with the UN and NATO, as well as EU missions.

Spain joined the EEC after forty years under Francisco Franco's fascist dictatorship. Like Rome and Bonn before it, when Madrid emerged from isolation, the government adopted an ambitious policy of normalization of international relations, beginning with its three closest neighbors: Portugal, France, and the United Kingdom. The record of Spain's membership in the European Union has proved to be truly impressive. The best and the brightest of Spain's government cadres joined the EC's expanded institutions, taking on positions of responsibility in EC/EU institutions and leading to the formulation of the bloc's policies toward Latin America, which have become one of the most important areas for the EU's foreign policy.

In Poland, too, the EU was pivotal for the modernization of the infrastructure system, regional development, and the reduction of the income gap with Western Europe. Poland has rapidly come to be a highly proactive, assertive, and pragmatic member of the EU. Warsaw has also used the EU tactically to pursue its own interests and to acquire more leverage within the EU and Central and Eastern Europe. It promoted the Eastern Partnership (EaP) and the reconfiguration of the EU-Russia partnership, and it is deeply committed to the development of the European Security and Defense Policy (ESDP). Warsaw has participated in several EU operations across the world—especially after the arrival of Donald Trump in the United States.

On the contrary, the Czech Republic has not yet emerged as a policy shaper inside EU foreign policy structures; as for Czech policymakers, the Atlantic Alliance remains the alpha and omega for security and defense and for foreign policy more broadly. Thus the Czech Republic initially welcomed the development of the EU's Common Security and Defense Policy (CSDP) with suspicion. This initial reluctance has been mostly overcome, and Prague has been increasingly investing in a particular civilian leg of the CSDP. Nevertheless, this gradual interest in CSDP remains mainly confined to a small group of experts within Czech EU-minded foreign policy elites and has yet to penetrate broader policymaking circles, let alone the political class. Czech policymakers tend *not* to regard the EU as a foreign policy actor, let alone a global player.

Membership in the Communities also had an influence on relations with the USSR. From the beginning, the USSR-EEC relationship has been problematic. With the advent of Mikhail Gorbachev's perestroika, the Soviet Union finally formally recognized the EEC. The first step in the "normalization" of relations between Brussels and Moscow, which encompassed Moscow's adaptation to EU legislation, was the signing in 1994 of a Partnership and Cooperation Agreement. At the Saint Petersburg summit in May 2003, the EU and Russia agreed to reinforce their cooperation by creating over the long term four "common spaces." In a few years, however, the relationship deteriorated. The main causes of tension were the alleged Western support for the so-called Color Revolutions and the recognition of Kosovo's independence in 2008 by two-thirds of EU members. However, the issue that creates the most conflict with the EU has been competition over the post-Soviet space: the 2004 EU European Neighborhood Policy (ENP) and the launch in 2009 of the EaP. Although the ENP does not offer participants membership in the EU, its economic, political, and social dimensions were perceived by Moscow as an attempt to carve out a

Western sphere of influence in Russia's traditional backyard. In this climate of mounting competition between Brussels and Moscow for "control" of the post-Soviet space, violent protests in Kiev's Maidan Square in November 2013 led rapidly to regime change in Ukraine. In reaction to the annexation of Crimea and violation of Ukraine's sovereignty and territorial integrity by Russian armed forces, the EU canceled the summit with Russia. However, because of EU-Russia interdependence, economic confrontation damages both. Russia is the third trading partner of the EU, and the EU is the first trading partner of Russia. For Russia, which holds the world's largest proven reserves of natural gas and is the EU's most important single supplier of energy products, energy is not simply about commercial interests. Energy has been an extraordinary political tool in the country's effort to return to its status as a great power, allowing it to continue to exert its influence in the post-Soviet space. Yet, in turn, Russia's economy remains highly dependent on the export of energy raw materials, and the EU is its most important destination.

EEC/EU-U.S. relations have also been contradictory. While the United States supported European integration during the Cold War, since the 1970s, there has been a gradual erosion in the significance of the relationship. Cultural differences widened. U.S. military interventionism, especially the war in Iraq in the early twenty-first century, further exacerbated the growing pattern of alienation. Although Barack Obama came into office with an outpouring of goodwill from Europeans, it would be a mistake to assume that Obama's popularity in Europe was an outgrowth of a substantial overhaul in U.S. policy. NATO intervention in Libya in 2011, initially seen in the United States as textbook-case transatlantic cooperation, confirmed the structural gap between U.S. and European military capabilities and eventually evolved into total failure. As Americans grumble that there is no true transatlantic burden-sharing in the security field, Europeans retort that they are too often expected to follow Washington's lead blindly and that there is no true sharing of power when it comes down to making decisions. What is most interesting, however, is the correlation between these periods of antagonization and the EU strengthening in foreign and defense policies: the creation of European Political Cooperation (EPC) in the 1970s, the Maastricht Treaty in the 1990s, the Lisbon Treaty during the George W. Bush presidency, PESCO and the Trump presidency—all are cases in point.

Russia

Often misunderstood in the United States, the relations between EU member states and Russia run deep because of historical, cultural, and economic reasons. During the Cold War, the USSR strictly controlled the Central and Eastern European countries (CEECs) and was perceived as the gravest danger for Western Europe. Despite being part of NATO, however, most Western European countries had no choice but to entertain relations with Moscow. Since the resurgence of Russia, relations are equally deep but also more ambiguous. However, no matter how strong the U.S. pressure or discontent may be, there will never be—in peacetime at least—a total break with Moscow.

Take Germany's relationship with Russia: On the one hand, Russia's geographic proximity and Germany's increasing dependence on Russian energy supplies mandated a cooperative and friendly relationship with Moscow. Economic ties with German companies in the energy sector have been very tight since at least the late 1970s and early 1980s, when large gas pipeline projects between Russia and Western Europe were planned and implemented. Also, traditional historical and cultural ties, rooted in hundreds of years of shared history, have given German-Russian relations a basically amicable character even during the coldest of Cold War periods. A fundamental shift occurred in Germany's Russia policy after Moscow's annexation of Crimea and the subsequent downing of Malaysian Airlines Flight MH17 over Ukrainian territory. Germany, at first reluctantly and then with much determination, became the front-runner on the Western sanctions imposed against Russia. After Crimea and the war in eastern Ukraine, trust in Vladimir Putin and his regime is low, but Germany's historic reluctance to risk conflict with Russia also still exists. Both on the political left and the political right, influential Russia-friendly groups exist. German business leaders—including the former German Chancellor Gerhard Schröder—lobbied very hard to keep relations with Russia on a soft footing. A case in point is the Nord Stream 2 pipeline project, designed to increase the direct transit capacity of Russian gas to Germany, which led to heated discussions in German and European energy circles, and to a German-American dispute, but which was ultimately given the green light by the German government.

Similar is the situation for Italy, whose relations with St. Petersburg date back centuries. During the Cold War, Italy viewed itself as a bridge between the East and West and pursued open dialogue and economic partnerships with the Soviet Union. The fall of the Berlin Wall in 1989, and of the Soviet Union in 1991, caused some policy confusion in Italy but did not fundamentally harm the Russo-Italian relationship. Relations suffered after Russia's controversial decision to occupy and annex the Crimean region while antagonizing Ukraine in its eastern provinces. Italy supported the European consensus that Russia's actions were unlawful and participated in the sanction program, despite the vocal protests of industrial areas like Veneto in northern Italy, which suffered greatly because of the sanctions. Yet Russia remains Italy's largest supplier of gas, and both countries still have large investments in each other's economies.

World War II winner France has at times tried to play the Russia card to counterbalance U.S. power. In 1966, de Gaulle was the first Western head of state to pay an official visit to Moscow, and a telephone hotline was established between the Kremlin and the Élysée. Despite this symbolism, this strategy paid off less than France would have liked. Fast-forward to 2015, President François Hollande and German chancellor Angela Merkel tried to mediate in the Crimea conflict. Failing that, France voted for a U.S.-sponsored resolution (vetoed by Russia) in the UN Security Council that declared the seizure of Crimea an illegal violation of Ukraine's political independence and territorial integrity. With French support, Russia was also excluded from the G-8, while Paris supported the EU's economic sanctions on Russia.

Denmark, too, has had a long historical relationship with Russia, with intermarriages between the Danish royal family and the czars. With the fall of the Soviet Union and the anchoring of a reunified Germany in the EU, Denmark no longer had to be wary of any large neighbors. Denmark thus started pursuing a much more active foreign policy—for example, actively engaging in early diplomatic recognition of the Baltic states, while still allowing one of Russia's natural gas pipelines to Europe pass through Danish territorial waters. However, since Russia's annexation of Crimea and ensuing destabilization of eastern Ukraine, relations with Moscow have deteriorated. Denmark supported the sanctions on Russia enacted by the EU. In the Arctic, unsettled boundary claims remain between the Kingdom of Denmark (on Greenland's behalf) and Russia around the North Pole, with Denmark striving to maintain the Arctic as a conflict-free, cooperative zone.

Having been under USSR control during the Cold War, Poland initially opposed reconciling with Russia. During the government of the Kaczyński brothers, Poland vetoed opening negotiations for the renovation of the Partnership and Cooperation Agreement (PCA) between Brussels and Moscow. With the arrival of Donald Tusk from the Civic Platform party (2007), emphasis was put on building a constructive relationship with Russia. Warsaw stopped objecting to Russia's bid to join the Organization for Economic Cooperation and Development (OECD) and to veto EU-Russia negotiations on the PCA; in return, Moscow lifted its ban on Polish meat imports. Poland proposed to serve as a bridge between the EU and Russia and pressed the EU toward a more effective Ostpolitik; in June 2008, Poland and Sweden proposed boosting the eastern dimension of the European Neighborhood Policy. Following the August 2008 five-day Georgia War, Poland was among the countries advocating for sanctions against Russia. The U.S.-Russia reset in 2009 benefited Polish-Russian relations, too. However, with the eruption of the Ukraine crisis, relations have become tense again, with Warsaw again advocating for strong sanctions against Russia and a more consistent NATO presence on the eastern flank of the alliance.

In the twentieth century, Russia constituted one of the two poles of the geopolitical equation for Czech national survival. Since the end of the Soviet Union, two independent states, Slovakia and Ukraine, have been restored in the space in-between Prague and Moscow, while the Czech Republic is now anchored within NATO and the EU. From an economic point of view, Czech-Russian relations have been steady and consequential. On the political and rhetorical side, by contrast, they have been rocky. While relations were good in the years immediately after the Velvet Revolution, they deteriorated over the question of the Czech accession to NATO. More tensions emerged around the American Ballistic Missile Defense (BMD) plan and, conversely, on Russia's "new assertiveness" in regional affairs. Yet Russia is probably the issue where the division of domestic actors is the most acute and paralyzing for foreign policy. This was particularly obvious during the Ukraine crisis of 2014, with the prime minister, the minister of foreign affairs, and the president all adopting different attitudes toward the crisis.

Middle East

The Middle East is an area where European and U.S. interests and policies at the same time intersect and contrast the most. The transatlantic partners were divided on the Six-Day War in 1967, the 1973 Arab-Israeli War, and the subsequent OPEC oil embargo on the United States and the Neth-erlands. The nine EEC members even greeted the Camp David peace talks without any noticeable enthusiasm, reaffirming the Palestinians' right to self-determination and asking for the PLO to be included in peace ne-gotiations. Similarly, with the Iran hostage crisis in 1979, while the EEC called for the release of the hostages, it did not support the U.S. call for sanctions. Only on April 22, 1980, did the EEC finally agree to sanctions, although only if implemented by the individual states. U.S.-EU relations on the Middle East reached a historic low with the 2003 invasion of Iraq. With the arrival of Barack Obama, on the contrary, the European Union and the United States cooperated—albeit not always with positive results—on a number of relevant issues: Afghanistan, the nuclear deal with Iran, the 2011 failed NATO operation in Libya, and counterterrorism.

As a consequence of World War II atrocities, German involvement in the Middle East has traditionally been dominated by its relationship with Israel. However, Chancellor Angela Merkel has gradually grown visibly cold toward Prime Minister Benjamin Netanyahu, considering his decision to press ahead with the building of new settlements in the Palestinian West Bank as detrimental to the proposed two-state solution. In an unprece-dented move, Germany abstained in the UN General Assembly vote on Palestinian statehood in November 2012. Germany has also been a signifi-cant contributor of development aid and acted as a diplomatic mediator. It is an important arms exporter to Saudi Arabia, Qatar, Kuwait, Omar, and Bahrain, and it is a financier of the Palestinian Authority. Berlin also played a major role in the negotiation of the Iran nuclear deal (or Joint Compre-hensive Plan of Action, JCPA) and has a strong national interest in stability in the region, which would include reducing Islamist terrorism, limiting the prospect of mass migration from the region to Europe, and securing access to the energy resources of the region. At the same time, it is not a primary geopolitical player in the region's diplomacy, preferring to embed its diplomatic involvement in the region in the multilateral approaches of the EU and the UN.

Arms sales have also been one of France's leitmotifs in dealing with the Middle East. De Gaulle developed good relations with several Arab coun-tries that benefited from French arms sales and diplomatic support against Israel. However, in the late 1950s, France became a main sponsor of Israel, supplying it with advanced conventional weapons and aiding the devel-opment of its nuclear weapons program. Israel, in turn, participated in the ill-fated invasion of Egypt (1956). Georges Pompidou developed close economic ties with many Arab countries, which commissioned French firms to build infrastructure (power plants) and bought French weapons (from small arms to tanks, airplanes, and missiles). Giscard d'Estaing allowed the Palestinian Liberation Organization (PLO), which the United States considered a terrorist group, to establish an office in Paris in 1975. The first French president to visit Israel, Mitterrand gave a speech in the Knesset where he called for Israel to grant Palestinians statehood and for Arab states to recognize Israel's right to exist. While condemning the terrorist attacks carried out by the PLO, he organized the evacuation of Yasser Arafat's fighters from Beirut during the Israeli invasion of Lebanon in 1982. In the 1970s, Saddam Hussein borrowed money from French banks, allowed French companies to develop Iraqi oil fields, and bought the nuclear reactor at Osirak. After some hesitation, France took part in the 1991 Gulf War; after the war, it supported economic sanctions against Iraq but lobbied the UN for an "Oil for Food" program. In 1998, however, France declined to participate in the U.S. and British air strikes against Iraq, arguing that they would be counterproductive. France also opposed the second Gulf War (2003), believing that Iraq served as a vital counterweight to Iran in the volatile Gulf region and that its destruction would unleash sectarian violence between the Sunnis and Shias. When the United States, supported by Britain and Spain, asked the UN Security Council for an authorization to disarm Iraq by force, France, supported by Russia, Germany, and China, threatened to cast a veto. After the United States and Britain, with the support of a motley "coalition of the willing," invaded Iraq and overthrew Saddam Hussein, the French president, Jacques Chirac, criticized the United States for undermining respect for international law and the principle of multilateralism. Outside Iraq, however, France cooperated with the United States in the global "war on terror." France sent 5,000 troops to Afghanistan, including special forces that participated in combat operations against al Qaeda and the Taliban, while French intelligence services shared data on jihadist groups with their U.S. counterparts. Chirac also worked to improve relations with Israel. Both Sarkozy and Holland embraced the idea of regime change in Arab countries that were not allied with the West. In the spring of 2011, France and Britain cosponsored the UN Security Council Resolution 1973 that authorized NATO to create a no-fly zone over Libya. Interpreting the resolution as widely as possible, Britain, France, and the United States then bombed Libyan airfields and ground forces, giving a decisive military advantage to the rebels, thus helping overthrow and kill Muammar Qaddafi, but ultimately leading to a civil war and Tuareg tribesmen fleeing Libya to start a revolt against the government of neighboring Mali. The intervention in Mali (2013–14) restored the government to power in the capital city but could not defeat the insurgency, which now involved the Islamic State of Iraq and Syria (ISIS), al Qaeda, and Boko Haram. François Hollande tried to build a coalition to launch air strikes against Syria in 2013, but he had to step back when Barack Obama decided to seek congressional approval before taking action. France has, however, provided political and logistical support to the Free Syrian Army, the main opponent of the Syrian government; France also bombed ISIS positions in Iraq and Syria, while its special forces have captured and killed ISIS operatives in Libya. At the same time, France continued to support the pro-Western monarchies in the Gulf region, such as Qatar and the United Arab Emirates, and Abu Dhabi, home to France's newest military base, and showed strong support for Israel.

In 1956, the British-France-Israel invasion of Egypt proved a major disaster: Britain thus discovered that it was no longer in a position to embark on military adventures abroad solo. By the late 1970s, Britain had given up most of its colonial possessions and military bases abroad, but with a majority of British politicians regretting the loss of Britain's global role. The invasion of Iraq in 2003 was in many respects a real turning point in British foreign policy that can be compared in its significance to the fateful Suez adventure in 1956. Bush's war on terror and the war in Afghanistan strengthened Blair's relationship with Washington. The hostile attitude of Germany and France toward the war in Iraq and much of Europe's only lukewarm support drove a wedge between Blair's Britain and the EU, leading to an increasingly antagonistic relationship with the German and French leaders and a close cooperation with U.S.-friendly governments such as Poland, José María Aznar's Spain, and Berlusconi's Italy. The following decade, the United Kingdom cautiously supported developments in the Arab Spring, but this was largely restricted to rhetorical support. London strongly condemned the civil war in Syria but refused to get drawn into the conflict militarily. Similarly, the counterrevolution in Egypt was at first viewed skeptically in London, but this quickly changed once it became clear that the replacement of democratically elected President Mohamed Morsi in July 2013 by military leader Fattah el-Sisi had positive results for Western policy. London was however pivotal, alongside France, for the intervention in Libya in 2011, the cause of the subsequent power vacuum and vicious civil war.

Even more than for political and economic reasons (oil especially), the Middle East and the North Mediterranean shores are important to Italy because of geographic proximity. Italy's chief concerns have thus been maintaining stability and peace in the wider Mediterranean region, as well as securing safety and durability of its major energy suppliers. During the Cold War, Italy's geostrategic position, its dependence on Arab oil markets, its activism in North Africa, and its only partial subordination to American pro-Israel policies enabled Rome to play a bridge role, counterbalancing the spreading Soviet influence within the Arab world. Italy's special relation is with Libya, a former colony from 1912 to 1947: by the end of the 1990s, one-fourth of Italy's petroleum needs were met by Libya, and Italy had become Libya's largest trading partner. Curbing illegal immigration was also a major part of negotiations for the Friendship Treaty signed by Italy and Libya in 2008, which measurably decreased illegal immigration but was voided by the war that began when France attacked Libya in 2011. Prime Minister Silvio Berlusconi offered to serve as a negotiator between Libya and the West, to no avail. Despite diverging views within the government, Italy eventually joined the war, which however left Libya a failed state and a terrorist haven, as well as a point of departure for the massive numbers of people fleeing the wars in the Middle East and widespread poverty and violence in African states such as Sudan, Nigeria, and others.

Like Italy, Spain shares a maritime border with the Middle East. Not surprising, therefore, Morocco has always been a priority in Spain's foreign policy. Besides illegal immigration, an important concern is the issue of the Spanish cities of Ceuta and Melilla, which are located on the Moroccan coast on territory claimed by Morocco. When Spain joined the EC in 1986, Ceuta and Melilla were considered Spanish cities and European territory, and the two cities claimed to be candidates for financial assistance from the EC's Regional Development Fund. Spain hoped that its membership in NATO, while providing no security guarantee to Ceuta and Melilla, would make Morocco's King Hassan II less likely to move against the territory. However, Spanish demands for the return of Gibraltar have consistently reinforced Moroccan ambitions to regain Ceuta and Melilla. The Arab countries have been a strategic priority for Spain because they are a source of oil and natural gas, and several Arab countries are important investors in Spain. Spain was thus late in recognizing the state of Israel and has provided steady support for Palestinian claims of statehood. When the Iraq War exploded, the Spanish government, led by Prime Minister Aznar, sent a small military unit to join the U.S.-led coalition. However, after the defeat of Aznar's party in the 2004 election, the new president, José Luis Rodríguez Zapatero, abruptly withdrew the troops, causing a major upset in the Bush administration. Last but not least, the Spanish military participated in an array of peacemaking and peacekeeping missions, as well as programs to train the armed forces of countries in need of democratic order and political consolidation, foremost through the UN Interim Force in Lebanon (UNIFIL).

Denmark is geographically remote from the Middle East. However, in 2005 the publication of satirical cartoons in the Danish daily *Jyllands-Posten* sparked angry popular reactions in Muslim countries. The Danish government perceived its response to the cartoon crisis primarily as a defense of internal rights, particularly freedom of expression. Since the cartoon crisis, Denmark has increased its engagement in the Middle East, opening new embassies in the region and enlarging funding for its Arab initiative, which focuses on supporting reform in areas such as women's rights in Arab and North African countries. Denmark, a staunch U.S. and U.K. ally, also took part in the air campaign in Libya in the spring of 2011, with broad parliamentary support. In 2013–14, Denmark took part in eliminating Syria's chemical weapons by providing a transport ship. Also in 2014, Denmark joined the American-led coalition campaign against ISIS in Iraq with both fighter planes and military trainers.

China

China has been the object of Washington's interest in past and current administrations. Regardless of who occupies the White House, China's economic success prompts jealousy and frequent complaints about unfair trading practices and currency manipulation. At the same time, the consistent annual increases in Chinese defense expenditures and its tense relationship with a number of its neighbors and regional players has caused much speculation about Beijing's imperial designs. China presents a potentially massive headache for American policy planners. In recent years, this has been most evident in the context of the South China Sea, where the Chinese have flexed their muscles to an unprecedented degree, intimidating other regional players (the Philippines, Vietnam, Taiwan, Malaysia, and Brunei, among others) with naval patrols and by constructing artificial islands that the Chinese claim have belonged to China for millennia. Although many of the nations subject to the PRC's coercive action are American allies, the Trump administration, much like the Obama administration before it, has chosen not to risk a direct military confrontation over the question. Instead, the president offered, while visiting Vietnam on November 12, 2017, to "mediate" the dispute.

Putin has also been cultivating the idea of extending Russia's geopolitical sphere of influence to include the Asia-Pacific region. Both Russia and China are members of BRICS (Brazil, Russia, India, China, and South Africa), which in turn depend mainly on the continuation of a good relationship between Moscow and Beijing. Moscow and Beijing, in fact, share similar views on the most critical issues, such as the turbulence in the Middle East, Iran's nuclear program, cross-border security, and the North Korean nuclear issue. China and Russia, as North Korea's neighbors, have the common goal of resuming the six-party talks and urging North Korea to return to the negotiating table.

Despite American rhetoric and Russian ambitions, however, China is the largest trading partner for EU imports, and the second largest partner for EU exports. In particular, China was Germany's top trading partner in 2017, steaming past the United States for the second consecutive year. Germany established a diplomatic relationship with China in 1972, following the thawing of relations between China and the United States. In 1972, the German trade volume with China was US$274 million. In 2017, it was US$230 billion. Today, Germany's relations with China are the best example of Germany's focus on the promotion of business interests, few security and defense concerns, clear focus on realpolitik, some references to human rights and democracy issues, and little meaningful dialogue with its partners over a common approach. The "special relationship" (Angela Merkel's words) that has formed between the two countries is based on a fundamental overlapping of interests. China considers Germany to be the country most useful for its own economic development. For some of Germany's Western partners, its robust, mercantile China strategy has created uneasiness. After an episode in which Germany tried to prevent an EU Commission antitrust procedure against China over distortions in the solar panel market, a sector with strong German business interests in China, some observers suggested that Germany is ready to undermine EU unity and solidarity in favor of lucrative business possibilities.

Curiously, Denmark was one of the first Western countries to recognize the People's Republic, having established diplomatic relations with China in 1950. In spite of some friction on human rights, Denmark signed a strategic partnership with China in 2008 to expand cooperation in a range of fields, from climate change to expanded economic relations and university cooperation. Denmark is the smallest EU member state to enter into such a partnership, which had been reserved for heavyweights like Germany, France, and the United Kingdom. Denmark has tried to Europeanize its policies on China, though divisions inside the EU make it difficult to agree on a common line.

Latin America

The Monroe Doctrine was elaborated as a reaction to the independence of Spain and Portugal's Latin America colonies. Yet the two countries managed to maintain a "special relationship" with their former colonies, as the Ibero-American Community—comprising the nineteen Spanish- and Portuguese-speaking countries in Latin America in addition to Spain, Portugal, and Andorra—testifies. When the Socialists came to power in Spain in 1982, they created generous development aid programs for Latin America. The EEC/EU provided the framework to further strengthen the relations; in fact, the EEC policies in Latin America were created thanks to Spanish and Portuguese efforts, and the tireless work of two Spanish EEC commissioners, Abel Matutes and Manuel Marín. Spain spearheaded the EU's new Latin American policy by promoting peace, democracy, and regional economic and political integration, in particular in Central America, a region riddled with internal conflict. The Spanish military also participated in an array of peacemaking and peacekeeping missions in Central America. While the U.S. government was skeptical about this novel European involvement, in time Washington welcomed the support in areas where U.S. influence was lagging. For instance, Spain was the main actor in promoting the Dominican Republic's accession to the African, Caribbean, and Pacific Group of States (ACP). As a result, the Dominican Republic has received an impressive volume of development aid from the EU. Another interesting case is Spain's relationship with its former colony Cuba: Spain has led the EU to important diplomatic overtures toward the Castro regime. In addition, Spain led the opposition against the United States' Helms-Burton Act.

The new actor in the continent, however, is Russia, keen to make economic deals with Latin America, starting with its forgiveness of the Soviet-era debt. The Kremlin in planning to build GLONASS navigation stations in the region, possibly in Nicaragua, Cuba, or Brazil. Russia also is ready to become a security guard to "protect against possible provocations," presumably by the United States, at a Chinese-led project to build a canal between the Pacific and the Atlantic across Nicaragua. However, it is Argentina that Moscow sees as an especially promising partner. In contrast to the Chinese expansion to Latin America, which is concerned almost entirely with economics, Russia's engagement is increasingly intertwined with its geopolitical agenda.

Africa

The United States has only relative interest in Africa as compared to the Europeans, who preserve strong ties because of the colonial past (France and the United Kingdom), geographic proximity (Spain), or economic and political interest (USSR/Russia).

France's engagement with French-speaking African countries is both of an economic and military kind, in a way that is very different from the rest of Europe and more like U.S. engagement. After a failed attempt to create a Franco-African Community, France quickly had to recognize its former colonies as independent states. In 1960–63 two sets of military treaties with the new states were signed, with France pledging to "protect" the former colonies' territorial integrity and political independence, while training and equipping their armies. The African franc was pegged to the French franc, and France remained the main trading partner for its former colonies, which also gained preferential access to the EEC market. Finally, France provided generous development aid to Francophone Africa, funding infrastructure development and sending teachers, doctors, and engineers to work there. In 1973, Georges Pompidou held the first Franco-African summit in Paris; France also remained the biggest donor of development aid to its former colonies, but much of it was spent on public sector contracts awarded to French companies. In 1975, Giscard d'Estaing hosted the Conference on International Economic Cooperation, which resulted in an agreement between the EEC and the countries of sub-Saharan Africa on the price of raw materials. In the aftermath of the Angolan revolution (1975), Giscard sponsored military interventions in Mauritania (1977), Chad (1978, 1980), and Zaire (1978) to keep in power anticommunist governments in the one theater of the Cold War where France continued to actively contest Soviet influence. François Mitterrand increased economic aid for Africa, but he continued his predecessors' policy of supporting anticommunist dictatorships, intervening twice (in 1983 and 1986) in Chad against Libya. In Rwanda, Hutu militias killed 800,000 Tutsis while French diplomats and military advisers stood by or even encouraged the massacres. In 1997, France intervened in the civil war in Congo-Brazzaville. Nicolas Sarkozy renegotiated the defense treaties with the former colonies and closed the French military bases in Senegal and the Ivory Coast. Nevertheless, he continued to support authoritarian leaders in countries that were strategically or economically important for France, such as Chad. François Hollande's main legacy is also France's use of military force: As Islamist terrorism spread to Central Africa, Hollande launched military interventions in the Central African Republic, Mali, and the entire Sahel region of Burkina Faso, Chad, Mali, Mauritania, and Niger.

During the Cold War, France's main rival in Africa was the USSR. Although the USSR/Russia never had African colonies, it has had a long history of interactions with the continent. Today, Russia's interest in Africa lies primarily in the continent's economic potential. It is rich in natural resources, and its population of over 1 billion can serve as a market for Russian goods and services. Russian and African approaches to international affairs are devoid of any antagonism: in fact, on many issues their positions are fairly close. Despite this favorable background, so far Africa has not been considered a priority for Russian foreign policy. However, its status might rapidly change if the Kremlin's relations with the West deteriorate further. President Putin has already shown a renewed interest in the continent, especially as far as the northern shores of the Mediterranean and South Africa are concerned. South Africa's inclusion in BRICS became a stimulus for strengthening the African vector. Moscow's return to Africa is also a response to the Chinese growing presence in the continent. Although Russia is not able to compete with China in exporting cheap goods, it also maintains an important position as an arms exporter to the continent.

Spain is the only European country almost sharing a border with Africa. Spain therefore has an interest in the Sahel region, with its only former colony, Equatorial Guinea, and maintains close relations with countries like Senegal, Mauritania, and Mali to control illegal immigration to the Canary Islands.

Transatlantic Relations

The relations between Washington and the European capitals have been fluctuating over time.

The German Fundamental Law was inspired by the United States, which at the time occupied part of the country. Today, the most important factor that needs to be understood in German-U.S. relations is the large extent to which they are multilateralized. In defense matters, Germany's membership in NATO dictates large parts of the relationship between the U.S. and German militaries. In trade relations, Germany is part of the EU's common trade policy. For Germany, multilateralism is raison d'état. The Trump Doctrine, which stipulates the exact opposite approach—that is, every country is on its own and has to see after its own interests first—came as a shock to Germany. In the past years, three topics have dominated the agenda in relations between Berlin and Washington: the European currency and economic crisis; Germany's role as a provider of military security in the NATO framework; and the project of a Transatlantic Free Trade Agreement (TAFTA). Germany's centrality in the euro crisis has made Germany America's most important partner in Europe, a role once reserved for the United Kingdom, though the positions of the German and U.S. teams differed significantly on how to best deal with the crisis. Even more profound, and more geopolitically relevant, are lingering rifts between Washington and Germany on Berlin's contribution in the military sector. American criticism was strong when German seemed to be uninterested in developing a new Strategic Concept for the North Atlantic Alliance. Later on, Washington was shocked when Germany abstained in the UN Security Council vote authorizing a military mission in Libya. President Trump has made the issue of 2 percent defense spending in NATO a central speaking point, on occasion singling out Germany as a free-rider. On trade, however, the image is reversed. Here it is the United States, under Trump, that blocks progress. Germany, like other European countries, had been a staunch supporter of the Transatlantic Trade and Investment Partnership (TTIP), formerly known as TAFTA.

Relations with France have historically been rockier. De Gaulle's complicated relationship with the United States was rooted in his view of France exceptionalism. He first supported French membership in NATO as the best way of containing the expansion of Russian influence. He quickly concluded, however, that NATO's military protection came at the price of subordinating European foreign and defense policy to the United States. He first withdrew from NATO's Mediterranean command and Atlantic fleet; then he asked the United States to remove its tactical nuclear weapons from France and turned down a request to increase American troops in France; finally, in 1966, he withdrew France from all of NATO's integrated commands (but not the political organization) and asked U.S. troops to leave France. De Gaulle's successors during the Cold War adopted a more conciliatory approach toward the United States, but they continued to pursue an independent foreign and defense policy. Georges Pompidou insisted that Europe must be able to defend itself, instead of relying on American protection. Giscard d'Estaing increased military spending and made French conventional troops available for "forward defense" of Germany against a possible Soviet attack. It was France's first socialist president, François Mitterrand, who significantly improved relations with the United States, welcoming Ronald Reagan's decision to place Pershing II and Cruise intermediate-range ballistic missiles in Germany and starting secret negotiations for reintegrating France into NATO's military command. With the fall of the Berlin Wall, Mitterrand was among the few to realize that the Old Continent would become strategically less relevant for the United States, and worked tirelessly to reinforce the European Communities, transforming them into the European Union (1992). Jacques Chirac worked with President Bill Clinton on the Dayton peace agreement on Bosnia (1995) and in 1999, France participated in NATO's military intervention in Kosovo. Chirac also supported the expansion of the EU and NATO to Eastern Europe and, in response to 9/11, sent French troops to Afghanistan as part of a broader NATO mission (2001). However, the Chirac vigorously opposed the U.S.-led invasion of Iraq (2003), defining it a violation of international law. Compared with Mitterrand and Chirac, Nicolas Sarkozy and François Hollande followed a more consistently pro-American foreign policy. France formally rejoined NATO's integrated command (2009) and took the lead in NATO's bombing campaign against Libya (2011). Sarkozy supported the 2008 Bucharest declaration, promising Ukraine that it would become a member of NATO, and the EU Association Agreement with Ukraine in 2012. Hollande, who criticized Sarkozy's hyperactive foreign policy as a candidate, launched more interventions abroad than any other French president since the end of the Cold War. With U.S. technical and logistical support, he sent troops to battle Islamist insurgencies in Mali (2013), the Central African Republic (2013), and the Sahel region (2015). He also participated in the U.S.-led air strikes against ISIS positions in Iraq and Syria and (unsuccessfully) lobbied the United States for a military intervention against the government of Bashar al-Assad of Syria. In fact, French counterterrorism operations in its former colonies in Central Africa depend on intelligence, logistical assistance, and weapons provided by the United States, while French support is of limited significance for U.S. operations in the Middle East.

At the time of the signature of the North Atlantic Treaty, most Italian political parties were opposed to it: not only the Communist and Socialist parties, but even the left fringes of the Christian Democrats. The first covered operation aimed at influencing a foreign country's election was the CIA operation to influence the 1947 Italian parliamentary and prevent a victory of the Communists and their Socialist allies. Since then, transatlantic relations and subordination to the United States have remained pillars of Italian foreign policy, though not without tensions. Italy's Middle East and energy policies have been frequent thorns, especially since the 1970s. It peaked in 1985 with the Sigonella crises, when the Italian army prevented the U.S. Navy Seals—who entered the small Italian island illegally—from seizing the plane transporting the *Achille Lauro* cruise ship's hijackers. In the late 1990s, Rome opened to Libya, North Korea, and Iran—which in addition to the Ocalan affair and the Cermis incident, the negotiations in Rambouillet over Serbia, and Italy's withdrawal from Iraq, further led Italy and the United States apart. In contrast, Silvio Berlusconi's close relationship with George W. Bush led to tensions with EU institutions and partners. The Obama administration played a role in bringing down the Berlusconi government; among Berlusconi's successors, Obama was said to be particularly fond of Enrico Letta and then Matteo Renzi. Renzi in turn idolized the forty-fourth American president and, eager to prove himself, committed to pro-U.S. policies without prior parliamentary scrutiny. The purchase of the F-24 fighter-bombers and Italy's support in Iraq are cases in point.

Opposite to Italy, the United Kingdom entered the Cold War as a winner. The United States, however, had no intention of sharing its global leadership role with the British. The United Kingdom was only consulted and cooperation only occurred when Washington believed this was in its interests. The United States had a much less romantic and a much more hard-nosed approach than the British to the "special relationship." Washington was pivotal in convincing London to join the EEC, arguing that if Britain were to become a full member of the European Community, this would increase rather than weaken Britain's role in world affairs, as well as its importance for the United States. Britain's 1982 victory in the Falklands War and the ensuing wave of British nationalism ensured Margaret Thatcher's reelection in a landslide victory in 1983. However, without U.S. satellite information about the whereabouts of Argentinian naval forces, victory would likely have been impossible. When Reagan began negotiations with the new and progressive Soviet leader Mikhail Gorbachev in 1985, the British were hardly consulted. By late 2002, Tony Blair refocused his foreign policy on the "special relationship" with the United States, so much that the United Kingdom joined Bush's war on terror, creating a wedge with the EU. David Cameron's misguided interpretation of the "special relationship" was one of the many reasons leading to Brexit, while in fact the Obama administration vehemently lobbied against it.

Transatlantic ties are a pillar of Danish foreign policy, too. Neutrality was shed in return for membership in NATO in 1949 and for a "mini" special relationship with the United States based on U.S. overflight rights and access to bases in Greenland, which were especially vital during the Cold War. Transatlantic ties have been strong since then, particularly since Denmark has demonstrated a consistent willingness to contribute to international challenges in the post–Cold War era. Denmark strongly supported the UN-authorized intervention in Afghanistan and early on supplied both troops and development assistance. Before that and for several years, Denmark had over 700 battle troops on the ground in the difficult Afghan province of Helmand. The U.S. invasion of Iraq in 2003 was more divisive in Denmark, as it was across Europe. The Danish government ultimately decided to join the Americans in Iraq and maintained soldiers in the country until 2007. Danish soldiers were back in Iraq in 2014, in a new role as trainers for the Iraqi army, a testimony to Denmark's strong transatlantic ties. When an unexpected opening arose to eliminate Syrian chemical weapons, Denmark provided a ship to transport chemical components out of Syria. In 2016, Denmark was again the maritime lead with a transport ship on a U.S.-supported mission to remove and destroy Libya's remaining chemical stockpile.

Spain's relations with the United States offer a contrast between contemporary diplomatic declarations and the historical record. While officials consistently claim that the two countries have been steady allies since U.S. independence, the historical evidence shows that Spain and the United States often took different sides, remained distanced from and indifferent to each other, and, at times, went to war with each other. During the first years of the Spanish political transition to democracy, there was no unanimous backing for Spain's accession to NATO. In 1981, the PSOE (Partido Socialista Obrero Español), otherwise known as the Socialist Workers' Party, organized an aggressive campaign against joining NATO. However, once Felipe González became prime minister, he had second thoughts and eventually advocated for limited NATO membership, which was eventually confirmed by popular vote. After Gonzales, the conservative leader, Jose María Aznar, opted to follow Bush's agenda, based on hard power. The Aznar period was an exception in recent Spanish history. The terrorist attacks in Madrid, on March 11, 2004, were a retaliation by al Qaeda for the intervention of Spanish armed forces in Iraq and the close relationship between Aznar and Bush, leading to the unexpected election of the young socialist leader José Luis Rodríguez Zapatero. His foreign policy strategy was composed of innovative measures and decisions, among them the design of the Alliance of Civilizations, in contrast with Bush's war on terror. The government announced an increase in Spain's foreign aid to reach the 0.7 percent of GDP set in the UN Millennium Development Goals. Zapatero joined the Conservative–Social Democratic alliance formed by France and Germany, in contrast to Aznar, who linked Spain with the United States and the United Kingdom. On top of that, a new defense policy favored a European security arrangement, downsizing defense links with NATO and the United States.

Diametrically opposed is the situation of Poland. As a reaction to its communist past, Poland turned to its defense cooperation with the United States, in which it has two main priorities: to improve transatlantic ties and to provide visible evidence of U.S. engagement and a U.S. presence on the ground. Preserving the traditional and core aim of the alliance—that is, collective defense—is in fact fundamental to Poland. Consequently, Poland strongly supports the accession to NATO of Moldova, the Western Balkans, and the South Caucasus. However, Poland's Atlanticism is also pragmatic, with Warsaw acknowledging that NATO must engage Russia on challenges such as Afghanistan, Iran, nonproliferation, and discussions about Conventional Forces in Europe (CFE).

The Czech Republic is, if possible, even more pro-Atlantic than Poland, with successive governments not hesitating to go against public opinion in supporting U.S. policies. In more recent years, Czech Atlanticism has become less vocal but remains largely unquestioned. A sustained American military presence in Europe has long been seen by Czech policymakers as the only way out of the geopolitical dilemma that placed the country between two powerful neighbors (Germany and Russia) and that, historically, often determined the fate of their country. Czech support for the U.S. campaign in Iraq, a region beyond its traditional zone of geopolitical interest, can be understood in these terms.

Finally, what is Moscow and Washington's take on each other? Russia-U.S. relations have been shaped as much as by stereotypes, misperceptions, distrust, and recriminations as by concrete interests. Famously Truman, after meeting with Stalin, said of the Russians, "They are only twenty-five years old. We are over a hundred,"[13] thereby ignoring centuries of Russian (imperial) history, which are a founding part of Russian self-perception. At the end of the Cold War, Russia worked with Washington on various delicate dossiers, including Iraq, German unification, Eastern Europe's new course, and the USSR's nuclear arsenal. The vision of President George H. W. Bush of a "new world order" was founded on a stable partnership with Moscow, which shared the aim of establishing a common security community stretching from Vancouver to Vladivostok. The events of 9/11 provided an extraordinary and unexpected opportunity for Russia to rebrand itself as a close ally of the United States in the fight against international terrorism. In 2002, the Russia-NATO Council was established with the aim of promoting cooperation among the parties on issues such as terrorism, military affairs, Afghanistan, industrial concerns, and nonproliferation. Nevertheless, the relationship stiffened with the U.S. intervention in Iraq (2003) and U.S. support of the Color revolutions in the post-Soviet space. George W. Bush's proposal to extend NATO membership action plans to Georgia and Ukraine (which was blocked by France and Germany) and to build missile defense installations in Eastern Europe (which was later shelved by the Obama administration), turned the relationship into an overt confrontation. But it was the five-day Russia-Georgia war in August 2008 that brought relations between the Kremlin and Washington to their lowest point since the dark days of the Cold War.

The election of Barack Obama marked a new cooperative phase. Among the positive outcomes of the reset policy were the New START (Strategic

Arms Reduction Treaty); the reduction by half of the number of strategic nuclear missile launchers, and a new inspection and verification regime; NATO-Russia dialogue on antiballistic missile defense; the Russian president's participation in the NATO Lisbon summit in 2010; and creation of the U.S.-Russia Bilateral Presidential Commission. The new friendly climate was, however, very soon replaced by another wave of mistrust and conflict. Putin's highly contested reelection (2012), the row over the missile defense system in Europe, the approval of the Magnitsky Act, NATO's military intervention in Libya, and divergent approaches to the situation in Syria became the stumbling blocks that triggered and revealed the exhaustion of the reset policy. However, Russia presents no immediate threat to American interests. Rather, it is a potential useful partner for various U.S. policy initiatives, from nuclear nonproliferation to stabilizing Central Asia. The reality of the Russian-American relationship is a far cry from that of the Cold War years. Russia was pivotal in the Iran deal and collaborated with NATO on Afghanistan. On the other side, the Syrian Civil War, North Korea, the Russian annexation of Crimea, and the U.S. missile shield program in Europe are a few examples of the many issues that have inflamed relations between Moscow and Washington. Yet the Trump administration's apparent keenness to move beyond the Cold War mindset was voided by the reports of Russian meddling in U.S. elections, leaving the question of the future of the U.S.-Russia relationship wide open and uncertain.

Conclusions

What does all this say about the state of transatlantic relations, and their future perspective? Are the transatlantic partners going to go separate ways, or is there still hope? The answer is to be found in the determinants of the various transatlantic partners' foreign policies. Our comparative analysis shows that three main variables determine European foreign policy: geographic proximity, leadership, and, most of all, historical legacy.

Examples of the importance of geographic proximity include Italy's interest in the Balkans and the Middle East, or Spain's engagement with the Northern African states. Denmark's condition as a small state surrounded by big, powerful former enemies explains its staunch support for international norms and cooperation with international institutions, including strong transatlantic ties through NATO and membership in the

European Union. Another example is Warsaw's reassessment of its relations with countries that were once considered hostile, such as Germany and Russia, and its emphasis on its role as a bridge between East and West.

As for leadership, there are political leaders who left an indelible mark on their countries' foreign policies—for the good or for the bad: Charles de Gaulle's imprint, which still dominates France's contemporary foreign policy; Mikhail Gorbachev's reassessment of relations with the West; Vladimir Putin's assertiveness; Margaret Thatcher's decision to attack Argentina, or her fight with the EEC; David Cameron's decision to hold the Brexit referendum; and Felipe Gonzales's U-turn on NATO are all cases in point.

However, the main variable determining foreign policy decisions in Europe is historical legacy. Germany's reliance on economic power as a tool of foreign policy while overlooking its military aspects is a direct consequence of Germany's role in World War II. In similar ways, Italy's fascist legacy led to the negation of the "national interest," replaced with an undefined "European interest." At the same time, Italy's glorious Roman imperial past makes people believe Rome's role is greater and more universal than it really is. For the United Kingdom, France, and Spain, the historical legacy mostly comes from their colonial pasts. To date, British foreign policymakers continue to view the United Kingdom as a major international power; even Brexit—possibly the major mistake in modern British foreign policy—is in part due to such over-interpretation of reality. France has taken its colonial legacy to the extreme, with continued political, economic, and—most relevant—military interventions in Africa. Spain—allying with its former rival Portugal, thanks to common EU membership—has instead used cooperation to development to continue to exert influence in its former colonies in Latin America. Historical factors—primarily the straw of lost wars—shape Denmark's current perceptions and foreign policy outlook, while Central European countries, formerly embedded in successive empires, whether Habsburg or Soviet, reacted by anchoring into the EU and NATO.

Russia is no different from the other European countries when it comes to the influence of history, geography, and leadership on its foreign policy. The very identity of Russia has been forged by the country's capacity to spread out and conquer new territories; thus, contemporary Russian foreign policy is determined by both history (Russia's self-image as a great power) and the sense of frustration that the country felt after the implosion of the Soviet system, which was accompanied by a deep economic slump. Once

Putin's Russia returned to its place among the great powers, thanks to its energy revenues, its priority has been to consolidate its international role and expand its influence in strategic areas. The Kremlin is strengthening its leverage by widening its network of partners and creating new organizations, with the intent to carry more weight in all venues that have a significant impact on the international system.

On the contrary, the importance of history—and to a lesser extent of geography—is hard to conceptualize in the United States. The United States' main variables in foreign policy are in fact leadership and ideology. The early United States used its geographic remoteness to stay out of Europe's troubles; then with the Monroe Doctrine and its Corollary, it self-attributed a right to interfere in the domestic policies of its Latin American "neighbors." George Washington, Teddy Roosevelt, and Woodrow Wilson left a permanent mark on American foreign policy, so indelible that even the most charismatic or active presidents who followed have always used different blends and conjugations of the doctrines elaborated by these predecessors. The ideas of American moral superiority, America's greatness, and its right/duty to intervene globally are so entrenched in U.S. society and policymaking that they can be rightly defined as ideologies.

The United States emerged from the Cold War victorious, prosperous, and confident. The collapse of the Soviet Union was interpreted as proof of the superiority of liberal capitalism over totalitarian socialism and as an effective military victory, an interpretation of events that is not shared by the rest of the world. The United States was "bound to lead," Joseph Nye concluded. 9/11 and George W. Bush's decisions to essentially act unilaterally, however, alienated most of America's allies, in a way that is not yet properly understood in Washington. The war in Iraq created a multitude of long-term problems that still linger on. For all the unrealistically high expectations surrounding Barack Obama's election, matters remained the same: Obama's foreign policy can be regarded as a mixture of the Clinton administration's emphasis on multilateral engagement and democratic enlargement and the Bush Doctrine's assertions about the American need to reserve for itself the right to take unilateral military action, or a mix of Wilson's moral superiority and Roosevelt's right/duty to intervene. Notwithstanding the proliferation of 140- or 280-character messages, Donald Trump's foreign policy has not fundamentally transformed U.S. relations with the rest of the world. Continuity, not change, remains the fundamental characteristic of American foreign policy, coupled with a fundamental misunderstanding about the rest of the world's cultures, priorities, and legacies.

As the United States is looking inward, distracted by the sagas surrounding the Trump presidency, the world—and Europe within it—is, however, moving on, as this book shows. Russia is regaining a major role in world affairs, and for all the reprimands and the sanctions, the historical, geographic, and economic ties between Moscow and Europe—hereby including the countries that were once subjugated to it—will not be severed. On the contrary, countries like Austria are moving closer to Russia, well symbolized by Vladimir Putin waltzing with the newlywed Austrian foreign minister, Karin Meilinger-Kneissl.

Europe is finally realizing that most U.S. policies toward the Old Continent have been, and will continue to be, essentially self-serving. On the other side, as shown throughout this volume, the individual member states have been successfully able to use the European Union (and previously the EEC) to move forward their individual foreign policy goals. These factors, together with the realization that Europe might soon be on its own, provided the EU with an opportunity to do more. The decision to create PESCO in December 2017, which has gone largely unnoticed in Washington, is the most important case in point. It is also particularly significant since, as shown in this book, the United States had previously meddled—directly or indirectly—with any attempt to unify the EU's foreign and defense policies. PESCO will be a fundamental driver for integration in the field of defense, and for the European defense industry, by providing enhanced coordination and collaboration in the areas of investment, capability development, and operational readiness. Massive European financial investments and European-wide procurement procedures will benefit the European military industry and challenge the American one. As PESCO will help reinforce the EU's strategic autonomy to act alone, for the first time in seventy years the possibility of NATO subordination to the EU, rather than the contrary, is an eventual prospect, which would in turn lead to the end of transatlantic relations as we know them.

And yet, though the last twenty years of useless wars have dramatically decreased the moral capital the United States had accumulated in the twentieth century, the Europeans—with their history-based foreign policy—are still deeply thankful to those young soldiers who offered their lives to save them from Hitler. They are grateful for the inclusion of NATO—before the EU—after the end of communism. The past is often romanticized, and Europe is no exception. With a little Hollywood help, and against all evidence, Europeans are still faithful that the United States will go back to business as usual after twitterplomacy. Let's hope they are right, and not just delusional.

NOTES

1. George Washington's Farewell Address (1796), in P. B. Viotti, *American Foreign Policy and National Security: A Documentary Record* (Upper Saddle River, N.J.: Pearson Prentice Hall, 2005), pp. 151–52.

2. Viotti, *American Foreign Policy and National Security*, pp. 157–61.

3. H. Kissinger, *Diplomacy* (New York: Simon & Schuster, 1994), pp. 38–39.

4. Ibid., pp. 45–47.

5. Ibid., p. 49.

6. M. Mastanduno, "Preserving the Unipolar Moment: Realist Theories and U.S. Grand Strategy after the Cold War," *International Security* 21, no. 4 (April 1997), pp. 49–88.

7. K. W. Stiles, *Case Histories in International Politics*, 5th ed. (New York: Person Longman, 2008), p. 55.

8. Mastaduno, *Preserving the Unipolar World*.

9. Stiles, *Case Histories in International Politics*, p. 55.

10. Viotti, *American Foreign Policy and National Security*, pp. 244–49.

11. Stiles, *Case Histories in International Politics*, pp. 54–55.

12. Ibid., pp. 57–58.

13. Kissinger, *Diplomacy*, p. 426.

Contributors

FEDERIGA BINDI   Tor Vergata and the School of Advanced International Studies, Johns Hopkins University

DAVID CADIER   Sciences Po and LSE IDEAS

MICHELA CECCORULLI   University of Bologna

SERENA GIUSTI   Sant'Anna School of Advanced Studies and Italian Institute for International Political Studies

JUSSI M. HANHIMÄKI   Graduate Institute of International and Development Studies, Geneva

KLAUS LARRES   University of North Carolina at Chapel Hill

ALEKSANDER LUST   Appalachian State University

JONAS PARELLO-PLESNER   Hudson Institute

JOAQUÍN ROY   University of Miami

JAN TECHAU   German Marshall Fund, Berlin

Index

Abdelaziz, Ould, 54
Acheson, Dean, 5, 109
ACP. *See* African, Caribbean, and
 Pacific Group of States
Adenauer, Konrad, 45
Afghanistan, 16, 22, 39; AfPak, 255;
 Denmark in, 186; Germany in, 83;
 Spain and, 147; United States
 invading, 101, 244; United States
 withdrawing from, 254–55
Africa: Chirac policy, 54; de Gaulle
 on independent states, 51; France
 in, 51–55, 286–87; Giscard
 d'Estaing on, 53; Russia and,
 232, 287; Sarkozy on, 54; Spain
 and, 287–88
African, Caribbean, and Pacific
 Group of States (ACP), 145, 285
Albright, Madeleine, 18
Andreatta, Filippo, 99
Andreotti, Giulio, 95, 102
Apuntarse a todo agenda, 5–6, 137

Arab Spring, 8, 21, 24, 154, 229, 244;
 Germany and, 76; Sarkozy on, 58;
 as unresolved, 253–54
Arafat, Yasser, 56, 280
Arctic, 194, 195, 231
Aron, Leon, 231
ASEAN. *See* Association of Southeast
 Asian Nations
Ashton, Catherine, 22, 23
Al-Assad, Bashar, 41, 187, 201, 290
Association of Southeast Asian
 Nations (ASEAN), 147
Atlanticism: Brexit and, 213;
 Congenital Atlanticism, 6;
 Critical Atlanticism, 99; of Czech
 Republic, 6–7, 204–05, 213, 293;
 nationalism and, 100; of Poland,
 6, 167, 173, 205–06, 292; Russia
 and, 220
Atomausstieg, 85
Aznar, José María, 125–26, 145–46,
 153, 155, 281, 283

Babiš, Andrej, 204
Bachelet, Michelle, 145
Al-Baghdadi, Abu Bakr, 254
Balcerowicz, Leszek, 164
Ballistic Missile Defense (BMD), 7, 203, 205–08, 278
Baranovsky, Vladimir, 222
Barnier, Michel, 132
Berlin Wall, 46, 92–93, 95, 277, 289
Berlusconi, Silvio, 92, 125, 126, 282; Bush, G. W., and, 96, 100, 290; pro-American position of, 99–100; resignation of, 97
Bildt, Carl, 194
Bin Laden, Osama, 103, 244, 255
Blair, Tony, 9, 18, 47; Bush, G. W., and, 125; election of, 119; EU and, 126; European policy of, 122–27; foreign policy principles, 120–22; Iraq War and, 120, 125; NATO and, 120–21
BMS. See Ballistic Missile Defense
Bolivarian Alliance for the Americas, 145
Bongo, Omar, 54
Bossuat, Gérard, 35
Bozo, Frédéric, 34, 57
Brazil, Russia, India, China, South Africa (BRICS), 7, 190, 230–33, 260–61, 284, 287
Brexit, 109; Atlanticism and, 213; Cameron and, 130, 295; France and, 272; May and, 130–32; U.K. foreign policy and, 5, 26, 127–32, 184, 256, 258, 273, 295; United States and, 291
Brezhnev, Leonid, 39
BRICS. See Brazil, Russia, India, China, South Africa
Brown, Gordon, 21, 119, 123, 126
Brzezinski, Zbigniew, 253
Bush, George H. W., 40, 117

Bush, George W., 57, 120, 203, 275; Aznar and, 153; Berlusconi and, 96, 100, 290; Blair and, 125; BMD system of, 7; as bully, 242–43; doctrine of, 241, 296; election of, 19; on exporting democracy, 21; hard power and, 155, 292; Iraq War and, 11; new world order of, 227, 293; nightmare years of, 257. See also War on terror

Callaghan, James, 115
Cameron, David, 127–28, 129, 130, 291, 295
Campbell, Kurt, 253
Camp David Peace talks, 15, 102
CAP. See Common Agricultural Policy
CECs. See Central European countries
Central and Eastern European countries (CEECs), 6, 17–18, 164, 276
Central European countries (CECs), 162, 173
Central Intelligence Agency (CIA), 98, 290
Cermis incident, 99, 290
CFSP. See Common Foreign and Security Policy
Chafer, Tony, 53
Chávez, Hugo, 145
Cheney, Dick, 271
China: Denmark relations with, 191–92, 285; ECFR on, 82; Germany special relationship with, 81–83, 284; Merkel visiting, 81–82; Poland and, 173; Spain and, 147; trade war with, 8; Trump in, 251–52; United Kingdom returning Hong Kong to, 111; U.S. relations with, 250–53

Chirac, Jacques, 18, 20, 39, 40–41, 289; Africa policy, 54; Hussein and, 56; on international law, 57; on multilateralism, 57, 280; Saint-Malo Agreement and, 47, 123, 124; Treaty of Lisbon and, 47; War on terror and, 57–58

Christian Democrats, 94, 96, 98, 290

Churchill, Winston, 127

CIA. See Central Intelligence Agency

CIS. See Community of Independent States

Civic Democratic Party (ODS), 204, 208–10

Clegg, Nick, 127

Clinton, Bill, 8, 18, 40, 242, 245, 271, 289

Clinton, Hillary, 22, 104, 246

Cogan, Charles, 34

Cohen, Stephen, 247

Cohesion Policy, 164, 165

Cold War: de Gaulle during, 36–37; Denmark during, 182; EU at end of, 16–19; Germany during, 84; Italy during, 91, 100–101, 282; return of, 247; Soviet Union during, 276; Thatcher during, 115–18; United Kingdom during, 110–18, 290–91; USSR dominance in, 2

Color revolutions, 223, 227, 274, 293

Common Agricultural Policy (CAP), 43–45

Common Foreign and Security Policy (CFSP), 17, 19, 20, 70, 72, 211

Common Security and Defense Policy (CSDP), 7, 70, 274

Community of Independent States (CIS), 221

Compaoré, Blaise, 55

Conference on Security and Cooperation in Europe (CSCE), 163

Congenital Atlanticism, 6

Cook, Robin, 121

Cooper, Marianne, 26

Corbyn, Jeremy, 131

Council of Europe, 5, 94, 99, 101, 138, 185

Cox, Michael, 242

Crimea: Hollande and, 277; Russia annexing, 6, 74, 101, 128, 174, 193, 209, 226, 234, 275–77

CSCE. See Conference on Security and Cooperation in Europe

CSDP. See Common Security and Defense Policy

ČSSD. See Czech Social Democratic Party

Cuba, 200, 270; Cuban Missile Crisis of 1962, 113

Czech Republic: Atlanticism of, 6–7, 204–05, 213, 293; conclusion, 212–13; Cuba and, 200; in EU, 202, 213, 274; EU foreign policy and, 210–12; foreign policy of, 200–205; in NATO, 202, 205, 208, 213, 278; overview, 199–201; Russia relations with, 208–10; Syria and, 201; U.S. relations with, 205–08

Czech Social Democratic Party (ČSSD), 204, 206, 207, 209–10

Dalai Lama, 191–92

D'Alema, Massimo, 92, 99, 100

Dassù, Marta, 93

Davis, David, 131, 132

Dayton peace agreement, 40, 289

Déby, Idriss, 54, 55

Declaration on European Identity, 15

Defense: BMD, 7, 203, 205–08, 278;
CSDP, 7, 70, 274; EDA, 20, 167;
EDC, 13–14, 272; ESDI, 18–19;
ESDP, 19, 123, 166, 274; Germany
and, 83–85; IRBMs, 39–40;
military cooperation with Spain,
148–49; PESCO and, 26, 297;
Star Wars program, 40
De Gasperi, Alcide, 94, 98–99
De Gaulle, Charles, 272, 277, 289; on
African independent states, 51;
during Cold War, 36–37; colonial
empire and, 49–50; EU and, 35,
43; Europe of states and, 44, 59;
FLN negotiations by, 50–51;
Germany and, 45, 59; imprint of,
295; Israel and, 55; jealousy by,
113; legacy of, 31–36; national
sovereignty and, 34–35; NATO
and, 37–38, 58; nuclear program
as priority, 37; orchestrating
overthrows, 52
Delors Plan of 1989, 117
Deng Xiaoping, 250
Denmark: in Afghanistan, 186;
Arctic boundary of, 194, 195;
China relations with, 191–92, 285;
during Cold War, 182; conclusion,
194–95; in EC, 183; ECFR on,
192; EEC/EU and, 273; EU and,
183–85; euro and, 183–84; foreign
policy of, 185–94; green and
efficient energy in, 189–91; as
historically diminished power,
181–82; India relations with, 192;
international cooperation of,
182–83; international governance
and, 190–91; Iraq War and, 186;
ISIS and, 181; *Jyllands-Posten*
cartoons, 187–89, 283; in NATO,
13, 183, 291; Obama on, 5, 180;
overview, 179–81; relations with

emerging powers, 191–93; Russia
relations with, 192–93, 195, 277;
soft power in, 183; Syria and, 187;
terrorism in, 188–89; U.S. special
relationship with, 182, 291
De Villepin, Dominique, 57
Diori, Hamani, 53
Dossetti, Giuseppe, 99
Draft Treaty, 96

EAEU. *See* Eurasian Economic
Union
Eastern Partnership (EaP), 6, 170,
211, 223–24, 274
EC. *See* European Community
ECFR. *See* European Council on
Foreign Relations
ECSC. *See* European Coal and Steel
Community
EDA. *See* European Defense Agency
EDC. *See* European Defense
Community
Eden, Anthony, 14
EEAS. *See* European External
Action Service
EEC. *See* European Economic
Community
EEC/EU. *See* European Economic
Community/European Union
EED. *See* European Endowment for
Democracy
Eisenhower, Dwight D., 112, 143
EMS. *See* European Monetary
System
Energy: Denmark as green and
efficient, 189–91; Germany and,
85–86; Global Green Growth
Forum, 189; IAEA, 23–24; pricing
by Putin, 226; Russia losing
leverage, 229–30
ENP. *See* European Neighbourhood
Policy

EP. *See* European Parliament
EPAA. *See* European Phased Adaptive Approach
EPC. *See* European Political Cooperation
Erasmus generation, 97
ERRF. *See* European Reaction Force
ESDI. *See* European security and defense identity
ESDP. *See* European Security and Defense Policy
Eshkol, Levi, 55
ESS. *See* European Security Strategy
ETA. *See* Euskadi Ta Askatasuna
EU. *See* European Union
EU-3, 23
EU High Representative (EUHR), 22, 272
Eurasian Economic Union (EAEU), 230
Eurasianism, 221
Euro: creation of, 47, 95; Denmark and, 183–84; fate of, 258; France and, 48; Germany and, 69, 71–72, 79, 288; Spain and, 150; United Kingdom and, 123–24, 126
European Coal and Steel Community (ECSC), 43; creation of, 13, 112; Czech Republic and foreign policy, 210–12; France and, 94; Italy joining, 94; United Kingdom and, 113, 272–73. *See also* Schuman Declaration
European Commission, 43; Poland and, 162–63; regulating workers, 49; role of, 16–17
European Community (EC): Denmark in, 183; PCAs and, 222; Spain acceding to, 5–6, 138, 142; United Kingdom and, 114, 116–17
European Council on Foreign Relations (ECFR), 171, 210, 225;

on China, 82; on Denmark, 192; first formal meeting of, 46; Helsinki meeting, December 1999, 19; Milan meeting, June 1985, 95; Obama and, 86; role defined, 16; at Thessaloniki Summit, December 2003, 19–20
European Defense Agency (EDA), 20, 167
European Defense Community (EDC), 13–14, 272
European Economic Community (EEC), 112; Declaration on European Identity of, 15; development policy of, 14; France and, 33, 35; Greece joining, 46; revision of, 95; Russia and, 274; Spain joining, 273; Thatcher and, 295; trade agreements, 17; Treaty of Rome and, 43, 94; United Kingdom and, 44–45, 113; U.S. relations with, 14–16
European Economic Community/ European Union (EEC/EU): Denmark and, 273; as foreign policy actor, 2; France and, 272; Latin America and, 285–86; U.S. relations and, 275
European Endowment for Democracy (EED), 166
European Exchange Rate Mechanism, 118–19
European External Action Service (EEAS), 22, 25, 72, 155
European Monetary System (EMS), 95
European Neighbourhood Policy (ENP), 170, 211, 223–24, 274
European Parliament (EP), 46, 96, 203; powers of, 43; role of, 17
European Phased Adaptive Approach (EPAA), 168

European Political Cooperation (EPC), 16, 275
European Reaction Force (ERRF), 124
European security and defense identity (ESDI), 18–19
European Security and Defense Policy (ESDP), 19, 123, 166, 274
European Security Strategy (ESS), 19–20
European Union (EU): Blair and, 126; Cohesion Policy of, 164, 165; Constitutional Treaty of, 138; crises in, 14–16; CSDP of, 7; Czech Republic in, 202, 213, 274; de Gaulle and, 35, 43; Denmark and, 183–85; at end of Cold War, 16–19; eurozone and, 195; as foreign policy actor, 2; Germany and foreign policy, 70–73, 272; Hanover summit, 1988, 117; Italy foreign policy and, 94–98, 272; Lisbon Treaty and, 20–25; Maastricht Treaty and, 16–17; Mediterranean process founded by, 6; member relations in, 271–76; Mogherini and, 25–26; NATO and, 297–98; overview, 11–12; Poland and foreign policy, 165–67; Poland as member, 162–65, 273–74; Russia and, 221–25, 276–78; September 11, 2001, terrorist attacks and, 19–20; Spain in, 138, 140, 146, 156; transatlantic relations and, 11–13; U.S. relations with, 2
Europe of states, 44–49, 59
Eurozone, 72, 120, 165, 172, 195, 200, 230
Euskadi Ta Askatasuna (ETA), 139–40
Eyadema, Gnassingbé, 54

Fake news, 1, 246
FDI. *See* Foreign direct investment
FLN. *See* National Liberation Front
Flynn, Michael, 248
Foreign direct investment (FDI), 172
Foreign policy: of Blair, 120–22; Brexit and United Kingdom, 5, 26, 127–32, 184, 256, 258, 273, 295; of Czech Republic, 200–205; of Denmark, 185–94; EEC/EU as actor, 2; EU and Czech Republic, 210–12; EU and Germany, 70–73, 172; EU and Italy, 94–98, 272; EU and Mogherini, 25–26; EU and Poland, 165–67; Lisbon Treaty and EU, 20–25; multilateralism in Germany, 77–78, 288; of Obama, 296; Putin on, 226; September 11, 2001 terrorist attacks and EU, 19–20; September 11, 2001 terrorist attacks and United States, 19–20, 244; transatlantic relations and EU, 11–13; transatlantic relations and France, 36–43; transatlantic relations and Italy, 98–100; of Trump, 246, 296. *See also specific countries; specific topics*
Françafrique, 51–54
France: in Africa, 51–55, 286–87; in Arab world, 55–58; arms sales, 279; bombing ISIS, 58; Brexit and, 272; conclusion, 58–60; constitution of, 33–34; continuity and change in, 60; cooperating with Germany, 31–32; ECSC and, 94; EEC and, 33, 35; EEC/EU and, 272; EU and, 43–48; euro and, 48; eurozone and, 200; global role of, 49–51; historical legacy of, 4–5; legacy of de Gaulle, 31–36; Libya attack and, 104, 282; multiple governments of, 32–33; in NATO,

33, 289; nuclear program of, 37;
Oil for Food program, 56, 280;
overview, 31–32; PESCO approved
by, 272; Russia relations with, 277;
with Soviet Union, 38–39; Spain
relations with, 139–40; transatlantic
relations in, 36–43; UNSC member,
4–5, 36; U.S. special relationship
with, 59–60, 289
Franco, Francisco, 5, 13, 137
Friendship Treaty, 45, 104, 282

G-2, 251
G-7, 77, 92, 106, 259
G-8, 7, 42, 78, 92
G-20, 20–21, 78
Gaddis, John, 243
Gaiani, Massimo, 106
Gates, Robert, 19, 104, 257–58
GATT. See General Agreement on
Tariffs and Trade
Gazprom, 86, 172, 229
General Agreement on Tariffs and
Trade (GATT), 14, 271
Gentilini, Fernando, 106
Georgia: Russo-Georgian War, 6,
174, 201, 203, 209, 227; Sarkozy
negotiating with, 59, 171
Germany: in Afghanistan, 83; Arab
Spring and, 76; China special
relationship with, 81–83, 284;
during Cold War, 84; conclusion,
86–87; conditional solidarity of,
69; on defense, 83–85; de Gaulle
and, 45, 59; economic strength of,
69–70; energy and, 85–86; EU and
foreign policy, 70–73, 272; euro
and, 69, 71–72, 79, 288; eurozone
and, 72, 165, 200; France cooperating with, 31–32; German-Russian
gas flow, 86; global crisis management and, 81; as indispensable

nation, 67; on Libya, 83; in Middle
East, 75–77; missiles in, 39;
Mitterrand and, 59; multilateralism
in, 77–78, 288; NATO and, 3–4,
14, 70, 77, 78; overview, 67–70;
Poland relations with, 173–74;
reunification of, 16–17; Russia and,
73–75, 276; as servant leader, 87;
three plus three pillars approach,
3–4, 68, 81; unification of, 117;
U.S. relations with, 77–81, 288; as
Zivilmacht, 76
Ghani, Ashraf, 255
Gibraltar, 141
Giscard d'Estaing, Valéry, 280, 286,
289; Africa policy of, 53; economic
cooperation and, 46; election of,
39; on Palestinian homeland, 56
Global crisis management, 81
Global Green Growth Forum, 189
Global Navigational Satellite System
(GLONASS), 231
Global Strategy for the European
Union's Foreign and Security
Policy, 26
GLONASS. See Global Navigational
Satellite System
González, Felipe, 143, 148, 292, 295
Gorbachev, Mikhail, 169; German
unification and, 117; perestroika
of, 222; Reagan negotiations, 116
Great Depression, 245
Greece: economic crisis in, 69;
joining EEC, 46
Green March, 142
Gulf War of 1991, 17, 40, 56, 280
Gulf War of 2003, 57, 280

Haass, Richard, 260
Hallstein, Walter, 43
Hamilton, Daniel, 259
Hard power, 69, 147, 155, 244, 292

Hassan II, 142, 282
Havel, Václav, 201–03, 207
H-bomb, 111–12
Heath, Edward, 113, 122
Hedegaard, Connie, 189
Helms-Burton Act, 286
Heseltine, Michael, 118
Hollande, François, 47, 54–55, 58, 281, 287, 290; Crimea conflict and, 277; pro-American policies of, 289
Houghuët-Boigny, Félix, 51
Howe, Geoffrey, 118
Hoxha, Enver, 111
Hussein, Saddam, 19, 56, 57, 120, 126, 280

IAEA. *See* International Atomic Energy Agency
Iceland, 12, 13, 184
IGC. *See* Intergovernmental Conference
IMF. *See* International Monetary Fund
India, 21, 111, 127, 147, 192, 230
Intergovernmental Conference (IGC), 95
Intermediate-range ballistic missiles (IRBMs), 39–40
International Atomic Energy Agency (IAEA), 23–24
International Monetary Fund (IMF), 78, 115, 172
International Security Assistance Force (ISAF), 83, 149
Iran: hostage crisis of 1979, 15–16; nuclear agreement, 8, 246, 253–54, 272, 279; nuclear program, 22–24, 75, 258
Iraq War, 243, 253; Blair and, 120, 125; Bush, G. W., and, 11; Denmark and, 186; Spain and, 146; United States and end of, 254

IRBMs. *See* Intermediate-range ballistic missiles
Ireland, 114–15
ISAF. *See* International Security Assistance Force
Islamic State (ISIS), 281; Denmark and, 181; France bombing, 58; rise and decline of, 253; Russia and, 225; U.S. air strikes against, 41, 244, 246
Israel: de Gaulle and, 55; Israeli-Palestinian conflict, 253–54; Merkel and, 75, 77
Italy: in the Balkans, 105–06; borders of, 92–93; Christian Democrats and, 94, 96, 98, 290; CIA and, 98, 290; during Cold War, 91, 100–101, 282; conclusion, 106; EU and foreign policy, 94–98, 272; joining ECSC, 94; Libya and, 102, 103, 282; Lisbon Treaty and, 97; Maastricht Treaty and, 272; in Middle East, 101–04, 290; in NATO, 12, 105; Olive Tree coalition in, 96, 99; overview, 91–93; "Rapporto Italia 2020," 93; role in world affairs, 4; Roman imperial past of, 295; Russia and, 100–101, 276–77; in transatlantic relations, 98–100; U.S. special relationship with, 100

Japan as Number One (Vogel), 260
Jenkins, Roy, 113–14
Johnson, Boris, 130–31
Johnson, Lyndon, 38, 113
Jyllands-Posten cartoons, 187–89, 283

Kaczyński, Jaroslaw, 169, 277–78
Kaczyński, Lech, 169, 171
Kagame, Paul, 53

Kagan, Robert, 186
Kennedy, John F., 14, 37, 113
Kennedy, Paul, 242
Kerry, John, 22, 26
Kim Jong-un, 252
Kirchner, Néstor, 145
Kissinger, Henry, 15, 250–51, 256
Klaus, Václav, 201–04
Kohl, Helmut, 40, 46, 71, 95;
    Bush, G. H. W., and, 117; ousting
    of, 4, 68
Korean War, 13, 111
Kosovo War, 4, 84, 105, 124, 185
Kozyrev, Andrei, 222
Krastev, Ivan, 233
Krauthammer, Charles, 242
Kristol, William, 271
Kundera, Milan, 169
Kundnani, Hans, 82

Labour Party, 118–21, 126, 131
Latin America: EEC/EU and,
    285–86; Spain in, 144–46, 154
Law and Justice Party (PiS), 162,
    169
Leffler, Melvyn, 243
Le Pen, Marine, 48
Letta, Enrico, 97, 100, 290
Leveau, Rémy, 56
Libya: France attacking, 104, 282;
    Germany on, 83; immigration
    from, 103; Italy and, 102, 103, 282;
    NATO operation in, 22–25, 41, 80,
    257, 275, 279, 294; Obama and, 104;
    United Kingdom attacking, 129
Lisbon Treaty, 123, 209, 275; EU
    foreign policy and, 20–25; Italy
    and, 97; Obama and, 20–25
Loan, Rachel Lee, 41
Locher, Anna, 35
Luce, Edward, 240
Ludlow, Piers, 44

Maastricht Treaty, 46, 183, 275;
    chapters of, 123; EU created with,
    16–17; Italy and, 272; ratification
    of, 119; requirements of, 48,
    164–65
McCain, John, 248
Macmillan, Harold, 112–13, 193
Macron, Emmanuel, 42–43, 48–49,
    59, 184, 272
Magnitsky Act, 228, 247, 294
Major, John, 118–19, 124
Malaysian Airlines Flight MH17
    downing, 74, 276
Manafort, Paul, 248
Mankoff, Jeffrey, 221
Margrethe, Queen, 192–93
Marín, Manuel, 144, 285
Marshall Plan, 2, 94, 98
Martin, Garret, 35
Matutes, Abel, 144, 285
May, Theresa, 130–32, 273
Mba, Léon, 52
Mediterranean process, 6, 138
Medvedev, Dmitri, 233
Memoirs of Hope (de Gaulle), 37
Mendès-France, Pierre, 94
Merkel, Angela, 47, 279, 284; China
    visits by, 81–82; economics
    approach of, 79; Grand Coalition
    of, 73; Israel and, 75, 77; Merkel
    Doctrine, 76; negotiations by,
    41, 71; Putin and, 74; TTIP
    and, 80
Middle East, 278–83; Germany in,
    75–77; Italy in, 101–04, 290; Spain
    in, 146–47
Miliband, Ed, 128
Milošević, Slobodan, 40
Mitterrand, François, 39–40, 46–48,
    117, 287, 289; anticommunist
    dictatorships and, 53; Germany
    and, 59; power of, 95

Modernisierungspartnerschaft,
    73–74
Mogherini, Federica, 22, 25–26,
    97
Monnet, Jean, 13, 35, 43
Monroe Doctrine, 285, 296
Monti, Mario, 97
Morales, Evo, 145
Moravcsik, Andrew, 44
Morocco, 142
Morsi, Mohamed, 22, 128, 281
Moumi, Félix-Roland, 52
Multilateralism: Chirac on, 57, 280;
    Clinton, B., engagement, 8, 245;
    in Germany foreign policy, 77–78,
    288; Poland and, 171; Trump
    and, 78
Murdoch, Rupert, 130
Mussolini, Benito, 92, 105

NACC. *See* North Atlantic
    Cooperation Council
NAFTA, 271
Nasser, Gamal Abdel, 55, 112
Nationalism, 100, 156, 162, 220, 247,
    258, 291
National Liberation Front (FLN),
    33, 50–51
National Security Strategy (NSS), 241,
    243, 271
National sovereignty, 34–35
NATO. *See* North Atlantic Treaty
    Organization
Nenni, Pietro, 98
Neo-Keynesian economics, 79
Nester, William, 34
Netanyahu, Benjamin, 76–77, 254, 279
Nguesso, Denis Sassou, 54
Nixon, Richard, 15, 39, 249
Nolan, Mary, 256
Nord Stream 2 pipeline project,
    85–86, 276

North Atlantic Alliance, 12–14, 80,
    98, 288
North Atlantic Cooperation Council
    (NACC), 18, 59
North Atlantic Treaty Organization
    (NATO): Blair and, 120–21;
    Clinton, B., and, 18; Czech
    Republic in, 202, 205, 208, 213,
    278; de Gaulle and, 37–38, 58;
    Denmark as member, 13, 183, 291;
    dual-track policy, 68; ESDI
    endorsed by, 18–19; EU and,
    297–98; France in, 33, 289;
    Germany and, 3–4, 14, 70, 77, 78;
    Iceland as member, 13; ISAF, 83,
    149; Italy in, 12, 105; Libya
    operation, 2011, 22–25, 41, 80,
    257, 275, 279, 294; Poland in,
    163–65, 168–69; Portugal as
    member, 13; Russia and, 276;
    Spain in, 5, 13, 141–44, 147–49,
    282, 292; Syria strategy, 258;
    Trump and, 8, 42, 166, 240, 288;
    United Kingdom and, 110; Wales
    summit, 2014, 80
NSS. *See National Security Strategy*
Nuenlist, Christian, 35
Nye, Joseph, 183, 242, 296

Obama, Barack, 279, 281; America's
    priorities and, 8; cooperative
    phase of, 293–94; on Denmark, 5,
    180; doctrine of, 241; on eco-
    nomic recovery, 239–40; EPAA
    launched by, 168; European
    Council and, 86; foreign policy
    of, 296; German-Russian gas flow
    and, 86; Letta and, 100; letter to,
    206–07; Libya and, 104; Lisbon
    Treaty and, 20–25; neo-Keynesian
    economics and, 79; Nobel Prize
    to, 244, 245; pillars of change,

20–21; popularity of, 257, 275;
Renzi and, 100; reversal of,
243–46; Russia and, 227
Ocalan affair, 99, 290
ODS. *See* Civic Democratic Party
OECD. *See* Organization for
Economic Cooperation and
Development
Oil for Food program, 56, 280
Olive Tree coalition, 96, 99
OPEC oil embargo, 16, 279
Operation Sophia, 47–48
Organization for Economic Co-
operation and Development
(OECD), 170, 278
Organization for Security and
Cooperation in Europe (OSCE),
22, 174, 226
Ortega y Gasset, José, 138
OSCE. *See* Organization for
Security and Cooperation
Ostpolitik, 3, 68, 165, 170, 278

P5 + 1. *See* Permanent Five Plus
One
Palestinian Liberation Organization
(PLO), 15, 56, 279, 280
Paris climate accord, 24, 240
Paris Peace Treaties of 1947, 94
Partido Socialista Obrero Español
(PSOE), 143, 148, 153–54, 158,
292
Partnership and Cooperation
Agreement (PCA), 170, 222, 274,
278
Partnership for Modernization
(PfM), 223–24
Patrick, Stewart, 260
PCA. *See* Partnership and Co-
operation Agreement
Pence, Mike, 26
Pentagon Talks, 12

Pereira, Pedro, 13
Perle, Richard, 271
Permanent Five Plus One (P5 + 1),
23
Permanent Structured Cooperation
(PESCO), 275; creation of, 3;
defense and, 26–27, 297; France
approving, 272
Peyrefitte, Alain, 44–45
PfM. *See* Partnership for
Modernization
Piatkowski, Marcin, 164
Piñera, Sebastián, 145
PiS. *See* Law and Justice Party
Pleven, René, 13
Pleven Plan, 13–14
PLO. *See* Palestinian Liberation
Organization
Poland: Atlanticism of, 6, 167, 173,
205–06, 292; China and, 173;
conclusion, 173–74; economic
relations of, 172–73; EED
proposed by, 166; EU foreign
policy and, 165–67; as EU
member, 162–66, 273–74;
European Commission and,
162–63; eurozone and, 172;
Germany relations with, 173–74;
martial law in, 16; multilateralism
and, 171; in NATO, 163–65,
168–69; overview, 161–63; Russia
relations with, 169–72, 174,
277–78; Soviet Union control of,
161; strikes of 1980, 39; Ukraine
and, 171; U.S. relations with,
167–69
Pompeo, Mike, 256
Pompidou, Georges, 39, 45, 52–53,
280, 286
Populism, 199
Portugal, 13, 140–41, 295
Prizel, Ilya, 220

Prodi, Romano, 96, 100–101
PSOE. *See* Partido Socialista Obrero
    Español
Putin, Vladimir, 169; assertiveness of,
    295; on BRICS, 230; embargoes
    by, 224; energy pricing of, 226; on
    foreign policy, 226; loss of trust in,
    276; Merkel and, 74; power and,
    225; priorities of, 7; reelection of,
    228; on Soviet Union, 220; Trump
    and, 8, 248–49; U.S. adoptions and,
    247; U.S. elections and, 248–49

Qaddafi, Muammar, 24, 58, 83,
    102–03, 129, 281
Al-Qaeda, 57, 103, 129, 153, 241,
    280–81, 292
Quinlan, Joseph, 259

Raab, Dominic, 132
Rajoy, Mariano, 145, 155–56
Rasmussen, Anders Fogh, 180,
    185–86, 188
Rasmussen, Lars Løkke, 180, 192
Rather, Ely, 253
Reagan, Ronald, 15; Gorbachev
    negotiations, 116; missiles in
    Germany by, 39; in Spain, 143;
    Star Wars program, 40; Thatcher
    and, 115–16
Realism theory, 220
Renzi, Matteo, 97, 100, 290
Rieker, Pernille, 41
Rise and Fall of Great Powers
    (Kennedy, P.), 242
Rogers, William P., 256
Romano, Sergio, 93
Romney, Mitt, 257
Roosevelt, Theodore, 260, 270, 271,
    296
Ross, Robert, 251
Rumsfeld, Donald, 19, 126, 167

Russia: Africa and, 232, 287; Arctic
    and, 231; Asia as new horizon of,
    230–31; Atlanticism and, 220;
    conclusion, 232–34; Crimea
    annexation, 6, 74, 101, 128, 174,
    193, 209, 226, 234, 275–77; Czech
    Republic relations with, 208–10;
    Denmark relations with, 192–93,
    195, 277; EEC and, 274; EU and,
    221–25, 276–78; foreign policy of,
    2–3, 7; France relations with, 277;
    German-Russian gas flow, 86;
    Germany and, 73–75, 276; history,
    geography, leadership influences,
    295–96; ISIS and, 225; Italy and,
    100–101, 276–77; losing energy
    leverage, 229–30; NATO and, 276;
    Obama and, 227; overview, 219–21;
    Poland relations with, 169–72, 174,
    277–78; returning to post-soviet
    space, 225–26; Russo-Georgian
    War, 6, 174, 201, 203, 209, 227;
    Sarkozy negotiating with, 59, 171;
    September 11, 2001 terrorist
    attacks and, 227; sovereignization
    of, 233; U.S. relations with, 223,
    227–29, 247–50

Saint-Malo Agreement, 47, 123, 124
Sakaviev, Akhmed, 192
Salazar, António de Oliveira, 13, 140
Saramago, José, 141
Sarkozy, Nicolas, 21, 280, 290; on
    Africa, 54; on Arab Spring, 58;
    economic and immigration crises
    and, 47; NATO and, 59; negotiat-
    ing with Congo-Brazzaville, 287;
    negotiating with Russia and
    Georgia, 59, 171; pro-American
    policies, 289; U.S. visit, 41
Schmidt, Helmut, 46
Schröder, Gerhard, 71, 75, 276

Schuman Declaration, 94, 112

Schwarzenberg, Karel, 207

Scotland, 115, 129–30

SEA. *See* Single European Act of 1986

Senghor, Léopold, 52

September 11, 2001 terrorist attacks, 4, 84, 103; closure and, 244; EU foreign policy and, 19–20; reaction to, 8, 186, 242; Russia and, 227; transatlantic relations and, 19–20; U.S. foreign policy and, 19–20, 244; war on terror and, 125

Sequi, Ettore, 106

Sforza, Carlo, 94

Sharma, Ruchir, 260–61

Sikorski, Radoslaw, 85

Single European Act of 1986 (SEA), 16, 116, 272

Sinocentric bloc, 251

El-Sisi, Fattah, 128–29, 281

Six-Day War of 1967, 15, 55, 278

Slovakia, 17, 166, 204, 209, 278

Sobotka, Bohuslav, 207, 210

Soft power: in Denmark, 183; in Spain, 147, 155; in United States, 1, 243–44, 270

Solana, Javier, 19–20

Sotelo, Leopoldo Calvo, 143

Soutou, Georges-Henri, 35

Soviet Union: Afghanistan invaded by, 16, 39; during Cold War, 276; as evil empire, 40; France and, 38–39; Poland controlled by, 161; Putin on, 220

Spain: acceding to EC, 5–6, 138, 142; Afghanistan and, 147; Africa and, 287–88; *Apuntarse a todo* agenda, 5–6, 137; China and, 147; conclusion, 153–56; cooperation and development aid from, 151–53; defense and military cooperation with, 148–49; economy of, 150; in EU, 138, 140, 146, 156; euro and, 150; France relations with, 139–40; Gibraltar and, 141; Iraq War and, 146; joining EEC, 273; in Latin America, 144–46, 154; mediation role of, 6; in Middle East, 146–47; Morocco and, 142; in NATO, 5, 13, 141–44, 147–49, 282, 292; overview, 137–38; Portugal relations with, 140–41; Reagan in, 143; soft power in, 147, 155; trade and investment of, 150–51; as UNSC member, 5; U.S. relations with, 143–44, 292

Special relationships: China and Germany, 81–83, 284; Denmark and US, 182, 291; France and United States, 59–60; Italy and United States, 100; United Kingdom and United States, 5, 82, 113, 120, 127, 273, 291

START. *See* Strategic Arms Reduction Treaty

Star Wars program, 40

Strategic Arms Reduction Treaty (START), 8, 21, 228, 244, 248, 293–94

Suárez, Adolfo, 148

Suez Crisis of 1956, 11, 33, 37, 40, 112–13, 120, 281

Sutton, Michael, 35

Syria, 187, 201, 254, 258–59

TAFTA. *See* Transatlantic Free Trade Agreement

Tajani, Antonio, 96

Taksøe-Jensen, Peter, 194

Taliban, 57, 186, 255, 280

Thatcher, Margaret, 124, 291; during Cold War, 115–18; EEC and, 295; Reagan and, 115–16; resignation of, 95

Third Reich, 36
Thirty Years War, 269
Thorning-Schmidt, Helle, 180
Three plus three pillars approach, 3–4
Thucydides, 269
Tito, Josip, 105
Togliatti, Palmiro, 98
Tombalbaye, François, 52
Topolánek, Mirek, 209
Touré, Sékou, 52
Transatlantic Free Trade Agreement (TAFTA), 78, 80, 288
Transatlantic relations, 1; determinants of, 294–98; in EU foreign policy, 11–13; in France foreign policy, 36–43; in Italy foreign policy, 98–100; September 11, 2001 terrorist attacks and, 19–20; of United States, 256–59
Transatlantic Trade and Investment Partnership (TTIP), 24, 80, 182, 259, 288
Treaty of Brussels, 1948, 12, 14
Treaty of Lisbon, 47, 49
Treaty of Nice, 47
Treaty of Rome, 35, 43, 94, 125
Treaty of Versailles, 36
Trenin, Dmitri, 230
Truman, Harry, 210
Truman Doctrine, 111
Trump, Donald, 1, 72, 156, 228; in China, 251–52; continuity and, 262; credibility damaged by, 261; doctrine of, 78; election impact, 2, 11, 193, 208, 275; foreign policy of, 246, 296; at G-7 Summit, 259; German-Russian gas flow and, 86; military expenditures of, 258; multilateralism and, 78; NATO and, 8, 42, 166, 240, 288; Paris climate accord and, 24, 240; Putin

and, 8, 248–49; shock of, 243–46; trade agenda of, 80, 182
TTIP. *See* Transatlantic Trade and Investment Partnership
Tusk, Donald, 170–71, 278
Twitterplomacy, 1, 298

Ukraine: Association Agreement with, 41, 171; crisis in, 199; energy efficiency for, 189; Orange Revolution in, 211; Poland and, 171; violation of sovereignty, 275
UN. *See* United Nations
UN Declaration of Human Rights, 5
UNIFIL. *See* United Nations Interim Force in Lebanon
United Kingdom: Brexit and foreign policy, 5, 26, 127–32, 184, 256, 258, 273, 295; during Cold War, 110–18, 290–91; contradictions in, 5; EC and, 114, 116–17; ECSC and, 272–73; EEC and, 44–45, 113; euro and, 123–24, 126; eurozone and, 120; Great Recession in, 126; Libya attack, 129; NATO and, 110; New Labour era of, 119–27; overview, 109–10; during post-Cold War years, 118–27; returning Hong Kong to China, 111; splendid isolation of, 7; U.S. special relationship with, 5, 82, 113, 120, 127, 273, 291
United Nations (UN), 3, 138
United Nations Interim Force in Lebanon (UNIFIL), 76, 149, 283
United States: Afghanistan invasion, 101, 244; Afghanistan withdrawal, 254–55; arc of instability and, 253–56; Brexit and, 291; change and continuity in, 259–62; China relations with, 250–53;

Czech Republic relations with, 205–08; Denmark special relationship with, 182, 291; EEC/EU and, 275; EEC relations with, 14–16; EU relations with, 2; France special relationship with, 59–60, 289; geopolitics in, 247–59; Germany relations with, 77–81, 288; history's role in, 296; illusions of omnipotence in, 241–43; Iraq War end and, 254; ISIS air strikes, 41, 244, 246; Italy special relationship with, 100; Obama reversal and Trump shock in, 243–46; overview, 239–41; Poland relations with, 167–69; primacy in post Cold War, 241–47; Putin and Russian adoptions, 247; Russia relations with, 223, 227–29, 247–50; Sarkozy visiting, 41; September 11, 2001 terrorist attacks and foreign policy, 19–20, 244; soft power in, 1, 243–44, 270; Spain relations with, 143–44, 292; transatlantic relations of, 256–59; U.K. special relationship with, 5, 82, 113, 120, 127, 273, 291; unipolar moment of, 242

UN Security Council (UNSC), 21; France as member, 4–5, 36; reform of, 4; resolutions of, 248; Spain as member, 5

Vaisse, Maurice, 34
Vandenberg Resolution, 1948, 12
Varricchio, Armando, 106
Venice Declaration of 1980, 15

Verschave, Xavier-François, 52
Visegrad Group, 162, 165, 166, 200, 210–12
Vogel, Ezra, 260
Vondra, Alexandr, 203, 207

Wajda, Andrzej, 171
Walpole, Horace, 179
War on terror, 99, 125, 291, 292; Chirac and, 57–58
Washington, George, 269, 296
Western European Union (WEU), 14, 17–19, 148
Western liberalism, 240
WEU. See Western European Union
Wilson, Harold, 113–15
Wilson, Woodrow, 36, 296
Wolfovitz, Paul, 271
World Bank, 78, 164
World Trade Organization (WTO), 78, 182, 190, 248
World War I, 36, 92, 270
World War II, 34, 51, 92, 94, 102, 161, 295
WTO. See World Trade Organization

Xi Jinping, 231, 250

Yaoundé Convention, 14
Yeltsin, Boris, 222

Zakaria, Fareed, 239
Zaorálek, Lubomir, 210, 212
Zapatero, José Luis Rodríguez, 145–47, 153–55, 283, 292
Zeman, Miloš, 201, 203–04, 207–08